11.29.17
$49.95

Profit-Driven
Business Analytics

Wiley & SAS Business Series

The Wiley & SAS Business Series presents books that help senior-level managers with their critical management decisions.

Titles in the Wiley & SAS Business Series include:

Analytics: The Agile Way by Phil Simon

Analytics in a Big Data World: The Essential Guide to Data Science and its Applications by Bart Baesens

A Practical Guide to Analytics for Governments: Using Big Data for Good by Marie Lowman

Bank Fraud: Using Technology to Combat Losses by Revathi Subramanian

Big Data Analytics: Turning Big Data into Big Money by Frank Ohlhorst

Big Data, Big Innovation: Enabling Competitive Differentiation through Business Analytics by Evan Stubbs

Business Analytics for Customer Intelligence by Gert Laursen

Business Intelligence Applied: Implementing an Effective Information and Communications Technology Infrastructure by Michael Gendron

Business Intelligence and the Cloud: Strategic Implementation Guide by Michael S. Gendron

Business Transformation: A Roadmap for Maximizing Organizational Insights by Aiman Zeid

Connecting Organizational Silos: Taking Knowledge Flow Management to the Next Level with Social Media by Frank Leistner

Data-Driven Healthcare: How Analytics and BI are Transforming the Industry by Laura Madsen

Delivering Business Analytics: Practical Guidelines for Best Practice by Evan Stubbs

Demand-Driven Forecasting: A Structured Approach to Forecasting, Second Edition by Charles Chase

Demand-Driven Inventory Optimization and Replenishment: Creating a More Efficient Supply Chain by Robert A. Davis

Developing Human Capital: Using Analytics to Plan and Optimize Your Learning and Development Investments by Gene Pease, Barbara Beresford, and Lew Walker

The Executive's Guide to Enterprise Social Media Strategy: How Social Networks Are Radically Transforming Your Business by David Thomas and Mike Barlow

Economic and Business Forecasting: Analyzing and Interpreting Econometric Results by John Silvia, Azhar Iqbal, Kaylyn Swankoski, Sarah Watt, and Sam Bullard

Economic Modeling in the Post Great Recession Era: Incomplete Data, Imperfect Markets by John Silvia, Azhar Iqbal, and Sarah Watt House

Enhance Oil & Gas Exploration with Data-Driven Geophysical and Petrophysical Models by Keith Holdaway and Duncan Irving

Foreign Currency Financial Reporting from Euros to Yen to Yuan: A Guide to Fundamental Concepts and Practical Applications by Robert Rowan

Fraud Analytics Using Descriptive, Predictive, and Social Network Techniques: A Guide to Data Science for Fraud Detection by Bart Baesens, Veronique Van Vlasselaer, and Wouter Verbeke

Harness Oil and Gas Big Data with Analytics: Optimize Exploration and Production with Data-Driven Models by Keith Holdaway

Health Analytics: Gaining the Insights to Transform Health Care by Jason Burke

Heuristics in Analytics: A Practical Perspective of What Influences Our Analytical World by Carlos Andre Reis Pinheiro and Fiona McNeill

Human Capital Analytics: How to Harness the Potential of Your Organization's Greatest Asset by Gene Pease, Boyce Byerly, and Jac Fitz-enz

Implement, Improve and Expand Your Statewide Longitudinal Data System: Creating a Culture of Data in Education by Jamie McQuiggan and Armistead Sapp

Intelligent Credit Scoring: Building and Implementing Better Credit Risk Scorecards, Second Edition, by Naeem Siddiqi

Killer Analytics: Top 20 Metrics Missing from your Balance Sheet by Mark Brown

Profit-Driven Business Analytics

A Practitioner's Guide to Transforming
Big Data into Added Value

Wouter Verbeke
Bart Baesens
Cristián Bravo

WILEY

Published by John Wiley & Sons, Inc., Hoboken, New Jersey.
Published simultaneously in Canada.

For general information on our other products and services or for technical support,
please contact our Customer Care Department within the United States at (800)
762-2974, outside the United States at (317) 572-3993, or fax (317) 572-4002.

Wiley publishes in a variety of print and electronic formats and by print-on-demand.
Some material included with standard print versions of this book may not be included
in e-books or in print-on-demand. If this book refers to media such as a CD or DVD
that is not included in the version you purchased, you may download this material at
http://booksupport.wiley.com. For more information about Wiley products, visit
www.wiley.com.

Library of Congress Cataloging-in-Publication Data is Available:

ISBN 9781119286554 (Hardcover)
ISBN 9781119286998 (ePDF)
ISBN 9781119286981 (ePub)

Cover Design: Wiley
Cover Image: © Ricardo Reitmeyer/iStockphoto

Printed in the United States of America.

10 9 8 7 6 5 4 3 2 1

To Luit, Titus, and Fien.

To my wonderful wife, Katrien, and kids Ann-Sophie, Victor, and Hannelore.

To my parents and parents-in-law.

To Cindy, for her unwavering support.

Contents

Foreword   xv

Acknowledgments   xvii

Chapter 1   A Value-Centric Perspective Towards Analytics   1
  Introduction   1
    Business Analytics   3
  Profit-Driven Business Analytics   9
  Analytics Process Model   14
  Analytical Model Evaluation   17
  Analytics Team   19
    Profiles   19
    Data Scientists   20
  Conclusion   23
  Review Questions   24
    Multiple Choice Questions   24
    Open Questions   25
  References   25

Chapter 2   Analytical Techniques   28
  Introduction   28
  Data Preprocessing   29
    Denormalizing Data for Analysis   29
    Sampling   30
    Exploratory Analysis   31
    Missing Values   31
    Outlier Detection and Handling   32
    Principal Component Analysis   33
  Types of Analytics   37
  Predictive Analytics   37
    Introduction   37
    Linear Regression   38
    Logistic Regression   39
    Decision Trees   45
    Neural Networks   52

Ensemble Methods 56
  Bagging 57
  Boosting 57
  Random Forests 58
  Evaluating Ensemble Methods 59
Evaluating Predictive Models 59
  Splitting Up the Dataset 59
  Performance Measures for Classification Models 63
  Performance Measures for Regression Models 67
  Other Performance Measures for Predictive Analytical
    Models 68
Descriptive Analytics 69
  Introduction 69
  Association Rules 69
  Sequence Rules 72
  Clustering 74
Survival Analysis 81
  Introduction 81
  Survival Analysis Measurements 83
  Kaplan Meier Analysis 85
  Parametric Survival Analysis 87
  Proportional Hazards Regression 90
  Extensions of Survival Analysis Models 92
  Evaluating Survival Analysis Models 93
Social Network Analytics 93
  Introduction 93
  Social Network Definitions 94
  Social Network Metrics 95
  Social Network Learning 97
  Relational Neighbor Classifier 98
  Probabilistic Relational Neighbor Classifier 99
  Relational Logistic Regression 100
  Collective Inferencing 102
Conclusion 102
Review Questions 103
  Multiple Choice Questions 103
  Open Questions 108
Notes 110
References 110

Chapter 3 Business Applications 114
Introduction 114
Marketing Analytics 114
  Introduction 114

RFM Analysis   115
Response Modeling   116
Churn Prediction   118
X-selling   120
Customer Segmentation   121
Customer Lifetime Value   123
Customer Journey   129
Recommender Systems   131
Fraud Analytics   134
Credit Risk Analytics   139
HR Analytics   141
Conclusion   146
Review Questions   146
Multiple Choice Questions   146
Open Questions   150
Note   151
References   151

Chapter 4   Uplift Modeling   154
Introduction   154
The Case for Uplift Modeling: Response Modeling   155
Effects of a Treatment   158
Experimental Design, Data Collection, and Data
      Preprocessing   161
Experimental Design   161
Campaign Measurement of Model Effectiveness   164
Uplift Modeling Methods   170
Two-Model Approach   172
Regression-Based Approaches   174
Tree-Based Approaches   183
Ensembles   193
Continuous or Ordered Outcomes   198
Evaluation of Uplift Models   199
Visual Evaluation Approaches   200
Performance Metrics   207
Practical Guidelines   210
Two-Step Approach for Developing Uplift Models   210
Implementations and Software   212
Conclusion   213
Review Questions   214
Multiple Choice Questions   214
Open Questions   216
Note   217
References   217

Chapter 5   Profit-Driven Analytical Techniques 220
Introduction 220
Profit-Driven Predictive Analytics 221
   The Case for Profit-Driven Predictive Analytics 221
   Cost Matrix 222
   Cost-Sensitive Decision Making with Cost-Insensitive
      Classification Models 228
   Cost-Sensitive Classification Framework 231
Cost-Sensitive Classification 234
   Pre-Training Methods 235
   During-Training Methods 247
   Post-Training Methods 253
   Evaluation of Cost-Sensitive Classification Models 255
   Imbalanced Class Distribution 256
   Implementations 259
Cost-Sensitive Regression 259
   The Case for Profit-Driven Regression 259
Cost-Sensitive Learning for Regression 260
   During Training Methods 260
   Post-Training Methods 261
Profit-Driven Descriptive Analytics 267
   Profit-Driven Segmentation 267
   Profit-Driven Association Rules 280
Conclusion 283
Review Questions 284
   Multiple Choice Questions 284
   Open Questions 289
Notes 290
References 291

**Chapter 6   Profit-Driven Model Evaluation
              and Implementation 296**
Introduction 296
Profit-Driven Evaluation of Classification Models 298
   Average Misclassification Cost 298
   Cutoff Point Tuning 303
   ROC Curve-Based Measures 310
   Profit-Driven Evaluation with Observation-Dependent
      Costs 334
Profit-Driven Evaluation of Regression Models 338
   Loss Functions and Error-Based Evaluation Measures 339
   REC Curve and Surface 341
Conclusion 345

Review Questions   347
    Multiple Choice Questions   347
    Open Questions   350
  Notes   351
  References   352

Chapter 7   Economic Impact   355
  Introduction   355
  Economic Value of Big Data and Analytics   355
    Total Cost of Ownership (TCO)   355
    Return on Investment (ROI)   357
    Profit-Driven Business Analytics   359
  Key Economic Considerations   359
    In-Sourcing versus Outsourcing   359
    On Premise versus the Cloud   361
    Open-Source versus Commercial Software   362
  Improving the ROI of Big Data and Analytics   364
    New Sources of Data   364
    Data Quality   367
    Management Support   369
    Organizational Aspects   370
    Cross-Fertilization   371
  Conclusion   372
  Review Questions   373
    Multiple Choice Questions   373
    Open Questions   376
  Notes   377
  References   377

About the Authors   378

Index   381

Foreword

Sandra Wilikens

Secretary General, responsible for CSR and member of the Executive
Committee, BNP Paribas Fortis

In today's corporate world, strategic priorities tend to center on customer and shareholder value. One of the consequences is that analytics often focuses too much on complex technologies and statistics rather than long-term value creation. With their book *Profit-Driven Business Analytics*, Verbeke, Bravo, and Baesens pertinently bring forward a much-needed shift of focus that consists of turning analytics into a mature, value-adding technology. It further builds on the extensive research and industry experience of the author team, making it a must-read for anyone using analytics to create value and gain sustainable strategic leverage. This is even more true as we enter a new era of sustainable value creation in which the pursuit of long-term value has to be driven by sustainably strong organizations. The role of corporate employers is evolving as civic involvement and social contribution grow to be key strategic pillars.

Acknowledgments

It is a great pleasure to acknowledge the contributions and assistance of various colleagues, friends, and fellow analytics lovers to the writing of this book. This book is the result of many years of research and teaching in business analytics. We first would like to thank our publisher, Wiley, for accepting our book proposal.

We are grateful to the active and lively business analytics community for providing various user fora, blogs, online lectures, and tutorials, which proved very helpful.

We would also like to acknowledge the direct and indirect contributions of the many colleagues, fellow professors, students, researchers, and friends with whom we collaborated during the past years. Specifically, we would like to thank Floris Devriendt and George Petrides for contributing to the chapters on uplift modeling and profit-driven analytical techniques.

Last but not least, we are grateful to our partners, parents, and families for their love, support, and encouragement.

We have tried to make this book as complete, accurate, and enjoyable as possible. Of course, what really matters is what you, the reader, think of it. Please let us know your views by getting in touch. The authors welcome all feedback and comments—so do not hesitate to let us know your thoughts!

Wouter Verbeke
Bart Baesens
Cristián Bravo
May 2017

CHAPTER **1**

A Value-Centric Perspective Towards Analytics

INTRODUCTION

In this first chapter, we set the scene for what is ahead by broadly introducing profit-driven business analytics. The value-centric perspective toward analytics proposed in this book will be positioned and contrasted with a traditional statistical perspective. The implications of adopting a value-centric perspective toward the use of analytics in business are significant: a mind shift is needed both from managers and data scientists in developing, implementing, and operating analytical models. This, however, calls for deep insight into the underlying principles of advanced analytical approaches. Providing such insight is our general objective in writing this book and, more specifically:

- We aim to provide the reader with a structured overview of state-of-the art analytics for business applications.
- We want to assist the reader in gaining a deeper practical understanding of the inner workings and underlying principles of these approaches from a practitioner's perspective.

■ We wish to advance managerial thinking on the use of advanced analytics by offering insight into how these approaches may either generate significant added value or lower operational costs by increasing the efficiency of business processes.

■ We seek to prosper and facilitate the use of analytical approaches that are customized to needs and requirements in a business context.

As such, we envision that our book will facilitate organizations stepping up to a next level in the adoption of analytics for decision making by embracing the advanced methods introduced in the subsequent chapters of this book. Doing so requires an investment in terms of acquiring and developing knowledge and skills but, as is demonstrated throughout the book, also generates increased profits. An interesting feature of the approaches discussed in this book is that they have often been developed at the intersection of academia and business, by academics and practitioners joining forces for tuning a multitude of approaches to the particular needs and problem characteristics encountered and shared across diverse business settings.

Most of these approaches emerged only after the millennium, which should not be surprising. Since the millennium, we have witnessed a continuous and pace-gaining development and an expanding adoption of information, network, and database technologies. Key technological evolutions include the massive growth and success of the World Wide Web and Internet services, the introduction of smart phones, the standardization of enterprise resource planning systems, and many other applications of information technology. This dramatic change of scene has prospered the development of analytics for business applications as a rapidly growing and thriving branch of science and industry.

To achieve the stated objectives, we have chosen to adopt a pragmatic approach in explaining techniques and concepts. We do not focus on providing extensive mathematical proof or detailed algorithms. Instead, we pinpoint the crucial insights and underlying reasoning, as well as the advantages and disadvantages, related to the practical use of the discussed approaches in a business setting. For this, we ground our discourse on solid academic research expertise as well as on many years of practical experience in elaborating industrial analytics projects in close collaboration with data science professionals. Throughout the book, a plethora of illustrative examples and case studies are discussed. Example datasets, code, and implementations

are provided on the book's companion website, www.profit-analytics
.com, to further support the adoption of the discussed approaches.

In this chapter, we first introduce business analytics. Next, the
profit-driven perspective toward business analytics that will be elaborated in this book is presented. We then introduce the subsequent
chapters of this book and how the approaches introduced in these
chapters allow us to adopt a value-centric approach for maximizing
profitability and, as such, to increase the return on investment of
big data and analytics. Next, the analytics process model is discussed, detailing the subsequent steps in elaborating an analytics
project within an organization. Finally, the chapter concludes by
characterizing the ideal profile of a business data scientist.

Business Analytics

Data is the new oil is a popular quote pinpointing the increasing value of
data and—to our liking—accurately characterizes data as raw material.
Data are to be seen as an input or basic resource needing further
processing before actually being of use. In a subsequent section in
this chapter, we introduce the analytics process model that describes
the iterative chain of processing steps involved in turning *data* into
information or *decisions*, which is quite similar actually to an oil refinery
process. Note the subtle but significant difference between the words
data and *information* in the sentence above. Whereas data fundamen-
tally can be defined to be a sequence of zeroes and ones, information
essentially is the same but implies in addition a certain utility or value
to the *end user* or *recipient*. So, whether data are information depends
on whether the data have utility to the recipient. Typically, for raw
data to be information, the data first need to be processed, aggregated,
summarized, and compared. In summary, data typically need to be
analyzed, and insight, understanding, or knowledge should be added
for data to become useful.

Applying basic operations on a dataset may already provide useful
insight and support the end user or recipient in decision making. These
basic operations mainly involve selection and aggregation. Both selection and aggregation may be performed in many ways, leading to a
plentitude of indicators or statistics that can be distilled from raw data.
The following illustration elaborates a number of sales indicators in a
retail setting.

Providing insight by customized reporting is exactly what the field
of **business intelligence (BI)** is about. Typically, visualizations are
also adopted to represent indicators and their evolution in time, in
easy-to-interpret ways. Visualizations provide support by facilitating

EXAMPLE

For managerial purposes, a retailer requires the development of real-time sales reports. Such a report may include a wide variety of indicators that summarize raw sales data. Raw sales data, in fact, concern transactional data that can be extracted from the online transaction processing (OLTP) system that is operated by the retailer. Some example indicators and the required selection and aggregation operations for calculating these statistics are:

- *Total amount of revenues generated over the last 24 hours*: Select all transactions over the last 24 hours and sum the paid amounts, with *paid* meaning the price net of promotional offers.

- *Average paid amount in online store over the last seven days*: Select all online transactions over the last seven days and calculate the average paid amount;

- *Fraction of returning customers within one month*: Select all transactions over the last month and select customer IDs that appear more than once; count the number of IDs.

Remark that calculating these indicators involves basic selection operations on characteristics or dimensions of transactions stored in the database, as well as basic aggregation operations such as sum, count, and average, among others.

the user's ability to acquire understanding and insight in the blink of an eye. Personalized dashboards, for instance, are widely adopted in the industry and are very popular with managers to monitor and keep track of business performance. A formal definition of business intelligence is provided by Gartner (http://www.gartner.com/it-glossary):

> Business intelligence is an umbrella term that includes the applications, infrastructure and tools, and best practices that enable access to and analysis of information to improve and optimize decisions and performance.

Note that this definition explicitly mentions the required infrastructure and best practices as an essential component of BI, which is typically also provided as part of the package or solution offered by BI vendors and consultants. More advanced analysis of data may further support users and optimize decision making. This is exactly where analytics comes into play. *Analytics* is a catch-all term covering a wide variety of what are essentially data-processing techniques.

In its broadest sense, analytics strongly overlaps with data science, statistics, and related fields such as artificial intelligence (AI) and machine learning. Analytics, to us, is a toolbox containing a variety of instruments and methodologies allowing users to analyze data for a diverse range of well-specified purposes. Table 1.1 identifies a number of categories of analytical tools that cover diverse intended uses or, in other words, allow users to complete a diverse range of tasks.

A first main group of tasks identified in Table 1.1 concerns prediction. Based on observed variables, the aim is to accurately estimate or predict an unobserved value. The applicable subtype of predictive analytics depends on the type of target variable, which we intend to model as a function of a set of predictor variables. When the target variable is categorical in nature, meaning the variable can only take a limited number of possible values (e.g., churner or not, fraudster or not, defaulter or not), then we have a classification problem. When the task concerns the estimation of a continuous target variable (e.g., sales amount, customer lifetime value, credit loss), which can take any value over a certain range of possible values, we are dealing with regression. Survival analysis and forecasting explicitly account for the time dimension by either predicting the timing of events (e.g., churn, fraud, default) or the evolution of a target variable in time (e.g., churn rates, fraud rates, default rates). Table 1.2 provides simplified example datasets and analytical models for each type of predictive analytics for illustrative purposes.

The second main group of analytics comprises descriptive analytics that, rather than predicting a target variable, aim at identifying specific types of patterns. Clustering or segmentation aims at grouping **entities** (e.g., customers, transactions, employees, etc.) that are similar in nature. The objective of association analysis is to find groups of **events** that frequently co-occur and therefore appear to be associated. The basic **observations** that are being analyzed in this problem setting consist of variable groups of events; for instance, transactions involving various products that are being bought by a customer at a certain moment in time. The aim of sequence analysis

Table 1.1 Categories of Analytics from a Task-Oriented Perspective

Predictive Analytics	Descriptive Analytics
Classification	Clustering
Regression	Association analysis
Survival analysis	Sequence analysis
Forecasting	

Table 1.2 Example Datasets and Predictive Analytical Models

Example dataset	Predictive analytical model

Classification

ID	Recency	Frequency	Monetary	Churn
C1	26	4.2	126	Yes
C2	37	2.1	59	No
C3	2	8.5	256	No
C4	18	6.2	89	No
C5	46	1.1	37	Yes
...	...	...	...	...

Decision tree classification model:

Regression

ID	Recency	Frequency	Monetary	CLV
C1	26	4.2	126	3,817
C2	37	2.1	59	4,31
C3	2	8.5	256	2,187
C4	18	6.2	89	543
C5	46	1.1	37	1,548
...	...	...	...	...

Linear regression model:

$$CLV = 260 + 11 \cdot \text{Recency} + 6.1 \cdot \text{Frequency} + 3.4 \cdot \text{Monetary}$$

Survival analysis

ID	Recency	Churn or Censored	Time of churn or Censoring
C1	26	Churn	181
C2	37	Censored	253
C3	2	Censored	37
C4	18	Censored	172
C5	46	Churn	98
...	...	...	...

General parametric survival analysis model:

$$\log(T) = 13 + 5.3 \cdot \text{Recency}$$

Forecasting

Timestamp	Demand
January	513
February	652
March	435
April	578
May	601
...	...

Weighted moving average forecasting model:

$$\text{Demand}_t = 0.4 \cdot \text{Demand}_{t-1} + 0.3 \cdot \text{Demand}_{t-2} + 0.2 \cdot \text{Demand}_{t-3} + 0.1 \cdot \text{Demand}_{t-4}$$

Table 1.3 Example Datasets and Descriptive Analytical Models

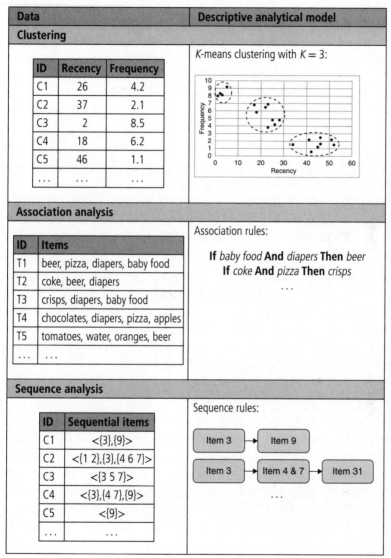

Data	Descriptive analytical model
Clustering	

K-means clustering with *K* = 3:

ID	Recency	Frequency
C1	26	4.2
C2	37	2.1
C3	2	8.5
C4	18	6.2
C5	46	1.1
...	...	...

Association analysis

Association rules:

If *baby food* **And** *diapers* **Then** *beer*
If *coke* **And** *pizza* **Then** *crisps*
. . .

ID	Items
T1	beer, pizza, diapers, baby food
T2	coke, beer, diapers
T3	crisps, diapers, baby food
T4	chocolates, diapers, pizza, apples
T5	tomatoes, water, oranges, beer
...	...

Sequence analysis

Sequence rules:

Item 3 → Item 9

Item 3 → Item 4 & 7 → Item 31

. . .

ID	Sequential items
C1	<{3},{9}>
C2	<{1 2},{3},{4 6 7}>
C3	<{3 5 7}>
C4	<{3},{4 7},{9}>
C5	<{9}>
...	...

is similar to association analysis but concerns the detection of events that frequently occur sequentially, rather than simultaneously as in association analysis. As such, sequence analysis explicitly accounts for the time dimension. Table 1.3 provides simplified examples of datasets and analytical models for each type of descriptive analytics.

Note that Tables 1.1 through 1.3 identify and illustrate categories of approaches that are able to complete a specific task from a *technical* rather than an *applied* perspective. These different types of analytics can be applied in quite diverse business and nonbusiness settings and consequently lead to many specialized applications. For instance, predictive analytics and, more specifically, classification techniques may be applied for detecting fraudulent credit-card transactions, for predicting customer churn, for assessing loan applications, and so forth. From an application perspective, this leads to various groups of analytics such as, respectively, fraud analytics, customer or marketing analytics, and credit risk analytics. A wide range of business applications of analytics across industries and business departments is discussed in detail in Chapter 3.

With respect to Table 1.1, it needs to be noted that these different types of analytics apply to **structured data.** An example of a structured dataset is shown in Table 1.4. The rows in such a dataset are typically called observations, instances, records, or lines, and represent or collect information on *basic entities* such as customers, transactions, accounts, or citizens. The columns are typically referred to as (explanatory or predictor) variables, characteristics, attributes, predictors, inputs, dimensions, effects, or features. The columns contain information on a particular entity as represented by a row in the table. In Table 1.4, the second column represents the age of a customer, the third column the postal code, and so on. In this book we consistently use the terms **observation** and **variable** (and sometimes more specifically, explanatory, predictor, or target variable).

Because of the structure that is present in the dataset in Table 1.4 and the well-defined meaning of rows and columns, it is much easier to analyze such a structured dataset compared to analyzing unstructured data such as text, video, or networks, to name a few. Specialized techniques exist that facilitate analysis of unstructured data—for instance, text analytics with applications such as sentiment analysis, video analytics that can be applied for face recognition and incident detection, and network analytics with applications such as community

Table 1.4 Structured Dataset

Customer	Age	Income	Gender	Duration	Churn
John	30	1,800	Male	620	Yes
Sarah	25	1,400	Female	12	No
Sophie	52	2,600	Female	830	No
David	42	2,200	Male	90	Yes

mining and relational learning (see Chapter 2). Given the rough estimate that over 90% of all data are unstructured, clearly there is a large potential for these types of analytics to be applied in business.

However, due to the inherent complexity of analyzing unstructured data, as well as because of the often-significant development costs that only appear to pay off in settings where adopting these techniques significantly adds to the easier-to-apply **structured analytics,** currently we see relatively few applications in business being developed and implemented. In this book, we therefore focus on analytics for analyzing structured data, and more specifically the subset listed in Table 1.1. For unstructured analytics, one may refer to the specialized literature (Elder IV and Thomas 2012; Chakraborty, Murali, and Satish 2013; Coussement 2014; Verbeke, Martens and Baesens 2014; Baesens, Van Vlasselaer, and Verbeke 2015).

PROFIT-DRIVEN BUSINESS ANALYTICS

The premise of this book is that analytics is to be adopted in business for *better decision making*—"better" meaning *optimal* in terms of maximizing the net profits, returns, payoff, or value resulting from the decisions that are made based on insights obtained from data by applying analytics. The incurred returns may stem from a gain in efficiency, lower costs or losses, and additional sales, among others. The decision level at which analytics is typically adopted is the operational level, where many customized decisions are to be made that are similar and granular in nature. High-level, ad hoc decision making at strategic and tactical levels in organizations also may benefit from analytics, but expectedly to a much lesser extent.

The decisions involved in developing a business strategy are highly complex in nature and do not match the elementary tasks enlisted in Table 1.1. A higher-level AI would be required for such purpose, which is not yet at our disposal. At the operational level, however, there are many *simple* decisions to be made, which exactly match with the tasks listed in Table 1.1. This is not surprising, since these approaches have often been developed with a specific application in mind. In Table 1.5, we provide a selection of example applications, most of which will be elaborated on in detail in Chapter 3.

Analytics facilitates optimization of the fine granular decision-making activities listed in Table 1.5, leading to lower costs or losses and higher revenues and profits. The level of optimization depends on the accuracy and validity of the predictions, estimates, or patterns derived from the data. Additionally, as we stress in this book, the quality

Table 1.5 Examples of Business Decisions Matching Analytics

Decision Making with Predictive Analytics	
Classification	Credit officers have to screen loan applications and decide on whether to accept or reject an application based on the involved risk. Based on historical data on the performance of past loan applications, a classification model may learn to distinguish *good* from *bad* loan applications using a number of well-chosen characteristics of the application as well as of the applicant. Analytics and, more specifically, classification techniques allow us to optimize the loan-granting process by more accurately assessing risk and reducing bad loan losses (Van Gestel and Baesens 2009; Verbraken et al. 2014). Similar applications of decision making based on classification techniques, which are discussed in more detail in Chapter 3 of this book, include customer churn prediction, response modeling, and fraud detection.
Regression	Regression models allow us to estimate a continuous target value and in practice are being adopted, for instance, to estimate customer lifetime value. Having an indication on the future worth in terms of revenues or profits a customer will generate is important to allow customization of marketing efforts, for pricing, etc. As is discussed in detail in Chapter 3, analyzing historical customer data allows estimating the future net value of current customers using a regression model.

Similar applications involve loss given default modeling as is discussed in Chapter 3, as well as the estimation of software development costs (Dejaeger et al. 2012). |
| Survival analysis | Survival analysis is being adopted in predictive maintenance applications for estimating when a machine component will fail. Such knowledge allows us to optimize decisions related to machine maintenance—for instance, to optimally plan when to replace a vital component. This decision requires striking a balance between the cost of machine failure during operations and the cost of the component, which is preferred to be operated as long as possible before replacing it (Widodo and Yang 2011).

Alternative business applications of survival analysis involve the prediction of time to churn and time to default where, compared to classification, the focus is on predicting *when* the event will occur rather than *whether* the event will occur. |
| Forecasting | A typical application of forecasting involves demand forecasting, which allows us to optimize production planning and supply chain management decisions. For instance, a power supplier needs to be able to balance electricity production and demand by the consumers and for this purpose adopts forecasting or time-series modeling techniques. These approaches allow an accurate prediction of the short-term evolution of demand based on historical demand patterns (Hyndman et al. 2008). |

Table 1.5 *(Continued)*

Decision Making with Descriptive Analytics	
Clustering	Clustering is applied in credit-card fraud detection to block suspicious transactions in real time or to select suspicious transactions for investigation in near-real time. Clustering facilitates automated decision making by comparing a new transaction to clusters or groups of historical nonfraudulent transactions and by labeling it as suspicious when it differs too much from these groups (Baesens et al. 2015). Clustering can also be used for identifying groups of similar customers, which facilitates the customization of marketing campaigns.
Association analysis Sequence analysis	Association analysis is often applied for detecting patterns within transactional data in terms of products that are often purchased together. Sequence analysis, on the other hand, allows the detection of which products are often bought subsequently. Knowledge of such associations allows smarter decisions to be made about which products to advertise, to bundle, to place together in a store, etc. (Agrawal and Srikant 1994).

of data-driven decision making depends on the extent to which the actual use of the predictions, estimates, or patterns is accounted for in developing and applying analytical approaches. We argue that the actual goal, which in a business setting is to generate profits, should be central when applying analytics in order to further increase the return on analytics. For this, we need to adopt what we call *profit-driven analytics*. These are adapted techniques specifically configured for use in a business context.

EXAMPLE

The following example highlights the tangible difference between a statistical approach to analytics and a profit-driven approach. Table 1.5 already indicated the use of analytics and, more specifically, classification techniques for predicting which customers are about to churn. Having such knowledge allows us to decide which customers are to be targeted in a retention campaign, thereby increasing the efficiency and returns of that campaign when compared to randomly or intuitively selecting customers. By offering a financial incentive to customers that are likely to churn—for instance, a temporary reduction of the monthly fee—they may be retained. Actively retaining customers has been shown by various studies to be much cheaper than acquiring new customers to replace those who defect (Athanassopoulos 2000; Bhattacharya 1998).

It needs to be noted, however, that not every customer generates the same amount of revenues and therefore represents the same value to a company. Hence, it is much more important to detect churn for the most valuable customers. In a basic customer churn prediction setup, which adopts what we call a statistical perspective, no differentiation is made between high-value and low-value customers when learning a classification model to detect future churn. However, when analyzing data and learning a classification model, it should be taken into account that missing a high-value churner is much costlier than missing a low-value churner. The aim of this would be to steer or tune the resulting predictive model so it accounts for value, and consequently for its actual end-use in a business context.

An additional difference between the statistical and business perspectives toward adopting classification and regression modeling concerns the difference between, respectively, *explaining* and *predicting* (Breiman 2001; Shmueli and Koppius 2011). The aim of estimating a model may be either of these two goals:

1. To establish the relation or detect dependencies between characteristics or independent variables and an observed dependent target variable(s) or outcome value.

2. To *estimate* or *predict* the unobserved or future value of the target variable as a function of the independent variables.

For instance, in a medical setting, the purpose of analyzing data may be to establish the impact of smoking behavior on the life expectancy of an individual. A regression model may be estimated that *explains* the observed age at death of a number of subjects in terms of characteristics such as gender and number of years that the subject smoked. Such a model will establish or quantify the impact or relation between each characteristic and the observed outcome, and allows for testing the statistical significance of the impact and measuring the uncertainty of the result (Cao 2016; Peto, Whitlock, and Jha 2010).

A clear distinction exists with estimating a regression model for, as an example, software effort prediction, as introduced in Table 1.5. In such applications where the aim is mainly to predict, essentially we are not interested in what drivers *explain* how much effort it will take to develop new software, although this may be a useful side result. Instead we mainly wish to predict as accurately as possible the effort that will be required for completing a project. Since the model's main use will be to produce an estimate allowing cost projection and planning, it is the exactness or accuracy of the prediction and the size of the errors that matters, rather than the exact relation between the effort and characteristics of the project.

Typically, in a business setting, the aim is to predict in order to facilitate improved or automated decision making. Explaining, as indicated for the case of software effort prediction, may have use as well since useful insights may be derived. For instance, from the predictive model, it may be found what the exact impact is of including more or less senior and junior programmers in a project team on the required effort to complete the project, allowing the team composition to be optimized as a function of project characteristics.

In this book, several versatile and powerful profit-driven approaches are discussed. These approaches facilitate the adoption of a value-centric business perspective toward analytics in order to boost the returns. Table 1.6 provides an overview of the structure of the book. First, we lay the foundation by providing a general introduction to analytics in Chapter 2, and by discussing the most important and popular business applications in detail in Chapter 3.

Chapter 4 discusses approaches toward uplift modeling, which in essence is about distilling or estimating the net effect of a decision and then contrasting the expected result for alternative scenarios. This allows, for instance, the optimization of marketing efforts by customizing the contact channel and the format of the incentive for the response to the campaign to be maximal in terms of returns being generated. Standard analytical approaches may be adopted to develop uplift models. However, specialized approaches tuned toward the particular problem characteristics of uplift modeling have also been developed, and they are discussed in Chapter 4.

Table 1.6 Outline of the Book

Book Structure
Chapter 1: A Value-Centric Perspective Towards Analytics
Chapter 2: Analytical Techniques
Chapter 3: Business Applications
Chapter 4: Uplift Modeling
Chapter 5: Profit-Driven Analytical Techniques
Chapter 6: Profit-Driven Model Evaluation and Implementation
Chapter 7: Economic Impact

As such, Chapter 4 forms a bridge to Chapter 5 of the book, which concentrates on various advanced analytical approaches that can be adopted for developing profit-driven models by allowing us to account for profit when learning or applying a predictive or descriptive model. Profit-driven predictive analytics for classification and regression are discussed in the first part of Chapter 5, whereas the second part focuses on descriptive analytics and introduces profit-oriented segmentation and association analysis.

Chapter 6 subsequently focuses on approaches that are tuned toward a business-oriented evaluation of predictive models—for example, in terms of profits. Note that traditional statistical measures, when applied to customer churn prediction models, for instance, do not differentiate among incorrectly predicted or classified customers, whereas it definitely makes sense from a business point of view to account for the value of the customers when evaluating a model. For instance, incorrectly predicting a customer who is about to churn with a high value represents a higher loss or cost than not detecting a customer with a low value who is about to churn. Both, however, are accounted for equally by nonbusiness and, more specifically, non-profit-oriented evaluation measures. Both Chapters 4 and 6 allow using *standard* analytical approaches as discussed in Chapter 2, with the aim to maximize profitability by adopting, respectively, a profit-centric setup or profit-driven evaluation. The particular business application of the model will appear to be an important factor to account for in maximizing profitability.

Finally, Chapter 7 concludes the book by adopting a broader perspective toward the use of analytics in an organization by looking into the economic impact, as well as by zooming into some practical concerns related to the development, implementation, and operation of analytics within an organization.

ANALYTICS PROCESS MODEL

Figure 1.1 provides a high-level overview of the analytics process model (Hand, Mannila, and Smyth 2001; Tan, Steinbach, and Kumar 2005; Han and Kamber 2011; Baesens 2014). This model defines the subsequent steps in the development, implementation, and operation of analytics within an organization.

As a first step, a thorough definition of the business problem to be addressed is needed. The objective of applying analytics needs to be unambiguously defined. Some examples are: customer segmentation

Overview of the Analytics Process Model

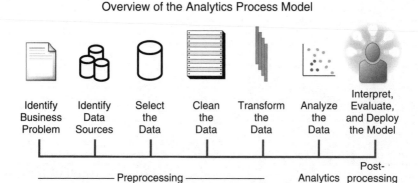

Figure 1.1 The analytics process model.
(Baesens 2014)

of a mortgage portfolio, retention modeling for a postpaid Telco subscription, or fraud detection for credit-cards. Defining the perimeter of the analytical modeling exercise requires a close collaboration between the data scientists and business experts. Both parties need to agree on a set of key concepts; these may include how we define a customer, transaction, churn, or fraud. Whereas this may seem self-evident, it appears to be a crucial success factor to make sure a common understanding of the goal and some key concepts is agreed on by all involved stakeholders.

Next, all source data that could be of potential interest need to be identified. This is a very important step as data are the key ingredient to any analytical exercise and the selection of data will have a deterministic impact on the analytical models that will be built in a subsequent step. The golden rule here is: the more data, the better! The analytical model itself will later decide which data are relevant and which are not for the task at hand. All data will then be gathered and consolidated in a staging area which could be, for example, a data warehouse, data mart, or even a simple spreadsheet file. Some basic exploratory data analysis can then be considered using for instance OLAP facilities for multidimensional analysis (e.g., roll-up, drill down, slicing and dicing). This will be followed by a data-cleaning step to get rid of all inconsistencies such as missing values, outliers and duplicate data. Additional transformations may also be considered such as binning, alphanumeric to numeric coding, geographical aggregation, to name a few, as well as deriving additional characteristics that are typically called features from the raw data. A simple example concerns the derivation of the age from the birth date; yet more complex examples are provided in Chapter 3.

In the analytics step, an analytical model will be estimated on the preprocessed and transformed data. Depending on the business objective and the exact task at hand, a particular analytical technique will be selected and implemented by the data scientist. In Table 1.1, an overview was provided of various tasks and types of analytics. Alternatively, one may consider the various types of analytics listed in Table 1.1 to be the basic building blocks or solution components that a data scientist employs to solve the problem at hand. In other words, the business problem needs to be reformulated in terms of the available tools enumerated in Table 1.1.

Finally, once the results are obtained, they will be interpreted and evaluated by the business experts. Results may be clusters, rules, patterns, or relations, among others, all of which will be called analytical models resulting from applying analytics. Trivial patterns (e.g., an association rule is found stating that spaghetti and spaghetti sauce are often purchased together) that may be detected by the analytical model are interesting as they help to validate the model. But of course, the key issue is to find the unknown yet interesting and actionable patterns (sometimes also referred to as knowledge diamonds) that can provide new insights into your data that can then be translated into new profit opportunities. Before putting the resulting model or patterns into operation, an important evaluation step is to consider the actual returns or profits that will be generated, and to compare these to a relevant base scenario such as a do-nothing decision or a change-nothing decision. In the next section, an overview of various evaluation criteria is provided; these are discussed to validate analytical models.

Once the analytical model has been appropriately validated and approved, it can be put into production as an analytics application (e.g., decision support system, scoring engine). Important considerations here are how to represent the model output in a user-friendly way, how to integrate it with other applications (e.g., marketing campaign management tools, risk engines), and how to make sure the analytical model can be appropriately monitored and backtested on an ongoing basis.

It is important to note that the process model outlined in Figure 1.1 is iterative in nature in the sense that one may have to return to previous steps during the exercise. For instance, during the analytics step, a need for additional data may be identified that will necessitate additional data selection, cleaning, and transformation. The most time-consuming step typically is the data selection and preprocessing step, which usually takes around 80% of the total efforts needed to build an analytical model.

ANALYTICAL MODEL EVALUATION

Before adopting an analytical model and making operational decisions based on the obtained clusters, rules, patterns, relations, or predictions, the model needs to be thoroughly evaluated. Depending on the exact type of output, the setting or business environment, and the particular usage characteristics, different aspects may need to be assessed during evaluation in order to ensure the model is *acceptable* for implementation.

A number of key characteristics of *successful* analytical models are defined and explained in Table 1.7. These broadly defined evaluation criteria may or may not apply, depending on the exact application setting, and will have to be further specified in practice.

Various challenges may occur when developing and implementing analytical models, possibly leading to difficulties in meeting the objectives as expressed by the key characteristics of successful analytical models discussed in Table 1.7. One such challenge may concern the dynamic nature of the relations or patterns retrieved from the data, impacting the usability and lifetime of the model. For instance, in a fraud detection setting, it is observed that fraudsters constantly try to out-beat detection and prevention systems by developing new strategies and methods (Baesens et al. 2015). Therefore, adaptive analytical models and detection and prevention systems are required in order to detect and resolve fraud as soon as possible. Closely monitoring the performance of the model in such a setting is an absolute must.

Another common challenge in a binary classification setting such as predicting customer churn concerns the imbalanced class distribution, meaning that one class or type of entity is much more prevalent than the other. When developing a customer churn prediction model typically many more nonchurners are present in the historical dataset than there are churners. Furthermore, the costs and benefits related to detecting or missing either class are often strongly imbalanced and may need to be accounted for to optimize decision making in the particular business context. In this book, various approaches are

Table 1.7 Key Characteristics of Successful Business Analytics Models

Accuracy	Refers to the predictive power or the correctness of the analytical model. Several statistical evaluation criteria exist and may be applied to assess this aspect, such as the hit rate, lift curve, or AUC. A number of profit-driven evaluation measures will be discussed in detail in Chapter 6. Accuracy may also refer to statistical significance, meaning that the patterns that have been found in the data have to be real, robust, and not the consequence of coincidence. In other words, we need to make sure that the model *generalizes* well (to other entities, to the future, etc.) and is not overfitted to the historical dataset that was used for deriving or estimating the model.
Interpretability	When a deeper understanding of the retrieved patterns is required—for instance, to validate the model before it is adopted for use—a model needs to be interpretable. This aspect involves a certain degree of subjectivism, since interpretability may depend on the user's knowledge or skills. The interpretability of a model depends on its format, which, in turn, is determined by the adopted analytical technique. Models that allow the user to understand the underlying reasons as to why the model arrives at a certain result are called white-box models, whereas complex incomprehensible mathematical models are often referred to as black-box models. White-box approaches include, for instance, decision trees and linear regression models, examples of which have been provided in Table 1.2. A typical example of a black-box approach concerns neural networks, which are discussed in Chapter 2.
	It may well be that in a business setting, black-box models are acceptable, although in most settings some level of understanding and in fact validation, which is facilitated by interpretability, is required for the management to have confidence and allow the effective operationalization of the model.
Operational efficiency	Operational efficiency refers to the time that is required to evaluate the model or, in other words, the time required to make a business decision based on the output of the model. When a decision needs to be made in real time or near-real time, for instance to signal possible credit-card fraud or to decide on a rate or banner to advertise on a website, operational efficiency is crucial and is a main concern during model performance assessment. Operational efficiency also entails the efforts needed to collect and preprocess the data, evaluate the model, monitor and back-test the model, and reestimate it when necessary.
Regulatory compliance	Depending on the context, there may be internal or organization-specific as well as external regulation and legislation that apply to the development and application of a model. Clearly, a model should be in line and comply with all applicable regulations and legislation—for instance, with respect to privacy or the use of cookies in a web browser.

Table 1.7 *(Continued)*

Economical cost	Developing and implementing an analytical model involves significant costs to an organization. The total cost includes, among others, the costs to gather, preprocess, and analyze the data, and the costs to put the resulting analytical models into production. In addition, the software costs, as well as human and computing resources, should be taken into account. Possibly also external data have to be purchased to enrich the available in-house data. On the other hand, benefits can be expected as a result of the adoption of the model. Clearly, it is important to perform a thorough cost-benefit analysis at the start of the project, and to gain insight into the constituent factors of the return-on-investment of building a more advanced system. The profitability of adopting analytics is the central theme of this book. The final chapter concludes by elaborating on the economic impact of analytics.

discussed for dealing with these specific challenges. Other issues may arise as well, often requiring ingenuity and creativity to be solved. Hence, both are key characteristics of a good data scientist, as is discussed in the following section.

ANALYTICS TEAM

Profiles

The analytics process is essentially a multidisciplinary exercise where many different job profiles need to collaborate. First of all, there is the database or data warehouse administrator (DBA). The DBA ideally is aware of all the data available within the firm, the storage details and the data definitions. Hence, the DBA plays a crucial role in feeding the analytical modeling exercise with its key ingredient, which is data. Since analytics is an iterative exercise, the DBA may continue to play an important role as the modeling exercise proceeds.

Another very important profile is the business expert. This could, for instance, be a credit portfolio manager, brand manager, fraud investigator, or e-commerce manager. The business expert has extensive business experience and business common sense, which usually proves very valuable and crucial for success. It is precisely this knowledge that will help to steer the analytical modeling exercise and interpret its key findings. A key challenge here is that much of the expert knowledge is tacit and may be hard to elicit at the start of the modeling exercise.

Legal experts are gaining in importance since not all data can be used in an analytical model because of factors such as privacy and discrimination. For instance, in credit risk modeling, one typically cannot discriminate good and bad customers based on gender, beliefs, ethnic origin, or religion. In Web analytics, information is typically gathered by means of cookies, which are files that are stored on the user's browsing computer. However, when gathering information using cookies, users should be appropriately informed. This is subject to regulation at various levels (regional and national, and supranational, e.g., at the European level). A key challenge here is that privacy and other regulatory issues vary highly depending on the geographical region. Hence, the legal expert should have good knowledge about which data can be used when, and which regulation applies in which location.

The software tool vendors should also be mentioned as an important part of the analytics team. Different types of tool vendors can be distinguished here. Some vendors only provide tools to automate specific steps of the analytical modeling process (e.g., data preprocessing). Others sell software that covers the entire analytical modeling process. Some vendors also provide analytics-based solutions for specific application areas, such as risk management, marketing analytics, or campaign management.

The data scientist, modeler, or analyst is the person responsible for doing the actual analytics. The data scientist should possess a thorough understanding of all big data and analytical techniques involved and know how to implement them in a business setting using the appropriate technology. In the next section, we discuss the ideal profile of a data scientist.

Data Scientists

Whereas in a previous section we discussed the characteristics of a good analytical model, in this paragraph we elaborate on the key characteristics of a good data scientist from the perspective of the hiring manager. It is based on our consulting and research experience, having collaborated with many companies worldwide on the topic of big data and analytics.

A Data Scientist Should Have Solid Quantitative Skills

Obviously, a data scientist should have a thorough background in statistics, machine learning and/or data mining. The distinction between these various disciplines is becoming more and more blurred and is actually no longer that relevant. They all provide a set of quantitative techniques to analyze data and find business-relevant patterns within a particular context such as fraud detection or credit risk management. A data scientist should be aware of which technique can be applied, when, and how, and should not focus too much on the underlying mathematical (e.g., optimization) details but, rather, have a good understanding of what analytical problem a technique solves, and how its results should be interpreted. In this context, the education of engineers in computer science and/or business/industrial engineering should aim at an integrated, multidisciplinary view, with graduates formed in both the use of the techniques, and with the business acumen necessary to bring new endeavors to fruition. Also important is to spend enough time validating the analytical results obtained so as to avoid situations often referred to as data massage and/or data torture, whereby data are (intentionally) misrepresented and/or too much time is expended in discussing spurious correlations. When selecting the optimal quantitative technique, the data scientist should consider the specificities of the context and the business problem at hand. Key requirements for business models have been discussed in the previous section, and the data scientist should have a basic understanding of, and intuition for, all of those. Based on a combination of these requirements, the data scientist should be capable of selecting the best analytical technique to solve the particular business problem.

A Data Scientist Should Be a Good Programmer

As per definition, data scientists work with data. This involves plenty of activities such as sampling and preprocessing of data, model estimation, and post-processing (e.g., sensitivity analysis, model deployment, backtesting, model validation). Although many user-friendly software tools are on the market nowadays to automate and support these tasks, every analytical exercise requires tailored steps to tackle the specificities of a particular business problem and setting. In order to successfully perform these steps, programming needs to be done. Hence, a good data scientist should possess sound programming skills in, for example, SAS, R, or Python, among others. The programming language itself is not that important, as long as the data scientist is familiar with the basic concepts of programming and knows how to use these to automate repetitive tasks or perform specific routines.

A Data Scientist Should Excel in Communication and Visualization Skills

Like it or not, analytics is a technical exercise. At this moment, there is a huge gap between the analytical models and the business users. To bridge this gap, communication and visualization facilities are key! Hence, a data scientist should know how to represent analytical models and their accompanying statistics and reports in user-friendly ways by using, for example, traffic light approaches, OLAP (online analytical processing) facilities, or if-then business rules, among others. A data scientist should be capable of communicating the right amount of information without getting lost in complex (e.g., statistical) details, which will inhibit a model's successful deployment. By doing so, business users will better understand the characteristics and behavior in their (big) data, which will improve their attitude toward and acceptance of the resulting analytical models. Educational institutions must learn to balance between theory and practice, since it is known that many academic degrees mold students who are skewed to either too much analytical or too much practical knowledge.

A Data Scientist Should Have a Solid Business Understanding

While this might seem obvious, we have witnessed (too) many data science projects that failed since the respective data scientist did not understand the business problem at hand. By *business* we refer to the respective application area. Several examples of such application areas have been introduced in Table 1.5. Each of those fields has its own particularities that are important for a data scientist to know and understand in order to be able to design and implement a customized solution. The more aligned the solution with the environment, the better its performance will be, as evaluated according to each of the dimensions or criteria discussed in Table 1.7.

A Data Scientist Should Be Creative!

A data scientist needs creativity on at least two levels. First, on a technical level, it is important to be creative with regard to feature selection,

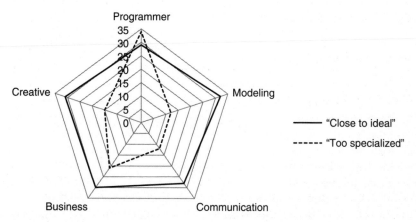

Figure 1.2 Profile of a data scientist.

data transformation and cleaning. These steps of the standard analytics process have to be adapted to each particular application and often the *right guess* could make a big difference. Second, big data and analytics is a fast-evolving field. New problems, technologies, and corresponding challenges pop up on an ongoing basis. Therefore, it is crucial that a data scientist keeps up with these new evolutions and technologies and has enough creativity to see how they can create new opportunities. Figure 1.2 summarizes the key characteristics and strengths constituting the ideal data scientist profile.

CONCLUSION

Profit-driven business analytics is about analyzing data for making optimized operational business decisions. In this first chapter, we discussed how adopting a business perspective toward analytics diverges from a purely technical or statistical perspective. Adopting such a business perspective leads to a real need for approaches that allow data scientists to take into account the specificities of the business context. The objective of this book therefore is to provide an in-depth overview of selected sets of such approaches, which may serve a wide and diverse range of business purposes. The book adopts a practitioner's perspective in detailing how to practically apply and implement these approaches, with example datasets, code, and implementations provided on the book's companion website, www .profit-analytics.com.

REVIEW QUESTIONS

Multiple Choice Questions

Question 1

Which is not a possible evaluation criterion for assessing an analytical model?

  a. Interpretability
  b. Economical cost
  c. Operational efficiency
  d. All of the above are possible evaluation criteria.

Question 2

Which statement is false?

  a. Clustering is a type of predictive analytics.
  b. Forecasting in essence concerns regression in function of time.
  c. Association analysis is a type of descriptive analytics.
  d. Survival analysis in essence concerns predicting the timing of an event.

Question 3

Which statement is true?

  a. Customer lifetime value estimation is an example of classification.
  b. Demand estimation is an example of classification.
  c. Customer churn prediction concerns regression.
  d. Detecting fraudulent credit-card transactions concerns classification.

Question 4

Which is not a characteristic of a good data scientist? A good data scientist:

  a. Has a solid business understanding.
  b. Is creative.
  c. Has thorough knowledge on legal aspects of applying analytics.
  d. Excels in communication and visualization of results.

Question 5

Which statement is true?

a. All analytical models are profit-driven when applied in a business setting.
b. Only predictive analytics are profit-driven, whereas descriptive analytics are not.
c. There is a difference between analyzing data for the purpose of explaining or predicting.
d. Descriptive analytics aims to explain what is observed, whereas predictive analytics aims to predict as accurately as possible.

Open Questions

Question 1

Discuss the difference between a statistical perspective and a business perspective toward analytics.

Question 2

Discuss the difference between modeling to explain and to predict.

Question 3

List and discuss the key characteristics of an analytical model.

Question 4

List and discuss the ideal characteristics and skills of a data scientist.

Question 5

Draw the analytics process model and briefly discuss the subsequent steps.

REFERENCES

Agrawal, R., and R. Srikant. 1994, September. "Fast algorithms for mining association rules." In *Proceedings of the 20th international conference on very large data bases, VLDB* (Volume 1215, pp. 487–499).

Athanassopoulos, A. 2000. "Customer Satisfaction Cues to Support Market Segmentation and Explain Switching Behavior." *Journal of Business Research* 47 (3): 191–207.

Baesens, B. 2014. *Analytics in a Big Data World: The Essential Guide to Data Science and Its Applications.* Hoboken, NJ: John Wiley and Sons.

Baesens, B., V. Van Vlasselaer, W. Verbeke. 2015. *Fraud Analytics Using Descriptive, Predictive, and Social Network Techniques: A Guide to Data Science for Fraud Detection.* Hoboken, NJ: John Wiley and Sons.

Bhattacharya, C. B. 1998. "When Customers Are Members: Customer Retention in Paid Membership Contexts." *Journal of the Academy of Marketing Science* 26 (1): 31–44.

Breiman, L. 2001. "Statistical Modeling: The Two Cultures." *Statistical Science* 16 (3): 199–215.

Cao, B. 2016. "Future Healthy Life Expectancy among Older Adults in the US: A Forecast Based on Cohort Smoking and Obesity History." *Population Health Metrics,* 14 (1), 1–14.

Chakraborty, G., P. Murali, and G. Satish. 2013. *Text Mining and Analysis: Practical Methods, Examples, and Case Studies Using SAS.* SAS Institute.

Coussement, K. 2014. "Improving Customer Retention Management through Cost-Sensitive Learning." *European Journal of Marketing* 48 (3/4): 477–495.

Dejaeger, K., W. Verbeke, D.Martens, and B. Baesens. 2012. "Data Mining Techniques for Software Effort Estimation: A Comparative Study." *IEEE Transactions on Software Engineering* 38: 375–397.

Elder IV, J., and H. Thomas. 2012. *Practical Text Mining and Statistical Analysis for Non-Structured Text Data Applications.* Cambridge, MA: Academic Press.

Han, J., and M. Kamber. 2011. *Data Mining: Concepts and Techniques.* Amsterdam: Elsevier.

Hand, D. J., H. Mannila, and P. Smyth. 2001. *Principles of Data Mining.* Cambridge, MA: MIT Press.

Hyndman, R. J., A. B. Koehler, J. K. Ord, and R. D. Snyder. 2008. "Forecasting with Exponential Smoothing." *Springer Series in Statistics,* 1–356.

Peto, R., G. Whitlock, and P. Jha. 2010. "Effects of Obesity and Smoking on U.S. Life Expectancy." *The New England Journal of Medicine* 362 (9): 855–857.

Shmueli, G., and O. R. Koppius. 2011. "Predictive Analytics in Information Systems Research." *MIS Quarterly* 35 (3): 553–572.

Tan, P.-N., M. Steinbach, and V. Kumar. 2005. *Introduction to Data Mining*. Reading, MA: Addison Wesley.

Van Gestel, T., and B. Baesens. 2009. *Credit Risk Management: Basic Concepts: Financial Risk Components, Rating Analysis, Models, Economic and Regulatory Capital*. Oxford: Oxford University Press.

Verbeke, W., D. Martens, and B. Baesens. 2014. "Social Network Analysis for Customer Churn Prediction." *Applied Soft Computing* 14: 431–446.

Verbraken, T., C. Bravo, R. Weber, and B. Baesens. 2014. "Development and Application of Consumer Credit Scoring Models Using Profit-Based Classification Measures." *European Journal of Operational Research* 238 (2): 505–513.

Widodo, A., and B. S. Yang. 2011. "Machine Health Prognostics Using Survival Probability and Support Vector Machine." *Expert Systems with Applications* 38 (7): 8430–8437.

CHAPTER 2

Analytical Techniques

INTRODUCTION

Data are everywhere. IBM projects that every day we generate 2.5 quintillion bytes of data. In relative terms, this means 90% of the data in the world has been created in the last two years. These massive amounts of data yield an unprecedented treasure of internal knowledge, ready to be analyzed using state-of-the-art analytical techniques to better understand and exploit behavior about, for example, your customers or employees by identifying new business opportunities together with new strategies. In this chapter, we zoom into **analytical techniques.** As such, the chapter provides the backbone for all other subsequent chapters. We build on the analytics process model reviewed in the introductory chapter to structure the discussions in this chapter and start by highlighting a number of key activities that take place during data preprocessing. Next, the data analysis stage is elaborated. We turn our attention to predictive analytics and discuss linear regression, logistic regression, decision trees, neural networks, and random forests. A subsequent section elaborates on descriptive analytics such as association rules, sequence rules and clustering. Survival analysis techniques are also discussed, where the aim is to predict the timing of events instead of only event occurrence. The chapter concludes by zooming into social network analytics, where the goal is to incorporate network information into descriptive or predictive analytical models. Throughout the chapter, we discuss standard approaches for evaluating these different types of analytical techniques, as highlighted in the final stage of the analytical process model.

DATA PREPROCESSING

Data are the key ingredient for any analytical exercise. Hence, it is important to thoroughly consider and gather all data sources that are potentially of interest and relevant before starting the analysis. Large experiments as well as a broad experience in different fields indicate that when it comes to data, bigger is better. However, real life data can be (typically are) dirty because of inconsistencies, incompleteness, duplication, merging, and many other problems. Hence, throughout the analytical modeling steps, various data preprocessing checks are applied to clean up and reduce the data to a manageable and relevant size. Worth mentioning here is the *garbage in, garbage out* (GIGO) principle that essentially states that messy data will yield messy analytical models. Hence, it is of utmost importance that every data preprocessing step is carefully justified, carried out, validated, and documented before proceeding with further analysis. Even the slightest mistake can make the data totally unusable for further analysis, and completely invalidate the results. In what follows, we briefly zoom into some of the most important data preprocessing activities.

Denormalizing Data for Analysis

The application of analytics typically requires or presumes the data to be presented in a single table, containing and representing all the data in some structured way. A structured data table allows straightforward processing and analysis, as briefly discussed in Chapter 1. Typically, the rows of a data table represent the basic entities to which the analysis applies (e.g., customers, transactions, firms, claims, or cases). The rows are also referred to as observations, instances, records, or lines. The columns in the data table contain information about the basic entities. Plenty of synonyms are used to denote the columns of the data table, such as (explanatory or predictor) variables, inputs, fields, characteristics, attributes, indicators, and features, among others. In this book, we will consistently use the terms observation and variable.

Several normalized source data tables have to be merged in order to construct the aggregated, denormalized data table. Merging tables involves selecting information from different tables related to an individual entity, and copying it to the aggregated data table. The individual entity can be recognized and selected in the different tables by making use of (primary) keys, which are attributes that have specifically been included in the table to allow identifying and relating observations from different source tables pertaining to the same entity. Figure 2.1 illustrates the process of merging two tables—that is, transaction

Customer data		
ID	Age	Start date
XWV	31	01-01-15
BBC	49	10-02-15
VVQ	21	15-02-15

Transactions		
ID	Date	Amount
XWV	02-01-15	52 €
XWV	06-02-15	21 €
XWV	03-03-15	13 €
BBC	17-02-15	45 €
BBC	01-03-15	75 €
VVQ	02-03-15	56 €

Non-normalized data table				
ID	Date	Amount	Age	Start date
XWV	02-01-15	52 €	31	01-01-15
XWV	06-02-15	21 €	31	01-01-15
XWV	03-03-15	13 €	31	01-01-15
BBC	17-02-15	45 €	49	10-02-15
BBC	01-03-15	75 €	49	10-02-15
VVQ	02-03-15	56 €	21	15-02-15

Figure 2.1 Aggregating normalized data tables into a non-normalized data table.

data and customer data—into a single, non-normalized data table by making use of the key attribute ID, which allows connecting observations in the transactions table with observations in the customer table. The same approach can be followed to merge as many tables as required, but clearly the more tables are merged, the more duplicate data might be included in the resulting table. It is crucial that no errors are introduced during this process, so some checks should be applied to control the resulting table and to make sure that all information is correctly integrated.

Sampling

The aim of sampling is to take a subset of historical data (e.g., past transactions), and use that to build an analytical model. A first obvious question that comes to mind concerns the need for sampling. Obviously, with the availability of high performance computing facilities (e.g., grid and cloud computing), one could also try to directly analyze the full dataset. However, a key requirement for a good sample is that it should be representative for the future entities on which the analytical model will be run. Hence, the timing aspect becomes important since, for instance, transactions of today are more similar to transactions of tomorrow than they are to transactions of yesterday. Choosing the optimal time window of the sample involves a trade-off between lots of data (and hence a more robust analytical model) and recent data (which may be more representative). The sample should also be taken from an average business period to get as accurate as possible a picture of the target population.

Exploratory Analysis

Exploratory analysis is a very important part of getting to know your data in an "informal" way. It allows gaining some initial insights into the data, which can then be usefully adopted throughout the analytical modeling stage. Different plots/graphs can be useful here such as bar charts, pie charts, and scatter plots, for example. A next step is to summarize the data by using some descriptive statistics, which all summarize or provide information with respect to a particular characteristic of the data. Hence, they should be assessed together (i.e., in support and completion of each other). Basic descriptive statistics are the mean and median values of continuous variables, with the median value less sensitive to extreme values but then, as well, not providing as much information with respect to the full distribution. Complementary to the mean value, the variation or the standard deviation provide insight with respect to how much the data are spread around the mean value. Likewise, percentile values such as the 10th, 25th, 75th, and 90th percentile provide further information with respect to the distribution and as a complement to the median value. For categorical variables, other measures need to be considered such as the mode or most frequently occurring value.

Missing Values

Missing values (see Table 2.1) can occur for various reasons. The information can be nonapplicable—for example, when modeling the amount of fraud, this information is only available for the fraudulent accounts and not for the nonfraudulent accounts since it is not applicable there (Baesens et al. 2015). The information can also be undisclosed. For example, a customer decided not to disclose his or her income because of privacy. Missing data can also originate because of an error during merging (e.g., typos in name or ID). Missing values can be very meaningful from an analytical perspective since they may indicate a particular pattern. As an example, a missing value

Table 2.1 Missing Values in a Dataset

Customer	Age	Income	Gender	Duration	Churn
John	30	1,800	?	620	Yes
Sarah	25	?	Female	12	No
Sophie	52	?	Female	830	No
David	?	2,200	Male	90	Yes
Peter	34	2,000	Male	270	No
Titus	44	?	?	39	No
Josephine	22	?	Female	5	No
Victor	26	1,500	Male	350	No
Hannah	34	?	Female	159	Yes
Catherine	50	2,100	Female	352	No

for income could imply unemployment, which may be related to, for example, default or churn. Some analytical techniques (e.g., decision trees) can directly deal with missing values. Other techniques need some additional preprocessing. Popular missing value handling schemes are removal of the observation or variable, and replacement (e.g., by the mean/median for continuous variables and by the mode for categorical variables).

Outlier Detection and Handling

Outliers are extreme observations that are very dissimilar to the rest of the population. Two types of outliers can be considered: valid observations (e.g., salary of boss is €1.000.000) and invalid observations (e.g., age is 300 years). Two important steps in dealing with outliers are detection and treatment. A first obvious check for outliers is to calculate the minimum and maximum values for each of the data elements. Various graphical tools can also be used to detect outliers, such as histograms, box plots, and scatter plots. Some analytical techniques (e.g., decision trees) are fairly robust with respect to outliers. Others (e.g., linear/logistic regression) are more sensitive to them. Various schemes exist to deal with outliers; these are highly dependent on whether the outlier represents a valid or an invalid observation. For invalid observations (e.g., age is 300 years), one could treat the outlier as a missing value by using any of the schemes (i.e., removal or replacement) mentioned in the previous section. For valid observations (e.g., income is €1,000,000), other schemes are needed such as capping whereby lower and upper limits are defined for each data element.

Principal Component Analysis

A popular technique for reducing dimensionality, studying linear correlations, and visualizing complex datasets is principal component analysis (PCA). This technique has been known since the beginning of the last century (Jolliffe 2002), and it is based on the concept of constructing an uncorrelated, orthogonal basis of the original dataset.

Throughout this section, we will assume that the observation matrix X is normalized to zero mean, so that $E[X] = 0$. We do this so the covariance matrix of X is exactly equal to $X^T X$. In case the matrix is not normalized, then the only consequence is that the calculations have an extra (constant) term, so assuming a centered dataset will simplify the analyses.

The idea for PCA is simple: is it possible to engulf our data in an ellipsoid? If so, what would that ellipsoid look like? We would like four properties to hold:

1. Each principal component should capture as much variance as possible.
2. The variance that each principal component captures should decrease in each step.
3. The transformation should respect the distances between the observations and the angles that they form (i.e., should be orthogonal).
4. The coordinates should not be correlated with each other.

The answer to these questions lies in the eigenvectors and eigenvalues of the data matrix. The orthogonal basis of a matrix is the set of eigenvectors (coordinates) so that each one is orthogonal to each other, or, from a statistical point of view, uncorrelated with each other. The order of the components comes from a property of the covariance matrix $X^T X$: if the eigenvectors are ordered by the eigenvalues of $X^T X$, then the highest eigenvalue will be associated with the coordinate that represents the most variance. Another interesting property of the eigenvalues and the eigenvectors, proven below, is that the eigenvalues of $X^T X$ are equal to the square of the eigenvalues of X, and that the eigenvectors of X and $X^T X$ are the same. This will simplify our analyses, as finding the orthogonal basis of X will be the same as finding the orthogonal basis of $X^T X$.

The principal component transformation of X will then calculate a new matrix P from the eigenvectors of X (or $X^T X$). If V is the matrix with the eigenvectors of X, then the transformation will calculate a new matrix $P = XV$. The question is how to calculate this orthogonal basis in an efficient way.

The **singular value decomposition (SVD)** of the original dataset X is the most efficient method of obtaining its principal components. The idea of the SVD is to decompose the dataset (matrix) X into a set of three matrices, U, D, and V, such that $X = UDV^T$, where V^T is the transpose of the matrix V^1, and U and V are **unitary matrices**, so $U^TU = V^TV = I$. The matrix D is a diagonal matrix so that each element d_i is the **singular value** of matrix X.

Now we can calculate the principal component transformation P of X. If $X = UDV^T$, then $P = XV = UDV^TV$. But, from $X = UDV^T$ we can calculate the expression $X^TX = VDU^TUDV^T = VD^2V^T$, and identifying terms we can see that matrix V is composed by the eigenvectors of X^TX, which are equal to the eigenvectors of X, and the eigenvalues of X will be equal to the square root of the eigenvalues of X^TX, D^2, as we previously stated. Thus, $P = UDV^TV = UD$, with D the eigenvalues of X and U the eigenvectors, or left singular vectors, of X.

Each vector in the matrix U will contain the corresponding weights for each variable in the dataset X, giving an interpretation of its relevance for that particular component. Each eigenvalue d_j will give an indication of the total variance explained by that component, so the percentage of explained variance of component j will be equal to $\mathrm{Var}_j = \dfrac{d_j}{\sum_k d_k}$.

To show how PCA can help with the analysis of our data, consider a dataset composed of two variables, x and y, as shown in Figure 2.2. This dataset is a simple one showing a 2D ellipsoid, i.e., an ellipse,

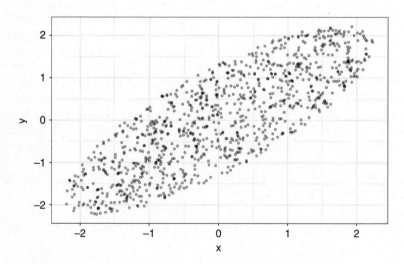

Figure 2.2 Example dataset showing an ellipse rotated in 45 degrees.

rotated 45° with respect to the *x* axis, and with proportion 3:1 between the large and the small axis. We would like to study the correlation between *x* and *y*, obtain the uncorrelated components, and calculate how much variance these components can capture.

Calculating the PCA of the dataset yields the following results:

$$D = \begin{pmatrix} 1.527 \\ 0.487 \end{pmatrix} \qquad\qquad U = \begin{bmatrix} 0.70 & -0.71 \\ 0.71 & 0.71 \end{bmatrix}$$

These results show that the first component is

$$PC1 = U_1 \cdot \begin{pmatrix} x \\ y \end{pmatrix} = 0.70x + 0.71y,$$

and the second one is

$$PC2 = U_2 \cdot \begin{pmatrix} x \\ y \end{pmatrix} = -0.71x + 0.71y.$$

As the two variables appear in the first component, there is some correlation between the values of *x* and *y* (as it is easily seen in Figure 2.2). The percentage of variance explained for each principal component can be calculated from the singular values: $Var_1 = 1.527/(1.527 + 0.487) = 0.7582$, so the first component explains 75.82% of the total variance, and the remaining component explains 24.18%. These values are not at all surprising: The data come from a simulation of 1,000 points over the surface of an ellipse with proportion 3:1 between the main axis and the second axis, rotated 45°. This means the rotation has to follow $\cos(\pi/4) = \sqrt{2}/2 \approx 0.707$ and that the variance has to follow the 3:1 proportion. We can also visualize the results of the PCA algorithm. We expect uncorrelated values (so no rotation) and scaled components so that the first one is more important (so no ellipse, just a circle). Figure 2.3 shows the resulting rotation.

Figure 2.3 shows exactly what we expect, and gives an idea of how the algorithm works. We have created an overlay of the original *x* and *y* axes as well, which are just rotated 45°. On the book's website, we have provided the code to generate this example and to experiment with different rotations and variance proportions.

PCA is one of the most important techniques for data analysis, and should be in the toolbox of every data scientist. Even though it is a very simple technique dealing only with linear correlations, it helps in getting a quick overview of the data and the most important variables in the dataset. Here are some application areas of PCA:

- ◼ *Dimensionality reduction:* The percentage of variance explained by each PCA component is a way to reduce the dimensions of

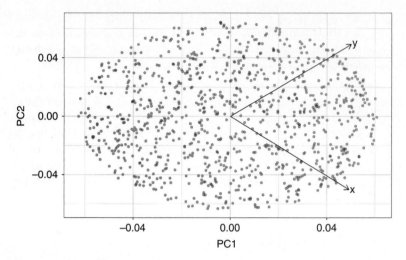

Figure 2.3 PCA of the simulated data.

a dataset. A PCA transform can be calculated from the original dataset, and then the first k components can be used by setting a cutoff T on the variance so that $D_k = \arg\min_k \left\{ \sum_i^k \text{Var}_i < T \right\}$. We can then use the reduced dataset as input for further analyses.

■ *Input selection:* Studying the output of the matrix **P** can give an idea of which inputs are the more relevant from a variance perspective. If variable j is not part of any of the first components, $v_{k'}^j = 0$ for all $k' \in \{1 \ldots k\}$, with k the component such that the variance explained is considered sufficient, then that variable can be discarded with high certainty. Note that this does not consider nonlinear relationships in the data, though, so it should be used with care.

■ *Visualization:* One popular application of PCA is to visualize complex datasets. If the first two or three components accurately represent a large part of the variance, then the dataset can be plotted, and thus multivariate relationships can be observed in a 2D or 3D plot. For an example of this, see Chapter 5 on Profit-Driven Analytical Techniques.

■ *Text mining and information retrieval:* An important technique for the analysis of text documents is latent semantic analysis (Landauer 2006). This technique estimates the SVD transform (principal components) of the term-document matrix, a matrix that summarizes the importance of different words across a set of documents, and drops components that are not relevant for their comparison. This way, complex texts with thousands of words are reduced to a much smaller set of important components.

PCA is a powerful tool for the analysis of datasets—in particular for exploratory and descriptive data analysis. The idea of PCA can be extended to non-linear relationships as well. For example, **Kernel PCA** (Schölkopf et al. 1998) is a procedure that allows transforming complex nonlinear spaces using kernel functions, following a methodology similar to Support Vector Machines. Vidal et al. (2005) also generalized the idea of PCA to multiple space segments, to construct a more complex partition of the data.

TYPES OF ANALYTICS

Once the preprocessing step is finished, we can move on to the next step, which is analytics. Synonyms of analytics are data science, data mining, knowledge discovery, and predictive or descriptive modeling. The aim here is to extract valid and useful business patterns or mathematical decision models from a preprocessed dataset. Depending on the aim of the modeling exercise, various analytical techniques can be used coming from a variety of different background disciplines, such as machine learning and statistics. In what follows, we discuss predictive analytics, descriptive analytics, survival analysis, and social network analytics.

PREDICTIVE ANALYTICS

Introduction

In predictive analytics, the aim is to build an analytical model predicting a target measure of interest (Hastie, Tibshirani et al. 2011). The target is then typically used to steer the learning process during an optimization procedure. Two types of predictive analytics can be distinguished: regression and classification. In regression, the target variable is continuous. Popular examples are predicting customer lifetime value, sales, stock prices, or loss given default. In classification, the target is categorical. Popular examples are predicting churn, response, fraud, and credit default. Different types of predictive analytics techniques have been suggested in the literature. In what follows, we discuss a selection of techniques with a particular focus on the practitioner's perspective.

Linear Regression

Linear regression is undoubtedly the most commonly used technique to model a continuous target variable: for example, in a customer lifetime value (CLV) context, a linear regression model can be defined to model the CLV in terms of the age of the customer, income, gender, etc.:

$$CLV = \beta_0 + \beta_1 Age + \beta_2 Income + \beta_3 Gender + \cdots$$

The general formulation of the linear regression model then becomes:

$$y = \beta_0 + \beta_1 x_1 + \cdots + \beta_k x_k,$$

whereby y represents the target variable, and $x_i, \ldots x_k$ the explanatory variables. The $\boldsymbol{\beta} = [\beta_1; \beta_2 \ldots; \beta_k]$ parameters measure the impact on the target variable y of each of the individual explanatory variables. Let us now assume we start with a dataset $D = \{(\boldsymbol{x}_i, y_i)\}_{i=1}^n$ with n observations and k explanatory variables structured as depicted in Table 2.2.

The $\boldsymbol{\beta}$ parameters of the linear regression model can then be estimated by minimizing the following squared error function:

$$\frac{1}{2}\sum_{i=1}^n e_i^2 = \frac{1}{2}\sum_{i=1}^n (y_i - \hat{y}_i)^2 = \frac{1}{2}\sum_{i=1}^n (y_i - (\beta_0 + \boldsymbol{\beta}^T \boldsymbol{x}_i))^2,$$

whereby y_i represents the target value for observation i, $\hat{y}_i$ the prediction made by the linear regression model for observation i, and $\boldsymbol{x}_i$ the vector with the predictive variables. Graphically, this idea corresponds to minimizing the sum of all error squares as represented in Figure 2.4.

Straightforward mathematical calculus then yields the following closed-form formula for the weight parameter vector $\hat{\boldsymbol{\beta}}$:

$$\hat{\boldsymbol{\beta}} = \begin{bmatrix} \hat{\beta}_0 \\ \hat{\beta}_1 \\ \cdots \\ \hat{\beta}_k \end{bmatrix} = (\boldsymbol{X}^T \boldsymbol{X})^{-1} \boldsymbol{X}^T \boldsymbol{y},$$

Table 2.2 Dataset for Linear Regression

Observation	x_1	x_2	...	x_k	Y
$\boldsymbol{x}_1$	$\boldsymbol{x}_1(1)$	$\boldsymbol{x}_1(2)$	...	$\boldsymbol{x}_1(k)$	y_1
$\boldsymbol{x}_2$	$\boldsymbol{x}_2(1)$	$\boldsymbol{x}_2(2)$	....	$\boldsymbol{x}_2(k)$	y_2
....	....	....	....	....	....
$\boldsymbol{x}_n$	$\boldsymbol{x}_n(1)$	$\boldsymbol{x}_n(2)$	....	$\boldsymbol{x}_n(k)$	y_n

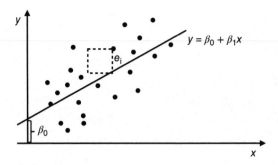

Figure 2.4 OLS regression.

whereby X represents the matrix with the explanatory variable values augmented with an additional column of ones to account for the intercept term β_0, and y represents the target value vector. This model and corresponding parameter optimization procedure are often referred to as ordinary least squares (OLS) regression. A key advantage of OLS regression is that it is simple and thus easy to understand. Once the parameters have been estimated, the model can be evaluated in a straightforward way, hereby contributing to its operational efficiency. Note that more sophisticated variants have been suggested in the literature—for example, ridge regression, lasso regression, time series models (ARIMA, VAR, GARCH), and multivariate adaptive regression splines (MARS). Most of these relax the linearity assumption by introducing additional transformations, albeit at the cost of increased complexity.

Logistic Regression

Basic Concepts

Consider a classification dataset in a response modeling setting, as depicted in Table 2.3.

When modeling the binary response target using linear regression, one gets:

$$y = \beta_0 + \beta_1 Age + \beta_2 Income + \beta_3 Gender$$

When estimating this using OLS, two key problems arise:

- The errors/target are not normally distributed but follow a Bernoulli distribution with only two values.
- There is no guarantee that the target is between 0 and 1, which would be handy since it can then be interpreted as a probability.

Table 2.3 Example Classification Dataset

Customer	Age	Income	Gender	...	Response	y
John	30	1,200	M	....	No	0
Sarah	25	800	F	....	Yes	1
Sophie	52	2,200	F	....	Yes	1
David	48	2,000	M	....	No	0
Peter	34	1,800	M	....	Yes	1

Consider now the following bounding function,

$$f(z) = \frac{1}{1 + e^{-z}}$$

which looks as shown in Figure 2.5. For every possible value of z, the outcome is always between 0 and 1. Hence, by combining the linear regression with the bounding function, we get the following logistic regression model:

$$p(response = yes|Age, Income, Gender) = \frac{1}{1 + e^{-(\beta_0 + \beta_1 Age + \beta_2 Income + \beta_3 Gender)}}$$

The outcome of the above model is always bounded between 0 and 1, no matter which values of age, income, and gender are being used, and can as such be interpreted as a probability.

The general formulation of the logistic regression model then becomes (Allison 2001):

$$p(y = 1|x_1, \ldots, x_k) = \frac{1}{1 + e^{-(\beta_0 + \beta_1 x_1 + \cdots + \beta_k x_k)}}.$$

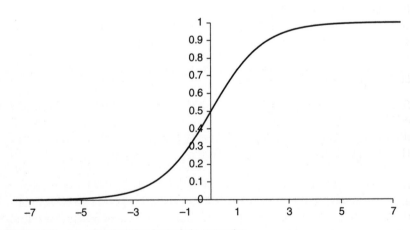

Figure 2.5 Bounding function for logistic regression.

Since $p(y = 0|x_1, \ldots, x_k) = 1 - p(y = 1|x_1, \ldots, x_k)$, we have

$$p(y = 0|x_1, \ldots, x_k) = 1 - \frac{1}{1 + e^{-(\beta_0 + \beta_1 x_1 + \cdots + \beta_k x_k)}} = \frac{1}{1 + e^{(\beta_0 + \beta_1 x_1 + \cdots + \beta_k x_k)}}.$$

Hence, both $p(y = 1|x_1, \ldots, x_k)$ and $p(y = 0|x_1, \ldots, x_k)$ are bounded between 0 and 1. Reformulating in terms of the odds, the model becomes:

$$\frac{p(y = 1|x_1, \ldots, x_k)}{p(y = 0|x_1, \ldots, x_k)} = e^{(\beta_0 + \beta_1 x_1 + \cdots + \beta_k x_k)}$$

or in terms of the log odds, also called the logit,

$$\ln\left(\frac{p(y = 1|x_1, \ldots, x_k)}{p(y = 0|x_1, \ldots, x_k)}\right) = \beta_0 + \beta_1 x_1 + \cdots + \beta_k x_k$$

The β parameters of a logistic regression model are then estimated using the idea of maximum likelihood. Maximum likelihood optimization chooses the parameters in such a way so as to maximize the probability of getting the sample at hand. First, the likelihood function is constructed. For observation i, the probability of observing either class equals

$$p(y = 1|x_i)^{y_i}(1 - p(y = 1|x_i))^{1-y_i},$$

whereby y_i represents the target value (either 0 or 1) for observation i. The likelihood function across all n observations then becomes

$$\prod_{i=1}^{n} p(y = 1|x_i)^{y_i}(1 - p(y = 1|x_i))^{1-y_i}.$$

To simplify the optimization, the logarithmic transformation of the likelihood function is taken and the corresponding log-likelihood can then be optimized using, for instance, the iteratively reweighted least squares method (Hastie, Tibshirani et al. 2011).

Logistic Regression Properties

Since logistic regression is linear in the log odds (logit), it basically estimates a linear decision boundary to separate both classes. This is illustrated in Figure 2.6 whereby Y (N) corresponds to Response = Yes (Response = No).

To interpret a logistic regression model, one can calculate the odds ratio. Suppose variable x_i increases with one unit with all other variables being kept constant (ceteris paribus), then the new logit becomes the old logit increased with β_i. Likewise, the new odds become the old odds multiplied by e^{β_i}. The latter represents the odds ratio—that is,

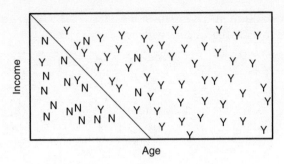

Figure 2.6 Linear decision boundary of logistic regression.

the multiplicative increase in the odds when x_i increases by 1 (ceteris paribus). Hence,

- $\beta_i > 0$ implies $e^{\beta_i} > 1$ and the odds and probability increase with x_i.
- $\beta_i < 0$ implies $e^{\beta_i} < 1$ and the odds and probability decrease with x_i.

Another way of interpreting a logistic regression model is by calculating the doubling amount. This represents the amount of change required for doubling the primary outcome odds. It can be easily seen that, for a particular variable x_i, the doubling amount equals $\log(2)/\beta_i$.

Variable Selection for Linear and Logistic Regression

Variable selection aims at reducing the number of variables in a model. It will make the model more concise and thus interpretable, faster to evaluate, and more robust or stable by reducing collinearity. Both linear and logistic regressions have built-in procedures to perform variable selection. These are based on statistical hypotheses tests to verify whether the coefficient of a variable i is significantly different from zero:

$$H_0: \beta_i = 0$$
$$H_A: \beta_i \neq 0$$

In linear regression, the test statistic becomes

$$t = \frac{\widehat{\beta_i}}{s.e.(\widehat{\beta_i})},$$

and follows a Student's t-distribution with $n - 2$ degrees of freedom, whereas in logistic regression, the test statistic is

$$\chi^2 = \left(\frac{\hat{\beta}_i}{s.e.(\hat{\beta}_i)} \right)^2$$

and follows a chi-squared distribution with 1 degree of freedom. Note that both test statistics are intuitive in the sense that they will reject the null hypothesis H_0 if the estimated coefficient $\hat{\beta}_i$ is high in absolute value compared to its standard error $s.e.(\hat{\beta}_i)$. The latter can be easily obtained as a byproduct of the optimization procedure. Based on the value of the test statistic, one calculates the p-value, which is the probability of getting a more extreme value than the one observed. This is visualized in Figure 2.7, assuming a value of 3 for the test statistic. Note that since the hypothesis test is two-sided, the p-value adds the areas to the right of 3 and to the left of –3.

In other words, a low (high) p-value represents a(n) (in)significant variable. From a practical viewpoint, the p-value can be compared against a significance level. Table 2.4 presents some commonly used values to decide on the degree of variable significance. Various variable selection procedures can now be used based on the p-value. Suppose one has four variables $x_1, x_2, x_3,$ and x_4 (e.g., income, age, gender, amount of transaction). The number of optimal variable subsets equals $2^4 - 1$, or 15, as displayed in Figure 2.8.

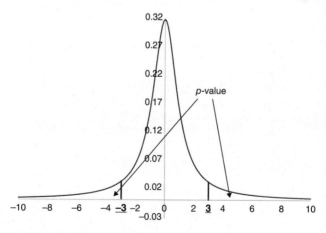

Figure 2.7 Calculating the p-value with a Student's t-distribution.

Table 2.4 Reference Values for Variable Significance

p-value < 0.01	Highly significant
0.01 < p-value < 0.05	Significant
0.05 < p-value < 0.10	Weakly significant
p-value > 0.10	Not significant

When the number of variables is small, an exhaustive search amongst all variable subsets can be performed. However, as the number of variables increases, the search space grows exponentially and heuristic search procedures are needed. Using the p-values, the variable space can be navigated in three possible ways. Forward regression starts from the empty model and always adds variables based on low p-values. Backward regression starts from the full model and always removes variables based on high p-values. Stepwise regression is a combination of both. It starts off like forward regression, but once the second variable has been added, it will always check the other variables in the model and remove them if they turn out to be insignificant according to their p-value. Obviously, all three procedures assume preset significance levels, which should be established by the user before the variable selection procedure starts.

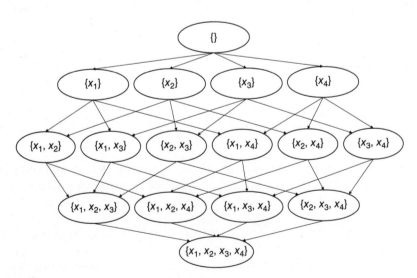

Figure 2.8 Variable subsets for four variables x_1, x_2, x_3, and x_4.

In many customer analytics settings, it is very important to be aware that statistical significance is only one evaluation criterion to do variable selection. As mentioned before, interpretability is also an important criterion. In both linear and logistic regression, this can be easily evaluated by inspecting the sign of the regression coefficient. It is hereby highly preferable that a coefficient has the same sign as anticipated by the business expert; otherwise he/she will be reluctant to use the model. Coefficients can have unexpected signs due to multicollinearity issues, noise, or small sample effects. Sign restrictions can be easily enforced in a forward regression set-up by preventing variables with the wrong sign from entering the model. Another criterion for variable selection is operational efficiency. This refers to the amount of resources that are needed for the collection and preprocessing of a variable. As an example, although trend variables are typically very predictive, they require a lot of effort to calculate and may thus not be suitable to be used in an online, real-time scoring environment such as credit-card fraud detection. The same applies to external data, where the latency might hamper a timely decision. Also, the economic cost of variables needs to be considered. Externally obtained variables (e.g., from credit bureaus, data poolers, etc.) can be useful and predictive, but usually come at a price that must be factored in when evaluating the model. When considering both operational efficiency and economic impact, it might sometimes be worthwhile to look for a correlated, less predictive but easier and cheaper-to-collect variable instead. Finally, legal issues also need to be properly taken into account. For example, some variables cannot be used in fraud detection and credit risk applications because of privacy or discrimination concerns.

Decision Trees

Basic Concepts

Decision trees are recursive partitioning algorithms (RPAs) that come up with a tree-like structure representing patterns in an underlying dataset (Duda, Hart et al. 2001). Figure 2.9 provides an example of a decision tree in a response modeling setting.

The top node is the root node specifying a testing condition of which the outcome corresponds to a branch leading up to an internal node. The terminal nodes of the tree assign the classifications (in our case response labels) and are also referred to as the leaf nodes.

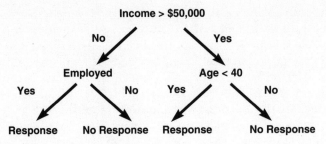

Figure 2.9 Example decision tree.

Many algorithms have been suggested in the literature to construct decision trees. Among the most popular are C4.5 (See5) (Quinlan 1993), CART (Breiman, Friedman et al. 1984), and CHAID (Hartigan 1975). These algorithms differ in the ways they answer the key decisions to build a tree, which are:

- *Splitting decision:* Which variable to split at what value (e.g., Income is > $50,000 or not, Age is < 40 or not, Employed is Yes or No, . . .).
- *Stopping decision:* When should you stop adding nodes to the tree? What is the optimal size of the tree?
- *Assignment decision:* What class (e.g., response or no response) should be assigned to a leaf node?

Usually, the assignment decision is the most straightforward to make since one typically looks at the majority class within the leaf node to make the decision. This idea is also referred to as winner-take-all learning. Alternatively, one may estimate class membership probabilities in a leaf node equal to the observed fractions of the classes. The other two decisions are less straightforward and are elaborated upon in what follows.

Splitting Decision

In order to answer the splitting decision, one needs to define the concept of impurity or chaos. Consider, for example, the three datasets of Figure 2.10, each containing good customers (e.g., responders, nonchurners, legitimates, etc.) represented by the unfilled circles and bad customers (e.g., nonresponders, churners, fraudsters, etc.) represented by the filled circles.[2] Minimal impurity occurs when all customers are either good or bad. Maximal impurity occurs when one has the same number of good and bad customers (i.e., the dataset in the middle).

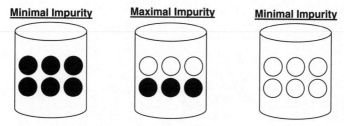

Figure 2.10 Example datasets for calculating impurity.

Decision trees will now aim at minimizing the impurity in the data. In order to do so appropriately, one needs a measure to quantify impurity. The most popular measures in the literature are as follows:

- Entropy: $E(S) = -p_G log_2(p_G) - p_B log_2(p_B)$ (C4.5/See5)
- Gini: $Gini(S) = -2p_G p_B$ (CART)
- Chi-squared analysis (CHAID)

with $p_G(p_B)$ being the proportions of good and bad, respectively. Both measures are depicted in Figure 2.11, where it can be clearly seen that the entropy (Gini) is minimal when all customers are either good or bad, and maximal in case of the same number of good and bad customers.

In order to answer the splitting decision, various candidate splits are now be evaluated in terms of their decrease in impurity. Consider, for example, a split on age as depicted in Figure 2.12.

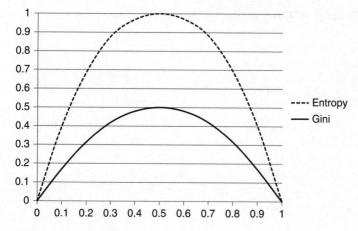

Figure 2.11 Entropy versus Gini.

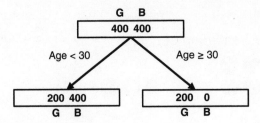

Figure 2.12 Calculating the entropy for age split.

The original dataset had maximum entropy since the amounts of goods and bads were the same. The entropy calculations now look like this:

- Entropy top node $= -\frac{1}{2} \cdot log_2 \left(\frac{1}{2}\right) - \frac{1}{2} \cdot log_2 \left(\frac{1}{2}\right) = 1$
- Entropy left node $= -\frac{1}{3} \cdot log_2 \left(\frac{1}{3}\right) - \frac{2}{3} \cdot log_2 \left(\frac{2}{3}\right) = 0.91$
- Entropy right node $= -1 \cdot log_2(1) - 0 \cdot log_2(0) = 0$

The weighted decrease in entropy, also known as the **gain,** can then be calculated as follows:

$$Gain = 1 - \left(\frac{600}{800}\right) \cdot 0.91 - \left(\frac{200}{800}\right) \cdot 0.32$$

The gain measures the weighted decrease in entropy thanks to the split. It speaks for itself that a higher gain is to be preferred. The decision tree algorithm will now consider different candidate splits for its root node and adopt a greedy strategy by picking the one with the biggest gain. Once the root node has been decided on, the procedure continues in a recursive way, each time adding splits with the biggest gain. In fact, this can be perfectly parallelized and both sides of the tree can grow in parallel, hereby increasing the efficiency of the tree construction algorithm.

Stopping Decision

The third decision relates to the stopping criterion. Obviously, if the tree continues to split, it will become very detailed with leaf nodes containing only a few observations. In the most extreme case, the tree will have one leaf node per observation and as such perfectly fit the data. However, by doing so, the tree will start to fit the specificities or noise in the data, which is also referred to as **overfitting.** In other words, the tree has become too complex and fails to correctly model the noise-free pattern or trend in the data. As such, it will generalize

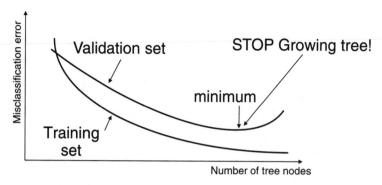

Figure 2.13   Using a validation set to stop growing a decision tree.

poorly to new unseen data. In order to avoid this happening, the dataset will be split into a training set and a validation set. The training set will be used to make the splitting decision. The validation set is an independent sample, set aside to monitor the misclassification error (or any other performance metric such as a profit-based measure) as the tree is grown. A commonly used split up is a 70% training set and 30% validation set. One then typically observes a pattern as depicted in Figure 2.13.

The error on the training set keeps on decreasing as the splits become more and more specific and tailored toward it. On the validation set, the error will initially decrease, which indicates that the tree splits generalize well. However, at some point the error will increase since the splits become too specific for the training set as the tree starts to memorize it. Where the validation set curve reaches its minimum, the procedure should be stopped, as otherwise overfitting will occur. Note that, as already mentioned, besides classification error, one might also use accuracy or profit-based measures on the y-axis to make the stopping decision. Also note that sometimes, simplicity is preferred above accuracy, and one can select a tree that does not necessarily have minimum validation set error, but a lower number of nodes or levels.

Decision-Tree Properties

In the example of Figure 2.9, every node had only two branches. The advantage of this is that the testing condition can be implemented as a simple yes/no question. Multiway splits allow for more than two branches and can provide trees that are wider but less deep. In a read-once decision tree, a particular attribute can be used only once in a certain tree path. Every tree can also be represented as a rule set since every path from a root note to a leaf node makes up a simple if-then rule. For the tree depicted in Figure 2.9, the corresponding rules are:

- **If** Income > $50,000 **And** Age < 40, **Then** Response = Yes
- **If** Income > $50,000 **And** Age ≥ 40, **Then** Response = No
- **If** Income ≤ $50,000 **And** Employed = Yes, **Then** Response = Yes
- **If** Income ≤ $50,000 **And** Employed = No, **Then** Response = No

These rules can then be easily implemented in all kinds of software packages (e.g., Microsoft Excel). Decision trees essentially model decision boundaries orthogonal to the axes. Figure 2.14 illustrates an example decision tree.

Regression Trees

Decision trees can also be used to predict continuous targets. Consider the example of Figure 2.15, where a regression tree is used to predict the fraud percentage (FP). The latter can be expressed as the percentage of a predefined limit based on, for example, the maximum transaction amount.

Other criteria now need to be used to make the splitting decision since the impurity will need to be measured in another way. One way to measure impurity in a node is by calculating the mean squared error (MSE) as follows:

$$MSE = \frac{1}{n} \sum_{i=1}^{n} (y_i - \bar{y})^2,$$

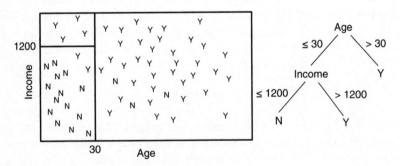

Figure 2.14 Decision boundary of a decision tree.

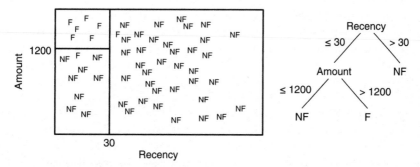

Figure 2.15 Example regression tree for predicting the fraud percentage.

whereby n represents the number of observations in a leaf node, y_i the value of observation i, and $\bar{y}$, the average of all values in the leaf node. Obviously, it is desirable to have a low MSE in a leaf node since this indicates that the node is more homogeneous.

Another way to make the splitting decision is by conducting a simple analysis of variance (ANOVA) test and then calculating an F-statistic as follows:

$$F = \frac{SS_{between}/(B-1)}{SS_{within}/(n-B)} \sim F_{n-B,B-1},$$

whereby

$$SS_{between} = \sum_{b=1}^{B} n_b (\bar{y}_b - \bar{y})^2$$

$$SS_{within} = \sum_{b=1}^{B} \sum_{i=1}^{n_b} (y_{bi} - \bar{y}_b)^2$$

with B the number of branches of the split, n_b the number of observations in branch b, $\bar{y}_b$ the average in branch b, y_{bi} the value of observation i in branch b, and $\bar{y}$ the overall average. Good splits favor homogeneity within a node (low SS_{within}) and heterogeneity between nodes (high $SS_{between}$). In other words, good splits should have a high F-value, or low corresponding p-value.

The stopping decision can be made in a similar way as for classification trees but using a regression-based performance measure (e.g., mean squared error, mean absolute deviation, coefficient of determination, etc.) on the y-axis. The assignment decision can be made by assigning the mean (or median) to each leaf node. Note that standard deviations and thus confidence intervals may also be computed for each of the leaf nodes.

Neural Networks

Basic Concepts

A first perspective on the origin of neural networks states that they are mathematical representations inspired by the functioning of the human brain. Although this may sound appealing, another more realistic perspective sees neural networks as generalizations of existing statistical models (Zurada 1992; Bishop 1995). Let us take logistic regression as an example:

$$p(y = 1 | x_1, \ldots, x_k) = \frac{1}{1 + e^{-(\beta_0 + \beta_1 x_1 + \cdots + \beta_k x_k)}},$$

We could visualize this model as follows:

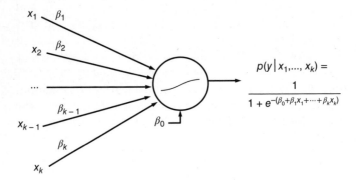

Figure 2.16 Neural network representation of logistic regression.

The processing element or neuron in the middle basically performs two operations: it takes the inputs and multiplies them with the weights (including the intercept term β_0, which is called the bias term in neural networks) and then puts this into a nonlinear transformation function similar to the one we discussed in the section on logistic regression. So logistic regression is a neural network with one neuron. Similarly, we could visualize linear regression as a one neuron neural network with the identity transformation $f(z) = z$. We can now generalize the above picture to a multilayer perceptron (MLP) neural network by adding more layers and neurons as follows (Bishop 1995; Zurada, 1992; Bishop 1995).

The example in Figure 2.17 is an MLP with one input layer, one hidden layer, and one output layer. The hidden layer essentially works like a feature extractor by combining the inputs into features that are then subsequently offered to the output layer to make the optimal

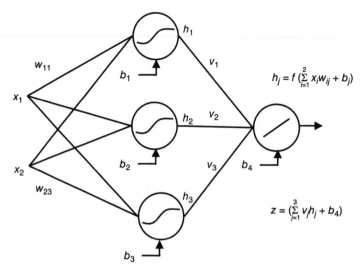

$$h_j = f\left(\sum_{i=1}^{2} x_i w_{ij} + b_j\right)$$

$$z = \left(\sum_{j=1}^{3} v_j h_j + b_4\right)$$

Figure 2.17 A Multilayer Perceptron (MLP) neural network.

prediction. The hidden layer has a non-linear transformation function f and the output layer a linear transformation function. The most popular transformation functions (also called squashing or activation functions) are:

- Logistic, $f(z) = \frac{1}{1+e^{-z}}$, ranging between 0 and 1
- Hyperbolic tangent, $f(z) = \frac{e^z - e^{-z}}{e^z + e^{-z}}$, ranging between -1 and $+1$
- Linear, $f(z) = z$, ranging between $-\infty$ and $+\infty$

Although theoretically the activation functions may differ per neuron, they are typically fixed for each layer. For classification (e.g., churn), it is common practice to adopt a logistic transformation in the output layer, since the outputs can then be interpreted as probabilities (Baesens et al. 2002). For regression targets (e.g., CLV), one could use any of the transformation functions listed above. Typically, one will use the hyperbolic tangent activation function in the hidden layer.

In terms of hidden layers, theoretical works have shown that neural networks with one hidden layer are universal approximators, capable of approximating any function to any desired degree of accuracy on a compact interval (Hornik et al., 1989). Only for discontinuous functions (e.g., a saw tooth pattern) or in a deep learning context, it could make sense to try out more hidden layers. Note, however, that these complex patterns rarely occur in practice. In a customer analytics setting, it is recommended to continue the analysis with one hidden layer.

Weight Learning

As discussed earlier, for simple statistical models such as linear regression, there exists a closed-form mathematical formula for the optimal parameter values. However, for neural networks, the optimization is a lot more complex and the weights sitting on the various connections need to be estimated using an iterative algorithm. The objective of the algorithm is to find the weights that optimize a cost function, also called an objective or error function. Similarly to linear regression, when the target variable is continuous, a mean squared error (MSE) cost function will be optimized as follows:

$$\frac{1}{2}\sum_{i=1}^{n} e_i^2 = \frac{1}{2}\sum_{i=1}^{n}(y_i - \hat{y}_l)^2,$$

where y_i now represents the neural network prediction for observation i. In case of a binary target variable, a likelihood cost function can be optimized as follows:

$$\prod_{i=1}^{n} p(y = 1|x_i)^{y_i}(1 - p(y = 1|x_i))^{1-y_i}$$

where $p(y = 1|x_i)$ represents the conditional positive class probability prediction for observation i obtained from the neural network.

The optimization procedure typically starts from a set of random weights (e.g., drawn from a standard normal distribution), which are then iteratively adjusted to the patterns in the data by the optimization algorithm. Popular optimization algorithms for neural network learning are back propagation learning, Conjugate gradient and Levenberg-Marquardt. (See Bishop (1995) for more details.) A key issue to note here is the curvature of the cost function, which is not convex and may be multimodal as illustrated in Figure 2.18. The cost function can thus have multiple local minima but typically only one global minimum. Hence, if the starting weights are chosen in a suboptimal way, one may get stuck in a local minimum, which is clearly undesirable since yielding suboptimal performance. One way to deal with this is to try out different starting weights, start the optimization procedure for a few steps, and then continue with the best intermediate solution. This approach is sometimes referred to as preliminary training. The optimization procedure then continues until the cost function shows no further progress; the weights stop changing substantially; or after a fixed number of optimization steps (also called epochs).

Although multiple output neurons could be used (e.g., predicting response and amount simultaneously) it is highly advised to use only

Figure 2.18 Local versus global minima.

one to make sure that the optimization task is well focused. The hidden neurons however should be carefully tuned and depend on the nonlinearity in the data. More complex, nonlinear patterns will require more hidden neurons. Although scientific literature has suggested various procedures (e.g., cascade correlation, genetic algorithms, Bayesian methods) to do this, the most straightforward, yet efficient procedure is as follows (Moody and Utans 1994):

1. Split the data into a training, validation, and test sets.
2. Vary the number of hidden neurons from 1 to 10 in steps of 1 or more.
3. Train a neural network on the training set and measure the performance on the validation set (maybe train multiple neural networks to deal with the local minimum issue).
4. Choose the number of hidden neurons with optimal validation set performance.
5. Measure the performance on the independent test set.

Note that in many customer analytics settings, the number of hidden neurons typically varies between 6 and 12.

Neural networks can model very complex patterns and decision boundaries in the data and are as such very powerful. Just as with decision trees, they are so powerful that they can even model the noise in the training set, which is something that definitely should be avoided. One way to avoid this overfitting is by using a validation set in a similar way as decision trees. This is illustrated in Figure 2.19. The training set is used here to estimate the weights and the validation set is again an independent dataset used to decide when to stop training.

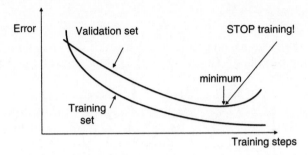

Figure 2.19 Using a validation set for stopping neural network training.

Another scheme to prevent a neural network from overfitting is weight regularization, whereby the idea is to keep the weights small in the absolute sense since otherwise they may be fitting the noise in the data. This idea is closely related to Lasso regression (Hastie, Tibshirani et al. 2011) and is implemented by adding a weight size term (e.g., Euclidean norm) to the cost function of the neural network (Bartlett, 1997; Baesens et al. 2002). In case of a continuous output (and thus mean squared error), the cost function then becomes

$$\frac{1}{2}\sum_{i=1}^{n} e_i^2 + \lambda\sum_{j=1}^{m} w_j^2,$$

whereby m represents the number of weights in the network and λ a weight decay (also referred to as weight regularization) parameter to weigh the importance of error versus weight minimization. Setting λ too low will cause overfitting, whereas setting it to high will cause underfitting. A practical approach to determine λ is to try out different values on an independent validation set and select the one with the best performance.

ENSEMBLE METHODS

Ensemble methods aim at estimating multiple analytical models instead of using only one. The idea here is that multiple models can cover different parts of the data input space and as such complement each other's deficiencies. In order to successfully accomplish this, the analytical technique needs to be sensitive to changes in the underlying data. This is particularly the case for decision trees and that is why they are commonly used in ensemble methods. In what follows, we discuss bagging, boosting, and random forests.

Bagging

Bagging (bootstrap aggregating) starts by taking **B** bootstraps from the underlying sample (Breima 1996). Note that a bootstrap is a sample with replacement (see section on evaluating predictive models). The idea is then to build a classifier (e.g., decision tree) for every bootstrap. For classification, a new observation will be classified by letting all B classifiers vote, using for example a majority voting scheme whereby ties are resolved arbitrarily. For regression, the prediction is the average of the outcome of the B models (e.g., regression trees). Note that, here also, a standard error and thus confidence interval can be calculated. The number of bootstraps B can either be fixed (e.g., 30) or tuned via an independent validation dataset.

The key element for bagging to be successful is the instability of the analytical technique. If perturbing the dataset by means of the bootstrapping procedure can alter the model constructed, then bagging will improve the accuracy (Breiman 1996). However, for models that are robust with respect to the underlying dataset, it will not give much added value.

Boosting

Boosting works by estimating multiple models using a weighted sample of the data (Freund and Schapire 1997; 1999). Starting from uniform weights, boosting will iteratively reweight the data according to the classification error whereby misclassified cases get higher weights. The idea here is that difficult observations should get more attention. Either the analytical technique can directly work with weighted observations, or if not, we can just sample a new dataset according to the weight distribution. The final ensemble model is then a weighted combination of all the individual models. A popular implementation of this is the Adaptive Boosting/Adaboost procedure, which works as indicated by Algorithm 2.1.

Note that in Algorithm 2.1, T represents the number of boosting runs, α_t measures the importance that is assigned to classifier C_t and increases as ε_t gets smaller, z_t is a normalization factor needed to make sure that the weights in step t make up a distribution and as such sum to 1, and $C_t(x)$ represents the classification of the classifier built in step t for observation x. Multiple loss functions may be used to calculate the error ε_t although the misclassification rate is undoubtedly the most popular. In substep i of step d, it can be seen that correctly classified observations get lower weights, whereas substep ii assigns higher weights to the incorrectly classified cases. Again, the number of boosting runs T can be fixed or tuned using an independent validation set.

Algorithm 2.1 AdaBoost

1: Given a dataset $D = \{(x_i, y_i)\}_{i=1}^{n}$ with $y_i \in \{1, -1\}$,

2: Initialize the weights as follows: $w_1(i) = \frac{1}{n}, i = 1, \ldots, n$

3: For $t = 1 \ldots T$

4:     Train a weak classifier (e.g., decision tree) using the weights w_t

5:     Get a weak classifier C_t with classification error ε_t

6:     Choose $\alpha_t = \frac{1}{2} \ln\left(\frac{1-\varepsilon_t}{\varepsilon_t}\right)$

7:     Update the weights for each observation x as follows:

$$w_{t+1}(i) = \frac{w_t(i)}{z_t} e^{-\alpha_t} \text{ if } C_t(x_i) = y_i$$

$$w_{t+1}(i) = \frac{w_t(i)}{z_t} e^{\alpha_t} \text{ if } C_t(x_i) \neq y_i$$

8: Output the final ensemble model: $E(x) = sign\left(\sum_{t=1}^{T}(\alpha_t C_t(x))\right)$

Note that different variants of this Adaboost procedure exist, such as Adaboost.M1 and Adaboost.M2 (both for multiclass classification), and Adaboost.R1 and Adaboost.R2 (both for regression). [See Freund and Schapire 1997; 1999 for more details.] A key advantage of boosting is that it is really easy to implement. A potential drawback is that there may be a risk of overfitting to the hard (potentially noisy) examples in the data, which will get higher weights as the algorithm proceeds.

Random Forests

The concept of random forests was first introduced by Breiman (2001). It creates a forest of decision trees as roughly described in Algorithm 2.2.

Common choices for m are 1, 2, or $floor(log_2(k) + 1)$, which is recommended. Random forests can be used with both classification trees

Algorithm 2.2 Random forests

1: Given a dataset with n observations and k inputs

2: m = constant chosen on beforehand

3: For $t = 1 \ldots T$

4:     Take a bootstrap sample with n observations

5:     Build a decision tree whereby, for each node of the tree, randomly choose m variables on which to base the splitting decision

6:     Split on the best of this subset

7:     Fully grow each tree without pruning

---

and regression trees. Key in this approach is the dissimilarity amongst the base classifiers (i.e., decision trees), which is obtained by adopting a bootstrapping procedure to select the training sets of the individual base classifiers, the selection of a random subset of attributes at each node, and the strength of the individual base models. As such, the diversity of the base classifiers creates an ensemble that is superior in performance compared to the single models.

Evaluating Ensemble Methods

Various benchmarking studies have shown that random forests can achieve excellent predictive performance. Actually, they generally rank amongst the best performing models across a wide variety of prediction tasks (Dejaeger et al. 2012). They are also perfectly capable of dealing with datasets that only have a few observations, but lots of variables. They are highly recommended when high performing analytical methods are needed. However, the price that is paid for this is that they are essentially black-box models. Due to the multitude of decision trees that make up the ensemble, it is very hard to see how the final classification is made. One way to shed some light on the internal workings of an ensemble is by calculating the variable importance. A popular procedure to do so is as follows:

1. Permute the values of the variable under consideration (e.g., x_j) on the validation or test set.
2. For each tree, calculate the difference between the error on the original, unpermutated data and the error on the data with x_j permutated as follows:

$$VI(x_j) = \frac{1}{ntree} \sum_t (error_t(D) - error_t(\tilde{D}_J)),$$

   whereby *ntree* represents the number of trees in the ensemble, D the original data, and $\tilde{D}_J$ the data with variable x_j permutated. In a regression setting, the error can be the mean squared error (MSE), whereas in a classification setting, the error can be the misclassification rate.
3. Order all variables according to their VI value. The variable with the highest VI value is the most important.

EVALUATING PREDICTIVE MODELS

Splitting Up the Dataset

When evaluating predictive models two key decisions need to be made. A first decision concerns the dataset split up, which specifies on what part of the data the performance will be measured. A second decision concerns the performance metric. In what follows, we elaborate on both.

The decision how to split up the dataset for performance measurement depends on its size. In case of large datasets (say more than 1,000 observations), the data can be split up into a training and a test set. The training set (also called development or estimation sample) will be used to build the model whereas the test set (also called the hold out set) will be used to calculate its performance (see Figure 2.20). A commonly applied split up is a 70% training set and a 30% test set. There should be a strict separation between training set and test set. No observation that was used for model development can be used for independent testing. Note that in the case of decision trees or neural networks, the validation set is a separate sample since it is actively being used during model development (i.e., to make the stopping decision). A typical split up in this case is a 40% training set, 30% validation set, and 30% test set.

In the case of small datasets (say less than 1,000 observations) special schemes need to be adopted. A very popular scheme is cross-validation. In cross-validation, the data are split into K folds (e.g., 5 or 10). An analytical model is then trained on $K - 1$ training folds and tested on the remaining validation fold. This is repeated for all possible validation folds resulting in K performance estimates, which can then be averaged. Note that also, a standard deviation and/or confidence interval can be calculated if desired. In its most extreme case, cross-validation becomes leave-one-out cross-validation whereby every observation is left out in turn and a model is estimated on the remaining $K - 1$ observations. This gives K analytical models in total.

A key question to answer when doing cross-validation is: What should be the final model that is being outputted from the procedure? Since cross-validation gives multiple models, this is not an obvious question. Of course, one could let all models collaborate in an ensemble set-up by using a (weighted) voting procedure. A more pragmatic answer would be to, for example, do leave-one-out cross-validation and pick one of the models at random. Since the models differ up to one observation only, they will be quite similar anyway. Alternatively, one may also choose to build one final model on all observations but report the performance coming out of the cross-validation procedure as the best independent estimate.

For small datasets, one may also adopt bootstrapping procedures (Efron 1979). In bootstrapping, one takes samples with replacement from a dataset D (see Figure 2.22).

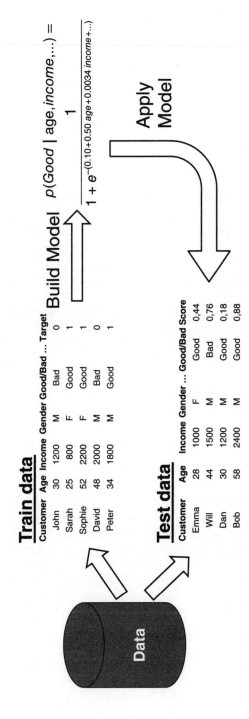

Figure 2.20 Training and test set split-up for performance estimation.

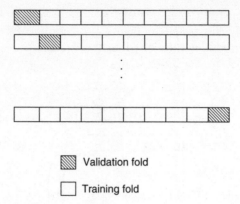

Figure 2.21 Cross-validation for performance measurement.

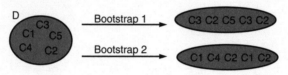

Figure 2.22 Bootstrapping.

The probability that a customer is sampled equals $1/n$, with n the number of observations in the dataset. Hence, the probability that a customer is not sampled equals $1 - 1/n$. Assuming a bootstrap with n sampled observations, the fraction of customers that is not sampled equals

$$\left(1 - \frac{1}{n}\right)^{n}.$$

We then have:

$$\lim_{n \to \infty} \left(1 - \frac{1}{n}\right)^{n} = e^{-1} = 0.368$$

whereby the approximation already works well for small values of n. So, 0.368 is the probability that a customer does not appear in the sample and 0.632 is the probability that a customer does appear. If we then take the bootstrap sample as the training set, and the test set as all observations in D but not in the bootstrap (e.g., for the first bootstrap of Figure 2.22, the test set consists of C1 and C4), we can approximate the performance as follows:

Error estimate = $0.368 \cdot$ Error(Training) $+ 0.632 \cdot$ Error(Test), whereby obviously, a higher weight is being put on the test set performance. As illustrated in Figure 2.22, multiple bootstraps can then be considered to get the distribution of the error estimate.

Performance Measures for Classification Models

Consider, for example, the following churn prediction example for a five-customer dataset. The second column in Table 2.5 depicts the churn status, whereas the third column depicts the churn score as it comes from a logistic regression, decision tree, neural network or other.

The scores have then been turned into predicted classes by adopting a default cutoff score of 0.50, as shown in Table 2.5. A confusion matrix can then be calculated as shown in Table 2.6.

Based on the confusion matrix, we can now calculate the following performance measures:

- Classification accuracy = (TP + TN)/(TP + FP + FN + TN) = 3/5
- Classification error = (FP + FN)/(TP + FP + FN + TN) = 2/5
- Sensitivity = Recall = Hit rate = TP/(TP + FN) = 1/2
- Specificity = TN/(FP + TN) = 2/3
- Precision = TP/(TP + FP) = 1/2
- F-measure = 2 · (Precision · Recall)/(Precision + Recall) = 1/2

Table 2.5 Example Dataset for Performance Calculation

Customer	Churn	Score		Predicted Class
John	Yes	0.72		Yes
Sophie	No	0.56	**Cutoff = 0.50**	Yes
David	Yes	0.44	→	No
Emma	No	0.18		No
Bob	No	0.36		No

Table 2.6 The Confusion Matrix

	Actual Negative (no churn)	Actual Positive (churn)
Predicted Negative (no churn)	True negative (TN) (Emma, Bob)	False negative (TN) (David)
Predicted Positive (churn)	False positive (FP) (Sophie)	True positive (TP) (John)

The classification accuracy is the percentage of correctly classified observations. The classification error is the complement thereof and also referred to as the misclassification rate. The sensitivity, recall, or hit rate measures how many of the churners are correctly labeled by the model as a churner. The specificity looks at how many of the nonchurners are correctly labeled by the model as nonchurner. The precision indicates how many of the predicted churners are actually churners.

Note that all these classification measures depend on the cutoff. For example: for a cutoff of 0 (1), the classification accuracy becomes 40% (60%), the error 60% (40%), the sensitivity 100% (0), the specificity 0 (100%), the precision 40% (0), and the F-measure 57% (0). Given this dependence, it would be nice to have a performance measure that is independent from the cutoff. We could construct a table with the sensitivity, specificity, and 1 − Specificity for various cutoffs as shown in the receiver operating characteristic (ROC) analysis in Table 2.7.

The ROC curve then plots the sensitivity versus 1 − Specificity, as illustrated in Figure 2.23 (Fawcett 2003).

Note that a perfect model detects all the churners and nonchurners at the same time, which results in a sensitivity of one and a specificity of one, and is thus represented by the upper-left corner. The closer the curve approaches this point, the better the performance. In Figure 2.23, model A has a better performance than model B. A problem, however, arises if the curves intersect. In this case, one can calculate the area under the ROC curve (AUC) as a performance metric. The AUC provides a simple figure-of-merit for the performance of the constructed classifier; the higher the AUC the better the performance. The AUC is always bounded between 0 and 1 and can be interpreted as a probability. In fact, it represents the probability that a randomly chosen churner gets a higher score than a randomly chosen nonchurner (Hanley and McNeil 1982; DeLong, DeLong et al. 1988).

Table 2.7 Receiver Operating Characteristic (ROC) Analysis

Cutoff	Sensitivity	Specificity	1 − Specificity
0	1	0	1
0.01	0.99	0.01	0.99
0.02	0.97	0.04	0.96
....	....	....	....
0.99	0.04	0.99	0.01
1	0	1	0

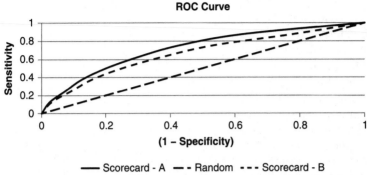

Figure 2.23 Receiver operating characteristic curve.

Note that the diagonal represents a random scorecard whereby sensitivity equals 1 − Specificity for all cutoff points. Hence, a good classifier should have an ROC above the diagonal and AUC bigger than 50%.

A lift curve is another important performance evaluation approach. It starts by sorting the population from high score to low score. Suppose now that in the top 10% highest scores, there are 60% churners, whereas the total population has 10% churners. The lift value in the top decile then becomes 60%/10%, or 6. In other words, the lift curve represents the cumulative percentage of churners per decile, divided by the overall population percentage of churners. Using no model, or a random sorting, the churners would be equally spread across the entire range and the lift value would always equal 1. The lift curve typically exponentially decreases as one cumulatively considers bigger deciles, until it reaches 1. This is illustrated in Figure 2.24.

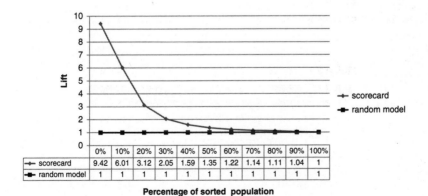

	0%	10%	20%	30%	40%	50%	60%	70%	80%	90%	100%
scorecard	9.42	6.01	3.12	2.05	1.59	1.35	1.22	1.14	1.11	1.04	1
random model	1	1	1	1	1	1	1	1	1	1	1

Percentage of sorted population

Figure 2.24 The lift curve.

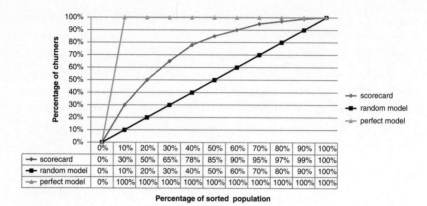

	0%	10%	20%	30%	40%	50%	60%	70%	80%	90%	100%
scorecard	0%	30%	50%	65%	78%	85%	90%	95%	97%	99%	100%
random model	0%	10%	20%	30%	40%	50%	60%	70%	80%	90%	100%
perfect model	0%	100%	100%	100%	100%	100%	100%	100%	100%	100%	100%

Percentage of sorted population

Figure 2.25 The cumulative accuracy profile (CAP).

Note that a lift curve can also be expressed in a noncumulative way, and is also often summarized by reporting top decile lift.

The cumulative accuracy profile (CAP), Lorenz, or Power curve is very closely related to the lift curve. It also starts by sorting the population from high score to low score and then measures the cumulative percentage of churners for each decile on the y-axis. The perfect model gives a linearly increasing curve up to the sample churn rate and then flattens out. The diagonal again represents the random model.

The CAP curve can be summarized in an accuracy ratio (AR), as depicted in Figure 2.26.

The accuracy ratio is defined as the ratio of (1) the area below the power curve for the model minus the area below the power curve of the random model, and (2) the area below the power curve for the perfect model minus the area below the power curve for random model. A perfect model will thus have an AR of 1 and a random model an AR of 0. Note that the accuracy ratio is also often referred to as the

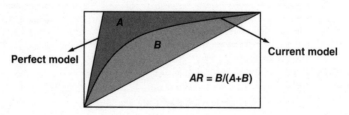

Figure 2.26 Calculating the accuracy ratio.

Gini coefficient. There is also a linear relation between the AR and the AUC as follows:

$$AR = 2 \cdot AUC - 1$$

As an alternative to these statistical measures, in Chapter 6 profit-driven performance measures will be extensively discussed, which allow us to evaluate a classification model in a cost-sensitive manner.

Performance Measures for Regression Models

A first way to evaluate the predictive performance of a regression model is by visualizing the predicted target against the actual target using a scatter plot (see Figure 2.27). The more the plot approaches a straight line through the origin, the better the performance of the regression model. It can be summarized by calculating the Pearson correlation coefficient as follows:

$$corr(\hat{y}, y) = \frac{\sum_{i=1}^{n} (\hat{y}_i - \overline{\hat{y}})(y_i - \overline{y})}{\sqrt{\sum_{i=1}^{n} (\hat{y}_i - \overline{\hat{y}})^2} \sqrt{\sum_{i=1}^{n} (y_i - \overline{y})^2}},$$

whereby $\hat{y}_i$ represents the predicted value for observation i, $\overline{\hat{y}}$ the average of the predicted values, y_i the actual value for observation i, and $\overline{y}$ the average of the actual values. The Pearson correlation always varies between -1 and $+1$. Values closer to $+1$ indicate better agreement and thus better fit between the predicted and actual values of the target variable.

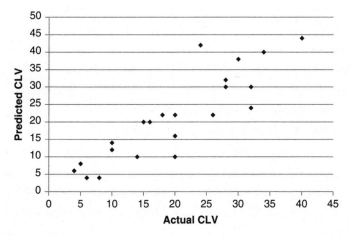

Figure 2.27 Scatter plot.

Another key performance metric is the coefficient of determination or R^2 defined as follows:

$$R^2 = \frac{\sum_{i=1}^{n}(\hat{y}_i - \bar{y})^2}{\sum_{i=1}^{n}(y_i - \bar{y})^2} = 1 - \frac{\sum_{i=1}^{n}(y_i - \hat{y}_l)^2}{\sum_{i=1}^{n}(y_i - \bar{y})^2},$$

The R^2 always varies between 0 and 1, and higher values are to be preferred. Basically, this measure tells us how much better we can make predictions by using the analytical model to compute $\hat{y}_i$ than by using the mean $\bar{y}$ as predictor. To compensate for the variables in the model, an adjusted R^2, R^2_{adj}, has been suggested as follows:

$$R^2_{adj} = 1 - \frac{n-1}{n-k-1}(1-R^2) = 1 - \frac{n-1}{n-k-1}\frac{\sum_{i=1}^{n}(y_i - \hat{y}_l)^2}{\sum_{i=1}^{n}(y_i - \bar{y})^2},$$

whereby k represents the number of variables in the model. Note that although R^2 is usually a number between 0 and 1, it can also have negative values for non-OLS models when the model predictions are worse than always using the mean from the training set as the prediction.

Two other popular measures are the mean squared error (MSE) and mean absolute deviation (MAD), defined as follows:

$$MSE = \frac{\sum_{i=1}^{n}(y_i - \hat{y}_i)^2}{n},$$

$$MAD = \frac{\sum_{i=1}^{n}|y_i - \hat{y}_i|}{n}.$$

A perfect model would have an MSE and MAD of 0. Higher values for both MSE and MAD indicate less good performance. Note that the MSE is sometimes also reported as the root mean squared error (RMSE), whereby $RMSE = \sqrt{MSE}$.

Other Performance Measures for Predictive Analytical Models

As already mentioned, statistical performance is just one aspect of model performance. Other important criteria are comprehensibility, justifiability, and operational efficiency. Although comprehensibility is subjective and depends on the background and experience of the business user, linear and logistic regressions as well as decision trees are commonly referred to as white box, comprehensible techniques (Baesens et al. 2003; Verbeke et al. 2011). Neural networks and random forests methods are essentially opaque models and thus much harder to understand (Baesens et al. 2011). However, in settings where statistical performance is superior to interpretability, they are the method of choice. Justifiability goes one step further and verifies to what extent the relationships modeled are in line with prior business knowledge and/or expectations. In a practical setting, this often boils down to verifying the univariate impact of a variable on the model's output.

For example: For a linear/logistic regression model, the signs of the regression coefficients will be verified. Finally, the operational efficiency can also be an important evaluation criterion to consider when selecting the optimal analytical model. Operational efficiency represents the ease with which one can implement, use, and monitor the final model. An example: in a (near) real-time fraud environment, it is important to be able to quickly evaluate the fraud model (Baesens et al. 2015). With regards to implementation, rule-based models excel since implementing rules can be done very easily, even in spreadsheet software. Linear models are also quite easy to implement, whereas nonlinear models are much more difficult to implement, due to the complex transformations that are being used by the model.

DESCRIPTIVE ANALYTICS

Introduction

In descriptive analytics, the aim is to describe patterns of customer behavior. Contrary to predictive analytics, there is no real target variable (e.g., churn, response or fraud indicator) available. Hence, descriptive analytics is often referred to as unsupervised learning, since there is no target variable to steer the learning process. The three most common types of descriptive analytics are association rules, sequence rules, and clustering.

Association Rules

Basic Setting

Association rules typically start from a dataset of transactions D. Each transaction consists of a transaction identifier and a set of items $\{i_1, i_2, \ldots\}$ selected from all possible items I. Items can be, for example,

Table 2.8 Example Transaction Dataset

ID	Items
T1	beer, milk, diapers, baby food
T2	coke, beer, diapers
T3	cigarettes, diapers, baby food
T4	chocolates, diapers, milk, apples
T5	tomatoes, water, apples, beer
T6	spaghetti, diapers, baby food, beer
T7	water, beer, baby food
T8	diapers, baby food, spaghetti
T9	baby food, beer, diapers, milk
T10	apples, wine, baby food

products, web pages, or courses. Table 2.8 gives an example of a transaction dataset in a supermarket setting.

An association rule is then an implication of the form $X \to Y$, whereby $X \subset I, Y \subset I$ and $X \cap Y = \emptyset$. X is referred to as the rule antecedent whereas Y is referred to as the rule consequent. Examples of association rules are:

- If a customer has a car loan and car insurance, then the customer has a checking account in 80% of the cases.
- If a customer buys spaghetti, then the customer buys red wine in 70% of the cases.
- If a customer visits web page A, then the customer will visit web page B in 90% of the cases.

It is hereby important to note that association rules are stochastic in nature; that means they should not be interpreted as a universal truth and are characterized by statistical measures quantifying the strength of the association. Also, the rules measure correlational associations and should not be interpreted in a causal way.

Support, Confidence, and Lift

Support and confidence are two key measures to quantify the strength of an association rule. The support of an item set is defined as the percentage of total transactions in the database that contains the item set. Hence, the rule $X \to Y$ has support s if $100s\%$ of the transactions in D

contains $X \cup Y$. It can be formally defined as follows:

$$Support(X \cup Y) = \frac{Number\ of\ transactions\ supporting\ (X \cup Y)}{Total\ number\ of\ transactions}$$

When considering the transaction database in Table 2.8, the association rule baby food and diapers → beer has support 3/10, or 30%.

A frequent item set is an item set for which the support is higher than a threshold (minsup), which is typically specified up front by the business user or data scientist. A lower (higher) support will obviously generate more (less) frequent item sets. The confidence measures the strength of the association and is defined as the conditional probability of the rule consequent, given the rule antecedent. The rule $X \rightarrow Y$ has confidence c if $100c\%$ of the transactions in D that contain X also contain Y. It can be formally defined as follows:

$$Confidence(X \rightarrow Y) = p(Y|X) = \frac{Support(X \cup Y)}{Support(X)}$$

Again, the data scientist has to specify a minimum confidence (minconf) in order for an association rule to be considered interesting. When considering Table 2.8, the association rule baby food and diapers → beer has confidence 3/5 or 60%.

Consider now the following example from a supermarket transactions database, as shown in Table 2.9.

Let us now evaluate the association rule Tea → Coffee. The support of this rule is 100/1,000, or 10%. The confidence of the rule is 150/200, or 75%. At first sight, this association rule seems very appealing given its high confidence. However, closer inspection reveals that the prior probability of buying coffee equals 900/1000, or 90%. Hence, a customer who buys tea is less likely to buy coffee than a customer about whom we have no information. The lift, also referred to as the interestingness measure, takes this into account by incorporating the prior probability of the rule consequent as follows:

$$Lift(X \rightarrow Y) = \frac{support(X \cup Y)}{support(X) \cdot support(Y)}.$$

Table 2.9 The Lift Measure

	Tea	Not tea	Total
Coffee	150	750	900
Not coffee	50	50	100
Total	200	800	1000

A lift value less (larger) than 1 indicates a negative (positive) dependence or substitution (complementary) effect. In our example, the lift value equals 0.89, which clearly indicates the expected substitution effect between coffee and tea.

Post-Processing Association Rules

Typically, an association rule-mining exercise will yield lots of association rules such that post-processing will become a key activity. Example steps include the following:

- Filter out the trivial rules that contain already known patterns (e.g., buying spaghetti and spaghetti sauce). This should be done in collaboration with a business expert.

- Perform a sensitivity analysis by varying the minsup and minconf values. Particularly for rare but profitable items (e.g., Rolex watches), it could be interesting to lower the minsup value and find the interesting associations.

- Use appropriate visualization facilities (e.g., OLAP-based) to find the unexpected rules that might represent novel and actionable behavior in the data.

- Measure the economic impact (e.g., profit, cost) of the association rules.

Sequence Rules

Given a database D of customer transactions, the problem of mining sequential rules is to find the maximal sequences among all sequences that have certain user-specified minimum support and confidence. An example could be a sequence of web page visits in a Web analytics setting as follows:

Home page → Electronics → Cameras and Camcorders
→ Digital Cameras → Shopping cart → Order confirmation
→ Return to shopping.

It is important to note that a transaction time or sequence field will now be included in the analysis. Whereas association rules are concerned about what items appear together at the same time (intra-transaction patterns), sequence rules are concerned about what items appear at different times (inter-transaction patterns).

Table 2.10 Example Transaction Dataset (left) and Sequential Dataset (right) for Sequence Rule Mining

Session ID	Page	Sequence
1	A	1
1	B	2
1	C	3
2	B	1
2	C	2
3	A	1
3	C	2
3	D	3
4	A	1
4	B	2
4	D	3
5	D	1
5	C	1
5	A	1

→

Session ID	Pages
1	A, B, C
2	B, C
3	A, C, D
4	A, B, D
5	D, C, A

Consider the following example of a transactions dataset in a Web analytics setting (see Table 2.10). The letters A, B, C, ... refer to web pages. A sequential version can be obtained as shown in Table 2.10.

One can now calculate the support in two different ways. Consider, for example, the sequence rule A → C. A first approach would be to calculate the support whereby the consequent can appear in any subsequent stage of the sequence. In this case, the support becomes 2/5 (40%). Another approach would be to only consider sessions where the consequent appears right after the antecedent. In this case, the support becomes 1/5 (20%). A similar reasoning can now be followed for the confidence, which can then be 2/4 (50%) or 1/4 (25%), respectively.

Remember that the confidence of a rule $A_1 \rightarrow A_2$ is defined as the probability $p(A_2|A_1) = support(A_1 \cup A_2)/support(A_1))$. For a rule with multiple items, $A_1 \rightarrow A_2 \rightarrow \ldots A_{k-1} \rightarrow A_k$, the confidence is defined as $p(A_k|A_1, A_2, \ldots, A_{k-1}) = support(A_1 \cup A_2 \cup \ldots \cup A_{k-1} \cup A_k)/support(A_1 \cup A_2 \cup \ldots \cup A_{k-1})$.

Clustering

The aim of clustering or segmentation is to split up a set of observations into clusters such that the homogeneity within a cluster is maximized (cohesive), and the heterogeneity between clusters is maximized (separated). Clustering techniques can be categorized as either hierarchical or nonhierarchical (see Figure 2.28).

Hierarchical Clustering

In what follows, we will first discuss hierarchical clustering. Divisive hierarchical clustering starts from the whole dataset in one cluster, and then breaks this up each time in smaller clusters until one observation per cluster remains (right to left in Figure 2.29). Agglomerative

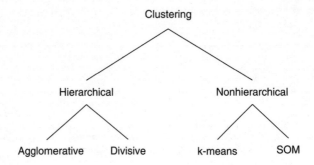

Figure 2.28 Hierarchical versus nonhierarchical clustering techniques.

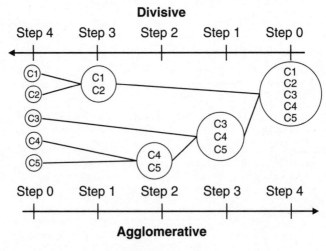

Figure 2.29 Divisive versus agglomerative hierarchical clustering.

clustering works the other way around, and starts from all observations in one cluster, continues to merge the ones that are most similar until all observations make up one big cluster (left to right in Figure 2.29). The optimal clustering solution then lies somewhere in between the extremes to the left and right, respectively.

In order to decide on the merger or splitting, a distance measure is needed. Examples of popular distance measures are the Euclidean distance and Manhattan (City Block) distance. For the example in Figure 2.30 both are calculated as follows:

- Euclidean: $\sqrt{(50-30)^2 + (20-10)^2} = 22$
- Manhattan: $|50 - 30| + |20 - 10| = 30$

It is obvious that the Euclidean distance will always be shorter than the Manhattan distance.

Various schemes can now be adopted to calculate the distance between two clusters (see Figure 2.31). The single linkage method defines the distance between two clusters as the shortest possible distance, or the distance between the two most similar objects. The complete linkage method defines the distance between two clusters as the biggest distance, or the distance between the two most dissimilar objects. The average linkage method calculates the average of all possible distances. The centroid method calculates the distance between the centroids of both clusters.

In order to decide on the optimal number of clusters, one could use a dendrogram or scree plot. A dendrogram is a tree-like diagram that records the sequences of merges. The vertical (or horizontal scale) then gives the distance between two amalgamated clusters. One can then cut the dendrogram at the desired level to find the optimal clustering. This is illustrated in Figure 2.32 and Figure 2.33 for a birds clustering

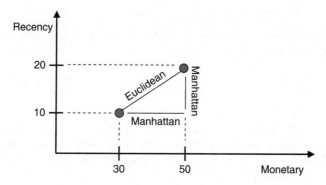

Figure 2.30 Euclidean versus Manhattan distance.

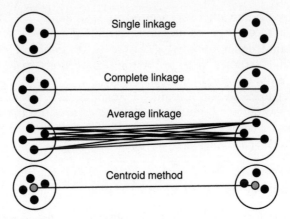

Figure 2.31 Calculating distances between clusters.

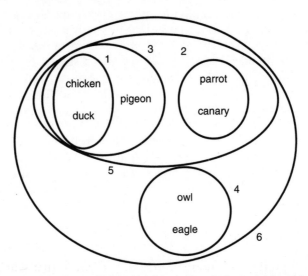

Figure 2.32 Example for clustering birds. The numbers indicate the clustering steps.

example. A scree plot is a plot of the distance at which clusters are merged. The elbow point then indicates the optimal clustering. This is illustrated in Figure 2.34.

A key advantage of hierarchical clustering is that the number of clusters does not need to be specified prior to the analysis. A disadvantage is that the methods do not scale very well to large datasets. Also, the interpretation of the clusters is often subjective and depends on the business expert and/or data scientist.

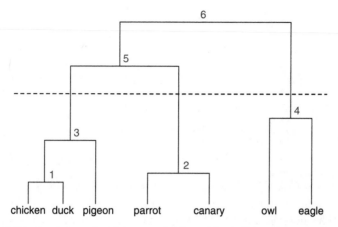

Figure 2.33 Dendrogram for birds example. The red line indicates the optimal clustering.

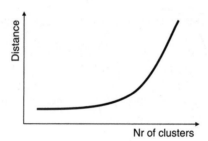

Figure 2.34 Scree plot for clustering.

K-means Clustering

K-means clustering is a nonhierarchical procedure that works along the following steps:

1. Select *K* observations as initial cluster centroids (seeds).
2. Assign each observation to the cluster that has the closest centroid (for example, in Euclidean sense).
3. When all observations have been assigned, recalculate the positions of the *k* centroids.
4. Repeat until the cluster centroids no longer change.

A key requirement here is that the number of clusters, *K*, needs to be specified before the start of the analysis. It is also advised to try out different seeds to verify the stability of the clustering solution. This decision can be made using expert-based input or based on the result of another (e.g., hierarchical) clustering procedure. Typically, multiple values of K are tried out and the resulting clusters evaluated in terms of their statistical characteristics and interpretation. It is also advised to try out different seeds to verify the stability of the clustering solution.

Self-Organizing Maps

A self-organizing map (SOM) is an unsupervised learning algorithm that allows users to visualize and cluster high-dimensional data on a low-dimensional grid of neurons (Kohonen 1982; Huysmans et al. 2006a; Seret et al. 2012). A SOM is a feedforward neural network with two layers. The neurons from the output layer are usually ordered in a two-dimensional rectangular or hexagonal grid. For the former, every neuron has at most eight neighbors, whereas for the latter every neuron has at most six neighbors.

Each input is connected to all neurons in the output layer. In other words, every output neuron has k weights, one for each input. As such, the output neurons can be thought of as prototype observations. All weights of the output neurons are randomly initialized. When a training vector x_i is presented, the weight vector w_s of each output neuron s is compared to x_i, using, for example, the Euclidean distance metric (beware to standardize the data to zero mean and unit standard deviation first!):

$$d(x_i, w_s) = \sqrt{\sum_{j=1}^{k} (x_i(j) - w_s(j))^2}.$$

The neuron that is most similar to x_i in Euclidean sense is called the best matching unit (BMU). The weight vector of each output neuron s

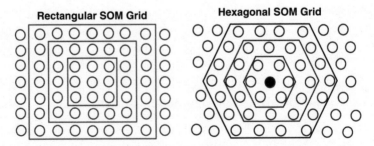

Figure 2.35 Rectangular versus hexagonal SOM grid.

is then updated using the following learning rule:

$$w_s(t+1) = w_s(t) + h_{bs}(t)[x(t) - w_s(t)],$$

where $t = 1, \ldots$ represents the training step, $w_s(t)$ the weight vector of output neuron s at step t, $x(t)$ the observation considered at step t, and $h_{bs}(t)$ the neighborhood function at step t. The neighborhood function $h_{bs}(t)$ specifies the region of influence and is dependent on the location of the BMU (say neuron b) and the neuron to be updated (i.e., neuron s). It should be a nonincreasing function of time t and the distance from the BMU. Some popular choices are:

$$h_{bs}(t) = \alpha(t) \exp\left(-\frac{\|r_b - r_s\|^2}{2\sigma^2(t)}\right),$$

$$h_{bs}(t) = \alpha(t) \text{ if } \|r_b - r_s\|^2 \leq threshold, 0 \text{ } otherwise,$$

whereby r_b and r_s represent the location of the BMU and neuron s on the map, $\sigma^2(t)$ represents the decreasing radius, and $0 \leq \alpha(t) \leq 1$ the learning rate (e.g., $\alpha(t) = 1/(t+B)$ or $\alpha(t) = \exp(-At)$). The decreasing learning rate and radius will give a stable map after a certain amount of training. Training is stopped when the BMUs remain stable, or after a fixed number of iterations (e.g., 500 times the number of SOM neurons). The output neurons will then move more and more toward the input observations, and interesting segments will emerge.

SOMs can be visualized by means of a U-matrix or component plane.

■ A **U (unified distance)-matrix** essentially superimposes a height dimension on top of each output neuron, visualizing the average distance between the output neuron and its neighbors, whereby typically dark colors indicate a large distance and can be interpreted as cluster boundaries.

■ A **component plane** visualizes the weights between each specific input neuron and its output neurons, and as such provides a visual overview of the relative contribution of each input to the output neurons.

Figure 2.36 provides an SOM example for clustering countries based on a corruption perception index (CPI) (Huysmans et al. 2006b). This is a score between 0 (highly corrupt) and 10 (highly clean), assigned to each country in the world. The CPI is combined with demographic and macroeconomic information for the years 1996, 2000, and 2004. Upper case countries (e.g., BEL) denote the situation in 2004, lower case (e.g., bel) in 2000, and sentence case (e.g., Bel) in 1996. It can be seen that many of the European countries are situated in the upper-right corner of the map. Figure 2.37 provides

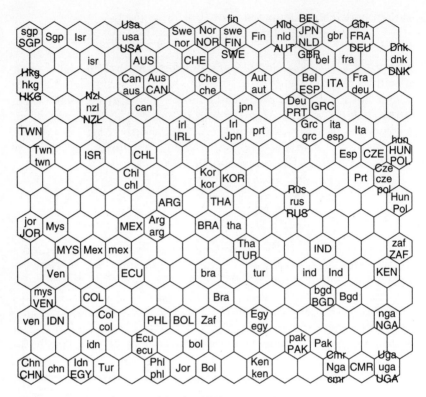

Figure 2.36 Clustering countries using SOMs.

Figure 2.37 Component plane for literacy.

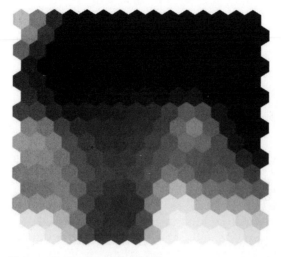

Figure 2.38 Component plane for political rights.

the component plane for literacy whereby darker regions score worse on literacy. Figure 2.38 provides the component plane for political rights whereby darker regions correspond to better political rights. It can be seen that many of the European countries score good on both literacy and political rights.

SOMs are a very handy tool for clustering high dimensional datasets because of the visualization facilities. However, since there is no real objective function to minimize, it is harder to compare various SOM solutions against each other. Also, experimental evaluation and expert interpretation is needed to decide on the optimal size of the SOM. Unlike K-means clustering, a SOM does not force the number of clusters to be equal to the number of output neurons.

SURVIVAL ANALYSIS

Introduction

Survival analysis is a set of statistical techniques focusing on the occurrence and timing of events (Cox 1972; Cox and Oakes 1984; Allison 1995). As the name suggests, it originates from a medical context where it was used to study survival times of patients who had received certain treatments. In fact, many classification problems we have discussed before also have a time aspect included, which can be analyzed using survival analysis techniques. Some examples are:

- Predict when customers churn.
- Predict when customers make their next purchase.
- Predict when customers default.
- Predict when customers pay off their loan early.
- Predict when customer will visit a website again.

Two typical problems complicate the usage of classical statistical techniques such as linear regression. A first key problem is censoring. Censoring refers to the fact that the target time variable is not always known since not all customers may have undergone the event yet at the time of the analysis. Consider the example depicted in Figure 2.39. At time T, Laura and John have not churned yet and thus have no value for the target time indicator. The only information available is that they will churn at some later date after T. Note that also Sophie is censored at the time she moved to Australia. In fact, these are all examples of right censoring. An observation on a variable T is right-censored if all you know about T is that it is greater than some value c. Likewise, an observation on a variable T is left-censored if all you know about T is that it is smaller than some value c. An example here could be a study investigating smoking behavior where some participants at age 18 already began smoking but can no longer remember the exact date they started. Interval censoring means the only information available on T is that it belongs to some interval $a < T < b$. Returning to the previous smoking example, one could be more precise and say $14 < T < 18$. Censoring occurs because many databases only contain current or rather recent customers for whom the behavior has not yet been completely observed, or because of database errors when, for example, the event dates are missing.

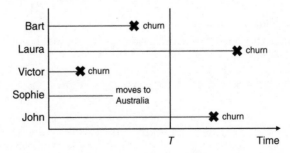

Figure 2.39 Example of right censoring for churn prediction.

Using classical statistical analysis techniques such as linear regression, the censored observations would have to be left out from the analysis, since they have no value for the target time variable. However, with survival analysis, the partial information available for the censored observations giving a lower and/or upper bound on the timing of the event will be included in the estimation.

Time-varying covariates are variables that change value during the course of the study. Examples are account balance, income, and credit scores, among others. Survival analysis techniques will be able to accommodate this in the model formulation, as is discussed in what follows.

Survival Analysis Measurements

A first important concept is the event time distribution defined as a continuous probability distribution, as follows:

$$f(t) = \lim_{\Delta t \to 0} \frac{P(t \le T < t + \Delta T)}{\Delta t}.$$

The corresponding cumulative event time distribution is then defined as follows:

$$F(t) = P(T \le t) = \int_0^t f(u)du.$$

Closely related is the survival function:

$$S(t) = 1 - F(t) = P(T > t) - \int_t^\infty f(u)du.$$

$S(t)$ is a monotonically decreasing function with $S(0) = 1$ and $S(\infty) = 0$. The following relationships hold:

$$f(t) = \frac{dF(t)}{dt} = -\frac{dS(t)}{dt}.$$

Figure 2.40 provides an example of a discrete event time distribution, with the corresponding cumulative event time and survival distribution depicted in Figure 2.41.

Another important measure in survival analysis is the hazard function defined as follows:

$$h(t) = \lim_{\Delta t \to 0} \frac{P(t \le T < t + \Delta T | T \ge t)}{\Delta t}.$$

The hazard function tries to quantify the instantaneous risk that an event will occur at time t, given that the individual has survived up

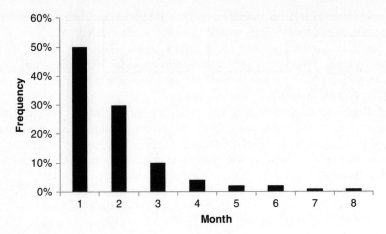

Figure 2.40 Example of a discrete event time distribution.

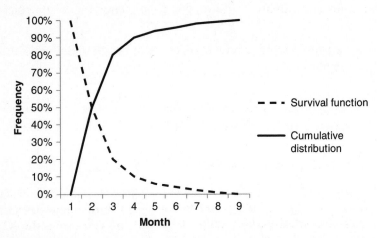

Figure 2.41 Cumulative distribution and survival function for the event time distribution in Figure 2.40.

to time t. Hence, it tries to measure the risk of the event occurring at time point t. The hazard function is closely related to the event time distribution up to the conditioning on $T \geq t$. That is why it is often also referred to as a conditional density.

Figure 2.42 provides some examples of hazard shapes as follows:

■ Constant hazard whereby the risk remains the same at all times.
■ Increasing hazard reflects an aging effect.

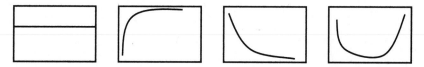

Figure 2.42 Sample hazard shapes.

- Decreasing hazard reflects a curing effect.
- A convex bathtub shape is typically the case when studying human mortality, since mortality declines after birth and infancy, remains low for a while, and increases with elder years. It is also a property of some mechanical systems to either fail soon after operation or much later, as the system ages.

The probability density function $f(t)$, survivor function $S(t)$, and the hazard function $h(t)$ are mathematically equivalent ways of describing a continuous probability distribution with the following relationships:

$$h(t) = \frac{f(t)}{S(t)},$$

$$h(t) = -\frac{d\log S(t)}{dt},$$

$$S(t) = \exp\left(-\int_0^t h(u)du\right).$$

Kaplan Meier Analysis

A first type of survival analysis is Kaplan Meier (KM) analysis, which is also known as the product limit estimator, or nonparametric maximum likelihood estimator for $S(t)$. If there is no censoring, the KM estimator for t is just the sample proportion with event times greater than t. If there is censoring, the KM estimator starts by ordering the event times in ascending order $t_1 \le t_2 \le \ldots \le t_k$. At each time t_j, there are n_j individuals who are at risk of the event. *At risk* means that they have not undergone the event, nor have they been censored prior to t_j. Let d_j be the number of individuals who die (e.g., churn, respond, default) at t_j. The KM estimator is then defined as follows:

$$\hat{S}(t) = \prod_{j:t_j \le t}\left(1 - \frac{d_j}{n_j}\right) = \hat{S}(t-1) \cdot \left(1 - \frac{d_t}{n_t}\right) = \hat{S}(t-1) \cdot (1 - h(t)),$$

for $t_1 \le t \le t_k$. The intuition of the KM estimator is very straightforward, as it basically states that in order to survive time t, one must

Customer	Time of Churn or Censoring	Churn or Censored
C1	6	Churn
C2	3	Censored
C3	12	Churn
C4	15	Censored
C5	18	Censored
C6	12	Churn
C7	3	Churn
C8	12	Churn
C9	9	Censored
C10	15	Churn

Time	Customers at Risk at t (n_t)	Churned at t (d_t)	Customers Censored at t	$S(t)$
0	10	0	0	1
3	10	1	1	0.9
6	8	1	0	0.9·7/8=0.79
9	7	0	1	0.79·7/7=0.79
12	6	3	0	0.79·3/6=0.39
15	3	1	1	0.39·2/3=0.26
18	1	0	1	0.26·1/1=0.26

Figure 2.43 Kaplan Meier example.

survive time $t - 1$ and cannot die during time t. Figure 2.43 gives an example of Kaplan Meier analysis for churn prediction.

If there are many unique event times, the KM estimator can be adjusted by using the life-table (also known as actuarial) method to group event times into intervals as follows:

$$\widehat{S}(t) = \prod_{j:t_j \leq t} \left[1 - \frac{d_j}{n_j - c_{j/2}} \right],$$

which basically assumes that censoring occurs uniform across the time interval, such that the average number at risk equals $(n_j + (n_j - c_j))/2$ or $n_j - c_j/2$, with c_j the number of censored observations during time interval j.

Kaplan Meier analysis can also be extended with hypothesis testing to see whether the survival curves of different groups (e.g., men versus women, employed versus unemployed) are statistically different. Popular test statistics here are the log-rank test (also known as the Mantel-Haenzel test), the Wilcoxon test, and the likelihood-ratio statistic, which are all readily available in any commercial analytics software.

Kaplan Meier analysis is a good way to start doing some exploratory survival analysis. However, it would be nice to be able to also build predictive survival analysis models that take into account customer heterogeneity by including predictive variables or covariates.

Parametric Survival Analysis

As the name suggests, parametric survival analysis models assume a parametric shape for the event time distribution. A first popular choice is an exponential distribution defined as follows:

$$f(t) = \lambda e^{-\lambda t}.$$

Using the relationships defined earlier, the survival function then becomes:

$$S(t) = e^{-\lambda t},$$

and the hazard rate

$$h(t) = \frac{f(t)}{S(t)} = \lambda.$$

It is worth noting that the hazard rate is independent of time such that the risk always remains the same. This is often referred to as the *memoryless property* of an exponential distribution.

When taking into account covariates, the model becomes:

$$\log(h(t|x_i)) = \mu + \beta^T x_i.$$

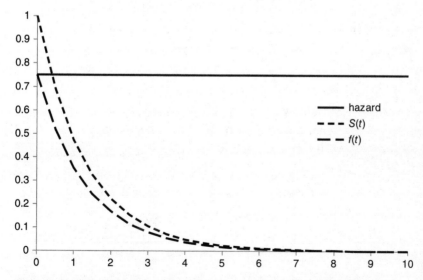

Figure 2.44 Exponential event time distribution, with cumulative distribution and hazard function.

Remember that β represents the parameter vector and x_i the vector of predictor variables. Note that the logarithmic transform is used here to make sure that the hazard rate is always positive.

The Weibull distribution is another popular choice for a parametric survival analysis model. It is defined as follows:

$$f(t) = \kappa \rho (\rho t)^{\kappa-1} \exp[-(\rho t)^{\kappa}].$$

The survival function then becomes:

$$S(t) = \exp[-(\rho t)^{\kappa}],$$

and the hazard rate becomes

$$h(t) = \frac{f(t)}{S(t)} = \kappa \rho (\rho t)^{\kappa-1}.$$

Note that, in this case, the hazard rate does depend on time and can be either increasing or decreasing (depending on κ and ρ). Figure 2.45 illustrates some examples of Weibull distributions. It can be seen that it is a very versatile distribution that can fit various shapes.

When including covariates, the model becomes:

$$\log(h(t|x_i)) = \mu + \alpha \log(t) + \beta^T x_i$$

Other popular choices for the event time distribution are gamma, log-logistic, and log-normal distributions (Allison, 1995). Parametric

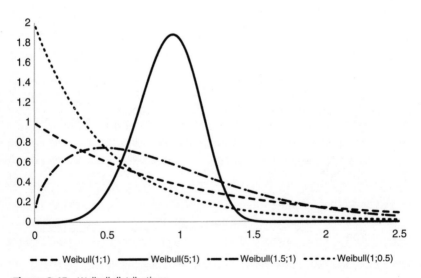

Figure 2.45 Weibull distributions.

survival analysis models are typically estimated using maximum likelihood procedures. In case of no censored observations, the likelihood function becomes:

$$L = \prod_{i=1}^{n} f(t_i).$$

When censoring is present, the likelihood function becomes:

$$L = \prod_{i=1}^{n} f(t_i)^{\delta_s} S(t_i)^{1-\delta_i},$$

whereby δ_i equals 0 if observation i is censored, and 1 if the observation dies at time t_i. It is important to note here that the censored observations do enter the likelihood function and, as such, have an impact on the estimates. For example, for the exponential distribution, the likelihood function becomes:

$$L = \prod_{i=1}^{n} [\lambda e^{-\lambda t_i}]^{\delta_i} [e^{-\lambda t_i}]^{1-\delta_i}.$$

This maximum likelihood function is then typically optimized by further taking the logarithm and then using a Newton Raphson optimization procedure.

A key question concerns the appropriate event time distribution for a given set of survival data. This question can be answered both graphically and statistically. In order to solve it graphically, we can start from the following relationships:

$$h(t) = -\frac{d\log S(t)}{dt}$$

or,

$$-\log(S(t)) = \int_{0}^{t} h(u)du.$$

Because of this relationship, the log survivor function is commonly referred to as the cumulative hazard function, denoted as $\Lambda(t)$. It can be interpreted as the sum of the risks that are faced when going from time 0 to time t. If the survival times are exponentially distributed, then the hazard is constant $h(t) = \lambda$, hence $\Lambda(t) = \lambda t$ and a plot of $-\log(S(t))$ versus t should yield a straight line through the origin at 0. Similarly, it can be shown that if the survival times are Weibull distributed, then a plot of $\log(-\log(S(t)))$ versus $\log(t)$ should yield a straight line (not through the origin) with a slope of κ. These plots can typically be asked for in any commercial analytics software implementing survival analysis. Note, however, that this graphical method is not a very precise method, as the lines will never be perfectly linear or go through the origin.

A more precise method for testing the appropriate event time distribution is a likelihood ratio test. In fact the likelihood ratio test can be used to compare models if one model is a special case of another (nested models). Consider the following generalized Gamma distribution:

$$f(t) = \frac{\beta}{\Gamma(t)\theta}\left(\frac{t}{\theta}\right)^{k\beta-1} e^{-\left(\frac{t}{\theta}\right)^{\beta}}.$$

Let's now use the following short-cut notations: $\sigma = 1/\beta\sqrt{k}$ and $\delta = 1/\sqrt{k}$, then the Weibull, exponential, standard gamma and log-normal model are all special versions of the generalized gamma model as follows:

- $\sigma = \delta$: standard gamma
- $\delta = 1$: Weibull
- $\sigma = \delta = 1$: exponential
- $\delta = 0$: log normal

Let L_{full} now be the likelihood of the full model (e.g., generalized gamma) and L_{red} be the likelihood of the reduced (specialized) model (e.g., exponential). The likelihood ratio test statistic then becomes:

$$-2\log\left(\frac{L_{\text{red}}}{L_{\text{full}}}\right) \sim \chi^2(k),$$

whereby the degrees of freedom k depends on the number of parameters that need to be set to go from the full model to the reduced model. In other words, it is set as follows:

- Exponential versus Weibull: 1 degree of freedom
- Exponential versus standard gamma: 1 degree of freedom
- Exponential versus generalized gamma: 2 degrees of freedom
- Weibull versus generalized gamma: 1 degree of freedom
- Log-normal versus generalized gamma: 1 degree of freedom
- Standard gamma versus generalized gamma: 1 degree of freedom

The χ^2-test statistic can then be calculated together with the corresponding p-value and a decision can be made about what is the most appropriate event time distribution.

Proportional Hazards Regression

The proportional hazards model is formulated as follows:

$$h(t, x_i) = h_0(t)\exp(\beta^T x_i),$$

so the hazard of an individual i with characteristics x_i at time t is the product of a baseline hazard function $h_0(t)$ and a linear function of a set of fixed covariates, which is exponentiated. In fact, $h_0(t)$ can be considered as the hazard for an individual with all covariates equal to zero. Note that if a variable x_j increases with one unit and all other variables keep their values (ceteris paribus), then the hazards for all t increase with $\exp(\beta_j)$, which is called the hazard ratio (HR). If $\beta_j > 0$, then HR > 1, $\beta_j < 0$ then HR < 1; $\beta_j = 0$ then HR $= 1$. This is one of the most popular models for doing survival analysis.

The term *proportional hazards* stems from the fact that the hazard of any individual is a fixed proportion of the hazard of any other individual.

$$\frac{h_i(t)}{h_j(t)} = \exp(\boldsymbol{\beta}^T(x_i - x_j)).$$

Hence, the subjects most at risk at any one time remain the subjects most at risk at any one other time (see also Figure 2.46).

Taking logarithms from the original proportional hazards model gives:

$$\log h(t, x_i) = \alpha(t) + \boldsymbol{\beta}^T x_i.$$

Note that if one chooses $\alpha(t) = \alpha$, one gets the exponential model, whereas if $\alpha(t) = \alpha \log(t)$, the Weibull model is obtained. A nice property of the proportional hazards model is that, using the idea of partial likelihood, the $\boldsymbol{\beta}$ coefficients can be estimated without having to explicitly specify the baseline hazard function $h_0(t)$ (Allison 1995; Cox 1972; Cox and Oakes 1984). This is useful if one is only interested in analyzing the impact of the covariates on the hazard rates and/or survival probabilities. However, if one wants to make predictions with the proportional hazards model, the baseline hazard needs to be explicitly specified.

The survival function that comes with the proportional hazards model looks as follows:

$$S(t, x_i) = \exp\left[-\int_0^t h_0(u)\exp(\boldsymbol{\beta}^T x_i)du\right],$$

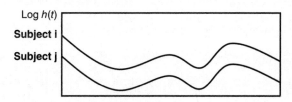

Figure 2.46 The proportional hazards model.

or

$$S(t, x_i) = S_0(t)^{\exp(\beta^T x_i)},$$

With

$$S_0(t) = \exp\left(-\int_0^t h_0(u)du\right).$$

$S_0(t)$ is referred to as the baseline survivor function, that is the survivor function for an individual whose covariates are all zero. Note that if a variable x_j increases with one unit (ceteris paribus), the survival probabilities are raised to the power $\exp(\beta_j)$, which is the hazard ratio (HR).

Extensions of Survival Analysis Models

A first extension of the models we discussed above is the inclusion of time varying covariates. These are variables that change value throughout the course of the study. The model then becomes:

$$h(t, x_i) = h_0(t) \exp(\beta^T x_i(t)),$$

where $x_i(t)$ is the vector of time-dependent covariates for individual i. Note that the proportional hazards assumption here no longer holds because the time-varying covariates may change at different rates for different subjects, so the ratios of their hazards will not remain constant. One could also let the β parameters vary in time as follows:

$$h(t, x_i) = h_0(t) \exp(\beta^T(t)x_i(t)).$$

The partial likelihood estimation method referred to earlier can easily be extended to accommodate these changes in the model formulation, such that the coefficients here can also be estimated without explicitly specifying the baseline hazard $h_0(t)$.

Another extension is the idea of competing risks (Crowder 2001). Often, an observation can experience any of k competing events. In medicine, customers may die because of cancer or aging. In a bank setting, a customer can default, pay off early, or churn at any given time. As long as a customer has not undergone any of the events, he/she remains at risk for any event. Once a customer has undergone the event, he/she is no longer included in the population at risk for any of the other risk groups; hence, the customer becomes censored for the other risks.

Although the ideas of time-varying covariates and competing risks seem attractive at first sight, the number of successful business applications of both remains very limited, due to the extra complexity introduced in the model(s).

Evaluating Survival Analysis Models

A survival analysis model can be evaluated by first considering the statistical significance of both the model as a whole, as well as the individual covariates (remember: significant covariates have low p-values). One could also predict the time of the event when the survival curve $S(t)$ drops below 0.50 and compare this with the real event time. Another option is to take a snapshot of the survival probabilities at a specific time t (e.g., 12 months), compare this with the event time indicator, and calculate the corresponding ROC curve and its area beneath. The AUC will then indicate how well the model ranks the observations for a specific timestamp t. Finally, one could also evaluate the interpretability of the survival analysis model by using univariate sign checks on the covariates and seeing whether they correspond to business expert knowledge.

The survival analysis models we have discussed in this chapter are classical statistical models. Hence, some important drawbacks are that the functional relationship remains linear or some mild extension thereof, interaction and nonlinear terms have to be specified ad hoc, extreme hazards may occur for outlying observations, and the assumption of proportional hazards may not always be the case. Other methods have been described in the literature to tackle these shortcomings, based on, for example, splines and neural networks (Baesens et al. 2005).

SOCIAL NETWORK ANALYTICS

Introduction

In the last decades, the use of social media websites in everybody's daily life is booming. People can continue their conversations on online social network sites such as Facebook, Twitter, LinkedIn, Google+, and Instagram, and share their experiences with their acquaintances, friends, and family. It only takes one click to update your whereabouts to the rest of the world. Plenty of options exist to broadcast your current activities: by picture, video, geo-location, links, or just plain text.

Users of online social network sites explicitly reveal their relationships with other people. As a consequence, social network sites are an (almost) perfect mapping of the relationships that exist in the real world. We know who you are, what your hobbies and interests are, to whom you are married, how many children you have, your buddies with whom you run every week, your friends in the wine club, and more. This whole interconnected network of people knowing each other somehow is an extremely interesting source of information and knowledge. Marketing managers no longer have to guess who might influence whom to create the appropriate campaign. It is all there—and that is exactly the problem. Social network sites acknowledge the richness of the data sources they have, and are not willing to share them as such and free of cost. Moreover, those data are often privatized and regulated, and well-hidden from commercial use. On the other hand, social network sites offer many good built-in facilities to managers and other interested parties to launch and manage their marketing campaigns by exploiting the social network, without publishing the exact network representation.

However, companies often forget that they can reconstruct (a part of) the social network using in-house data. Telecommunication providers, for example, have a massive transactional database where they record call behavior of their customers. Under the assumption that good friends call each other more often, we can recreate the network and indicate the tie strength between people based on the frequency and/or duration of calls. Internet infrastructure providers might map the relationships between people using their customers' IP addresses. IP addresses that frequently communicate are represented by a stronger relationship. In the end, the IP network will envisage the relational structure between people from another point of view, but to a certain extent as observed in reality. Many more examples can be found in the banking, retail, and online gaming industries. In this section, we discuss how social networks can be leveraged for analytics.

Social Network Definitions

A social network consists of both nodes (vertices) and edges. Both need to be clearly defined at the outset of the analysis. A node (vertex) could be defined as a customer (private/professional), household/family, patient, doctor, paper, author, terrorist, or website. An edge can be defined as a friend's relationship, a call, transmission of a disease, or reference. Note that the edges can also be weighted based on interaction frequency, importance of information exchange, intimacy, emotional intensity, and so on. For example: In a churn prediction setting, the edge can be weighted according to the time two customers called each other during a specific period. Social networks can be represented as a sociogram. This is illustrated in Figure 2.47 whereby the color of the nodes corresponds to a specific status (e.g., churner or nonchurner).

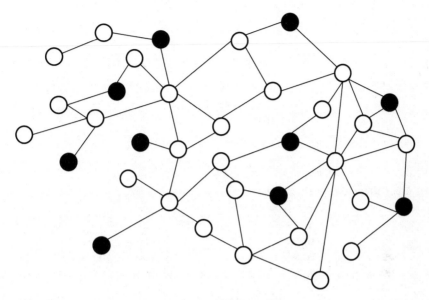

Figure 2.47 Sociogram representation of a social network.

Table 2.11 Matrix Representation of a Social Network

	C1	C2	C3	C4
C1	-	1	1	0
C2	1	-	0	1
C3	1	0	-	0
C4	0	1	0	-

Sociograms are useful for representing small-scale networks. For larger-scale networks, the network will typically be represented as a matrix, as illustrated in Table 2.11. These matrices will be symmetrical[3] and typically very sparse (with lots of zeros). The matrix can also contain the weights in case of weighted connections.

Social Network Metrics

A social network can be characterized by various social network metrics. The most important centrality measures are depicted in Table 2.12. Assume a network with g nodes $N_i, i = 1, \ldots, g . g_{jk}$ represents the number of geodesics from node N_j to node N_k, whereas

Table 2.12 Network Centrality Measures

Geodesic	Shortest path between two nodes in the network.	
Degree	Number of connections of a node (in- versus out-degree if the connections are directed).	
Closeness	The average distance of a node to all other nodes in the network (reciprocal of farness).	$\left[\dfrac{\sum_{j=1}^{g} d(N_i, N_j)}{g} \right]^{-1}$
Betweenness	Counts the number of times a node or connection lies on the shortest path between any two nodes in the network.	$\sum_{j<k} \dfrac{g_{jk}(N_i)}{g_{jk}}$
Graph theoretic center	The node with the smallest maximum distance to all other nodes in the network.	

$g_{jk}(N_i)$ represents the number of geodesics from node N_j to node N_k, passing through node N_i. The formulas in Table 2.12 each time calculate the metric for node N_i.

These metrics can now be illustrated for the well-known Kite network toy example depicted in Figure 2.48.

Table 2.13 reports the centrality measures for the Kite network. Based on degree, Diane is most central since she has the most connections. She works as a connector or hub. Note, however, that she only connects those already connected to each other. Fernando and Garth are the closest to all others. They are the best positioned to

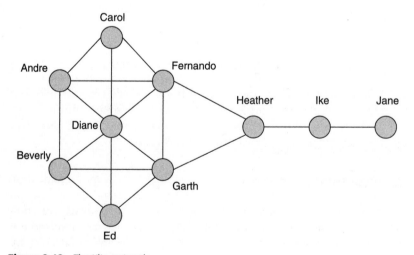

Figure 2.48 The Kite network.

Table 2.13 Centrality measures for the Kite network.

Degree		Closeness		Betweenness	
6	Diane	0.64	Fernando	14	Heather
5	Fernando	0.64	Garth	8.33	Fernando
5	Garth	0.6	Diane	8.33	Garth
4	Andre	0.6	Heather	8	Ike
4	Beverly	0.53	Andre	3.67	Diane
3	Carol	0.53	Beverly	0.83	Andre
3	Ed	0.5	Carol	0.83	Beverly
3	Heather	0.5	Ed	0	Carol
2	Ike	0.43	Ike	0	Ed
1	Jane	0.31	Jane	0	Jane

communicate messages that need to flow quickly through to all other nodes in the network. Heather has the highest betweenness. She sits in between two important communities (Ike and Jane versus the rest). She plays a broker role between both communities but is also a single point of failure. Note that the betweenness measure is often used for community mining. A popular technique here is the Girvan-Newman algorithm, which works as follows (Girvan, Newman, 2002):

1. The betweenness of all existing edges in the network is calculated first.
2. The edge with the highest betweenness is removed.
3. The betweenness of all edges affected by the removal is recalculated.
4. Steps 2 and 3 are repeated until no edges remain.

The result of this procedure is essentially a dendrogram, which can then be used to decide on the optimal number of communities.

Social Network Learning

In social network learning, the goal is within-network classification to compute the marginal class membership probability of a particular node given the other nodes in the network. Various important challenges arise when learning in social networks. A first key challenge is that the data are not independent and identically distributed (IID), an assumption often made in classical statistical models (e.g., linear and logistic regression). The correlational behavior between nodes implies that the class membership of one node might influence the class membership of a related node. Next, it is not easy to come up with a separation into a training set for model development and a test set for model validation, since the whole network is interconnected and cannot just be cut into two parts. Also, there is a strong need for collective inferencing procedures since inferences about nodes can mutually influence one another. Moreover, many networks are huge in scale (e.g., a call graph from a Telco provider), and efficient computational procedures need to be developed to do the learning (Verbeke, Martens et al., 2013). Finally, one should not forget the traditional way of doing analytics using only node-specific information, since this can still prove to be very valuable information for prediction as well.

Given the above remarks, a social network learner will usually consist of the following components (Macskassy and Provost 2007; Verbeke et al. 2014; Verbraken et al. 2014):

- A local model: This is a model using only node-specific characteristics, typically estimated using a classical predictive analytics model (e.g., logistic regression, decision tree).
- A network model: This is a model that will make use of the connections in the network to do the inferencing.
- A collective inferencing procedure: This is a procedure to determine how the unknown nodes are estimated together, hereby influencing each other.

In order to facilitate the computations, one often makes use of the Markov property, stating that the class of a node in the network only depends on the class of its direct neighbors (and not of the neighbors of the neighbors). Although this assumption may seem limiting at first sight, empirical evaluation has demonstrated that it is a reasonable assumption.

Relational Neighbor Classifier

The relational neighbor classifier is a network model that makes use of the homophily assumption stating that connected nodes have a propensity to belong to the same class. This idea is also referred to as *guilt by association*. If two nodes are associated, they tend to exhibit similar behavior. The posterior class probability for node N to belong to class c is then calculated as follows:

$$p(c|N) = \frac{1}{Z} \sum_{\{N_j \in Neighborhood_N | class(N_j) = c\}} w(N, N_j),$$

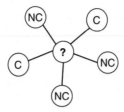

Figure 2.49 Example social network for relational neighbor classifier.

whereby $Neighborhood_N$ represents the neighborhood of node N, $w(N, N_j)$ the weight of the connection between N and N_j, and z is a normalization factor to make sure all probabilities sum to one.

Consider the example network depicted in Figure 2.49 whereby C and NC represent churner and nonchurner nodes, respectively, and where each relation has weight 1 (i.e., the network is unweighted).

The calculations then become:

$$p(C|?) = 1/z(1 + 1),$$
$$p(NC|?) = 1/z(1 + 1 + 1).$$

Since both probabilities have to sum to 1, z equals 5, so the probabilities become:

$$p(C|?) = 2/5,$$
$$p(NC|?) = 3/5.$$

Probabilistic Relational Neighbor Classifier

The probabilistic relational neighbor classifier is a straightforward extension of the relational neighbor classifier whereby the posterior class probability for node N to belong to class c is calculated as follows:

$$p(c|N) = \frac{1}{z} \sum_{\{N_j \in Neighborhood_N\}} w(N, N_j) p(c|N_j).$$

Note that the summation now ranges over the entire neighborhood of nodes. The probabilities $p(c|N_j)$ can be the result of a local model (e.g., logistic regression), or of a previously applied network model. Consider the network of Figure 2.50.

The calculations then become:

$$p(C|?) = 1/z(0.25 + 0.80 + 0.10 + 0.20 + 0.90) = 2.25/z,$$
$$p(NC|?) = 1/z(0.75 + 0.20 + 0.90 + 0.80 + 0.10) = 275/z.$$

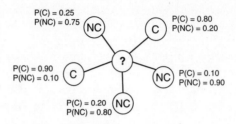

Figure 2.50 Example social network for probabilistic relational neighbor classifier.

Since both probabilities have to sum to 1, z equals 5, so the probabilities become:

$$p(C|?) = 2.25/5 = 0.45,$$
$$p(NC|?) = 2.75/5 = 0.55.$$

Relational Logistic Regression

Relational logistic regression was introduced by Lu and Getoor (2003). It basically starts off from a dataset with local node-specific characteristics and adds network characteristics to it as follows:

- Most frequently occurring class of neighbor (mode-link)
- Frequency of the classes of the neighbors (count-link)
- Binary indicators indicating class presence (binary-link)

This is illustrated in Figure 2.51.

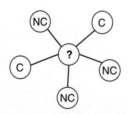

CID	Age	Income	...	Mode link	Frequency no churn	Frequency churn	Binary no churn	Binary churn
Bart	38	2400	...	NC	3	2	1	1

Figure 2.51 Relational logistic regression.

A logistic regression model is then estimated using the dataset with both local and network characteristics. Note that there is some correlation between the network characteristics added, which should be filtered out during an input selection procedure (using, for example, stepwise logistic regression). This idea is also referred to as *featurization*, since the network characteristics are basically added as special features to the dataset. These features can measure the behavior of the neighbors in terms of the target variable (e.g., churn or not) or in terms of the local node-specific characteristics (e.g., age, promotions, RFM, etc.).

Figure 2.52 provides an example whereby features are added describing the target behavior (i.e., churn) of the neighbors. Figure 2.53 provides an example whereby, additionally, features are added describing the local node behavior of the neighbors.

| | Local variables | | | Network variables | | |
Customer	Age	Recency	Number of contacts	Contacts with churners	Contacts with contacts of churners	Churn
John	35	5	18	3	9	Yes
Sophie	18	10	7	1	6	No
Victor	38	28	11	1	5	No
Laura	44	12	9	0	7	Yes

First order   Second order

Figure 2.52 Example of featurization with features describing target behavior of neighbors.

Customer	Age	Average duration	Average revenue	Average age friends	Average duration friends	Average revenue friends	Churn
John	25	50	123	20	55	250	Yes
Sophie	35	65	55	18	44	66	No
Victor	50	12	85	50	33	50	No
Laura	18	66	230	65	55	189	No

Figure 2.53 Example of featurization with features describing local node behavior of neighbors.

Algorithm 2.3 Gibbs sampling

1: Given a network with known and unknown nodes.
2: Initialize every unknown node using the local classifier to obtain the (local) posterior probabilities $p(y = j), j = 1, \ldots, J$
   (J = number of classes).
3: Sample a class value for each node according to the probabilities $p(y = j)$.
4: Generate a random ordering for the unknown nodes.
5: For each node in the ordering:
   a. Apply the relational learner to obtain new posterior probabilities $p(y = j)$.
   b. Sample the class value according to the new probabilities $p(y = j)$.
6: Repeat step 5 during 200 iterations without keeping any statistics (burn-in period).
7: Repeat step 5 during 2000 iterations counting the number of times each class is assigned to a particular node. Normalizing these counts gives us the final class probability estimates.

Collective Inferencing

Given a network initialized by a local model and a relational model, a collective inference procedure infers a set of class labels/probabilities for the unknown nodes by taking into account the fact that inferences about nodes can mutually affect one another. Following are some popular examples of collective inferencing procedures:

- Gibbs sampling (Geman and Geman 1984)
- Iterative classification (Lu and Getoor 2003)
- Relaxation labeling (Chakrabarti et al. 1998)
- Loopy belief propagation (Pearl 1988)

As an example, Gibbs sampling works as described in Algorithm 2.3.

Note, however, that empirical evidence has shown that collective inferencing usually does not substantially add to the performance of a social network learner.

CONCLUSION

In this chapter, we provided a broad overview of various analytical techniques. We started by zooming in on data preprocessing. This is a very important set of activities, since data are the key ingredient to any analytical model. We then elaborated on predictive analytics where the aim is to predict a categorical or continuous target measure of interest. We reviewed linear regression, logistic regression, decision trees, neural networks, and ensemble methods such as bagging, boosting, and random forests. We extensively discussed how to evaluate predictive models by adopting the right dataset split-up and performance measure. The next topic was descriptive analytics where no target variable is available. We discussed association rules, sequence rules, and clustering. The aim of survival analysis is to predict the timing of events. We discussed Kaplan Meier analysis, parametric survival analysis, and proportional hazards regression. The chapter concluded by zooming into social network analytics. The idea here is to study how relationships between nodes (e.g., customers) can be used for either predictive or descriptive purposes. After having introduced some key definitions and metrics, we elaborated on social network learning, network classifiers, and collective inference. Many of the techniques discussed in this chapter will be used in subsequent chapters in a profit setting.

REVIEW QUESTIONS

Multiple Choice Questions

Question 1

Which of the following strategies can be used to deal with missing values?

    a. Keep
    b. Delete
    c. Replace/impute
    d. All of the above

Question 2

Outlying observations that represent erroneous data are treated using

    a. missing value procedures
    b. truncation or capping·

Question 3

Clustering, association rules and sequence rules are examples of

    a. Predictive analytics
    b. Descriptive analytics

Question 4

Given the following transactions dataset:

ID	Items
T1	{K, A, D, B}
T2	{D, A, C, E, B}
T3	{C, A, B, D}
T4	{B, A, E}
T5	{B, E, D}

Consider the association rule R: A → BD. Which statement is correct?

a. The support of R is 100% and the confidence is 75%.
b. The support of R is 60% and the confidence is 100%.
c. The support of R is 75% and the confidence is 60%.
d. The support of R is 60% and the confidence is 75%.

Question 5

The aim of clustering is to come up with clusters such that the

a. homogeneity within a cluster is minimized and the heterogeneity between clusters is maximized.
b. homogeneity within a cluster is maximized and the heterogeneity between clusters is minimized.
c. homogeneity within a cluster is minimized and the heterogeneity between clusters is minimized.
d. homogeneity within a cluster is maximized and the heterogeneity between clusters is maximized.

Question 6

Given the following decision tree:

According to the decision tree, an applicant with Income > $50,000 and High Debt = Yes is classified as:

a. good risk
b. bad risk

Question 7

Consider a dataset with a multiclass target variable as follows: 25% bad payers, 25% poor payers, 25% medium payers, and 25% good payers. In this case, the entropy will be:

a. minimal.
b. maximal.
c. nonexistent.
d. dependent on the number of payers.

Question 8

Which of the following measures cannot be used to make the splitting decision in a regression tree?

a. mean squared error (MSE)
b. ANOVA/F-test
c. entropy
d. All of the measures can be used to make the splitting decision.

Question 9

Which of the following statements is true about decisions trees?

a. They are stable classifiers.
b. They are unstable classifiers.
c. They are sensitive to outliers.
d. They are recursive patterned algorithms.

Question 10

What is bootstrapping?

a. drawing samples with replacement
b. drawing samples without replacement
c. estimating multiple models using a weighted data sample
d. a process for building a replacement sample for random forests

Question 11

Which of the following steps in the random forests algorithm is not correct?

a. Step 1: Take a bootstrap sample with n observations.
b. Step 2: For each node of a tree, randomly choose m inputs on which to base the splitting decision.
c. Step 3: Split on the best of this subset.
d. Step 4: Fully grow each tree and prune.

Question 12

Which statement is correct?

a. An observation on a variable T is left-censored if all you know about T is that it is greater than some value c.
b. An observation on a variable T is right-censored if all you know about T is that it is smaller than some value c.
c. An observation on a variable T is interval-censored if all you know about T is that $a < T < b$.
d. A time-dependent covariate is always censored.

Question 13

Which formula is not correct?

a. $f(t) = \lim\limits_{\Delta t \to 0} \frac{P(t \leq T < t + \Delta t)}{\Delta t}$

b. $S(t) = 1 - F(t) = P(T > t) = \int\limits_{t}^{\infty} f(u)du$

c. $h(t) = \lim\limits_{\Delta t \to 0} \frac{P(t \leq T < t + \Delta t | T \geq t)}{\Delta t}$

d. $h(t) = \frac{S(t)}{f(t)}$

Question 14

Consider the survival data in the table below. Which statement is correct?

a. $S(6) = 4/5$
b. $S(9) = 3/4$
c. $S(12) = 1/2$
d. $S(15) = 1/2 \cdot 3/5$

Customer	Time of Churn or Censoring	Churn or Censored
C1	3	Churn
C2	6	Churn
C3	9	Censored
C4	12	Churn
C5	15	Censored

Question 15

Which statement is correct?

a. If the survival times are Weibull-distributed, then the hazard is constant and a plot of $-log(S(t))$ versus t should yield a straight line through the origin at 0.

b. If the survival times are Weibull-distributed, then a plot of $log(-log(S(t)))$ versus $log(t)$ is a straight line (not through the origin) with a slope of κ.

c. If the survival times are exponentially distributed, then a plot of $log(-log(S(t)))$ versus $log(t)$ is a straight line (not through the origin) with a slope of κ.

d. If the survival times are Weibull-distributed, then a plot of $-log(S(t))$ versus is a straight line (not through the origin) with a slope of κ.

Question 16

The proportional hazards model assumes that

a. the subjects most at risk at any one time remain the subjects most at risk at any one other time.

b. the subjects most at risk at any one time remain the subjects least at risk at any one other time.

Question 17

What statement about the adjacency matrix representing a social network is not true?

a. It is a symmetric matrix.

b. It is sparse since it contains a lot of nonzero elements.

c. It can include weights.

d. It has the same number of rows and columns.

Question 18

Which statement is correct?

    a. The geodesic represents the longest path between two nodes.
    b. The betweenness counts the number of the times that a node or edge occurs in the geodesics of the network.
    c. The graph theoretic center is the node with the highest minimum distance to all other nodes.
    d. The closeness is always higher than the betweenness.

Question 19

Given the following social network:

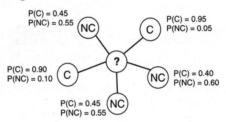

According to the probabilistic relational neighbor classifier, the probability that the node in the middle is a churner equals:

    a. 0.37
    b. 0.63
    c. 0.60
    d. 0.40

Question 20

Featurization refers to

    a. selecting the most predictive features.
    b. adding more local features to the dataset.
    c. making features (= inputs) out of the network characteristics.
    d. adding more nodes to the network.

Open Questions

Question 1

Discuss the key activities when preprocessing data for credit scoring. Remember, credit scoring aims at distinguishing good payers from bad payers using application characteristics such as age, income, and employment status. Why is data preprocessing considered important?

Question 2

What are the key differences between logistic regression and decision trees? Give examples of when to prefer one above the other.

Question 3

Consider the following dataset of predicted scores and actual target values (you can assume higher scores should be assigned to the goods).

Score	Actual
100	Bad
110	Bad
120	Good
130	Bad
140	Bad
150	Good
160	Bad
170	Good
180	Good
190	Bad
200	Good
210	Good
220	Bad

Score	Actual
230	Good
230	Good
240	Good
250	Bad
260	Good
270	Good
280	Good
290	Bad
300	Good
310	Bad
320	Good
330	Good
340	Good

a. Calculate the classification accuracy, sensitivity, and specificity for a classification cutoff of 205.
b. Draw the ROC curve. How would you estimate the area under the ROC curve?
c. Draw the CAP curve and estimate the AR.
d. Draw the lift curve. What is the top decile lift?

Question 4

Why are random forests called random? Do they usually perform better than decision trees? Why or why not?

Question 5

Discuss how association and sequence rules can be used to build recommender systems such as the ones adopted by Amazon, eBay, and Netflix. How would you evaluate the performance of a recommender system?

Question 6

Explain K-means clustering using a small (artificial) dataset. What is the impact of K? What preprocessing steps are needed?

Question 7

What differentiates survival analysis methods from classical statistical methods such as linear or logistic regression? How can you evaluate the performance of a survival analysis model, and how is this different from classical regression models?

Question 8

Discuss the most important types of social network classifiers using a real-life example.

NOTES

1. In detail, we would like the matrices U and V to be unitary, that is, that the inverse of the matrix is its conjugate transpose. The conjugate transform of a matrix A is such that $a_{ij} = \overline{a_{ij}}$, with $\bar{a}$ the complex conjugate of a. If all elements a_{ij} of matrix A are real, then $A^* = A^T$ the transpose of matrix A.

2. Note that we will frequently adopt the term *positives* to refer to the minority class (e.g., churners, defaulters, fraudsters, responders) and *negatives* to refer to the majority class (e.g., nonchurners, nondefaulters, nonfraudsters, nonresponders, and so on).

3. Note that this is only the case for undirected networks. For directed networks, the matrix will not necessarily be symmetrical.

REFERENCES

Allison, P. D. 2001. *Logistic Regression Using the SAS® System: Theory and Application*. Hoboken, NJ: Wiley-SAS.

Allison, P. D. 1995. *Survival Analysis Using the SAS System*. SAS Institute Inc.

Baesens, B. 2014. *Analytics in a Big Data World*. Hoboken, NJ: Wiley.

Baesens, B., D. Martens, R. Setiono, and J. Zurada. 2011. "White Box Nonlinear Prediction Models," editorial special issue. *IEEE Transactions on Neural Networks* 22 (12): 2406–2408.

Baesens, B., R. Setiono, C. Mues, and J. Vanthienen. 2003. "Using Neural Network Rule Extraction and Decision Tables for Credit-Risk Evaluation." *Management Science* 49 (3): 312–329.

Baesens, B., T. Van Gestel, M. Stepanova, D. Van den Poel, and J. Vanthienen. 2005. "Neural Network Survival Analysis for Personal Loan Data." *Journal of the Operational Research Society, Special Issue on Credit Scoring* 59 (9): 1089–1098.

Baesens, B., W, Verbeke, and V. Van Vlasselaer. 2015. *Fraud Analytics Using Descriptive, Predictive, and Social Network Techniques: A Guide to Data Science for Fraud Detection*. Hoboken, NJ: John Wiley & Sons.

Baesens, B., S. Viaene, D. Van den Poel, J. Vanthienen, and G. Dedene. 2002. "Bayesian Neural Network Learning for Repeat Purchase Modelling in Direct Marketing." *European Journal of Operational Research* 138 (1): 191–211.

Bartlett, P. L. 1997. "For Valid Generalization, the Size of the Weights Is More Important than the Size of the Network." In Mozer, M. C., Jordan, M. I., and Petsche, T. (eds.), *Advances in Neural Information Processing Systems 9*, Cambridge, MA: the MIT Press, pp. 134–140.

Bishop, C. M. 1995. *Neural Networks for Pattern Recognition*. Oxford: Oxford University Press.

Breiman, L. 1996. "Bagging Predictors." *Machine Learning* 24 (2): 123–140.

Breiman, L., J. H. Friedman, R, A. Olshen, and C. J. Stone.1984. *Classification and Regression Trees*. Monterey, CA: Wadsworth & Brooks/Cole Advanced Books & Software.

Breiman, L. 2001. "Random Forests." *Machine Learning* 45 (1): 5–32.

Chakrabarti, S., B. Dom, and P. Indyk.1998, June. "Enhanced Hypertext Categorization Using Hyperlinks." In *ACM SIGMOD Record* 27 (2): 307–318. ACM.

Cox, D. R., and D. Oakes. 1984. *Analysis of Survival Data*. Chapman and Hall.

Cox, D. R. 1972. "Regression Models and Life Tables." *Journal of the Royal Statistical Society, Series B.*

Crowder, M. J. 2001. *Classical Competing Risks*. London: Chapman and Hall.

Dejaeger, K., W. Verbeke, D. Martens, and B. Baesens. 2012. "Data Mining Techniques for Software Effort Estimation: a Comparative Study." *IEEE Transactions on Software Engineering* 38 (2): 375–397.

DeLong, E. R., D. M. DeLong, and D. L. Clarke-Pearson. 1988. "Comparing the Areas Under Two or More Correlated Receiver Operating Characteristic Curves: A Nonparametric Approach." *Biometrics* 44: 837–845.

Duda, R. O., P. E. Hart, and D. G. Stork. 2001. *Pattern Classification*. New York: John Wiley & Sons.

Efron, B. 1979. "Bootstrap Methods: Another Look at the Jackknife." *The Annals of Statistics* 7 (1): 1–26.

Fawcett, T. 2003. "ROC Graphs: Notes and Practical Considerations for Researchers." *HP Labs Tech Report* HPL-2003–4.

Freund, Y., and R. E. Schapire. 1997. "A Decision-Theoretic Generalization of On-Line Learning and an Application to Boosting." *Journal of Computer and System Sciences* 55 (1): 119–139, August.

Freund, Y., and R. E. Schapire. 1999. "A Short Introduction to Boosting." *Journal of Japanese Society for Artificial Intelligence* 14 (5): 771–780, September.

Geman S., and D. Geman. 1984. "Stochastic Relaxation, Gibbs Distributions, and the Bayesian Restoration of Images." *IEEE Transactions on Pattern Analysis and Machine Intelligence* 6: 721–741.

Girvan, M., and M. E. J. Newman. 2002. "Community Structure in Social and Biological Networks." *Proceedings of the National Academy of Sciences, USA* 99: 7821–7826.

Hanley, J. A., and B. J. McNeil. 1982. "The Meaning and Use of Area under the ROC Curve." *Radiology* 143: 29–36.

Hartigan, J. A.1975. *Clustering Algorithms*. New York: John Wiley & Sons.

Hastie, T., R. Tibshirani, and J. Friedman. 2011. *The Elements of Statistical Learning: Data Mining, Inference, and Prediction*, Second Edition (Springer Series in Statistics). New York: Springer.

Hornik, K., M. Stinchcombe, and H. White. 1989. "Multilayer Feedforward Networks Are Universal Approximators." *Neural Networks* 2 (5): 359–366.

Huysmans, J., B. Baesens, T. Van Gestel, and J. Vanthienen. 2006a. "Using Self Organizing Maps for Credit Scoring." *Expert Systems with Applications, Special Issue on Intelligent Information Systems for Financial Engineering* 30 (3): 479–487.

Huysmans, J., D. Martens, B. Baesens, and J. Vanthienen. 2006a. "Country Corruption Analysis with Self Organizing Maps and Support Vector Machines." *Proceedings of the Tenth Pacific-Asia Conference on Knowledge Discovery and Data Mining (PAKDD 2006), Workshop on Intelligence and Security Informatics (WISI)*, Lecture Notes in Computer Science 3917: 103–114. Singapore, Springer-Verlag, April 9.

Jolliffe, I. 2002. *Principal Component Analysis*. Hoboken, NJ: John Wiley & Sons, Ltd.

Kohonen, T. 1982. "Self-Organized Formation of Topologically Correct Feature Maps." *Biological Cybernetics* 43: 59–69.

Landauer, T. K. 2006. *Latent Semantic Analysis.* Hoboken, NJ: John Wiley & Sons, Ltd.

Lu, Q., and L. Getoor. 2003. "Link-based Classification." *Proceeding of the Twentieth Conference on Machine Learning (ICML-2003),* Washington DC.

Macskassy, S. A., and F. Provost. 2007. "Classification in Networked Data: A Toolkit and a Univariate Case Study." *Journal of Machine Learning Research* 8: 935–983.

Moody, J., and J. Utans. 1994. "Architecture Selection Strategies for Neural Networks: Application to Corporate Bond Rating Prediction." In *Neural Networks in the Capital Markets.* New York: John Wiley & Sons.

Pearl, J. 1988. *Probabilistic Reasoning in Intelligent Systems.* San Francisco: Morgan Kaufmann Publishers.

Quinlan, J. R. 1993. *C4.5 Programs for Machine Learning.* San Francisco: Morgan Kauffman Publishers.

Schölkopf, B., A. Smola, and K. R. Müller. 1998. "Nonlinear Component Analysis as a Kernel Eigenvalue Problem." *Neural Computation* 10 (5): 1299–1319.

Seret, A., T. Verbraken, S. Versailles, and B. Baesens. 2012. "A New SOM-Based Method for Profile Generation: Theory and an Application in Direct Marketing." *European Journal of Operational Research* 220 (1): 199–209.

Verbeke W., D. Martens, and B. Baesens. 2014. "Social Network Analysis for Customer Churn Prediction." *Applied Soft Computing* 14: 341–446.

Verbeke W., D. Martens, C. Mues, and B. Baesens. 2011. "Building Comprehensible Customer Churn Prediction Models with Advanced Rule Induction Techniques." *Expert Systems with Applications* 38: 2354–2364.

Verbraken, T., Goethals, F., Verbeke, W., & Baesens, B. (2014). Predicting online channel acceptance with social network data. *Decision Support Systems,* 63, 104–114.

Vidal, R., Y. Ma, and S. Sastry. 2005. "Generalized Principal Component Analysis (GPCA)." *IEEE Transactions on Pattern Analysis and Machine Intelligence* 27 (12): 1945–1959.

Zurada, J. M. 1992. *Introduction to Artificial Neural Systems.* Boston: PWS Publishing.

CHAPTER 3

Business Applications

INTRODUCTION

Big data can be leveraged in various ways using analytics. In this chapter, we elaborate on some popular examples of applications without claiming to be exhaustive. More specifically, we zoom in on marketing analytics, fraud analytics, credit risk analytics, and HR analytics. For each of these areas, we define the overall modeling problem, the target to be optimized (if any), and the business implications. We also relate back to the key characteristics of successful analytical models in each of these settings as discussed in Chapter 1: accuracy, interpretability, operational efficiency, regulatory compliance, and economical cost. We give recommendations concerning which of the analytical techniques discussed in the previous chapters can be used to tackle each of the applications. Subsequent chapters then further elaborate by introducing the profit perspective.

MARKETING ANALYTICS

Introduction

Various types of marketing analytics can be distinguished. A key characteristic is that they all center on the customer as the basic entity of analytical modeling. Therefore, marketing analytics is sometimes also referred to as customer analytics. By carefully analyzing historical data and transactions, analytics can help us to understand customer behavior from an acquisition, retention, selling, segmentation, lifetime value, journey, or recommendation perspective as we discuss next.

RFM Analysis

As illustrated in Chapter 2 (see Tables 2.2 and 2.3), a commonly used set of features in marketing analytics are the RFM variables. RFM stands for recency, frequency, and monetary and has been popularized by Cullinan (1977) as follows:

- Recency: time frame (days, weeks, months) since last purchase
- Frequency: number of purchases within a given time frame
- Monetary: value (€) of purchases

The RFM variables are not readily available as such, but need to be distilled from your historical transaction data. Each of the RFM constructs can be operationalized in various ways (Baesens et al. 2002). For example, one can consider the minimum/maximum/average/most recent monetary value of purchases. The constructs can be used separately or combined into an RFM score by either independent or dependent sorting. For the former (see Figure 3.1), the customer

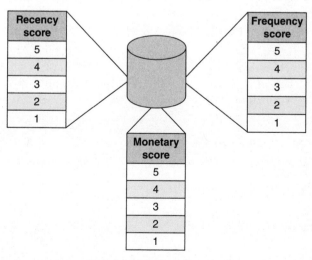

Figure 3.1 Constructing an RFM score (independent sorting).

database is sorted into independent quintiles or deciles based on recency, frequency, and monetary (e.g., recency quintile 1 represents the 20% most ancient buyers). The final RFM score then combines the three quintiles into one number (e.g., 325) and can be used as a quantitative, continuous variable in your marketing analytics models. For dependent sorting, the customer database is first sorted into quintiles based on recency (see Figure 3.2). Each recency quintile is then further divided into frequency quintiles and then into monetary quintiles. This again yields a combined RFM score (e.g., 335), which can be used for marketing analytics. The RFM variables or scores can be used for response modeling, churn prediction, customer segmentation, and customer lifetime value modeling. They have also been successfully used in fraud analytics (see below).

Response Modeling

When you are running a marketing campaign, it is not always possible or even desirable to target your entire customer base. A first obvious reason is limited marketing budgets. Sending out irrelevant campaigns to uninterested customers is a waste of money. Moreover, some customers might even get so annoyed that it creates an adverse effect toward your product, brand, or company (also called *wearout*). Hence, it would be ideal if we could send out the marketing message only to those customers who are positively impacted. The analytical solution to this is called response modeling. The goal hereby is to develop a classification model (e.g., logistic regression or decision tree) that selects the customers who are most likely to respond and take action. Put differently, response modeling focuses on deepening or recovering customer relationships using analytically based models.

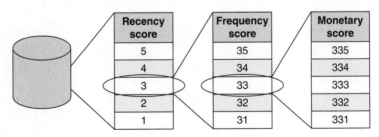

Figure 3.2 Constructing an RFM score (dependent sorting).

Various types of responses can be considered. Assume you invested in an email marketing message or a Facebook ad that has a fancy title, together with a link to your website. The response can now be qualified in various ways. More specifically, we can make a distinction between a soft response and a hard response. Seeing the ad could be a first type of response that is of interest since it will create product and/or brand awareness. A next type of response would be someone clicking the link. This already illustrates more engagement with your offer. Responses may then come in a variety of forms. Examples are opening a web page or pdf with a product description, or leaving your contact details together with a request for a price quote. These are all examples of soft responses with increasing interest in your message and offer. The ultimate, hard response would be a product or service purchase. Hence, as a first step in response modeling, the data scientist needs to discuss with the business expert what target (e.g., ad impression, click link, pdf download, or actual purchase) needs to be modeled.

Once the response target has been appropriately defined, the historical data for analytical modeling must be gathered from previous marketing campaigns in order to properly understand customer response behavior. Popular examples of data that might be useful include the following:

- Demographic variables (e.g., age, gender, marital status, employment status)
- Relationship variables (e.g., length of relationship, number of products purchased)
- RFM variables (see above)
- Social network information (e.g., purchase behavior of friends, product reviews from friends)

These variables can then be gathered into a dataset to build your analytical response model. Given the multitude of variables available, it will be important to perform variable selection to make the model compact and powerful.

Various analytical techniques can be used for response modeling such as logistic regression, decision trees, neural networks, and random forests. In fact, many companies feel comfortable using black-box analytical models (e.g., random forests, neural networks) for response modeling since their primary goal is to find out who will respond rather than understand why customers respond. Note that besides classification, response modeling can also be approached from a regression angle, whereby the aim is to build a regression model predicting the amount (or intensity) of the response. In Chapter 4, we extend this traditional response modeling setup by introducing uplift modeling.

Churn Prediction

Customer churn, also called attrition or defection, is the loss of customers (Baesens 2014). In saturated markets, there are limited opportunities to attract new customers, so retaining existing customers is essential to profitability and stability. In Telco, it is estimated that attracting a new customer costs five to six times more than retaining an existing customer (Athanassopoulos 2000; Verbeke et al. 2012, 2014). Established customers are more profitable due to a lower cost to serve them, and the brand loyalty they have developed over time makes them less likely to churn. Satisfied customers also serve as word-of-mouth advertisement, referring new customers to the company.

The first step in analytical churn prediction is to define churn for the particular business context. This may be naturally present in the data: contract termination, service cancellation, or nonrenewal. In other settings, it will not be so clear: A customer no longer shops at the store or website, or a customer stops purchasing credits. In these cases, the data scientist must choose a definition of churn that makes sense in the given business setting. One common solution is to select an appropriate length of time of inactivity on the account. In the examples above, a number of days or months (e.g., three months) without a purchase might define churn. Of course, a customer may not buy something within that time frame but might still return at a later date, so the churn definition might never be perfect. Setting the time period too short may lead to nonchurn customers being targeted as potential churners. Setting it too long may mean that churning customers are not identified in a timely manner. In most cases, a shorter time period may be preferable, if the cost of the intervention campaign is much lower than the cost of a lost customer.

A further distinction can be made between active, passive, forced, and expected churn. Active churn implies that the customer severs the relationship with the firm. This can be quite easily determined in a contractual setting but is less evident in a noncontractual setting, as mentioned above. Passive churn refers to a decrease in product or service usage. As an example, consider a customer churning from Bank A to Bank B. Instead of canceling his/her checking account at Bank A, the customer decides to keep it alive but now concentrates his/her banking activities to Bank B. Hence, this implies that the account at Bank A becomes a dormant or sleeping account. Timely detecting these accounts could also be a goal of churn prediction. Forced churn occurs when the company rather than the customer stops the relationship due to, for example, fraud. Finally, expected churn implies that a customer no longer needs a product or service. As an example, consider the consumption of baby products.

Various types of data can be used for churn prediction, such as demographic data, product/service usage data, and RFM data. Two other very interesting sources of data are complaints data and social network data. Examples of the former are number of filed complaints and number of contacts with the service desk. These are clear signs of growing customer dissatisfaction, which may finally result in churn. Another very interesting piece of information concerns social network data. Earlier research (Verbeke et al. 2014) in telecommunications (telco) has shown a clear pattern in call detail record data, implying that churners are likely to be connected to other churners in the call graph. This phenomenon clearly illustrates a viral effect of customer drain. Hence, appropriately featurizing these call graphs will definitely contribute to the performance of the analytical churn models. Although a call graph gives us a quite natural social network in telco, defining networks in other customer churn settings may not be that obvious.

An important attention point from a business perspective concerns the distinction between a characteristic predictor for future churn and a symptom of occurring churn. As an example, in a prepaid telco setting, a sudden peak in phone usage often occurs right before churn because the customer has already decided to churn and wants to consume all his/her credits. Although these variables are highly predictive, they are not very actionable in terms of churn prevention. Hence, when developing churn prediction models, it is important to focus on early-warning signs of customer dissatisfaction such that the churn event might possibly be halted by a timely targeting of the customer with the appropriate marketing action.

From an analytical perspective, churn can be tackled in various ways. A first approach is by developing a classification model (e.g., logistic regression, decision trees). These models will assign each customer an expected probability of churn. Then it is relatively straightforward to offer those customers with the highest churn probability a discount or other promotion to encourage them to extend their contract or keep their account active. Accurate predictions are perhaps the most apparent goal, but learning the reasons, or at least indicators, for churn is also invaluable to the company. More comprehensible models can offer novel insights into the correlation between customer behavior and propensity to churn (Verbeke et al. 2011), allowing management to address the factors leading to churn in addition to targeting the customers before they decide to churn. Besides classification, churn can also be tackled using survival analysis techniques. The idea here is to not only predict if a customer will churn but also when the churn event will take place. This will afford valuable information to calculate the customer lifetime value, as we discuss in what follows. Finally, as discussed before, social network analytics can also be used to appropriately take into account homophilic patterns in churn behavior.

X-selling

The aim of X-selling is to change the intended purchase behavior of a customer. X-selling can be done in three possible ways: up-selling, cross-selling, or down-selling. The idea of **up-selling** is to sell more of a given product, usually at the time of purchase. An example of this is if you order a lager beer (e.g., Stella Artois) and the waiter recommends an upscale, more expensive beer instead (e.g., a specialty Trappist beer such as Westmalle). **Cross-selling** aims at selling an additional product or service. For example, the waiter might also recommend some abbey cheese as it pairs well with a Westmalle. Finally, **down-selling** means selling less of a product or service in order to maintain a sustainable, long-lasting customer relationship. For example, if you had too many beers and order yet another one, the waiter might discourage you from doing so and recommend water instead.

From an analytical perspective, X-selling applications are usually developed using descriptive analytics techniques. As an example, association rules can be used to detect frequently occurring patterns between purchased items and, as such, recommend products or services for cross-selling. The resulting associations can be used for product bundling, catalog design, store layout, and/or shelf organization. Association rules can also be used to develop recommender systems as we discuss next.

Customer Segmentation

The aim of customer segmentation is to segment a set of customers or transactions into clusters that can be used for marketing purposes. Applications could accomplish these goals, for example:

- Understand a customer population—for example, targeted marketing or advertising (mass customization).
- Efficiently allocate marketing resources.
- Differentiate between brands in a portfolio.
- Identify the most profitable customers.
- Identify shopping patterns (e.g., based on the RFM variables).
- Identify the need for new products.

Various types of clustering data can be used, such as demographic, lifestyle, attitudinal, behavioral, RFM, acquisitional and social network, among others. A critical parameter to be decided on during clustering concerns the number of clusters (e.g., the "K" in a K-means clustering procedure). Usually, it is determined in close collaboration between the data scientist and business expert whereby both the statistical separation and marketing interpretation of a clustering solution are considered.

Contrary to, for example, response modeling, interpretation in customer segmentation is key. The marketer needs to clearly understand the characteristics of each segment so that it can be targeted with the appropriate campaign. To facilitate the interpretation of a clustering solution, various options are available (Baesens et al. 2015). A first one is to compare cluster distributions with the population distribution across all variables on a cluster-by-cluster basis. This is illustrated in Figure 3.3, where the distribution of a cluster C1 is contrasted with the overall population distribution for the recency, frequency, and monetary variables. It can clearly be observed that cluster C1 has mainly observations with low recency values and high monetary values, whereas the frequency is relatively similar to that of the original population.

Another way to explain a given clustering solution is by building a decision tree with the cluster ID as the target variable. Assume we have the output shown in Table 3.1 from a K-means clustering exercise with K equal to 4.

We can now build a decision tree with the Cluster ID as the target variable, as shown in Figure 3.4.

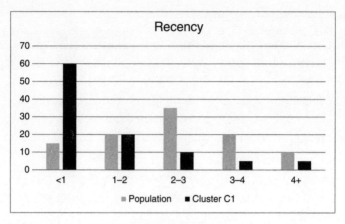

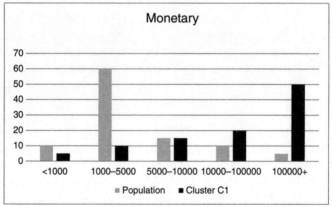

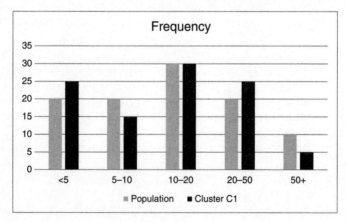

Figure 3.3   Cluster profiling using histograms.

Table 3.1 *K*-Means Clustering Sample Output

Customer	Recency	Frequency	Monetary	. . . .	Cluster ID
John	3	1	2,100	. . .	C2
Sophie	5	7	850	. . .	C4
Bob	0.5	15	100	. . .	C3
Josephine	18	2	1,200	. . .	C2
Bart	1	4	400	. . .	C1
Robert	12	6	500	. . .	C4
. . .	. . .	. . .	. . .	. . .	. . .

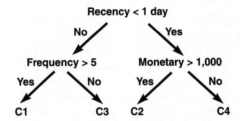

Figure 3.4 Using decision trees for clustering interpretation.

The decision tree in Figure 3.4 gives us a clear insight into the distinguishing characteristics of the various clusters. For example, cluster 2 is characterized by customers having recency < 1 day and monetary > 1,000. Hence, using decision trees, we can clearly understand the characteristics of each cluster and work out corresponding marketing strategies. It also allows us to classify new observations into existing clusters without having to rerun the clustering solution. This is a nice example of how predictive techniques can be used to explain the solution of a descriptive analytics exercise. We revisit this in Chapter 5, where we talk about profit-driven analytics.

Customer Lifetime Value

Customer lifetime value is the net present value of the profit generated by an individual customer. It can be measured in various ways depending on how the customer relationship is conceptualized. Two common alternatives are the *lost for good* and the *always a share* perspective (Jackson 1985). The former assumes that when customers churn at some point during their lifecycle, they become permanently lost to the firm. A popular example of a lost-for-good approach is the CLV formula suggested by Gupta et al. (2006) as follows:

$$CLV_i = \sum_{t=1}^{n} \frac{(R_{it} - C_{it})s_{it}}{(1 + r)^t}$$

where CLV_i represents the customer lifetime value of customer i, R_{it} is the revenue generated by customer i at time t, C_{it} is the cost to serve customer i at time t, S_{it} is the survival probability of customer i at time t, r is the discount factor, and n is the period under study. A key characteristic of the lost-for-good approach is the inclusion of the survival probability, S_{it}, which is the compliment of the churn probability and can be estimated using for example a parametric or proportional hazards model as discussed in Chapter 2. Lost-for-good CLV models can make sense in, for example, telco where switching customers usually never return. If, for some reason, a customer would reactivate the relationship with the firm, (s)he would be considered as a new customer in this approach. Hence, this approach has an intrinsic bias to underestimate the CLV at customer level since one customer may be represented by multiple observations.

The always-a-share approach assumes that customers allocate their purchasing across several firms and can always return to a firm, even after a long period of inactivity. In other words, customers never terminate the relationship with the firm. Examples of this are online retailers (e.g., Amazon, Netflix, etc.) and airlines where purchases may take place with big inter-purchase times. This approach will not explicitly account for the survival probability, S_{it}, but rather, calculate the CLV as follows:

$$CLV_i = \sum_{t=1}^{n} \frac{(R_{it} - C_{it})}{(1 + r)^t}$$

CLV can be calculated for both your existing customer base as well as for prospects or potential future customers, in which case it is sometimes also referred to as the prospect lifetime value (PLV). The difference is important when it comes to factoring in the acquisitions costs (e.g., costs of marketing campaigns, lead generation) to initialize the customer relationship. For your current customers, these are sunk costs and hence of no influence on managerial decision making. However, acquisition costs represent a material investment for prospects that should be accounted for in the calculation of the PLV.

Besides the survival probabilities and acquisition costs, the other components of the CLV also require closer attention. A first issue concerns the choice of the time horizon, n. Although theoretically this should be infinity or at least the remaining part of the customer life cycle, many firms will work with a two-to-three-year time period, since this is usually considered to be representative for a relatively stable business environment. Forecasting with longer time horizons will be a lot more difficult and cause bigger forecasting errors, making the CLV models less useful. The time granularity adopted will depend on the transaction intensity. Many firms measure time on a monthly basis.

Also the revenues R_{it} and C_{it} should be properly quantified. Ideally, both direct and indirect revenues and costs should be accounted for. Direct revenues are the income from sales whereas examples of indirect revenues are word of mouth potential, recommendations to fellow customers or prospects, and even social impact or presence in influential customer communities (see the section on social networks in Chapter 2). Direct costs are the costs to produce the goods or services whereas examples of indirect costs are the costs of marketing activities (e.g., retention or X-selling campaigns), costs of customer service and costs of returns, among others. Note that both indirect revenues and costs are often hard to precisely quantify. Hence, many firms will work with averages or even ignore both in their CLV calculation due to the unavailability of data.

Also the discount factor r needs some careful thought. A common practice is to use the weighted average cost of capital (WACC) calculated as follows (Kumar, Ramani and Bohling 2004):

$$WACC = \frac{E}{E+D}C_E + \frac{D}{E+D}C_D(1-t)$$

where E represents the (market) value of the equity, D the (market) value of the total debt, C_E the cost of equity, C_D the cost of debt, and t the local tax rate. It represents the average cost of raising money, which is invested in building and extending customer relationships. For many firms, this will range around 7%.[1] Note that the WACC is usually expressed on a yearly basis, so when working with monthly time periods, the monthly discount factor becomes $\sqrt[12]{(1 + WACC)} - 1$.

Various approaches can be used to model and calculate CLV. A straightforward approach is to work with averages. This can be sufficient in simple and stable business environments. Consider the example of a newspaper vendor. The revenues or margins are fixed and the time of purchase is also known and stable. Only the length of the customer relationship needs to be determined for which a fixed time window (e.g., two to three years) can be adopted. Although this approach sounds appealing at first sight, it will be less suitable in volatile business environments with varying inter-purchase times and purchase amounts.

The Pareto/NBD (negative binomial distribution) model is a more sophisticated approach and uses observed past purchase behavior of customers to forecast future purchase behavior (Schmittlein et al. 1987). More specifically, it uses one submodel to predict the number of transactions in the future and another one to provide an estimate of the average profit per transaction. The CLV is then computed as the discounted product of the future number of transactions and the average profit per transaction. The Pareto/NBD model is highly parametric, as it makes the following assumptions:

- The number of purchases made by an active customer follows a Poisson process.

- The customer lifetime follows an exponential distribution.

- The purchasing rate and churn rate follow a Gamma distribution.

- The purchasing rate and churn rate are independent.

Using these assumptions, an expression can be derived to estimate the future number of transactions (Fader and Hardie 2005). The average profit per transaction can then be estimated using the Gamma/Gamma submodel as suggested by Fader et al. (2005b). Note that this model assumes that the profit per transaction is Gamma-distributed, constant over time, and independent of the number of transactions. Furthermore, the rate parameter of the former Gamma distribution is also Gamma-distributed across all customers. The various distribution parameters are then typically estimated using a maximum likelihood or method of moments procedure (Reinartz and Kumar 2003). Various extensions of the Pareto/NBD model have been developed by either relaxing or introducing other assumptions. A first example is the Beta-geometric/NBD submodel by Fader et al. (2005a). The Pareto/Dependent approach by Glady et al. (2009a) introduces a dependency between the number of transactions and the average profit per transaction and proves to be empirically superior to the original Pareto/NBD model which assumes independence. More recently, extensions have been provided to also calculate the variance of the CLV representing the degree of uncertainty associated with a customer's expected CLV (McCarthy et al. 2016).

From this discussion, it becomes clear that the assumptions of the Pareto/NBD model and its extensions are quite stringent and often unrealistic in many practical application settings. Moreover, estimating all the distribution parameters can be a cumbersome task. Another approach could be to use predictive analytics, as discussed before. The idea here is to split the modeling data into two periods:

one period for calculating all the predictors (e.g., sociodemographic, RFM, social network variables, etc.) and one period for calculating the target CLV. The relationship can then be modeled using any of the predictive analytical techniques discussed before, such as linear regression, neural networks, or random forests, among others. For example, in Glady et al. (2009a) a plain-vanilla linear regression already outperformed the Pareto/NBD model: 47.9% versus 40.5% Pearson correlation between predicted and actual CLV values.

Obviously, these models assume the availability of detailed historical data as well that the past is a meaningful predictor for the future. A key advantage is that they also afford us insight into how the various predictors contribute to the CLV. In fact, this predictive analytical approach is the most popular in industry.

A further analytical refinement would be to individually predict the values of R_{it} and C_{it} using regression or forecasting type of models, and S_{it} using survival analysis models, and combine all predictions into a predicted CLV. Although this approach would require more modeling efforts, it would yield further insight into the underlying dynamics of customer behavior.

Another approach to modeling CLV is by using Markov chain models (Pfeifer and Carraway 2000). The idea is to choose a number of states in which the customer can be. These could be based on the recency or number of periods since the last purchase. Consider the following example of a Markov chain (based on Pfeifer and Carraway 2000).

The five states are based on the recency. A customer is in state 1 if (s)he purchased one period ago, in state 2 if (s)he purchased two periods ago, and so on. The fifth state represents former customer or churner. The probabilities represent the likelihood to move from one state to another during one period of time. You can see that the transition probability for state 5 is 1, which makes it an absorbing state. Once in state 5, a customer remains in state 5. In other words, the customer

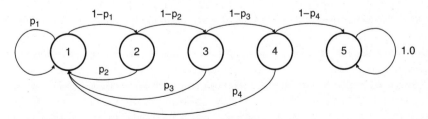

Figure 3.5 Example Markov chain (Pfeifer and Carraway 2000).

can be considered a permanent churner and the model is essentially a lost-for-good model. If we allowed a transition from state 5 back to state 1, the model would become an always-a-share model since a customer always had the option to return to the firm. The transition probabilities can be estimated from historical data and represented using a transition matrix **P** as follows:

$$P = \begin{bmatrix} p_1 & 1-p_1 & 0 & 0 & 0 \\ p_2 & 0 & 1-p_2 & 0 & 0 \\ p_3 & 0 & 0 & 1-p_3 & 0 \\ p_4 & 0 & 0 & 0 & 1-p_4 \\ 0 & 0 & 0 & 0 & 1 \end{bmatrix}$$

A key assumption in Markov chain analysis is that the probability to move to a state is only dependent upon the current state and not upon the entire historical trajectory of the customer. Hence, the t-step transition matrix specifying the probabilities of moving from one state to another in t steps can be obtained by multiplying P by itself t times, or P^t. The expected customer lifetime value for each of the initial states can then be calculated as

$$\sum_{t=1}^{n} \left(\frac{P}{1+r} \right)^t R$$

where R represents the profit vector for each of the states, which is assumed to be constant in time. A key advantage of Markov chains is that they are flexible and can be used for both current customers as well as prospects using either a lost-for-good or always-a-share approach. Furthermore, the approach can be extended to also account for the frequency and monetary values of the purchases by defining corresponding states.

CLV can be used for various purposes. The customer equity (CE) can be obtained by summing the CLV across all C customers:

$$CE = \sum_{i=1}^{C} CLV_i$$

Customer equity is one of the fundamental drivers of a firm's value or its stock price (Gupta et al. 2006; Gupta 2009). Furthermore, individual CLV or PLV values can be used to determine how much to spend to either retain an existing customer or acquire a new customer. Next, customer portfolios are often segmented based on CLV whereby marketing strategies can be tailored to individual CLV segments. CLV analysis is also useful to gauge the effect of marketing campaigns by evaluating the incremental change in CLV after versus before the campaign. Finally, CLV can also be used to define churn; for instance, Glady et al. (2009b) defined a churner as someone whose CLV is decreasing.

Although CLV is an attractive concept for analyzing customer relationships, various challenges remain. A first one concerns generalizing the concept to a multiproduct setting. This would imply taking into account inter-product dependencies such as cross-selling effects whereby a purchase of one product could trigger the purchase of another one, as well as cannibalism whereby the purchase of one product prohibits the purchase of another. Another challenge pertains to the multichannel aspect of modern business environments. Incorporating multichannel behavior into CLV requires complex modeling approaches. Hence, many firms start their CLV modeling exercise by focusing on one particular product and abstracting from the various channels through which transactions are initiated. We will revisit CLV in Chapters 5 and 6 on developing and evaluating analytical models in a profit-driven manner.

Customer Journey

A customer journey is a diagram representing the various steps the customers go through when engaging with a firm (Richardson 2010). Figure 3.6 shows an example of a simplified customer journey for a mortgage sales process. It illustrates the various activities, states, and transactions that a customer can be in when buying a mortgage. Transition probabilities and time indicators are usually added for further enrichment of the analysis. Customer journey analysis serves various business purposes. It can be used to get a clear and comprehensive picture of the overall process and highlight process deficiencies such as excessive processing times, deadlock situations, circular references, and unwanted customer leakage, among others. It can also be used to verify if the process is compliant with both internal and external regulations.

From an analytical perspective, sequence rules as discussed in Chapter 2 can be a first approach to discover customer journeys. A more mature discipline of analytical techniques for customer journey mapping is the field of process mining and discovery (van der Aalst 2016). The idea here is to start from an event log of activities, as depicted in Table 3.2. The event log depicts a unique customer identifier, the various activity names and timestamps. Process discovery techniques such as HeuristicsMiner (De Weerdt et al. 2012) or Fodina (vanden Broucke et al. 2017) can then be used to discover the

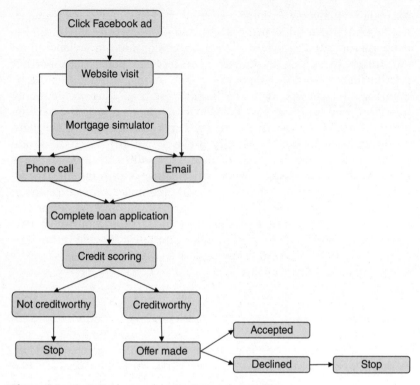

Figure 3.6 Customer journey in a mortgage sales process.

Table 3.2 Event Log of Customer Activities

Customer	Activity Name	Timestamp
...	...	...
Bart	Click Facebook Ad	20-06-2017 14:02:06
Wouter	Mortgage simulator	20-06-2017 15:15:54
Cristian	Creditworthy	21-06-2017 09:54:24
...	...	...

underlying process model or customer journey. For more information on process mining and discovery techniques, we refer to van der Aalst (2016).

Various challenges arise when doing customer journey analysis. First of all, it is important that all events are properly tracked across the various customer touch points using, for example, JavaScript plug-ins and cookies. It is recommended to capture all events at the lowest level of granularity. During the analysis, the complexity can be reduced by using appropriate aggregation operations as decided in collaboration with the business user. Furthermore, a customer should be uniquely identifiable across all touch points such that the corresponding information can be correctly matched.

Many firms will start doing customer journey analysis by focusing on one channel only, such as the web. Using data collected through JavaScript page tagging, web logs, and cookies, firms can do clickstream analysis and understand how customers navigate through their website. More specifically, they can find out where customers come from, what search engines and search terms they used (if any), what their first page was (also called landing page), what the other pages in their session or visit were, and where they dropped out and at what time. As another example, consider an online sales process that may consist of the following steps: Add items to basket, check out, provide personal details, provide payment details, review order, and confirm order. Customer journey analysis can be used to analyze how much time customers spend in each of these stages, where they drop out, and where they go. The analysis can be further enriched by performing segmentation and considering how different segments of customers in terms of, for example, geographic region, referrer, or gender (if available) may have different customer journeys.

Recommender Systems

Recommender systems have been defined by Ricci et al. (2011) as follows:

> Recommender systems are software tools and techniques providing suggestions for items to be of use to a user.

These kinds of systems are extensively used by companies like Amazon, Netflix, TripAdvisor, eBay, LinkedIn, Tinder, and Facebook, to name a few. Various types of items can be recommended, such as products or services, restaurants, jobs, friends, and even romantic partners. The main goal of recommender systems is to help users cope with the information overload they face when browsing massive product or service catalogs by offering them targeted recommendations (Ekstrand et al. 2010). They should not only help users to more quickly locate what they are looking for, but also facilitate serendipitous discovery by recommending items a customer would not have thought of himself or herself.

Recommendations can be impersonalized or personalized. In case of the former, all users get the same recommendations, which are typically based on popularity or novelty. Personalized recommender systems are more sophisticated and offer unique recommendations tailored to a user's interest or profile.

Accurately measuring user interest is key to the success of any recommender system. However, this can be quite challenging, as it is highly dependent on the context and type of items to be recommended. Examples of explicit user interest are ratings, likes/dislikes, repeated purchases, opinions, or reviews a user provides about a particular item. Unfortunately, this is not always available, in which case implicit user interest can be used as a proxy, such as the time a user spent visiting a particular website; the amount of mouse movements (e.g., clicks, scrolling), swipes; whether the user bookmarked the page or submitted his/her personal details for further information, and so on. Although measuring implicit user interest requires no user effort, it typically requires more data and is noisier than measuring explicit user interest. User interest can be represented in a rating matrix whereby the rows represent the users and the columns the items. The data cells can then contain one feedback indicator or a (weighted) combination of multiple indicators (e.g., ratings, like/dislike, number of clicks). Consider the example given in Table 3.3.

A quick inspection of Table 3.3 reveals that Bart, Wouter, and Cristian have very similar profiles so it could make sense to recommend the book on Belgian beers to Bart and the book on credit risk analytics to Wouter. We also see that it is probably not wise to recommend the book on fashion trends to Cristian or the book on salsa dancing to Wouter. This example is quite simple to analyze, since only a few users and items are considered. Real-life applications can have millions of

Table 3.3 Example User-Item Matrix

Name	Profit-Driven Analytics	Knitting for Dummies	The Secrets of Salsa Dancing	Credit Risk Analytics	Fashion Trends	Belgian Beers
Bart	5		1	5	2	
Anna		4	5	1	4	
Emma		4	5		5	1
Wouter	5	1			2	5
John		2	3			5
Cristian	5		2	4		4

users and items. Furthermore, contrary to the previous example, the user-item matrix is usually very sparse since, at best, a user only rates a few items. It is not uncommon to have user item matrices where less than 1% of the cells contain values. Hence, efficient solutions are needed to represent these sparse matrices in a compact way and analyze them.

The key challenge when building recommender systems is to infer values for the missing cells. For example, how would Bart rate the books *Knitting for Dummies* and *Belgian Beers*? Various techniques can be used to build recommender systems.

Collaborative filtering uses other users' ratings to do this (Ekstrand et al. 2010). Memory approaches start from user similarities (user–user collaborative filtering) or item similarities (item–item collaborative filtering). Model-based approaches use analytical techniques to uncover patterns in the data.

The basic intuition of user–user collaborative filtering is that users who were interested in similar items in the past will probably be interested in similar items in the future (and vice versa). It starts by finding like-minded users by calculating, for example, the Pearson correlation in case of continuous interest values (e.g., ratings) or the Jaccard index in case of binary interest values (e.g., like/dislike, clicked or not). In our example, we can see that both Wouter and Cristian are similar to Bart. A simple and straightforward way to calculate Bart's rating for *Belgian Beers* is then the average of Cristian's and Wouter's rating, or 4.5. The idea is very similar to a *k*-nearest neighbor approach. Note that other procedures to infer missing ratings have been suggested, which take into account the rating bias of a user (Ricci et al. 2011).

Item–item collaborative filtering assumes that items that were previously liked by the same users will likely continue to be liked by the same users. It starts by computing the item–item similarities using among others the Pearson correlation or Jaccard index. In our example, we can see that the books *Knitting for Dummies, The Secrets of Salsa Dancing,* and *Fashion Trends* have correlated ratings. Bart's rating for *Knitting for Dummies* can then be inferred as the average of his ratings for the books *The Secrets of Salsa Dancing* and *Fashion Trends*, or 1.5. Note again that more sophisticated procedures can be used to perform this inference (Ricci et al. 2011). Another example of item–item collaborative filtering is association rules, as discussed in Chapter 2. Remember, the idea here is to look for frequently occurring associations between items with sufficient support and confidence.

Both user–user and item–item collaborative filtering are easy to develop and explain and have been successfully applied in many applications. A main concern relates to the cold start problem, which means that new items cannot easily be recommended because they have not been rated yet, and new users cannot easily receive recommendations because they have not rated any items yet. Another issue worth noting is that the performance of the recommendations will significantly drop when the sparsity of the user–item matrix increases.

Model-based collaborative filtering uses analytical techniques to analyze the user–item matrix and provide recommendations. Popular examples are singular value decomposition (SVD), Bayesian networks, latent semantic models, latent Dirichlet allocation, and Markov decision processes (Ekstrand et al. 2010). Although these systems are more sophisticated, they are usually harder to explain.

Content filtering provides recommendations based on the content of items instead of other users' opinions. More specifically, it looks at—among others— author, artist, director, keywords, abstract, product description, and user tags. The basic intuition is that users who are interested in a specific item, will probably be interested in similar items, too. For example, if a user bought the book *Profit Driven Analytics*, (s)he might also be interested in credit risk analytics, since both deal with analytics, as can be seen from the title and/or abstract, and have one author in common. The cold start problem now only applies to new users, but not to new items. A disadvantage of this method is that user ratings or opinions are not taken into account.

Both collaborative and content filterings have their advantages and disadvantages. Hybrid recommender systems try to combine the best of both worlds. A first way of doing so is by combining recommendation scores of various recommenders using weights. Switching is a second hybrid technique in which recommendations are taken from alternating recommender systems.

FRAUD ANALYTICS

It is estimated that a typical organization loses about 5% of its revenues to fraud each year (www.acfe.com). A detailed characterization of the multifaceted phenomenon of fraud has been provided by Van Vlasselaer et al. (2016) as follows:

> Fraud is an uncommon, well-considered, imperceptibly concealed, time-evolving and often carefully organized crime which appears in many types of forms.

This definition highlights five characteristics that are associated with particular challenges related to developing an analytical fraud detection system. Fraud is uncommon, since only a minority of the involved population of cases typically engages in fraud, which makes it difficult to detect. Moreover, fraudsters will try to blend in to avoid being noticed, and to remain obscured by nonfraudsters. This effectively makes fraud imperceptibly concealed, since fraudsters aim to hide by carefully considering and planning how to precisely commit fraud without detection. Fraud detection systems improve and learn by example; therefore, the techniques and tricks that fraudsters adopt evolve in time along with or, better, ahead of fraud detection mechanisms.

Fraud is often a carefully organized crime as well, meaning that fraudsters often do not operate independently, have allies, and may induce copycats. A final element in the description of fraud provided by Van Vlasselaer et al. (2016) indicates the many different types of forms in which fraud occurs. This refers both to the wide set of techniques and approaches used by fraudsters and to the many different settings in which fraud occurs. Some popular examples are credit-card fraud, insurance claim fraud, anti-money laundering, identity theft, insurance fraud, corruption, counterfeit, product warranty fraud, telecommunications fraud, click fraud, and tax evasion (Baesens et al. 2016).

The classic approach to fraud detection is an expert-based approach, meaning that it builds on the experience and business knowledge of the fraud analyst. This approach typically involves a manual investigation of a suspicious case, which may have been signaled for instance by a customer complaining of being charged for transactions (s)he did not do. A disputed transaction may indicate a new fraud mechanism adopted by fraudsters, and therefore requires a detailed investigation to understand and subsequently address the new mechanism. Expert-based approaches to fraud detection typically make use of business rules, such as the following:

IF:

- Amount of claim is above threshold **OR**
- Severe injury, but no doctor report **OR**
- Claimant has multiple versions of the accident.

THEN:

- Flag claim as suspicious.

An expert approach suffers from a number of disadvantages. Rule bases are typically expensive to build, since they require advanced manual input and often turn out to be difficult to manage. Rules have to be kept up to date and only trigger real fraudulent cases, since every signaled case requires human follow-up. Therefore, the main challenge concerns keeping the rule base lean and effective; in other words, deciding on which rules to add, remove, update, or merge, and when to do so.

Given these problems, a shift is taking place toward analytical-based fraud detection approaches for three apparent reasons:

1. **Precision:** Analytical-based fraud detection offers an increased detection power compared to expert approaches.

2. **Operational efficiency:** An increasing amount of cases needs to be analyzed, requiring an automated process as offered by analytical fraud detection methods.

3. **Cost efficiency:** A more automated and by implication more cost-efficient approach to develop a fraud detection system, as offered by analytical methods, is preferred compared to maintaining an expensive rule base.

Various analytical techniques can be used for fraud detection. Detection mechanisms based on descriptive analytics aim at identifying behavior that deviates from normal behavior, or in other words, at detecting anomalies. Consider the example dataset of call detail records given in Table 3.4. Some calls are deviating from the normal behavior for this particular subscriber when looking at day, time of day, duration, and other characteristics. Hence, they are labeled as suspicious since this could be a case of identity theft.

Descriptive analytical techniques learn from historical observations and are also called unsupervised, since they do not require these observations to be labeled as either a fraudulent or a nonfraudulent example case. Popular examples are outlier or anomaly detection, peer group analysis, breakpoint analysis, and clustering (Baesens et al. 2015). Descriptive analytics, however, is prone to deception, by, for example, camouflage-like fraud strategies adopted by fraudsters.

Predictive analytics can also be used to tackle fraud. These techniques aim at finding silent alarms, the parts of their tracks that fraudsters cannot cover up. Predictive analytics can be applied both to predict fraud as well as to estimate the amount of fraud. Unfortunately, predictive analytics has its limitations as well. More specifically, it needs historical examples to learn from; that is, a labeled dataset of historically observed fraud behavior. This reduces its detection power with respect to drastically different fraud types based on new mechanisms, and which have not been detected thus

Table 3.4 Example Call Detail Record Dataset for Fraud Detection

Date	Time	Day	Duration	Caller	Callee	Fraud
16/11/2016	11:15	Wed	18 mins	Paris	Rome	
18/11/2016	9:44	Fri	15 mins	Paris	Prague	
21/11/2016	19:20	Mon	22 mins	Helsinki	Madrid	
22/11/2016	12:05	Tue	34 mins	Paris	Paris	
23/11/2016	14:34	Wed	12 mins	Dublin	Rome	
25/11/2016	15:58	Fri	10 mins	Paris	Paris	
26/11/2016	01:45	Sat	30 sec	Amsterdam	Moscow	Suspicious
26/11/2016	01:50	Sat	15 sec	Amsterdam	Moscow	Suspicious
27/11/2016	10:45	Sun	10 min	Dublin	Paris	
27/11/2016	23:20	Sun	24 sec	Madrid	Frankfurt	Suspicious
28/11/2016	15:18	Mon	14 min	Amsterdam	Amsterdam	
28/11/2016	23:54	Mon	18 sec	Amsterdam	Berlin	Suspicious

far and are hence not included in the historical database. Descriptive analytics may perform better with respect to detecting such new fraud mechanisms, at least if a new fraud mechanism leads to detectable deviations from normality. This illustrates the complementarity of predictive and descriptive analytics and motivates the use of both methods in developing a powerful fraud detection system.

A third type of complementary tool concerns social network analysis, which can further extend the abilities of a fraud detection system by learning and detecting characteristics of fraudulent behavior in a network of linked entities. Consider the example social network given in Figure 3.7.

This is an example of a unipartite network with only one type of node. These could represent companies, customers, credit cards, and bank accounts, among others. Filled nodes correspond to fraudsters and unfilled nodes to nonfraudsters. From the network, it becomes clear that the fraudsters are clustered in a community. The idea of social network analytics is to model this effect as accurately as possible using community mining or featurization (see Chapter 2). Note that besides unipartite networks, multipartite networks can also be considered whereby multiple types of nodes are distinguished. As an example, consider an insurance fraud detection setting. Here, the network may consist of nodes such as claimant, insured individual, car, car repair shop, and mobile phone. Studying the relationships between these nodes may give valuable insights into complex,

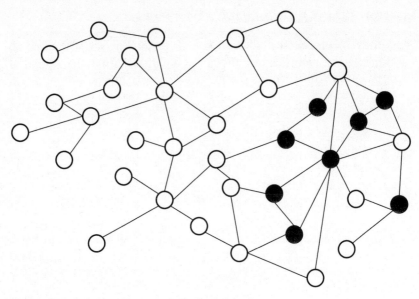

Figure 3.7 Example social network for fraud detection.

multipartite fraud patterns. In order to successfully leverage social networks for fraud detection, it is important to carefully design the network in terms of both its nodes and links. This will usually involve in-depth discussions with the fraud analyst whereby previous experience and background knowledge is a key input.

It is important to stress that descriptive, predictive, and social network analytics should complement each other since they possess different capabilities, and can focus on different aspects of fraud. More specifically, all three techniques reinforce each other when applied in a combined setup. When developing a fraud detection system, an organization will likely follow the order in which the different techniques have been introduced: as a first step, an expert-based rule engine may be developed, which in a second step may be complemented by descriptive analytics, and subsequently by predictive and social network analytics. Developing a fraud detection system in this order allows the organization to gain expertise and insight in a stepwise manner, hereby facilitating each next step. In terms of comprehensibility, it is advisable to use white box analytical techniques (e.g., logistic regression, decision trees) for fraud detection since the insights gained can then be used to work out fraud prevention strategies.

CREDIT RISK ANALYTICS

The introduction of compliance guidelines such as Basel II/Basel III and IFRS 9 has catalyzed the interest in credit risk analytics. Different types of analytical models are built to evaluate credit risk (Baesens et al. 2016). More specifically, credit risk is typically decomposed into three components as follows:

1. **Default risk** is the risk of defaulting on a loan obligation. It is measured by a 12-month forward-looking probability of default (PD) whereby default is commonly defined as being more than 90 days in payment arrears.

2. **Exposure risk** is the risk of increasing the exposure prior to default. It is measured by the exposure at default (EAD), which represents the outstanding debt in currency amount. It is readily available for on-balance sheet exposures (e.g., installment loans, mortgages) but needs to be estimated for off-balance-sheet exposures (e.g., credit cards and credit lines) to take into account which part of the undrawn amount is likely to be turned into credit upon default.

3. **Loss risk** is the economic loss due to default on an exposure. It is measured by the loss given default (LGD) expressed as a percentage of the EAD and should take into account both direct and indirect costs, as well as the timing of the cash flows through proper discounting.

These three risk parameters are then combined to calculate the expected loss (EL) as $EL = PD \cdot LGD \cdot EAD$ and the unexpected loss (UL), which is a complex function of PD, LGD, and EAD based on a value at risk (VaR) approximation (Baesens, Roesch and Scheule, 2016). Both EL and UL will then help a bank decide on its optimal capital buffers and provisions to protect it against the risks it is exposed to. Analytical models will be built to estimate the PD, LGD, and EAD. This will typically be done according to a multilevel model architecture, as depicted in Figure 3.8.

Level 0 constitutes the data level where various sources of data will be gathered and combined such as internal data, expert data, and external data obtained from data poolers such as Equifax, Experian, TransUnion, Dun & Bradstreet, Moody's, S&P, and Fitch. The models at level 1 will then rank or discriminate the credit exposures in terms of their default (PD), loss (LGD), and exposure (EAD) risks. For default, new customers will be evaluated using application scorecards, whereas existing customers will be monitored using behavioral scorecards.

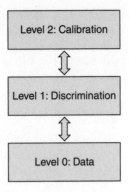

Figure 3.8 Multilevel credit risk model architecture.
(Baesens, Roesch, and Scheule 2016).

Besides the application characteristics (e.g., age, income, employment status), the latter can also make use of behavioral characteristics (e.g., checking account balance, delinquency history), which makes them usually more predictive. Given the regulatory need for transparency and model interpretability, both types of model will typically be built using logistic regression. Default risk can usually be quite accurately estimated with area under the ROC curve values ranging between 70% and 90% for the application and behavioral scorecards (Lessmann et al. 2015). For loss and exposure risks, both linear regression and regression trees are commonly used, as well as two-stage models (Loterman et al. 2012). As opposed to default risk, both loss and exposure risks are a lot harder to predict with R-squared performance benchmarks typically ranging between 15% and 25% (Loterman et al. 2012). The output of the analytical discrimination models at level 1 will then be used at level 2 to create default, loss, and exposure ratings with corresponding calibrated PD, LGD, and EAD risk measurements. The calibration procedure also takes into account the impact of the macroeconomic environment as measured by variables such as the gross domestic product (GDP), inflation, and unemployment. The Basel guidelines prescribe that the calibration should be done using five years of historical data for PD and seven years for LGD and EAD.

Because of the strategic impact of the analytical PD, LGD, and EAD models on banks, savings depositors, and the economy as a whole, they will be extensively validated by local bank regulators. Furthermore, local or international regulation may specify what input variables can or cannot be used for analytical credit risk modeling. As an example, the US Equal Credit Opportunities Act stipulates that one cannot discriminate credit based on age, gender, marital status, ethnic origin, or religion, so these variables should be left out from the analysis. Note that different regulations may apply in different geographical regions and hence should be checked before analytical credit modeling can start. Regulators will also require financial institutions to stress-test their analytical PD, LGD, and EAD models in order to understand their behavior and outcomes under adverse circumstances such as macroeconomic downturns or recessions. Two common approaches to stress testing are sensitivity and scenario analysis. The former usually performs a univariate sensitivity analysis (e.g., an income drop of 10%; an application or behavioral score decrease of 5%), whereas the latter elaborates an entire scenario (either historically based or hypothetical) involving multiple variables and their correlation to see how the PD, LGD, and EAD models are affected. In fact, many of the ideas and approaches developed in credit risk stress testing could also be successfully used for the other applications discussed in this chapter to see how the analytical models developed react to stress conditions.

HR ANALYTICS

Besides using big data and analytics to manage customer relationships, these can also prove beneficial to leverage a firm's other key assets: its employees! Various HR analytics (also called workforce analytics) examples can be considered (Baesens, De Winne, and Sels 2016; Baesens, De Winne, and Sels 2017).

A first application is analyzing employee churn or turnover, which is a major problem for many companies these days. Great talent is scarce, hard to retain, and highly solicited by headhunters. Hence, given the well-known direct relationship between happy employees and happy customers, it becomes of utmost importance to keep employees and understand the drivers of employee dissatisfaction. Similar to customer churn, analytics can also be used for this purpose. A first step to doing so is to collect historical data on employee churn. The more data the better, as this gives more opportunities to find previously unknown, interesting insights into employee behavior. Popular examples are staffing data, performance, and productivity data, engagement data (e.g., collected through surveys), payment data, and task-specific data, among other types. Following the analytics process model outlined previously, in a next step, the data will be consolidated, aggregated and cleaned such that it becomes ready for analysis. An analytical model can then be built to predict employee churn. From a pure analytical perspective, the cross-fertilization between customer churn and employee churn is immense, since it essentially also boils down to a classification exercise of which the results need to be evaluated in a business-relevant way using, among other tools, profit measures. Recommended techniques are logistic regression and decision trees since both are white-box techniques, which provide clear insights into why employees leave the firm. HR directors can then use these insights to work out employee retention strategies.

Another interesting application of HR analytics is analyzing employee absenteeism. Employees may be absent due to illness, accidents or burnout. The latter has recently received wide attention since various studies have shown that your highest motivated employees are particularly sensitive to it. Hence, using analytics, it now becomes possible to adequately understand the drivers of employee absenteeism and act upon this understanding before the problems start to occur. Employee absenteeism can be tackled using both classification (employee is absent or not) or regression (number of days absent) techniques. Both can also be combined to determine the expected number of days absent (EDA). More specifically, a classification model can predict the probability that an employee will be absent (PA), e.g., during the next 12 months. A regression model can then be used to predict the number of days absent for those employees that are absent—or in other words, days absent given absence (DAGA). The expected number of days absent (EDA) can then be calculated as follows:

$$EDA = PA \cdot DAGA + (1 - PA) \cdot 0 = PA \cdot DAGA$$

Besides predictive analytics, social network analytics can also be used for HR purposes. Understanding, modeling, and measuring your employee network should be key ingredients to your strategic HR decisions. As already noted by Adler and Kwon (2002), a well-designed employee network essentially comprises the social capital of a firm referring to all the assets or resources than can be mobilized through it. Let us take the case of firing, be it on an individual or collective basis, as an example.

The key question to answer first is how to build an employee network and leverage it when making firing decisions. Although the nodes are obviously the employees, the links are far less intuitive to define. These should be established based on two sources of information: communication patterns (e.g., emails, Skype calls) and joint project allocations. Obviously, there is a strong correlation between both, but state-of-the-art analytical techniques are nowadays perfectly capable to filter this out and determine the optimal blend of information. One way to quantify the links is by using the previously introduced RFM framework: recency (when was the most recent email exchange/joint project allocation?), frequency (frequency of emails or joint project allocations), and monetary (average size of emails, or average man-months of joint project allocations). It is hereby important to commit to anonymized analysis and respect privacy at all times. In other words, emails can only be analyzed in terms of sender and receiver (but not in terms of content!) and the necessary disclosure agreements should be properly agreed upon between the stakeholders involved.

Once the employee network has been defined, we can start analyzing it using various descriptive network metrics as discussed before. Two key measures to characterize the social and organizational impacts of an employee are his/her betweenness and closeness. We will illustrate both with the Kite network depicted in Figure 3.9, which we also discussed in Chapter 2. Recalling that betweenness quantifies how often an employee is situated on the shortest path between any two other employees in the network, whereas closeness measures the average distance from an employee to all other nodes in the network. Employees with a high betweenness (e.g., Heather in our example network) play a broker role between communities by bridging social capital, which is essential in terms of both innovation and efficiency improvement. Employees with a high closeness (e.g., Fernando and

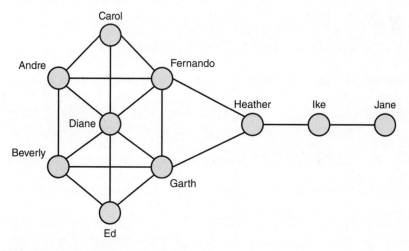

Figure 3.9 Example employee network.
(Kite network, see Chapter 2).

Garth in our example network) are the closest to everyone else and thus have the best position to monitor the information flow in the workforce network. They are key players when it comes to bonding social capital and catalyze collaboration, thereby improving workforce cohesion.

Both betweenness and closeness should be essential elements to the future decision making toolkit of any HR manager, both from proactive (i.e., risk mitigation) as well as reactive (i.e., damage control) perspectives. When making firing decisions, employees with a high betweenness (e.g., Heather) should be carefully approached. They act as community connectors, and can—if fired— functionally disconnect essential parts of your workforce network (e.g., Ike and Jane from the rest). This risk can be mitigated proactively, by doing the network analysis and measurement, identifying the weak spots (i.e., with high betweenness) and using that information when deciding on new project teams or maybe even new hires, in order to build the necessary relationships between loosely coupled employee communities. From a damage-control perspective, the firing of high-betweenness employees should be accommodated by establishing the necessary communication and collaboration bridges between disconnected communities. As an addendum, note that retention policies might also benefit from network analysis by designing tailored career paths for high betweenness employees.

Also the closeness should be closely monitored and evaluated. From a firing perspective, dismissing employees with a high closeness (i.e., Fernando and Garth) is risky because of social contagion. More specifically, they could cause ripple effects in terms of negative word-of-mouth, for example, resulting in potential talent drain. From a risk mitigation perspective, management should avoid closeness hot spots and aim for a uniform (or, say, less concentrated) closeness distribution across the entire workforce network. In case employees with a high closeness need to be fired, management should reactively intervene and ensure that the necessary and accurate information about its decisions is properly disseminated so as to maintain the cohesiveness of its workforce.

As with any analytical exercise or disruptive technology, it is important to start small but think big. The above discussion largely focuses on understanding your employee network in terms of descriptive social network analytics. A next obvious step would then also be to leverage it for predictive purposes whereby network information is used to, for example, predict employee churn or engagement, or even for recruitment purposes. This can be accomplished using any of the relational classifiers discussed in Chapter 2. An even more ambitious goal would be to directly link the employee network to the customer network. This could reveal new serendipitous insights into the relationship between employee and customer drain, which would allow a firm to create an unprecedented competitive advantage.

These are just a few applications of HR analytics; many others can be thought of. Examples are understanding workforce collaboration patterns using social network techniques, job recruitment based on intelligent recommender systems, career path analysis using sequence rules, and talent forecasting. Despite its potential, not many successful applications of HR analytics have been reported yet in the industry. This can be attributed to various reasons as we discuss below.

First of all, HR is still struggling with the perception of being less strategically important than—for instance—risk management, marketing, and logistics. Hence, it is usually the last in line to benefit from new technologies such as big data and analytics. This is unfortunate, given the tremendous potential of both for improving the HR function.

A next barrier, which also applies to the other analytics applications discussed before, concerns the skills needed to work with both technologies. The job profile aimed for is the one of a data scientist. In the industry, there are strong misconceptions and disagreements about what constitutes a good data scientist. As discussed in Chapter 1, a data scientist should possess a multidisciplinary mix of skills: quantitative modeling (e.g., statistics), ICT (e.g., programming), communication and visualization, business understanding, and creativity. It is quite obvious that this is a unique skillset and not many universities worldwide are offering educational programs for data scientists yet. This explains why there is currently a huge international shortage for this job profile. Some organizations are setting up in-house training and coaching initiatives to turn some of their employees into data scientists. Others are considering outsourcing as a possible solution. Despite the short-term benefits of the latter, it should be approached with a clear strategic vision and critical reflection with awareness of all risks involved.

Another attention point is the employees' union. In strongly unionized countries, companies have to provide clear justifications about how they intend to utilize big data and analytics to study their workforce behavior. It is in our human nature to approach any new technology with a certain degree of anxiety; hence, it can be anticipated that unions might also be skeptical. To remedy this, it is of key importance to introduce both technologies as facilitators or opportunities rather than a looming danger or treat, and clearly illustrate how working conditions and/or employee satisfaction can be improved as a result of their usage.

CONCLUSION

In this chapter, we discussed a selection of popular applications of analytics. In terms of maturity, analytical models for credit risk are the most sophisticated. This can be explained by the availability of various regulatory guidelines (e.g., Basel II/III, IFRS 9), which impose analytical credit risk modeling on financial institutions. In essence, these guidelines precisely specify how the inputs and outputs of an analytical credit risk model should be defined and what types of analytical techniques can be used to relate them (e.g., no black-box techniques can be used). This explains why state-of-the-art analytical models can be seen in credit risk and other regulated risk applications (e.g., market and operational risk). In marketing, fraud, and HR analytics, no regulations are available and thus the analytical models (if any at all!) are not developed because of external guidelines but because of internal strategic priorities. Hence, these models are typically far less mature from a technical perspective than their counterparts in credit risk analytics are. In fact, many of the modeling extensions and experiences from credit risk can be successfully transferred to the other application areas.

One perspective that was lacking throughout much of the discussion in this chapter relates to the economic impact of the models developed. At the end of the day, the analytical models should not only be evaluated in terms of their statistical performance, interpretability, operational efficiency, or regulatory compliance, but also in terms of their bottom-line impact. In other words, how much profit can be gained from using these models? This perspective is further elaborated in subsequent chapters.

REVIEW QUESTIONS

Multiple Choice Questions

Question 1

Which of the following statements about response modeling is not correct?

    a. Response modeling focuses on deepening or recovering customer relationships using analytical models.

b. Besides classification, response modeling can also be approached from a regression angle, whereby the aim is to build a regression model predicting the amount (or intensity) of the response.

c. The RFM variables can be used separately or combined into a single score by using either independent sorting or dependent sorting.

d. The RFM variables only make sense for response modeling and cannot be used in other marketing analytics applications.

Question 2

Which of the following is not correct?

a. Expected churn implies that a customer leaves the firm for a cheaper or better alternative.

b. Passive churn refers to a decrease in product or service usage.

c. Forced churn occurs when the company rather than the customer stops the relationship due to, for example, fraud.

d. Active churn implies that the customer cuts the relationship with the firm.

Question 3

Which of the following data can be used for churn prediction?

a. Demographic data
b. RFM data
c. Product/service usage data
d. All of the above

Question 4

Churn prediction can be tackled using

a. a classification model.
b. a survival analysis model.
c. a social network model.
d. all of the above.

Question 5

Which statement is not correct?

a. The idea of up-selling is to sell more of a given product, usually at the time of purchase.

b. X-selling applications are usually built using predictive analytics techniques.

    c. Cross-selling aims at selling an additional product or service.
    d. Down-selling means selling less of a product or service in order to maintain a sustainable, long-lasting customer relationship.

Question 6

A critical parameter to be decided on during customer segmentation concerns is

    a. the homogeneity metric used to measure cluster similarity.
    b. the number of clusters.
    c. the number of iteration steps.
    d. the cluster centroids.

Question 7

Which statement about customer lifetime value modeling is correct?

    a. When using Markov chains for CLV modeling, it is assumed that the current state of a customer depends on all previous states the customer has been in.
    b. A key advantage of the Pareto/NBD model is that it is a distribution-free model, which can be easily implemented using any real-life dataset.
    c. To parametrize CLV values, many firms will choose only one specific product, use a time horizon of two to three years, set the discount rate to the WACC, and ignore indirect revenues and costs.
    d. The always-a-share approach assumes that, upon churn, a customer never returns to the firm.

Question 8

In customer journey analysis, which of the following is important?

    a. All events are properly tracked across the various customer touch points using unique customer identifiers.
    b. Events are tracked at aggregated levels of detail.
    c. Events are stored in event logs, which only need two pieces of information: customer identifier and event type.
    d. Events related to customer disservice (e.g., complaints) are ignored.

Question 9

Which of the following statements about recommender systems is not correct?

    a. Although measuring implicit user interest requires no user effort, it typically requires more data and is noisier than measuring explicit user interest.

    b. Association rules are an example of user–user collaborative filtering.

    c. The basic intuition of user–user collaborative filtering is that users who were interested in similar items in the past will probably be interested in similar items in the future.

    d. Item–item collaborative filtering assumes that items that were previously liked by the same users will likely continue to be liked by the same users.

Question 10

Which of the following characteristics defines fraud?

    a. The crimes are uncommon and imperceptibly concealed.

    b. Fraud is well-considered and carefully organized.

    c. Strategies evolve over time.

    d. All of the above are defining characteristics.

Question 11

Which statement about credit risk analytics is correct?

    a. PD models usually perform worse than LGD and EAD models.

    b. The unexpected loss (UL) can be calculated as $UL = PD \cdot LGD \cdot EAD$.

    c. Credit risk models are usually developed according to a multilevel model architecture as follows: level 0: data; level 1: calibration, level 2: discrimination.

    d. Both application and behavioral scorecards are usually constructed using logistic regression.

Question 12

Which statement about HR analytics is correct?

    a. Only descriptive analytics can be used for HR purposes.

    b. Only predictive analytics can be used for HR purposes.

c. In strongly unionized countries, companies have to provide clear justifications about how they intend to utilize big data and analytics for studying their workforce behavior. Hence, this could create an important hurdle to successfully leverage HR analytics.

d. Many successful applications of HR analytics have already been reported in the industry.

Open Questions

Question 1

The Internet of Things (IoT) refers to the network of interconnected things such as electronic devices, sensors, software, and IT infrastructure which create and add value by exchanging data with various stakeholders such as manufacturers, service providers, customers, and other devices, hereby using the World Wide Web technology stack (e.g., Wifi, IPv6, etc.). In terms of devices, you can think about heartbeat monitors; motion, noise or temperature sensors; smart meters measuring utility (e.g., electricity, water) consumption; and so on. Some examples of applications are:

- Smart parking: automatically monitoring free parking spaces in a city
- Smart lighting: automatically adjusting street lights to weather conditions
- Smart traffic: optimizing driving and walking routes based on traffic and congestion
- Smart grid: automatically monitoring energy consumption
- Smart supply chains: automatically monitoring goods as they move through the supply chain
- Telematics: automatically monitoring driving behavior and linking it to insurance risk and premiums

It speaks for itself that the amount of data generated is enormous and offers an unseen potential for analytical applications. Pick one particular type of application of IoT and discuss the following:

a. How to use predictive, descriptive, and social network analytics
b. How to evaluate the performance of the analytical models
c. Key issues in post-processing and implementing the analytical models
d. Important challenges and opportunities

Question 2

Many companies nowadays are investing in analytics. Also, for universities, there are plenty of opportunities to use analytics for streamlining and/or optimizing processes. Examples of applications where analytics may have a role to play are:

- Analyzing student fail rates
- Timetabling of courses
- Finding jobs for graduates
- Recruiting new students
- Meal planning in the student restaurant

Identify some other possible applications of analytics in a university context. Discuss how analytics could contribute to these applications. In your discussion please make sure you clearly address:

a. The added value of analytics for analyzing the problems considered
b. The analytical techniques to be used
c. Key challenges
d. New opportunities

NOTE

1. See http://pages.stern.nyu.edu/~adamodar/New_Home_Page/datafile/wacc.htm.

REFERENCES

Adler P. S., and S. W. Kwon. 2002. "Social Capital: Prospects for a New Concept." *Academy of Management Review* 27 (1): 17–40.

Athanassopoulos, A. 2000. "Customer Satisfaction Cues to Support Market Segmentation and Explain Switching Behavior." *Journal of Business Research* 47 (3): 191–207.

Baesens B. 2014. *Analytics in a Big Data World*. Hoboken, NJ: John Wiley & Sons.

Baesens B., S. De Winne, and L. Sels. 2017. "Is Your Company Ready for HR Analytics?" *MIT Sloan Management Review*, forthcoming.

Baesens B., S. De Winne, and L. Sels. 2016. "What to Do Before You Fire a Pivotal Employee." *Harvard Business Review*.

Baesens B., D. Roesch D., and H. Scheule. 2016. *Credit Risk Analytics—Measurement Techniques, Applications and Examples in SAS.* Hoboken, NJ: John Wiley & Sons.

Baesens B., V. Van Vlasselaer, and W. Verbeke. 2015. *Fraud Analytics Using Descriptive, Predictive, and Social Network Techniques: A Guide to Data Science for Fraud Detection.* Hoboken, NJ: John Wiley & Sons.

Baesens B., S. Viaene, D. Van den Poel, J. Vanthienen, and G. Dedene. 2002. "Bayesian Neural Network Learning for Repeat Purchase Modelling in Direct Marketing." *European Journal of Operational Research* 138 (1): 191–211.

Cullinan G. J. 1977. *Picking Them by Their Batting Averages' Recency–Frequency–Monetary Method of Controlling Circulation,* Manual Release 2103 (Direct Mail/Marketing Association, NY).

De Weerdt, J., M. De Backer, J. Vanthienen, and B. Baesens. 2012. "A Multi-Dimensional Quality Assessment of State-of-the-Art Process Discovery Algorithms Using Real-Life Event Logs." *Information Systems* 37 (7): 654–676.

Ekstrand, M. D., J. T. Riedl, and J. A. Konstan. 2010. "Collaborative Filtering Recommender Systems." *Foundations and Trends in Human–Computer Interaction* 4 (2): 81–173.

Fader, P. S., and B. G. S. Hardie 2005. "A Note on Deriving the Pareto/NBD Model and Related Expressions." http://brucehardie.com/notes/009/.

Fader, P. S., B. G. S. Hardie, and K. L. Lee, 2005a. "Counting Your Customers the Easy Way: An Alternative to the Pareto/NBD Model." *Marketing Science* 24 (2): 275–284.

Fader, P. S., B. G. S. Hardie, and K. L. Lee. 2005b. "RFM and CLV: Using Iso-Value Curves for Customer Base Analysis." *Journal of Marketing Research* 42 (4): 415–430.

Glady, N., C. Croux, and B. Baesens. 2009a. "A Modified Pareto/NBD Approach for Predicting Customer Lifetime Value." *Expert Systems with Applications* 36 (2): 2062–2071.

Glady, N., C. Croux, and B. Baesens. 2009b. "Modeling Churn Using Customer Lifetime Value." *European Journal of Operational Research* 197 (1): 402–411.

Gupta, S. 2009. "Customer-Based Valuation." *Journal of Interactive Marketing* 23: 169–178.

Gupta, S., D. Hanssens, B. Hardie, V. Kumar, N. Lin, N. Ravishanker, and S. Sriram. 2006. "Modeling Customer Lifetime Value." *Journal of Service Research* 9 (2): 139–155.

Jackson B. 1985. *Winning and Keeping Industrial Customers.* Lexington, MA: Lexington Books.

Kumar V., G. Ramani, and T. Bohling. 2004. "Customer Lifetime Value Approaches and Best Practice Applications." *Journal of Interactive Marking* 18 (3): 60–72.

Lessmann S., B. Baesens, H. V. Seow, and L. C. Thomas. 2015. "Benchmarking State-of-the-Art Classification Algorithms for Credit Scoring: An Update of Research." *European Journal of Operational Research* 247 (1): 124–136.

Loterman G., I. Brown, D. Martens, C. Mues, and B. Baesens. 2012. "Benchmarking Regression Algorithms for Loss Given Default Modeling." *International Journal of Forecasting* 28 (1): 161–170.

McCarthy, D., P. Fader, and B. Hardie. 2016. "V(CLV): Examining Variance in Models of Customer Lifetime Value," work in progress.

Pfeifer P. E., and R. L. Carraway. 2000. "Modeling Customer Relationships as Markov Chains." *Journal of Interactive Marketing* 14 (2): 43–55.

Reinartz, W. J., and V. Kumar. 2003. "The Impact of Customer Relationship Characteristics on Profitable Lifetime Duration." *Journal of Marketing* 67 (1): 77–99.

Ricci, F., L. Rokach, B. Shapira, and P. B. Kantor. 2011. *Recommender Systems Handbook*. Heidelberg: Springer-Verlag.

Richardson, A. 2010. "Using Customer Journey Maps to Improve Customer Experience." *Harvard Business Review*.

Schmittlein, D. C., D. G. Morrison, and R. Colombo. 1987. "Counting Your Customers: Who Are They, and What Will They Do Next?" *Management Science* 33 (1): 1–24.

van der Aalst, W. M. P. 2012. *Process Mining: Data Science in Action*. Heidelberg: Springer-Verlag.

Van Vlasselaer V., T. Eliassi-Rad, L. Akoglu, M. Snoeck, and B. Baesens. 2016. "GOTCHA! Network-Based Fraud Detection for Security Fraud." *Management Science*, forthcoming.

vanden Broucke, S. K. L. M., and J. De Weerdt. 2017. "Fodina: A Robust and Flexible Process Discovery Technique." http://www.processmining.be/fodina/.

Verbeke W., K. Dejaeger, D. Martens, J. Hur, and B. Baesens. 2012. "New Insights into Churn Prediction in the Telecommunication Sector: A Profit-Driven Data Mining Approach." *European Journal of Operational Research* 218 (1): 211–229.

Verbeke W., D. Martens, and B. Baesens 2014. "Social Network Analysis for Customer Churn Prediction." *Applied Soft Computing* 14: 341–446.

Verbeke W. 2011. "Building Comprehensible Customer Churn Prediction Models with Advanced Rule Induction Techniques." *Expert Systems with Applications* 38: 2354–2364.

CHAPTER 4

Uplift Modeling

INTRODUCTION

When discussing customer churn prediction in Chapter 3, we explained that by developing and adopting a customer churn prediction model we can target the customers which are most likely to churn in a retention campaign. As such, the use of a predictive model significantly increases the efficiency and return of a retention campaign by allowing to select true would-be churners and to exclude nonchurners. The reader may have realized that a further improvement may be achieved by selecting customers that are not only likely to churn but as well likely to be retained when targeted in a retention campaign. If we exclude would-be churners from the campaign that have made up their minds and therefore cannot be retained, a further increase in profitability will be achieved.

To this end, we introduce uplift modeling approaches in this chapter, which aim at estimating the net effect of a *treatment*, such as a marketing campaign, on customer behavior. Uplift models allow users to optimize the selection of customers to include in marketing campaigns as well as a further customization at the individual customer level of the campaign design, for example, in terms of the contacting channel and the characteristics of the incentive that is offered. Such customization may even further increase the effect and return of the campaign.

In the first section of this chapter, we will broadly introduce and motivate the use of uplift modeling as an alternative approach to standard predictive analytics as discussed before in this book. As will be elaborated subsequently in the second section, specific data requirements hold to develop uplift models, which may require to run dedicated experiments. Next, in the third section, various uplift modeling approaches will be introduced and subsequently the evaluation of uplift models is discussed. Finally, practical guidelines and a two-step approach toward developing uplift models are discussed, before the conclusions of the chapter are presented.

The Case for Uplift Modeling: Response Modeling

Predictive analytics are widely adopted for developing response models as introduced in Chapter 3 of this book. Response models aim at predicting which customers are likely to respond. By targeting these customers, the efficiency and expected returns of a marketing campaign are boosted. Remember that various types of responses can be considered when developing response models, e.g., a soft response such as reading or clicking on an advertisement, or a hard response such as purchasing or converting.

Response modeling is used for setting up different types of marketing campaigns, for instance, campaigns aimed at the following (Lo 2002):

- **Acquisition:** predicting which prospects are most likely to become customers and therefore should be targeted in an acquisition campaign
- **Development:** predicting which customers might have interest in purchasing additional products or subscribing to additional services, which is the aim of cross-selling models, or which customers can be advanced to spend more on existing products, which is the aim of up-selling models
- **Retention:** predicting which customers among those with a high probability of churning are most likely to be retained when targeted in a retention campaign

The idea is to identify the customers who are most likely to respond and to offer these customers an incentive to effectively convert. Targeting a customer in a marketing campaign is referred to more generally as *treating* a customer, and a campaign or action toward a customer as a **treatment.** Typically, not all customers are targeted in a marketing campaign (i.e., are treated), because marketing budgets are limited and including a customer in a campaign comes at a cost—that is, the cost of setting up and developing the campaign and the cost involved in contacting the customer. Contacting the customer can occur through various channels, for example, by mail or email, by telephone, or by sales representatives visiting customers or addressing prospects in-store. Additionally, there is the cost of the incentive that is offered. Examples of incentives include coupons, vouchers, samples, promotional offers, and reductions.

Contacting costs are not necessarily uniform across the target population, although they often are assumed uniformly distributed for simplicity. For instance, some customers must be called multiple times before they are reached, or sales representatives might be required to travel longer to visit prospective customers living in remote areas. Incentives can also be diversified and customized in terms of contacting channel, type, and value of the incentive to optimize further the effect of the campaign. Predictive analytics are also used to customize campaign characteristics at the individual customer level, for instance to estimate the preferred channel or the minimum incentive for the campaign to be effective.

However, the use of such traditional response models is suboptimal because these models are developed to estimate **gross response** rather than **net response.** Estimating gross response consists of predicting all responders, whereas estimating net response consists of predicting those who will only respond when treated. In other words, traditional response models do not allow for distinguishing between customers who will respond or convert because of being targeted in the campaign and having received an incentive and those who would have responded anyway, even had they not been treated.

When examining the profitability of running targeted marketing campaigns, no net profit in fact results from including the second group in a marketing campaign—that is, those who would have responded anyway. Instead, a net loss is incurred by including these customers because no additional revenues are generated to cover the involved costs. For instance, when coupons offering a 10% discount are sent to customers who would have purchased a product anyway, they will pay less for the product or service compared with them not having been contacted. The marketing effort then leads to decreased revenues and hence a net loss.

Clearly, we must know the net effect of a *treatment* on a customer rather than the gross effect to optimize the concrete actions that are undertaken. Uplift modeling, also called net-lift, true-lift, or difference modeling, aims at precisely establishing the difference in customer behavior because of a specific treatment that is extended to a customer. In this chapter, we will discuss various approaches for uplift modeling.

In line with the literature and in line with a number of business applications discussed extensively in the previous chapter, the discussion on uplift modeling in this chapter will center on marketing applications. However, note that uplift modeling can have great use and generate significant added value beyond the marketing context. A number of example applications in other fields include the following:

- **Credit risk management** (Siegel 2011), in which uplift modeling can be applied to estimate the effect of a collection effort on the eventual loss that is incurred when an obligor has defaulted on a loan.

- **Dynamic pricing** (Siegel 2011), in which the objective of uplift modeling is to establish the net effect of changes in pricing on the intention of a customer to purchase. Price in general could be perceived as a characteristic of a marketing campaign that is expected to have an effect on customer behavior. Tuning the characteristics of a campaign to maximize its effect requires an advanced uplift modeling setup. Such tuning will be discussed in a later section in this chapter.

- **Biomedical clinical trial analysis** (Collett 2015; Goetghebeur and Lapp 1997; Holmgren and Koch 1997; Russek-Cohen and Simon 1997), in which the aim is to establish the net effect of a newly developed drug on a patient's health situation, possibly depending on patient characteristics.

- **Political campaigning** (Issenberg 2012), which obviously shows great resemblances to running marketing campaigns, in which the objective of uplift modeling is to address and stimulate in a customized manner the *right* citizens to vote. *Right* in this context means those citizens who will vote for the candidate that is running the campaign, or who might be convinced to vote for this candidate (i.e., so-called swing or switch voters).

Whenever data used for developing a predictive model are somehow affected or subject to change because of interactions between a business or organization and its customers, uplift modeling might be a more correct approach to reach unbiased conclusions. Uplift modeling allows distilling the effect of these interactions from the data and accounting for the effects of interactions within the model.

A key requirement for uplift modeling to distill the effects of inter-actions on the behavior of customers is availability of the *right* data. In the following section, we will discuss in detail what *right* exactly means and how these data can be gathered. A specific preliminary data collection strategy, which is indispensable and conditional for uplift modeling, will be extensively discussed. For uplift modeling, it is necessary to *actively* gather the required data by means of well-designed experiments or, alternatively, to passively gather the required data by tracking information on marketing campaigns at the customer level.

The remainder of this chapter is structured as follows. The next section discusses the effects of a campaign in terms of the achieved change in customer behavior. Subsequently, data requirements will be discussed for developing uplift models as an improved alternative to traditional response modeling. The third section discusses various approaches for developing uplift models. The fourth and final section of this chapter is dedicated to the evaluation of uplift models, which will appear even more challenging than evaluating traditional pre-dictive models and will require specific measures and approaches. Therefore, tailored evaluation procedures for assessing the effective-ness of uplift models will be extensively discussed and illustrated. Both visual evaluation approaches and performance metrics will be covered. To conclude, notes on optimally operating uplift models in practice from a profit-driven perspective are provided in line with discussions in the previous chapter.

Effects of a Treatment

As introduced previously, the aim of uplift modeling is to distinguish between responders and nonresponders and additionally to distin-guish within the group of responders between customers who respond because of the campaign and those who would respond even when not treated. In fact, within the group of nonresponders, a further and similar segmentation can and should be made in terms of response behavior when treated or not treated.

In some situations, it has been observed that customers can be adversely affected by targeting them in a marketing campaign. In other words, some customers do not respond when treated, whereas they would purchase when not treated. In Kane et al., (2014), four groups of customers have been identified. As seen in Figure 4.1, these groups are differentiated in two dimensions, based on response behavior and on being treated or not.

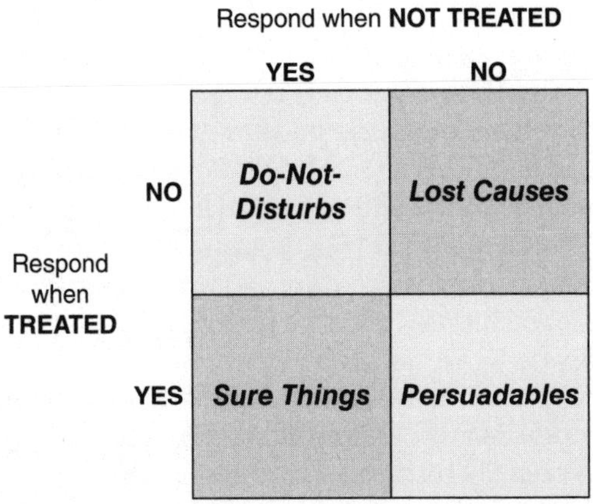

Respond when **NOT TREATED**

Figure 4.1 Four types of customers identified as a function of purchasing behavior when treated or not treated.
(Figure adopted from (Kane et al. 2014)).

The resulting four customer types are named *Sure Things*, *Lost Causes*, *Do-Not-Disturbs*, and *Persuadables*. In the remainder of this chapter, we will make extensive use of these customer types. Hence, the reader is advised to memorize them.

1. **Sure Things** respond or purchase whether or not they are treated. Treating *Sure Things* therefore does not generate additional returns but does generate additional costs (i.e., the fixed cost of contacting a customer and the cost related to the incentive offered to the targeted customers—for example, coupons that are sent to customers offering reduced prices aiming at converting customers to purchase a product or service). Note that this additional cost can generate positive second-order effects in strengthening the customer relationship and in increasing customer satisfaction, leading to a reduction of the risk of customer churn. Such second-order effects are ignored in this discussion for simplicity.

2. **Lost Causes** will not respond regardless of whether they are treated. Similar to *Sure Things*, targeting *Lost Causes* in a campaign does not generate additional revenues but again does generate additional costs. However, these additional costs are lower compared with the additional costs incurred when treating *Sure Things*. *Lost Causes* do not respond and do not take advantage of the incentive that is offered, whereas *Sure Things* do. Therefore, *Sure Things* are costlier when targeted in a campaign compared with *Lost Causes*.

3. **Do-Not-Disturbs** are adversely affected when targeted in a marketing campaign. They will not purchase if treated, whereas they do respond if they are not treated. For example, customers who are targeted in a retention campaign because they have been indicated by a standard customer churn prediction model to be at high risk of withdrawing from a product or service can actually be triggered to churn. Hence, the opposite effect of what is aimed for is achieved. Clearly, targeting *Do-Not-Disturbs* in a campaign generates no additional revenues but comes with large additional costs. Treating *Do-Not-Disturbs* is absolutely to be avoided because of these large associated costs. When many *Do-Not-Disturbs* are targeted in a campaign, it can even be better from a profitability perspective not to run the campaign because it will yield a net loss.

4. **Persuadables** respond when treated, and do not respond when not treated. These net-responders are those whom we are in fact seeking. They purchase only when contacted or, depending on the application, purchase more, purchase earlier, or continue purchasing. Including *Persuadables* generates additional revenues and, thus, after subtraction of the costs generated by including other types of customers, makes the campaign profitable. *Persuadables* are exactly the customers who must be treated; these customers should be identified by the model that is used to select the target population for the campaign.

Note that the actual behavior of a customer in terms of responding or not responding when treated or not treated likely depends on the various characteristics of the marketing campaign—that is, of the treatment that is applied. These characteristics can include, for example, the channel through which the customer is contacted and the type and size or amount of the financial incentive that is offered. It makes sense to optimize and customize these characteristics because we are in full control and can freely decide on these characteristics to maximize the returns of the campaign. In some settings, we might even customize these characteristics at the individual customer level. Given the important precondition of availability of the required data, uplift modeling approaches do accommodate such further optimization and customization at the individual customer level, as will be discussed in the section on uplift modeling approaches. Nonetheless, few case studies can be found in the literature elaborating such a setup, which is likely due to the involved complexity of gathering the required data, developing the appropriate uplift model, and implementing and operating the model for tuning and elaborating the marketing campaign.

Finally, note that the customer types might or might not *exist* in a customer base. More generally, within a particular customer base, any possible combination of the four customer types discussed above can be present. Whether these types exist and their exact combination depends on the characteristics of the population and of the campaign. For instance, there can be no *Do-Not-Disturbs* in a customer base for a particular type of campaign. In such a situation, there is no risk of adversely affecting the customers. Conversely, when there are no *Persuadables*, one should not run a campaign, because no profits will be generated. Although such an extreme situation might be rather exceptional, the fraction of *Persuadables* is often small. Performing a cost-benefit analysis therefore can be sensible.

EXPERIMENTAL DESIGN, DATA COLLECTION, AND DATA PREPROCESSING

Experimental Design

Specific data requirements hold for building uplift models and for identifying *Persuadables* in a customer population, which in essence is the objective of uplift modeling. Information must be available on a sample of customers, that is, whether they responded to a campaign in which they were targeted. This campaign preferably is identical or, if not, at least to the greatest possible extent similar to the campaign that is to be launched on a larger scale or that is to be reiterated and for which we intend developing the uplift model. If the campaign that is eventually run is significantly different from the campaign employed to gather response data for a sample of customers, then the eventual uplift model and estimates concerning the effects of the new campaign on the behavior of customers might be less trustworthy and accurate.

In addition to this first sample containing information on the behavior of treated customers, data are also needed describing or capturing the behavior of a *similar* sample of customers who were not treated. Information is needed concerning whether these customers responded or, more generally, whether these customers displayed the behavior we aim to instigate without being treated. The underlying idea of gathering these two samples is to contrast them and thus distill the net effect of the treatment as a function of individual customer characteristics.

The first sample of treated customers is called the **treatment group**, whereas the sample of customers who were not treated is called the **control group** (which is also called the reference group). The difference in behavior observed between the customers in the control and treatment group is what allows uplift modeling approaches to estimate the net effect of a treatment on individual customers. Ideally, both samples have been selected randomly and are similar in terms of all relevant characteristics.

Figure 4.2 provides a conceptual overview of both the data collection and uplift modeling and of the subsequent campaign setup. In a first step, a **development base** is randomly selected from the full customer base. Note that the full customer base as represented in the figure might or might not include prospective customers, depending on the application of the uplift model that is developed. For instance, customer acquisition modeling aims at evaluating prospective customers in terms of responsiveness to an acquisition campaign in which the goal of the acquisition campaign is to attract new customers. Therefore, the meaning of *full* depends on the application at hand and should be determined as appropriate in the particular application setting to ensure a *representative* sample is drawn.

The development base is randomly split into treatment and control groups of equal size. The treatment and control groups will and will not be treated, respectively, with the envisaged campaign. Response data are recorded for both samples and are then pooled and

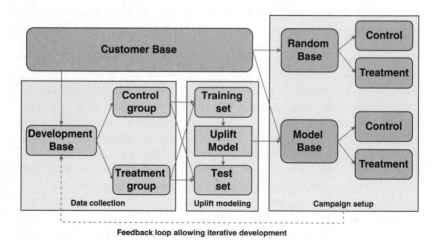

Figure 4.2 Experimental design to collect the required data for uplift modeling, allowing the selection of a model base for the campaign.

randomly split into training and test sets, as discussed in Chapter 2. An uplift model can then be developed using the training set, as will be discussed in the next section of this chapter. The resulting model is to be evaluated on the test set using the evaluation procedures, as will be discussed in a separate section at the end of this chapter. The evaluation procedure allows deciding whether the model is likely to perform well in terms of selecting an appropriate **model base** for running the actual campaign.

To measure the campaign and model effectiveness and to gather additional data for further uplift modeling purposes, a **random base** is also to be setup. The random base concerns a sample of customers that is randomly drawn from the customer base. The random base itself should be randomly split into treatment and control groups of equal size that respectively will and will not be treated by the campaign, similarly to the control and treatment groups in the development base.

Note that as previously discussed, the original development base sample used to develop the uplift model could be the combined model and random base sample of a previous similar campaign (if available). Alternatively, the development base can be the combined model and random base sample of a previous run of a campaign that is repeated on a regular basis.

It is recommended to setup the development of the uplift model and run the campaign as an iterative process. In each iteration, data are gathered that record the response behavior of a control and a treatment group selected using the model and of a control and a treatment group selected randomly from the customer base. In other words, a random base sample is randomly selected from the customer base, which is subsequently split into a control and a treatment group. The development base used for the next iteration then consists of the combined random base and model base samples.

One could argue that the model base sample should not be used for developing an uplift model, because the model base was not randomly selected. In fact, a random sample is always preferred when building analytical models because the randomness eliminates possible biases. However, the model base sample is too valuable and represents a *rich* source of information that should be explored and exploited for further improving the uplift model, for further optimizing the model base sample selection, and for further maximizing the returns of future campaigns.

To test and control for a possible bias due to the nonrandom selection of the model base, a dummy variable indicating whether a customer was selected for the campaign or the random base can be included in the data sample that is used for developing the uplift model. If the dummy indicator is an important, statistically significant variable, then the bias is controlled for.

Campaign Measurement of Model Effectiveness

Based on the observed response rates in the control and treatment groups in the random base and model base, a data scientist can measure the effectiveness of the uplift model and the effectiveness of the campaign (Lo 2002). Note that the effectiveness of the uplift model is not the same as the effectiveness of the campaign and that both should be well distinguished when assessing model effectiveness. Table 4.1 summarizes the response rates observed in the various groups or samples in the campaign setup as illustrated in Figure 4.1, allowing measurement of effectiveness. The effects of the campaign, the effects of the model, and the combined effects of model and campaign together can be assessed by comparing the response rates among the resulting four groups of customers.

The effect of the campaign can be evaluated by checking whether the difference in response rates in the treatment groups is greater than in the control groups for both the model base and the random base. For both bases, the treatment and control groups are similar except for the effect of the campaign, which affects the response rate. Therefore, the greater the difference in response rate that is observed between these fully comparable groups, the greater the effectiveness of the campaign.

Conversely, for the model to effectively contribute to increasing the effect of the campaign by improving the selection of customers to treat, the difference in response rates between the treatment and control groups in the model base ($R_{M,T} - R_{M,C}$) should be greater than the difference in response rate observed in the random base between the treatment and control groups ($R_{R,T} - R_{R,C}$). The difference in response rate in the random base measures the increase in response rate due to the campaign. For the model to be proved effective in

Table 4.1 Overview of Model and Campaign Effect Measurement

	Treatment Group	Control Group	Treatment Minus Control
Model Base	$R_{M,T}$	$R_{M,C}$	$R_{M,T} - R_{M,C}$
Random Base	$R_{R,T}$	$R_{R,C}$	$R_{R,T} - R_{R,C}$
Model minus Random	$R_{M,T} - R_{R,T}$	$R_{M,C} - R_{R,C}$	$(R_{M,T} - R_{R,C}) - (R_{M,C} - R_{R,C})$

selecting customers to treat, the increase in response rate in the model base should be greater than the increase attributable to the campaign. Hence, as proposed by (Lo 2002), the quantitative business objective of a response model, as measured by its effectiveness for running campaigns, is to maximize this difference, which is called the **true lift**:

$$\text{true lift} = (R_{M,T} - R_{M,C}) - (R_{R,T} - R_{R,C}).$$

The true lift evaluates the gain, for example in terms of response rate, revenues, and sales, that is achieved due to selecting the target population to be treated based on the model.

One can also reach the above equation for the true lift by adopting a perpendicular perspective to assessing model performance. The effectiveness of the model in identifying *Persuadables* can also be evaluated by contrasting the response rates in the treatment groups of the model and the random base. Both groups receive a treatment and only differ in terms of how they were selected, that is, by the model or in a random manner. Therefore, the larger the difference between the response rates $(R_{M,T} - R_{R,T})$ that is observed, the more effective the model is in selecting *Persuadables*.

The difference in response rates between the control groups of the model and the random base $(R_{M,C} - R_{R,C})$ can be expected to be negative because the uplift model aims at selecting *Persuadables* from the customer base who only respond when treated. Because no treatment is applied, the response rate in the control group of the model base $(R_{M,C})$ can be expected to be less than the average response rate, which is exactly what is observed in the random base control group. Hence, because $R_{M,C} < R_{R,C}$, the difference $R_{M,C} - R_{R,C}$ will be negative.

Comparing the difference in response rates for the treatment groups $(R_{M,T} - R_{R,T})$ with the difference in response rates for the control groups $(R_{M,C} - R_{R,C})$ provides a *net* measure for model effectiveness, the true lift:

$$\text{true lift} = (R_{M,T} - R_{R,T}) - (R_{M,C} - R_{R,C}).$$

Reworking this equation leads to the same equation of true lift provided above. Hence, both perspectives on assessing model effectiveness yield the same equation, as could be expected. Nonetheless, both rationales provide complementary insights.

Following the previous discussion, Table 4.2 provides a practical illustration of model and campaign effectiveness measurement by elaborating an example. As seen from the table, for the treatment group selected with the model, a response rate of 5.3% is achieved, whereas in the control group, a response rate of 1.2% is achieved. In the randomly selected treatment and control groups, the response

Table 4.2 Example Model and Campaign Effect Measurement

	Treatment Group	Control Group	Treatment − Control
Model Base	5.3%	1.2%	4.1%
Random Base	2.1%	0.8%	1.3%
Model − Random	3.2%	0.4%	**2.8%**

rates are 2.1% and 0.8%, respectively. Therefore, when randomly selecting customers to target, the treatment results in an increase in response rate or uplift equal to 2.1% − 0.8% = 1.3%. This result is considered the base effect of the campaign on which the model should further improve. Note that the campaign is effective in the sense that it boosts the response rate.

When examining the uplift effect of the campaign when selecting target customers by making use of the model, we observe a treatment effect equal to 5.3% − 1.2% = 4.1%, which is much greater than the benchmark effect of 1.3% uplift that is achieved when randomly selecting customers. The *True Lift* equals 4.1% − 1.3% = 2.8% and therefore, one can conclude that the model is effective and reinforces the effect of the campaign.

Practical Issues

Several practical issues and challenges emerge when setting up the experimental design for uplift modeling, as shown in Figure 4.2.

A first major challenge can be to convince management of the required shift in its modeling paradigm and to switch from a traditional response modeling approach to uplift modeling. A significant investment is required to develop and implement the proposed experimental setup and modeling process, which comes without a guarantee of yielding increased returns. Additionally, for the following reasons, management might be reluctant to elaborate the proposed experimental setup for gathering the required data:

1. Excluding a control group from the model base, although almost certainly containing many customers who are expected to purchase if treated (i.e., containing many *Persuadables*), might be hard to push through, because the immediate potential returns of the campaign are thus not maximized.

2. The returns of investing in data acquisition for uplift modeling are uncertain and will only become apparent (at least, to some extent) and tangible after some time, when the uplift model is up and running. Because as the saying goes, a *bird in the hand*

is worth two in the bush, management might opt for short-term results, whereas uplift modeling and more specifically investing in the collection of the required data is about going for the birds in the bush (i.e., likely to yield higher returns but in the longer term).

3. Additionally, targeting a randomly selected treatment group as part of setting up a random base might be deemed undesirable. Because such a sample is randomly selected from the customer base, a low net and possibly gross response rate might be expected. In other words, a low proportion of *Persuadables* might be selected as part of the random base treatment group. Again, investing in the random base treatment group will not yield immediate returns and will only generate indirect benefits in the longer term.

The investments and efforts to setup the experimental design and collect the required data will not immediately result in additional returns or benefits. Instead, immediate losses due to missed sales and suboptimal targeting are experienced. In fact, however, these losses relate to essential investments in data collection and model evaluation, which eventually will yield additional revenues and profits in subsequent campaigns.

When approval is obtained for implementing the experimental setup, a next challenge and important decision that must be made concerns the numbers of customers to select for the model and random base and for the control and treatment groups within the model and random base. As shown in the literature, the more observations available for developing a model, typically the better the result. However, practical limitations obviously exist:

1. The size of the model base is often decided based on the available marketing budget to run the campaign and the cost per included customer. However, the number of customers to be targeted by the campaign should be optimized to maximize the return of the campaign. How to practically optimize the size of the model base will be discussed in the section on evaluating uplift models. This discussion will not be straightforward but nonetheless potentially will have a significant effect on the generated revenues and thus be worth the effort. A utility or profit function must be developed that considers costs and benefits related to treating or not treating both responders and non-responders.

2. Because the customers in the treatment group of the random base represent an investment, pressure might exist to minimize

the size of the random base or, more specifically, that of the treatment group in the random base. As a general guideline, we recommend, based on experience rather than empirical evidence and in line with guidelines on minimum data sample sizes provided in Chapter 2, including at least 1,000 customers in the treatment group of the random base, but definitely not fewer than 100. The number of included customers can depend on the expected response rate, the size of the overall customer base, the costs and potential returns of the campaign, and other requirements or problem characteristics. With respect to the expected response rate, the lower this rate, the more observations should be included to address and compensate for the skewed class distribution.

The samples used to measure campaign effectiveness and, more specifically, to calculate the response rates shown in Table 4.1 and to test statistically the observed differences in response rates can be selected randomly from the available samples in the experimental setup to balance the sizes of these samples. This approach might be preferable from a statistical perspective or to address specific concerns related to the applied statistical tests. Conversely, if all samples used are sufficiently large, the effect of imbalanced sample sizes can be expected to be small. Practically speaking, the sample size of the random base treatment group and of the model base control group will be restrictive.

Extended Experimental Design

In the previous section, the possible effects of campaign characteristics on the behavior of customers were briefly mentioned. In addition to setting up an experiment and gathering data allowing the building of an uplift model for selecting the optimal set of customers to be targeted with a given campaign with fixed characteristics, the experimental design can be extended to accommodate optimization and customization of campaign characteristics at the individual customer level. Similar to the A/B testing discussed in the next section, this approach allows optimizing the campaign design to complement optimizing customer selection. Such an extended analysis requires treating multiple customer subsamples with different campaign characteristics. This requirement indeed further complicates both the setup and the analysis of these experiments, which might be even more costly and complex. Obviously, the added value might be greater but should, of course, compensate for the additional cost to be worth the effort.

Note that when extending the experimental design, there is a requirement to include sufficient customers in each subsample that is treated in a different manner—for example, with a unique combination of campaign characteristics such as contact channel and type and value of the incentive. As always, sufficiently large (preferably including more than 100 observations) subsamples are required to draw conclusions and derive patterns that are robust and hold for the full population of customers. *Robust* in this setting means that the findings do not depend on the exact observations selected in the treatment samples. In other words, if another sample of customers were selected as the development base for gathering data and developing an uplift model, the resulting uplift model should not be substantially different in terms of relationships and predictions.

A/B Testing

The experimental setup shown in Figure 4.2 and previously discussed, with two or more groups treated differently, might remind the reader of so-called *A/B testing*, which is also known as *split testing* or *bucket testing* (Kohavi and Longbotham 2015). A/B testing is a common practice in webpage design and more generally in software development. The aim is to compare different designs of a webpage or variations of application interfaces experimentally to decide on the *optimal* layout. Usually, two designs are compared, version A and version B, hence the name A/B testing. When more than two designs are compared, we speak of multivariate testing. In A/B testing, visitors to a webpage or users of an application are shown variations of the page or interface. Comparing the performance of the alternative setups in terms of appropriate performance indicators allows determining which design is preferred and eventually to be implemented. Example performance indicators that are often used are the *conversion rate,* which measures the fraction of visitors of a webpage who purchase the offered product or service, and the *click-through rate,* which measures the fraction of visitors of a webpage who click on a link that is shown on the webpage.

A/B testing is similar to uplift modeling in the sense that an experiment is set up in which different customers receive a different treatment. However, in uplift modeling, a predictive model is developed by analyzing the behavior of these customers, allowing subsequent customization of treatment given to individual customers. Whereas in A/B testing, a single design or treatment is selected, implemented, and applied to the full population of users. Hence, in A/B testing, the overall optimal design or treatment at the aggregated population level is selected, whereas uplift modeling aims at optimizing the treatment at the individual level by making use of advanced data analytics. For more information on A/B testing, one can refer to Kohavi and Longbotham (2015). Note that the practice of A/B testing is suboptimal and could theoretically be replaced by an uplift modeling approach. Rather than selecting a single layout of a webpage, the optimal layout might be customized depending on user characteristics to improve the performance of the website or application. This improvement is to some extent what recommender systems are about, as discussed in Chapters 2 and 3. However, from a practical perspective, such a dynamic, customized interface might be complex to develop and implement. In addition, the consistency of the interface that is shown to the users might be of importance, thereby limiting the practical use of uplift modeling.

UPLIFT MODELING METHODS

The purpose of uplift modeling is to estimate the expected net effect of a campaign or treatment on the behavior of individual customers. In a marketing campaign setting, the aim of uplift modeling is to identify *Persuadables* (i.e., customers who will purchase only if treated). Traditional response modeling approaches estimate gross response, leading to the identification and treatment of *Sure Things* and possibly *Do-Not-Disturbs*. These two groups should not be treated, but are labeled as positives in a traditional response modeling setup because they have been observed to purchase. Conversely, *Persuadables* who were not treated have not been observed to purchase and hence are labeled as *nonresponders*. Therefore, traditional response models are trained to predict the wrong targets for a campaign—*Sure Things* and *Do-Not-Disturbs* rather than *Persuadables*. This conceptual design error often goes unnoticed because response rates to campaigns indeed are higher when using a traditional response model than when randomly selecting target customers because of the *Sure Things* identified by the response model and included in the campaign.

Hence, the core issue with traditional response modeling is the objective function that is adopted for building the model and that does not capture the true objective because it is incorrectly specified. Response models aim at estimating *the probability of responding* instead of *the increase in probability of responding* based on a treatment. The increment in probability is exactly what uplift models estimate. In other words, uplift models estimate the change in behavior because of the marketing campaign, which is captured by the target variable y, defined as follows:

$$y = p(response \mid treatment) - (response \mid control).$$

However, note that the value of this target variable cannot be observed for individual customers because a customer cannot be treated and not treated simultaneously, i.e., belong to both the treatment and the control groups. Therefore, specific analytical techniques are required—that is, uplift modeling approaches. This section provides an overview of uplift modeling approaches that have been selected by assessing the following essential properties:

1. **Power**, in the sense that the application of these techniques has been shown in various case studies in the literature to effectively improve uplift and hence to increase returns and profits

2. **Interpretability**, which allows intuitive understanding of the resulting models and their output, which in a business setting is of crucial importance to successfully develop and implement uplift models

3. **Operational efficiency**, implying limited complexity and facilitating relatively straightforward implementation using standard data analytics tools and software

The selected approaches can be categorized in the following four groups:

1. Two-model approaches
2. Regression-based approaches
3. Tree-based approaches
4. Ensembles

This categorization is adopted to structure this section and allows the reader to further identify and frame approaches as proposed in the literature on uplift modeling. In this section, we will introduce and discuss the most representative, useful, powerful, and/or popular approaches from these different groups. References are provided throughout the text to the original works, presenting the selected approaches and providing full details, discussions, and experimental evaluations.

The approach that performs best and that should be applied in a particular setting depends on the exact application, the available data, the characteristics of the population, and the personal preferences and skills of the involved data scientists and management. Experimentation with different approaches is highly recommended if permitted by time and budget constraints because a relatively large variability is observed in the reported performance across different application settings. Even within similar application settings but for heterogeneous campaign and customer population characteristics, a strong variability has been observed. This observation leads to an important recommendation: Be cautious, and carefully and precisely test and monitor the performance of uplift models both when in development and even more so when in operation.

Two-Model Approach

A rather simple and intuitive approach for developing uplift models is called the two-model approach. The two-model approach builds on the traditional response modeling approach and combines two independent response models that are developed on two subsamples:

1. A first model is called the **treatment response model** (M_T) and estimates the response probability for a customer when treated, e.g., when targeted by a marketing campaign. The treatment response model is estimated using the observations in the treatment group of the development base as shown in Figure 4.2.

2. The second model is called the **control response model** (M_C) and aims at estimating the response probability for a customer when not treated. The control response model is estimated using observations from the control group in the development base.

The aggregated **uplift model** (M_U) combines these two models and estimates the net effect of a marketing campaign on the behavior of customers in terms of change in probability of responding. In other words, the uplift model estimates the uplift by subtracting the response probability when not treated, $p(response|control)$, estimated by the control response model, from the response probability when treated, $p(response|treatment)$, estimated by the treatment response model. The uplift model M_U is formulated as follows:

$$M_U = M_T - M_C.$$

In the literature, this approach is also known as the **naïve approach**, **difference score method**, or **double classifier approach** (Radcliffe 2007; Soltys, Jaroszewicz, and Rzepakowski 2015). The approach is indirect in the sense that uplift is not directly estimated by a model that is fitted to produce uplift scores. Instead, uplift is calculated indirectly from estimated response probabilities.

This approach has the benefit of being straightforward to implement. Two standard classification models must be developed, following the same methodology used for developing traditional response models estimating the gross response. For building the treatment and control response models, any supervised learning technique as discussed in Chapter 2 can be adopted. For instance, a two-model approach using logistic regression has been discussed and applied in Hansotia and Rukstales (2002a 2002b).

An important drawback of this approach is that the individual treatment and control response model constituting the uplift model is built using data from either the treatment group or the control group—without considering the other group (Chickering and Heckerman 2000; Hansotia and Rukstales 2002b; Radcliffe and Surry 2011). Uplift is then estimated by subtracting both model scores for each observation in the test set, as discussed above. By independently building the models, the model-building process does not actively search for and does not focus on finding patterns that are directly related to and hence indicative or predictive for uplift. The models are not built *directly* with the aim of estimating uplift but, rather, of estimating response behavior for two separate groups of customers.

The model-building process could result in one of the models selecting a rather different set of predictor variables than would a modeling approach directly estimating uplift (see below on direct estimation approaches). Moreover, to predict the uplift accurately, errors in the individual estimates of both models should not reinforce one another. Both models must therefore be highly accurate, since errors in one or both of the models could be amplified when predicting uplift and result in an inaccurate aggregate uplift model (Radcliffe and Surry 2011). However, highly accurate models appear difficult to achieve in practice. Consistency is not enforced among the models, and the effects are not directly assessed and modeled.

The two-model approach discussed in this section is considered an indirect means of estimating uplift, leading to associated issues and limitations. Instead, an estimation method that builds a *single* model to predict uplift *directly* using data from both control and treatment groups is preferred.

Several such approaches allowing direct estimation of uplift have been independently developed in the academic literature. Most of these approaches are either regression-based or tree-based. The next two sections introduce a series of methods stemming from these two respective classes of estimation approaches. A subsequent section will then discuss a selection of ensemble-based approaches for estimating uplift.

Regression-Based Approaches

In this section, two approaches will be presented. Lo's method is based on logistic regression, whereas Lai's method and the generalized Lai method reformulate the uplift modeling problem to allow standard approaches to be used, as discussed in Chapter 2. As will be shown, Lo's method can also be generalized for use in combination with any standard classification technique.

Lo's Method

A direct approach for uplift modeling that makes use of logistic regression was introduced in Lo (2002). The proposed methodology groups the treatment and control groups and incorporates a treatment dummy variable t, which indicates treatment or control group membership. See, for instance, the example dataset provided in Table 4.3, in which t is assigned a value of zero for control group membership and a value of one for treatment group membership.

Lo's method includes predictor variables x, treatment indicator t, and interaction variables $x \cdot t$ as predictor variables in a logistic regression model that is fitted to estimate target variable y that indicates whether a customer responded ($y = 1$) or did not respond ($y = 0$).

Similar to the discussed standard procedure for estimating a logistic regression model discussed in Chapter 2, Lo's method calls for a variable selection procedure to be applied in a forward, backward, or stepwise manner, depending on the data scientist's preference.

Table 4.3 Dataset Including Treatment Dummy Variable t, Predictor Variables x_i and Target Variable y

Customer	Age	Income	...	Treatment t	Target y
John	32	1,530	...	1	1
Sophie	48	2,680	...	1	0
...	...	...	...	...	...
Josephine	23	1,720	...	0	0
Bart	39	2,390	...	0	1
...	...	...	...	...	...

The number of candidate variables is doubled by including the interaction variables $x \cdot t$. Hence, the aim of the variable selection procedure is to reduce the included set of predictor variables, which allows reaching a stable or robust logistic regression model that includes only statistically significant variables, allows interpretation and validation of the incorporated relationships, and makes accurate predictions and generalizes well to new, unseen observations.

The interaction variables that are explicitly advanced in Lo's method and included in the set of candidate predictor variables allow the model to account for the heterogeneous effect of a treatment based on the characteristics of a customer, as expressed by the predictor variables x. If a treatment works well in a particular segment (i.e., significantly increases the response rates for instance in the customer segment with $age < 30$), then including the interaction variables allows the logistic regression model to pick up this pattern in the uplift model and to more accurately predict uplift. In other words, including these interaction variables increases the versatility of the approach.

Usually, interaction variables combining pairs of variables (or triplets, or more) are not preferred in business applications because of the reduced interpretability of the resulting model. For instance, the meaning of an interaction variable $x_1 \cdot x_2 = age \cdot income$ is arguably difficult to interpret unless you are to some extent trained in understanding the meaning of interaction effects. In Lo's method, however, the interaction effects $x \cdot t$ are less complex because t is a simple dummy variable, and the reason for adopting these interaction effects can be quite easily explained to a nonexpert.

Note that the interaction effects $x \cdot t$ allow data scientists and marketers or campaign developers to gain insight into the possibly divergent effects of a campaign on various subgroups in the customer base. By setting up well-designed experiments and by applying differentiated treatments to different samples of customers, one can customize the campaign characteristics in terms of, for example, channel or incentive to match the exact customer profile and allow further boosting of the returns to marketing efforts. This idea was discussed in the extended experimental design section earlier in this chapter.

Lo's method then applies logistic regression to model uplift as follows:

$$p(y = 1|x_1, \ldots, x_k) = \frac{1}{1 + e^{-(\beta_0 + \beta_1 x_1 + \cdots + \beta_k x_k + \beta_{k+1} x_1 t + \cdots + \beta_{k+k} x_k t + \beta_{k+k+1} t)}}.$$

As discussed in Chapter 2, β_0 represents the intercept, β_1 to β_k are coefficients measuring the main effects of the k predictor variables, and β_{k+1} to β_{k+k} capture the additional effects of the predictor variables due to the treatment. In other words, β_{k+1} to β_{k+k} measure the effect of the interaction effects between campaign and customer characteristics as discussed above. Finally, β_{k+k+1} captures the main treatment effect.

When applying a variable selection procedure (e.g., a forward, backward, or stepwise variable selection), the treatment dummy indicator t and interaction effects $x \cdot t$ can be eliminated from the model. However, for estimating uplift, the treatment indicator t should somehow be in the model. If not, then the model does not allow calculation of the difference between the probability of responding for $t = 1$ and $t = 0$—that is, the uplift for a customer when targeted in the campaign. If the selection procedure eliminates t and the interaction effects $x \cdot t$ from the final model, there are two possible explanations, which come with different solutions:

1. *The treatment or campaign is not significant or relevant in explaining response or purchasing behavior of customers.* In other words, the campaign is not working—the treatment has no effect. In this case, the campaign obviously should not be deployed, and a new campaign must be devised.

2. *The treatment variable and the interaction effects are not selected because they have less power in explaining the target variable than do other variables.* Alternatively, they are highly correlated with other variables and do not add predictive or explanatory power to the model in combination with the selected variables. A solution might be to force the most significant of the set of interaction effects and the treatment dummy in the model and to run the variable selection procedure in a complementary manner, meaning adding or removing variables to the model, which always includes the selected treatment variable.

Another possibility is that the coefficient of the treatment dummy indicator in the model is significant but negative. This result would actually mean that the treatment has a negative effect on the probability of responding, so the campaign achieves the opposite of what is aimed for. Clearly, then, an improved campaign should be designed that does positively affect customers.

The predicted lift is essentially the difference between the probability of a customer responding when treated minus the probability of a customer responding when not treated. This approach is similar to the two-model approach. However, a single integrated model is now estimated using both data from the treatment and control groups to produce both estimates, whereas in the two-model approach, two separate and therefore nonintegrated models were constructed. Additional advantages of Lo's method are the intuitiveness of the approach in accommodating the estimation of the effect of a campaign by including the treatment dummy indicator and the interpretability of the resulting model, which allows understanding and validating the relationships that are incorporated in the model and which explains the observed behavior.

The disadvantages of Lo's approach, according to Kane et al., (2014), are that some compound errors might remain when subtracting two model scores, and a substantial collinearity between variables might be present in the model because some characteristics might be included as both baseline and interaction variables. Full details on this approach are provided by Lo (2002) and Kane et al. (2014).

Note that the underlying principle of this approach (i.e., the inclusion of a treatment dummy indicator), is not restricted to logistic regression and can be implemented in combination with any supervised learning approach. For example, one can include the treatment dummy variable t and the interaction variables $x \cdot t$ in a neural network classification model and use this model similarly to obtain uplift estimates.

Finally, note that this approach might not work when adopting a base classifier that *inherently* incorporates a variable selection procedure, as discussed above. For instance, decision trees and ensembles of decision trees (e.g., obtained through bagging, boosting, or random forests) incorporate variable selection procedures. Therefore, the treatment dummy indicator t and the interaction variables $x \cdot t$ might not be selected in the final model, thus not allowing calculation of uplift estimates by setting t to zero and one. Again, this condition might or might not mean the treatment has no significant effect, as discussed above. Other variables that are correlated with the treatment variables might be more predictive for the target variable and therefore preferred, making the treatment variables redundant.

As will be discussed in the next sections on decision tree-based approaches for developing uplift models, when the treatment nonetheless is significant, the dummy or an interaction effect can be enforced in the model, facilitating the development of an uplift model. This approach comes with greater complexity than enforcing t in the logistic regression model and therefore might be less preferred.

Lai's Method and the Generalized Lai Method

Two alternative regression-based uplift modeling approaches are *Lai's method* and the *generalized Lai method* as introduced in Lai et al. (2006) and Kane et al. (2014), respectively. These models essentially redefine the target variable as follows.

In the introduction section of this chapter, the customer population was categorized into four groups based on whether a customer responds when treated or not treated: *Sure Things*, *Lost Causes*, *Persuadables*, and *Do-Not-Disturbs* (see Figure 4.1). Preferably, we would like to know for each customer individually to which group he or she belongs, which would allow us to treat all *Persuadables* and to maximize the returns of a campaign. However, we do not have this information; we therefore develop uplift models with the aim of identifying the *Persuadables*.

What we do know, based on previous campaign or experimental data that were gathered to build an uplift model, is whether a customer was treated and whether the customer responded. Hence, a customer can be grouped into one of the following four categories as discussed in Lai et al. (2006) and Kane et al. (2014); see Figure 4.3:

1. **Control responders (CR)** are the customers who responded without having received a treatment. Note that we do not know whether a control responder would have bought when treated. Therefore, we do not know whether a control responder is either a *Sure Thing* or a *Do-Not-Disturb*.

2. **Control nonresponders (CN)** are the customers who did not receive a treatment and did not respond. Because they might have responded had they been treated, we cannot tell whether a control nonresponder is either a *Lost Cause* or a *Persuadable*.

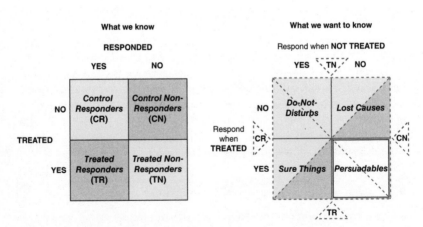

Figure 4.3 Categorization of customers based on whether a customer was treated and whether the customer responded.

(Figure adopted from (Kane et al. 2014)).

3. **Treatment responders (TR)** are customers who were treated and responded. They might or might not have responded without treatment; therefore, a treatment responder can be either a *Persuadable* or a *Sure Thing*.

4. **Treatment nonresponders (TN)** are customers who received a treatment but did not respond. They might be either *Lost Causes* or *Do-Not-Disturbs* because they might or might not have responded had they not received treatment.

Based on these four categories of customers, an alternative direct uplift modeling approach is proposed in Lai (2006) and Lai et al. (2006). This approach labels control nonresponders and treated responders as **good targets** because both groups together contain all *Persuadables* and do not contain *Do-Not-Disturbs*, who should not be treated. In addition to *Persuadables*, these groups (control nonresponders and treated responders) also contain *Lost Causes* and *Sure Things*. These groups should optimally not be treated, but only involve a minor cost compared with treating *Do-Not-Disturbs*.

Control responders and treated nonresponders are labeled **bad targets** because these groups only contain Do-Not-Disturbs, Lost Causes, and Sure Things. Targeting these groups always involves costs but never generates additional revenues. Hence, control responders and treated nonresponders should not be treated.

Thus, the uplift modeling problem is converted into a binary classification problem. Logistic regression or any other supervised learning technique as discussed in Chapter 2 can be applied to estimate the new target variable. The probability of being good resulting from the developed model allows ranking customers from high to low likelihood of being a *Persuadable* and selecting a target population for running the campaign by setting a cutoff score for a customer to be included in the campaign, as will be further discussed in a subsequent section. Note that including a treatment dummy in this approach is of no use because both the good and the bad targets stem from both the control and the treatment group.

Table 4.4 applies Lai's method to the example dataset provided in Table 4.3, with a value of the new target variable $y' = 1$ representing good customers (i.e., control nonresponders and treated responders) and $y' = 0$ representing bad customers (i.e., control responders and treated nonresponders). Applying a binary classification technique to the relabeled dataset excluding the treatment indicator and the original target variable then yields an uplift model.

In Kane et al. (2014), a variation of this approach is suggested by adopting a supervised learning model for predicting multiple nominal

Table 4.4 Relabeled Dataset of Table 4.3 Following Lai's Method

x_1	x_2	...	t	y		y'
32	1,530 €	...	1	1		1
48	2,680 €	...	1	0		0
...	...	...	...	...	⇒	...
23	1,720 €	...	0	0		1
39	2,390 €	...	0	1		0
...	...	...	...	...		...

outcomes (e.g., multinomial logistic regression or decision tree) to directly estimate probability scores for each quadrant of the left panel in Figure 4.3—for belonging to class TR, TN, CR, or CN. This approach might lead to more flexibility in model development compared with the original formulation and to a higher precision in estimating class membership and lift score. The drawback of this approach is an increase in complexity. Table 4.5 relabels the dataset provided in Table 4.3 following this approach. Subsequently, a multiclass classification technique can be applied, again excluding the treatment indicator and the original target variable from the dataset, which will yield a classification model that allows predicting a probability score for each of the classes (TR, TN, CR, and CN).

The resulting probability scores can then be combined in an unweighted fashion as follows:

$$\text{Lift score}(x) = [p(TR \mid x) + p(CN \mid x)] - [p(TN \mid x) + p(CR \mid x)].$$

The lift score again allows ranking and selecting a target population to be treated by setting a cutoff. Essentially, this process reduces to the original approach in the sense that the probabilities for belonging

Table 4.5 Relabeled Dataset of Table 4.3 Following the Generalized Lai Method

x_1	x_2	...	t	y		y'
32	1,530 €	...	1	1		TR
48	2,680 €	...	1	0		TN
...	...	...	...	...	⇒	...
23	1,720 €	...	0	0		CN
39	2,390 €	...	0	1		CT
...	...	...	...	...		...

to classes TR and TN are summed, thus representing the probability of good (i.e., the probability of being a *Persuadable*). In addition, the probabilities for belonging to groups TN and CR are summed, thus representing the probability of bad (i.e., the probability of not being a *Persuadable*). Hence, the lift score, with $p(good|x) = p(TR \mid x) + p(CN \mid x)$ and $p(bad \mid x) = p(TN \mid x) + p(CR \mid x)$, equals the following:

$$\text{Lift score}(x) = p(good \mid x) - p(bad \mid x).$$

The essential difference from Lai's approach is the moment of aggregation, which in Lai's method occurs *before estimating a model* by redefining the target variable; however, in Kane's variation, the aggregation occurs *after model estimation* by recombining the probabilities, thus yielding the lift scores.

EXAMPLE

A customer is scored yielding the following probability scores:

$p(TR \mid x) = 0.29,$

$p(TN \mid x) = 0.14, p(CR \mid x) = 0.18,$ and $p(CN \mid x) = 0.39.$

This scoring allows calculating the lift score as follows:

$p(good \mid x) = p(TR \mid x) + p(CN \mid x) = 0.29 + 0.39 = 0.68$

$p(bad \mid x) = p(TN \mid x) + p(CR \mid x) = 0.14 + 0.18 = 0.32$

$\text{Lift score}(x) = p(good \mid x) - p(bad \mid x) = 0.68 - 0.32 = 0.36$

The development of a multiclass model as in Kane's variation allows further refining and generalizing the above equation and is therefore preferred. This model leads to the *generalized Lai method*. In Kane et al. (2014), it is shown that an adjustment of the above equation for the lift score is required when using Kane's variation to account for different sample sizes of the control and treatment groups.

Only when both samples are randomly drawn from the customer base and include the same number of customers (which is often not true) is the above equation *statistically correct*. In other words, only then will the estimated models produce *tuned* probabilities for a customer to belong to a particular class that can be reliably used to calculate the lift score and for ranking and selecting customers. Tuned in this setting means that a probability can be interpreted as an exact estimate of the probability—that is, one representing the precise likelihood of belonging to either class.

Because of imbalanced sample sizes, probability estimates might become biased. To correct for this bias, the lift scores should be calculated using the following equation:

$$\text{Lift score}(x) = \frac{p(TR \mid x)}{p(T)} + \frac{p(CN \mid x)}{p(C)} - \frac{p(TN \mid x)}{p(T)} - \frac{p(CR \mid x)}{p(C)},$$

with $p(T)$ the proportion of treated customers, $p(C)$ the proportion of customers in the control group, and $p(C) = 1 - p(T)$. Intuitively, this correction makes sense. If the sample of treated customers is relatively small compared with the control group, then the fraction of treated responders will also be relatively small. The model will therefore produce small absolute probability estimates for customers to belong to the treated responders or treated nonresponders groups, whereas this probability should not depend on the original sample sizes of treatment and control groups. In essence, only the customer characteristics should determine the lift score; hence, the scaling in the above equation of the probability estimates produced by the model using the proportions of the samples used to develop the model.

EXAMPLE

For the previous example, we can estimate the relative sample sizes of the treatment and control groups:

$$p(T) = 0.29 + 0.14 = 0.43,$$

and

$$p(C) = 0.39 + 0.18 = 0.57.$$

This information then permits calculation of the lift score following the generalized Lai method as follows:

$$\text{Lift score}(x) = \frac{0.29}{0.43} + \frac{0.39}{0.57} - \frac{0.14}{0.43} - \frac{0.18}{0.57} = 0.72.$$

An advantage of the simple and the generalized Lai methods is that traditional supervised learning techniques and model estimation procedures can be applied for developing an uplift model. Conversely, the approach is rather rough because by design it does not exclude *Lost Causes* and *Sure Things* from the control nonresponders and treatment responders. Hence, a further optimization can be desirable to maximize returns.

The two-model approach, the simple and generalized Lai method, and Lo's approach were evaluated on three datasets in Kane et al. (2014). Overall, the generalized Lai method appeared to perform best given the imbalanced sizes of the different samples, whereas Lo's approach worked well for some but not all datasets.

Tree-Based Approaches

Most tree-based approaches for uplift modeling, such as *uplift trees*, are adaptations from popular classification tree algorithms such as C4.5 (Quinlan 1993), CART (Breiman et al. 1984), or CHAID (Kass 1980). Chapter 2 provided an introductory discussion of these standard classification-tree induction algorithms. The original setup of these approaches does not directly accommodate uplift estimation but is oriented toward class estimation. Nonetheless, it seems intuitive that classification trees can be altered in a relatively simple manner for uplift modeling purposes. In this section, a selected number of such adaptations are discussed in detail.

Standard classification trees consider a single sample with observations belonging to two or more classes. In uplift modeling, however, two samples exist: the treatment and control groups. To account for these two groups and to estimate lift rather than class membership, the proposed tree-based approaches alter the splitting criterion, the pruning technique, or both the splitting criterion and pruning technique involved in building a classification tree.

Significance-Based Uplift Tree

In Radcliffe and Surry (2011), a powerful tree-based uplift modeling approach is introduced called the significance-based uplift tree (SBUT), which is similar to the well-known CART and C4.5 decision tree induction algorithms.

As with most tree-based approaches, SBUT grows a tree by evaluating all potential splits. To do so, a quality measure is calculated for each potential split, indicating goodness. This approach allows iteratively selecting the best split and growing the tree until a stopping criterion is met or, alternatively, until a fully pure tree is obtained. SBUT aims at selecting for each node the split, which simultaneously does two things:

1. It maximizes the difference in uplift—the difference in response rates between the treatment and control groups, in all child nodes.

2. It minimizes the difference in size of the child nodes, with size meaning the number of observations, expressing a preference for splits that result in groups of equal size and a dispreference for splits leading to highly imbalanced groups.

Both properties are important determinants of the *quality* of a split because a split can quite easily be found that yields a large difference in uplift between the resulting child nodes by simply separating a small number of observations exhibiting a high response rate and uplift in a node. However, the strong uplift observed in the respective child node only applies to a very limited number of observations and therefore does not have broad validity or applicability. Hence, a good splitting quality criterion achieves strong uplift in the child nodes but also accounts for the size of the child nodes. Figure 4.4 provides an illustration of the trade-off between achieving high uplift in a child node and accounting for the number of observations, a *bad* and a *good* split.

Note that some methods proposed in the literature strongly simplify the split quality evaluation by for instance ignoring the sizes of the child nodes and selecting splits solely based on difference in uplift (Hansotia and Rukstales 2002b). As an alternative, the tree-based approach proposed by Chickering and Heckerman (2000) does not adapt the splitting criterion to accommodate the specific objective of uplift modeling but rather enforces the final splits in all leaf nodes to be on the treatment dummy indicator *t*. Remember that the treatment variable indicates whether a customer received a treatment. Hence, in each leaf node, a probability of responding when treated and when not treated by setting *t* to one or zero can be calculated. Thus, the uplift can be estimated as the difference between these probabilities. Note that this approach strongly resembles Lo's method discussed in the above section, which also forces the treatment indicator *t* in the model for uplift estimation. However, Lo's approach directly aims at distilling the effect of the campaign on the probability of responding. Conversely, this tree-based version of Lo's approach does

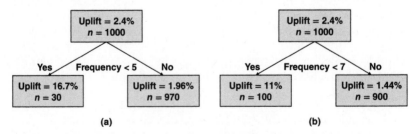

Figure 4.4 (a) High uplift but low number of observations in the left child node versus (b) lower uplift but applicable to a higher number of observations.

not fit trees that directly aim at estimating uplift but rather aim at estimating class membership (i.e., respond or not). Found responders and nonresponders are eventually split into treated and non-treated, but this split might not be meaningful.

Both simplified approaches (Hansotia and Rukstales, 2002b; Chickering and Heckerman, 2000) are intuitive but less well equipped to accommodate the specific modeling objective (i.e., estimating uplift). Consequently, as can be expected, they have already been reported to be less powerful in inducing uplift trees than the more refined decision tree approaches just discussed.

A measure similar to the standard information gain measure implemented in CART and C4.5 is proposed in Radcliffe and Surry (1999) and reported on more extensively in Radcliffe and Surry (2011). The measure, which we will call the *uplift gain* ($Gain_U$), evaluates the quality of a split by penalizing the difference in uplift between the left and right child node $\Delta = U_L - U_R$, which is to be maximized, by multiplying Δ with a factor between zero and one as a function of the difference in the sizes of the child nodes, n_L and n_R, respectively, representing the number of observations in the left and the right child node:

$$Gain_U = \Delta \cdot \left(1 - \left| \frac{n_L - n_R}{n_L + n_R} \right|^k \right).$$

Parameter k in the $Gain_U$ equation determines the importance or effect of the sample size difference in correcting the difference in uplift Δ. The larger k is, the smaller is the penalty factor for imbalanced node sizes (see the example of Figure 4.5). The value of parameter k is set heuristically (e.g., using a standard tuning approach).

When the child nodes are exactly balanced, then $n_L = n_R$ and the penalty factor equals 1, which then intuitively leads the uplift gain to be equal to the difference in uplift Δ between the child nodes. Note that we then essentially have the measure as proposed by Hansotia and Rukstales (2002b) as already explained. However, when the difference in child node sizes is large, the penalty factor shifts to zero. $Gain_U$ then becomes small, indicating a poor split quality and leading to imbalanced splits being penalized.

EXAMPLE

Figure 4.5 provides an example of a node in a tree that is split in a left (L) and right (R) child node. For each node, the response rate (R) and the number of observations (n) are indicated for both the treatment (T) and control (C) groups. The $Gain_U$ measure for evaluating this split can be calculated as follows. The uplift in the left child node equals the difference in response rate between the treatment and control groups in that node, i.e., $U_L = R_{L,T} - R_{L,C} = 3.1\% - 1.4\% = 1.7\%$. In the right child node, we have $U_R = R_{R,T} - R_{R,C} = 2.2\% - 2.0\% = 0.2\%$. Hence, the difference in uplift between the child nodes equals $\Delta = U_L - U_R = 1.7\% - 0.2\% = 1.5\%$. Moreover, n_L equals the total number of observations in the left child node, i.e., $125 + 146 = 266$, whereas n_R equals the total number of observations in the right child node, $89 + 102 = 191$.

The uplift gain for $k = 1$ thus equals the following:

$$Gain_U = \Delta \cdot \left(1 - \left|\frac{n_L - n_R}{n_L + n_R}\right|^k\right) = 1.5\% \cdot \left(1 - \left|\frac{266 - 191}{266 + 191}\right|^1\right) = 1.25\%.$$

Similarly, for $k = 2$, we obtain $Gain_U = 1.46\%$, and for $k = 3$, $Gain_U = 1.49\%$.

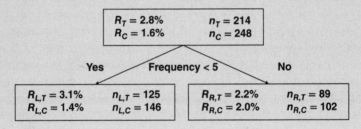

Figure 4.5 Illustration of **$Gain_U$** calculation.

The split with the largest $Gain_U$ is considered the optimal split because it balances between the two objectives introduced above; i.e., it maximizes the difference in uplift between the child nodes and minimizes the difference in size of the child nodes.

The split with the largest $Gain_U$ is iteratively selected when growing the tree. Alternative formulations for the uplift gain measure have been proposed in the literature but are beyond the scope of this chapter because these measures might or might not work well depending on the real world problem that must be solved (Radcliffe and Surry, 2011).

As an alternative to the above uplift gain measure, the **significance-based splitting criterion** is proposed in Radcliffe and Surry (2011). This measure is more complex and less intuitive but likely is also more powerful. When considering a candidate split, the SBUT approach fits a linear regression model that estimates the probability of responding for all observations in the Treatment and Control Groups in both child nodes as a function of a number of dummy variables indicating three things:

1. Left (L) or right (R) child node membership, that is, $N = 0$ or 1 respectively.
2. Control (C) or treatment (T) group membership, that is, $G = 0$ or 1 respectively.
3. Interaction between child node and group, $N \cdot G$. This is only different from zero when both N and G have value one (i.e., for the Treatment Group in the right child node).

The linear regression model then becomes the following:

$$p_{ij} = \beta_0 + \beta_N \cdot N + \beta_G \cdot G + \beta_{NG} \cdot N \cdot G.$$

β_0 is the intercept representing the baseline response probability for observations with all dummies having a value equal to zero (i.e., for control group customers in the left child node). β_N captures the effect of belonging to the right child node compared with the baseline response probability, and β_G of belonging to the treatment group. Finally, β_{NG} captures the difference in response probability for belonging to the treatment group in the right child node compared with all other groups. Hence, β_{NG} estimates the effects of both the split and the treatment in the right child node treatment group compared with all other subgroups, i.e., compared with the control groups in both the left and right child node and the treatment group in the left child node. Thus, β_{NG} captures the difference in uplift, which is exactly the effect we aim to distill. The significance of this coefficient is therefore indicative of the strength of the split. We can find the optimal split by evaluating for all possible splits the significance of the interaction term.

The significance of the interaction term can be tested with a t-statistic following a t-distribution, an approach that provides an indication of significance given the other variables in the model and isolates the effect of the split on uplift, which is exactly what we need in this setting (Radcliffe and Surry 2011). The expression used to evaluate split quality is the following:

$$t^2\{\beta_{NG}\} = \frac{(n-4) \cdot (U_R - U_L)^2}{C_{44} \cdot SSE},$$

where n is the number of observations in the node that is split, U_R and U_L are the uplift in the right and left child node, and C_{44} is the $(4, 4)$-element of the matrix $\mathbf{C} = (\mathbf{X'X})^{-1}$. The sum of squared errors, SSE, in the denominator of the statistic can be calculated as follows:

$$SSE = \sum_{i \in \{T,C\}} \sum_{j \in \{L,R\}} n_{ij} p_{ij} (1 - p_{ij}),$$

where n_{ij} is the size of the various groups in the child nodes, and p_{ij} is the estimated response probability in each node by the linear regression model.

Splits can be ranked according to the associated value of $t^2\{\beta_{NG}\}$, with a higher value of the statistic indicating a stronger significance of the coefficient.

One might wonder why a linear regression model is used in the significance-based splitting procedure instead of a logistic regression model, because the target variable is binary. Although not explicitly indicated by the developers, there are two main advantages to the use of linear regression over logistic regression in this setting:

1. Estimating a linear regression model is computationally less demanding than fitting a logistic regression model because a closed formula solution is available for estimating the coefficients in the linear regression model, whereas fitting a logistic regression model requires an optimization procedure for estimating the coefficients (see Chapter 2). In growing an uplift tree, many possible splits must be evaluated. Hence, linear regression accelerates the tree-growing process and is likely to perform equally well.

2. A linear regression model can also be applied when the target variable is continuous. Thus, linear regression is more flexible because it also allows fitting regression uplift trees. However, although explicitly mentioned in Radcliffe and Surry (2011), no practical cases of uplift regression trees have been documented in the literature. Uplift regression modeling can find practical use in customer lifetime value estimation, in which the aim can be to develop treatments for boosting CLV (see Chapter 3). A subsequent section in this chapter will briefly elaborate on uplift modeling for continuous targets.

Given the usually small effect of a treatment compared with the baseline or background effect and the often small size of the treatment group in the development base, a main challenge when developing uplift models concerns the stability of the resulting model. Stability or robustness refers to the generalization behavior and precision toward future applications on new customers different from those in the development sample. Particularly for decision-tree-based approaches, stability is a concern, and overfitting must actively be addressed. A pruning strategy involving a holdout validation sample as discussed in Chapter 2 can be used for this purpose.

In Radcliffe and Surry (2011), a variance-based pruning approach is proposed for application in combination with the significance-based splitting criterion discussed above. The training data for this purpose must be split randomly in k equally sized sets, with k by default equal to eight. The tree is grown *in full* by making use of one of these sets until, for example, all leaf nodes are pure, until a maximum depth is reached, or until a leaf node contains a minimum number of observations. In a second step, splits are removed if the uplift at a child node exhibits a standard deviation (as a measure of variability and thus of stability) greater than some predetermined threshold, with the standard deviation measured on the $k - 1$ sets that were not used for growing the tree. The exact value to use as a threshold is highly application dependent. It is recommended by the developers of this approach to experiment and tune this parameter to test the effect and sensitivity of the uplift tree and to optimize its value for reaching maximum performance. In Radcliffe and Surry (2011) an indication is provided, placing the pruning threshold in the range of 0.5% to 3% for a baseline response rate (i.e., the response rate in the control group) in the range of 1% to 3% and uplift (i.e., the difference between the response rate in the treatment and the control group) between 0.1% to 2%.

Given the inherent instability of decision trees, an alternative approach for improving the stability of the obtained uplift model is to grow an ensemble of uplift trees. Bagging, boosting, and random forests approaches for uplift modeling will be discussed in a later section.

Divergence-Based Uplift Tree

As an alternative to the significance-based splitting criterion, a number of divergence-based splitting criteria have been proposed in Rzepakowski and Jaroszewicz (2012), with the concept of distributional divergence drawn from the field of information theory. We will call these approaches *divergence-based uplift trees* (DBUT).

The aim of a split in an uplift tree is in essence to maximize the distance in the class distributions of the response between treatment and control groups in the child nodes. In other words, the fractions of responders and nonresponders (i.e., the class distribution of the target variable, with the fraction of nonresponders equal to one minus the fraction of responders) in the treatment groups should be *as different as possible* from the fractions of responders and nonresponders in the control group. When in a relative sense (i.e., in proportion to the group size), there are many more responders in the treatment group than in the control group in a node, then the uplift in that node is large. Remember that the fraction of responders in a group corresponds to the probability of responding in that group, and the difference in probability of responding between the treatment and control group is the uplift in that node.

Before putting forward specific candidate divergence measures D, we introduce the divergence-based splitting approach in general terms by defining the **weighted aggregate divergence** D over the left and right child nodes of a split S between the class distributions $P(y)$ of the response variable y in the treatment and control groups:

$$D(P_T(y)) : P_C(y)|S) = \frac{n_L \cdot D(P_{L,T}(y) : P_{L,C}(y)) + n_R \cdot D(P_{R,T}(y) : P_{R,T}(y))}{n_L + n_R}.$$

The subscripts T and C, respectively, indicate treatment and control, and subscripts L and R indicate left and right child node. Consequently, if $D(P_T(y) : P_C(y))$ represents the divergence as measured in the parent node of the split, then a gain measure based on the divergence measure D for evaluating the quality of a split can be defined as follows:

$$Gain_D(S) = D(P_T(y) : P_C(y)|S) - D(P_T(y) : P_C(y)).$$

$Gain_D(S)$ is called the **divergence gain** measure and is similar to the general information gain and uplift gain measures defined respectively in Chapter 2 and in the previous section. Again, each candidate split can be evaluated by calculating the divergence gain measure, and the split with the highest divergence gain is selected. The procedure is repeated recursively as in standard decision tree approaches until a stopping criterion is met or until the tree is grown in full, after which it is pruned (see below).

Several divergence measures D allowing quantifying the *difference* in the (discrete) distribution $P(y)$ of the response variable in the treatment and control groups have been proposed and tested in the literature for uplift modeling. These measures include the following (Rzepakowski and Jaroszewicz 2012):

1. Kullback-Leibler divergence (KL)
2. Squared Euclidean distance (E)
3. Chi-squared divergence (χ^2)

These measures are generally defined to express the divergence or distance from a distribution $Q = (q_1, \dots, q_n)$, which is the baseline distribution, to a distribution $P = (p_1, \ldots, p_n)$, which deviates to some extent from Q as quantified by the measure, as follows:

$$KL(P : Q) = \sum_{i=1..n} p_i \cdot log\frac{p_i}{q_i};$$

$$E(P : Q) = \sum_{i=1..n} (p_i - q_i)^2;$$

$$\chi^2(P : Q) = \sum_{i=1..n} \frac{(p_i - q_i)^2}{q_i}.$$

For a more elaborate discussion on these divergence measures, one may refer to Csiszar and Shields (2004); Lee (1999); and Rzepakowski and Jaroszewicz (2012).

Soltys, Jaroszewicz, and Rzepakowski (2015) introduced an equivalent approach to the pruning approach discussed in Chapter 2 for making divergence-based uplift trees robust. A validation set is to be held aside for pruning and is not used when growing the tree. The tree is grown on the training set, and the performance of the tree is monitored on the validation set in terms of an uplift performance metric that will be discussed in detail in the final section of this chapter—that is, the Qini measure or area under the uplift curve (AUUC). Note that this pruning approach permits the use of any preferred and suitable evaluation metric for pruning instead of the AUUC. Early stopping can be applied to determine the size of the tree and to stop adding splits when overfitting occurs. Preferably, however, post-pruning is employed to maximize simultaneously the performance and the generalization power of the final tree.

EXAMPLE

We reevaluate the uplift tree split shown in Figure 4.5 by calculating the divergence gain using the three divergence measures D already introduced. The respective class distributions of the response variable y in the parent and child nodes can be derived directly from the response rates shown in Figure 4.5:

$$P_C(y) = (0.984, 0.016) \qquad P_T(y) = (0.972, 0.028)$$
$$P_{L,C}(y) = (0.986, 0.014) \qquad P_{L,T}(y) = (0.969, 0.031)$$
$$P_{R,C}(y) = (0.980, 0.020) \qquad P_{R,T}(y) = (0.978, 0.022)$$

Next, we calculate the divergence in the parent node $D(P_T(Y) : P_C(Y))$ according to the various divergence measure definitions:

$$KL(P_T(y) : P_C(y))$$

$$= \sum_{i=1..n} p_{T,i} log\frac{p_{T,i}}{p_{C,i}} = 0.972 \cdot log\frac{0.972}{0.984} + 0.028 \cdot log\frac{0.028}{0.016} = 0.003;$$

$$E(P_T(y) : P_C(y))$$

$$= \sum_{i=1..n} (p_{T,i} - p_{C,i})^2 = (0.972 - 0.984)^2 + (0.028 - 0.016)^2$$

$$= 0.0003;$$

$$\chi^2(P_T(y) : P_C(y))$$

$$= \sum_{i=1..n} \frac{(p_{T,i} - p_{C,i})^2}{p_{C,i}} = \frac{(0.972 - 0.984)^2}{0.984} + \frac{(0.028 - 0.016)^2}{0.016}$$

$$= 0.0091.$$

Similarly, the divergence measures for the child nodes can be calculated, leading to the following:

$KL(P_{L,T}(y) : P_{L,C}(y)) = 0.0078$ $\quad KL(P_{R,T}(y) : P_{R,C}(y)) = 9.8866\text{e-}05$
$E(P_{L,T}(y) : P_{L,C}(y)) = 5.7800\text{e-}04$ $\quad E(P_{R,T}(y) : P_{R,C}(y)) = 8.0000\text{e-}06$
$\chi^2(P_{L,T}(y) : P_{L,C}(y)) = 0.0096$ $\quad \chi^2(P_{R,T}(y) : P_{R,C}(y)) = 1.8591\text{e-}04$

These results then allow calculation of the *weighted aggregate divergence* over the left and right child node of split S, with $n_L = 274$, $n_R = 191$, and the above divergence measures for the child nodes as follows:

$$KL(P_T(y) : P_C(y)|S) = \frac{274 \cdot 0.0078 + 191 \cdot 9.8866\text{e-}05}{274 + 191} = 0.0046;$$

$$E(P_T(y) : P_C(y)|S) = \frac{274 \cdot 5.7800\text{e-}04 + 191 \cdot 8.0000\text{e-}06}{274 + 191}$$

$$= 3.4387\text{e-}04;$$

$$\chi^2(P_T(y) : P_C(y)|S) = \frac{274 \cdot 0.0096 + 191 \cdot 1.8591\text{e-}04}{274 + 191} = 0.0057.$$

Finally, we calculate the divergence gain based on the following different divergence measures:

$$Gain_{KL}(S) = KL(P_T(y) : P_C(y)|S) - KL(P_T(y) : P_C(y))$$

$$= 0.0045 - 0.0037 = 0.0009;$$

$$Gain_E(S) = E(P_T(y) : P_C(y)|S) - E(P_T(y) : P_C(y))$$

$$= 3.4387\text{e-}04 - 0.0003 = 0.4387\text{e-}04;$$

$$Gain_{\chi^2}(S) = \chi^2(P_T(y) : P_C(y)|S) - \chi^2(P_T(y) : P_C(y))$$

$$= 0.0057 - 0.0091 = -0.0034.$$

Ensembles

The previous sections discussed stand-alone decision trees for estimating uplift. Inspired by ensemble methods such as bagging, boosting, and random forests (see Chapter 2), one can also construct an ensemble of decision trees for uplift estimation. This approach can be expected to improve the stability of the resulting uplift model and increase the precision of the predictions because in various benchmarking studies, ensembles have been shown to yield superior performance (Dejaeger et al. 2012; Verbeke et al. 2012). The basic idea is to construct a set of B uplift trees, each built on a randomly selected fraction v of the training data containing both treatment and control group observations. For learning the individual uplift trees, any of the approaches discussed in the previous section can be adopted.

In this section, a number of ensemble approaches for uplift modeling will be discussed that have recently been proposed in the literature (Radcliffe and Surry 2011; Guelman, Guillén, and Pérez-Marín 2012, 2014, 2015; Soltys et al. 2015). The key idea of these approaches is to replace the base learner in bagging, boosting, or random forests with an uplift decision-tree learner, with additional adjustments that are made to address specific uplift modeling challenges and to exploit opportunities offered by these meta-learning schemes.

Uplift Random Forests

Algorithm 4.1 was adopted from Guelman et al. (2012) and introduces the uplift random forests ensemble approach for uplift modeling.

Note that the variable/split-point selection in step 7 of Algorithm 4.1 in the original approach defined in Guelman et al. (2012) is performed with the Kullback-Leibler divergence-based splitting criterion, as discussed above. However, alternative-splitting criteria can be used in this step.

In step 8 of the algorithm, it is mentioned that nodes are split into two or more branches. The Kullback-Leibler divergence-based splitting criterion as proposed in Guelman et al. (2014) limits the uplift decision trees to two child nodes. However, the original formulation in Rzepakowski and Jaroszewicz (2012) and the later adoption for uplift ensembles in Soltys et al. (2015) allow for the possibility of having splits with more than two child nodes. This latter approach can be useful to induce more-compact trees by providing more flexibility when growing the trees.

Algorithm 4.1 Uplift Random Forests

 1: **for** $b = 1$ to B do
 2:   Sample a fraction v of the training observations L without replacement
 3:   Grow an uplift decision tree UT_b on the sampled data:
 4:   **for** each terminal node **do**
 5:     **repeat**
 6:       Select p variables at random from the k variables
 7:       Select the best variable/split-point among the p variables
 8:       Split the node into two branches (or more)
 9:     **until** a minimum node size l_{min} is reached
10:   **end for**
11: **end for**
12: Output the ensemble of uplift trees $UT_b; b = \{1 \ldots B\}$
13: The predicted personalized treatment effect for a new observation is obtained by averaging the predictions of the individual trees in the ensemble:

$$\hat{\tau}(x) = \frac{1}{B} \sum\nolimits_{b=1}^{B} UT_b(x)$$

Uplift random forests come with two important parameters that must be determined: the number of trees B and the minimum node size l_{min}:

- ■ The number of trees B is to be optimized to maximize the performance of the ensemble as a function of the real-world problem characteristics. In Guelman et al. (2014), B is set to 500, whereas the default value of B is 100 in the R package published by the same authors implementing uplift random forests.[1] Experiments by the authors are inconclusive concerning the optimal value of B, which appears to be highly application dependent. Hence, we recommend employing a tuning approach as discussed in Chapter 2.

- ■ The minimum node size l_{min} represents the stopping criterion that is applied in determining the tree size. The default value of l_{min} is 20 in the above-mentioned implementation, but again, this parameter can be tuned for achieving optimal performance. An alternative stopping criterion or pruning approach could be plugged into this general formulation for constructing an ensemble. However, a key characteristic of random forests is to grow trees to maximum depth to compensate for the random variable selection at each split.

The final predicted uplift is then calculated by averaging the uplift over all trees. Again, alternative aggregation functions could be used—for instance, a function similar to the approach applied in boosting that accounts for tree performance when combining the estimates.

Uplift Bagging

Algorithm 4.2 is obtained from Soltys et al. (2015) and adapts the standard bagging meta-learning scheme, as proposed by Leo Breiman (1996), for uplift modeling. D_T and D_C represent the datasets containing the observations of the treatment and the control groups, respectively.

Note that in step 7 of Algorithm 4.2, as in Algorithm 4.1, any splitting criterion can be used. In Soltys et al. (2015), the Euclidean divergence criterion as discussed in the previous section is used. Similar to Algorithm 4.1, the final predicted uplift is calculated by

---

Algorithm 4.2 Uplift Bagging

1: **for** $b = 1$ to B **do**

2:      Draw a sample with replacement $D_{T,b}$ from D_T

3:      Draw a sample with replacement $D_{C,b}$ from D_C

4:      Grow an uplift decision tree UT_b on the samples $D_{T,b}$ and $D_{C,b}$:

5:      **for** each terminal node **do**

6:          **repeat**

7:              Select the best variable/split-point among the k variables

8:              Split the node into two (or more) branches

9:          **until** a minimum node size l_{min} is reached

10:     **end for**

11: **end for**

12: Output the ensemble of uplift trees UT_b; $b = \{1 \dots B\}$

13: The predicted personalized treatment effect for a new observation is obtained by averaging the predictions of the individual trees in the ensemble:

$$\hat{\tau}(x) = \frac{1}{B} \sum_{b=1}^{B} UT_b(x)$$

---

averaging the uplift over all trees, and the same two parameters B and l_{min} steer the ensemble learning process. Other than a minimum node size l_{min}, no pruning or stopping criterion is used when building the ensemble, meaning that *full*, or unpruned, trees are trained and included in the final model. It has been shown in the literature that this strategy in general improves the performance of the uplift ensemble when compared with including pruned trees (Soltys et al. 2015). Note that in the standard bagging technique as discussed in Chapter 2, pruned trees are used.

Causal Conditional Inference Forests

Two aspects of uplift random forests have been further improved in the causal conditional inference tree (CCIT) and forests (CCIF) approaches as described in Algorithm 4.3, adopted from Guelman et al. (2014). The CCIT is a decision tree learner that can be applied for constructing an ensemble (e.g., using the random forests meta-learning scheme as used in the CCIF approach and described in Algorithm 4.3). The enhancements of the CCIT approach over the uplift tree implemented in the uplift tree ensemble approach address overfitting and variable selection bias of variables with many possible splits or missing values. Overfitting has been addressed in other approaches through standard pruning strategies as explained in Chapter 2 (Radcliffe and Surry 2011; Soltys et al. 2015) but can also be addressed in the specific context of uplift modeling by performing statistical tests on the significance of the interactions between the treatment and splitting variables. The significance of the interactions can be evaluated with a procedure based on the theoretical framework of permutation tests. Full details on the testing procedure applied in step 7 in Algorithm 4.3 are provided in Guelman et al. (2014) and are beyond the scope of this chapter on uplift modeling. Because the proposed enhancements disentangle the splitting criterion into a variable selection step (step 11 in Algorithm 4.3) and a variable splitting step (step 12 in Algorithm 4.3), this procedure also addresses the variable selection bias already mentioned.

If the tested null hypotheses—stating that no significant interactions exist between the treatment variable and the predictor variables—cannot be rejected at some significance level α, then there exists no significant difference between the treatment and control group in terms of response. Therefore, a split based on such a variable will not induce child nodes in which an actual difference in response between the treatment and control group exists. In other words, no uplift is observed because of applying the treatment.

Algorithm 4.3 Causal Conditional Inference Forests

1: **for** $b = 1$ to B do

2:   Sample a fraction v of the training observations L with replacement such that the number of Treatment Group observations equals the number of Control Group observations, i.e.,
$$p(t = 1) = p(t = 0) = 0.5$$

3:   Grow a conditional causal inference tree $CCIT_b$ on the sampled data:

4:   **for** each terminal node **do**

5:     **repeat**

6:       Select p variables at random from the k variables

7:       Test the global null hypothesis of no interaction effect between the treatment t and any of the p variables at a significance level α based on a permutation test

8:       **if** the null hypothesis H_0 cannot be rejected **then**

9:         **stop**

10:       **Else**

11:         Select the variable x_j with the strongest interaction effect

12:         Split x_j in two disjoint sets using $G^2(S)$ split criterion

13:       **end if**

14:     **until** a minimum node size l_{min} is reached

15:   **end for**

16: **end for**

17: Output the ensemble of uplift trees $CCIT_b; b = \{1 \dots B\}$

18: The predicted personalized treatment effect for a new observation is obtained by averaging the predictions of the individual trees in the ensemble:
$$\hat{\tau}(x) = \frac{1}{B}\sum_{b=1}^{B} UT_b(x)$$

Conversely, when the null hypothesis is rejected and significant interactions exist, the predictor variable with the most significant or strongest interaction effect is selected. Subsequently, a split is defined on this variable as indicated in step 12 of Algorithm 4.3 by applying the $G^2(S)$ split criterion as proposed by Su et al. (2009). The latter is essentially a chi-squared interaction test between the treatment variable and the selected variable, which is binned in two groups by a given split.

Continuous or Ordered Outcomes

The discussion on uplift modeling has thus far focused on binary outcome prediction and, more specifically, on response modeling. In the literature on uplift modeling, we almost exclusively find approaches and case studies aimed at estimating the effect of a treatment on a binary outcome variable. However, in many settings, the target variable of interest is continuous or ordinal in nature. For instance, we could setup a marketing campaign that aims at increasing customer spending rather than response. Alternatively, we could aim at increasing customer lifetime value, as discussed in Chapter 3.

It would be of great value and further boost the profitability of marketing campaigns and customer loyalty programs if we were able to model the long-term effects of such efforts on *partial* or *total* spending behavior. By *partial*, we refer to a single or limited selection of products or services over a short time span, whereas *total* refers to all products or services over a long time horizon.

Another example of a continuous target variable stems from the field of credit risk analytics, in which the loss given default related to a credit represents the fraction of the outstanding exposure that is not recovered in the case of default (Baesens, Roesch, Scheule 2016). From a profitability perspective, it is of great importance to know which collection strategies and actions effectively reduce the LGD. In this setting, uplift modeling with a continuous target variable has practical use to estimate the net effect of different treatments on the final loss. This use will allow minimization of the final loss by optimizing and customizing the exact treatments applied to defaulted obligors.

Except for Radcliffe and Surry (2011), who explicitly indicate the extensibility of the significance-based uplift tree approach for the continuous case, little effort appears to have been invested in developing uplift regression approaches. Hence, this field remains to be explored by scientists and practitioners.

Similar to regression trees, which define an alternative to classification trees for continuous target prediction (see Chapter 2), an equivalent approach has been proposed for the significance-based uplift tree. To find the optimal split, SBUT fits a linear regression model to predict the target variable in each child node as a function of treatment and child node membership and the interaction between these two. This technique allows testing for the significance of the treatment and uplift in increasing the response probability. Such a linear model can, of course, also be fitted in the case of a continuous outcome target variable. Thus, SBUT is directly applicable without any main adjustments to the continuous case.

Additionally, bagging, boosting, and random forests meta-learning schemes can be applied in combination with SBUT as a base learner leading to ensembles of uplift regression trees. Such schemes can lead to a more powerful uplift regression model than a stand-alone tree.

Alternatively, a two-model-based approach can be applied to the continuous case, fitting a separate regression model to both the treatment and control groups. The difference in the estimates is the uplift. The same drawbacks and advantages apply to the two-model approach for continuous target uplift modeling as discussed for the binary case.

Finally, Lo's approach can also be extended in a straightforward manner. For example, including the treatment variable and interaction terms with the treatment variable in a linear regression or neural network allows calculation of the difference in estimated output for the treatment variable taking a value of one and zero, respectively.

Evaluating these *continuous* uplift models will require the development of specific evaluation measures because, to our knowledge, no metrics have been defined in the literature on uplift modeling thus far that apply to the continuous case. This development could be challenging because evaluating *binary* uplift models is also not straightforward, as will be illustrated and discussed in the next section.

EVALUATION OF UPLIFT MODELS

A conventional classification or regression model is evaluated by comparing the predictions made by the model on observations in a holdout test set with the observed outcomes for these observations. The differences between predictions and outcomes—that is, the errors on the observations in the test set—can be aggregated or summarized by means of performance measures discussed in Chapter 2 such as AUC, accuracy ratio, or MSE. Further insight into the performance of the model is provided by plotting factors such as the receiver operating characteristic (ROC) curve, correlation plots, and lift curves. Such visualizations can offer more-detailed insight about the performance but are less handy for comparing or expressing the overall accuracy or precision, which is exactly when performance indices are useful.

Although the use of an independent test set is also recommended for evaluating uplift models, we need alternative evaluation measures and visual evaluation approaches because of the *fundamental problem of causal inference* (FPCI) (Holland 1986). The FPCI essentially reduces to the simple fact that we cannot *simultaneously* observe for a single individual or entity the outcome of all possible treatments. Note that in general, *no treatment* should also be considered one of the possible treatments.

Because of the FPCI, we cannot be certain whether a treatment has any effect on an individual's behavior. Consequently, we cannot observe the value of the target variable we aim to estimate with an uplift model. Because the target variable, or uplift, for a single entity is not observable, we cannot calculate the *error* that is made by an uplift model by comparing estimates with outcomes at the entity level.

What we can observe at the entity level and what we must use for evaluation is the post hoc outcome, given that a treatment was or was not applied. By grouping individuals accordingly and calculating the observed difference in behavior between *similar* groups of individuals who received and did not receive a treatment, an indicator of the performance of the model is obtained, as will be further elaborated below. The meaning of *similar* in this sentence will appear to be of crucial importance.

To evaluate an uplift model, the first step is to randomly select a test set consisting of observations from both the treatment and control groups as present in the development base; see Figure 4.2. The distribution of treatment and control group customers in the test set is preferably identical to the overall distribution in the development base and in the training set, thus avoiding possible sources of bias.

In the remainder of this section, we will initially discuss visual evaluation approaches, after which we will define a number of performance metrics.

Visual Evaluation Approaches

The uplift by decile graph and the gains charts are two intuitive visual evaluation approaches that are often used to gain insight into the performance of an uplift model.

Uplift by Decile Graph

To plot the uplift by decile graph, in a first step, all of the observations in both the treatment and control group in the test set are scored with the uplift model. Subsequently, observations from both groups together are ranked from high to low estimated uplift. The response rate can then be plotted separately for the observations of the treatment and control groups for each decile, as shown in the upper panel of Figure 4.6. Additionally, the difference in response rate in each decile (i.e., the *Uplift by decile* graph), can be plotted as shown in the lower panel of Figure 4.6.

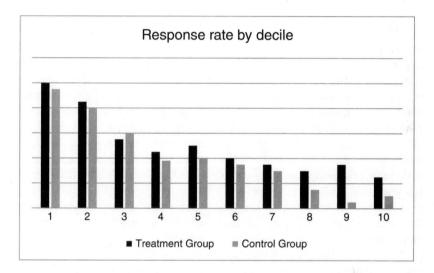

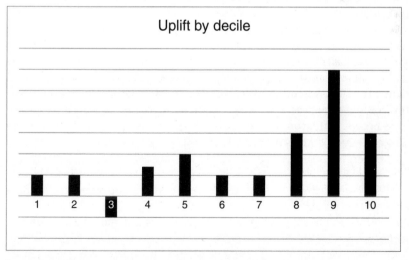

Figure 4.6 Response rate by decile graph for both treatment and control groups (upper panel) and uplift by deciles graph (lower panel).

The plots in Figure 4.6 allow analyzing the performance of an uplift model. Customers in the treatment group received a treatment to boost the response rate, whereas customers in the control group received no treatment. By comparing the response rates in both groups, the effect of the treatment can be observed. Two factors affect the differences in response rates observed in Figure 4.6:

1. Effectiveness of the campaign
2. Effectiveness of the model

The effectiveness of the campaign will affect the overall amount of uplift that is observed when comparing the full treatment group with the full control group. When the bars pertaining to the treatment group in the top panel of Figure 4.6 are of the same height as the bars pertaining to the control group, then the bars in the bottom panel of Figure 4.6 will be short, meaning that little uplift is achieved and the campaign appears to be ineffective. How much uplift is obtained or can be expected depends on the nature of the particular application. For some products, a strong uplift can be anticipated, whereas for other products (e.g., very expensive products), a limited uplift is to be expected.

The effectiveness of the model, conversely, becomes apparent from the bar plot in the lower panel of Figure 4.6. Ideally, the (positive) uplift should be situated as much as possible on the left side of the bar plot, meaning that the model assigns a high uplift score to customers who indeed display a higher response rate when treated (i.e., to the *Persuadables* in the customer base).

A good uplift model allows selecting treatment groups for which the treatment has a significant net effect on the response rate. Hence, if observations in both treatment and control groups are ranked using the uplift model, then by comparing the response rates in the treatment and control groups as a function of the uplift cutoff score, an indication of the quality of the model is obtained. The difference in response rate between treatment and control groups is expected to be relatively large for high cutoffs and decreases for decreasing cutoffs. The higher the difference at high cutoffs, the better the model manages to detect *Persuadables*.

By comparing the response rates in the treatment and control groups for the observations with the lowest predicted uplift scores, we can observe whether the treatment produces a negative effect on the propensity to respond. This result would occur if a lower response rate were observed among the treated versus the control groups, yielding a negative uplift or *downlift* because of the treatment.

Uplift can be negative for subgroups when the treatment has a negative effect on response behavior. This effect is observed for the so-called *Do-Not-Disturb* customers, as discussed previously in this chapter (see Figure 4.1). Observing downlift for the lowest ranked customers, that is, the observations with the lowest predicted uplift by the model, indicates good model quality because the model manages to identify *Do-Not-Disturb* customers accurately.

Between the *Persuadables*, who should be assigned the highest uplift values by the model, and the *Do-Not-Disturbs*, who should be assigned the lowest uplift by the model, the model should rank the *Sure Things* and *Lost Causes*. In an absolute sense, these last two groups should both be assigned a zero value for uplift because the treatment has no effect at all, in either a positive manner (e.g., for the *Persuadables*, who therefore should receive a positive uplift value) or in a negative manner (for example, for the *Do-Not-Disturbs*, who therefore should receive a negative uplift score).

This ranking leads to the response rate curve for a perfect uplift model, as displayed in Figure 4.7. The rationale behind the optimal response rate curve is the following: the perfect uplift model allows ranking customers according to expected effect. If we rank from high (left) to low (right) expected effect, then the optimal model initially ranks all *Persuadables*. The response rate can therefore initially be expected to equal zero in the control group and to equal 100% in the treatment group.

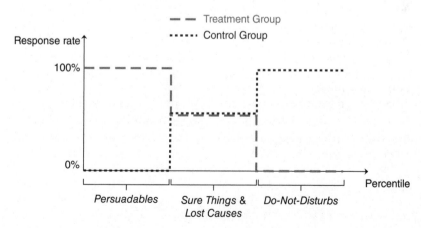

Figure 4.7 Response rate curve for the perfect uplift model, plotting the response rates for the treatment and control groups ranked according to estimated uplift.

Next, after the *Persuadables*, the optimal uplift model ranks the customers for whom the treatment has no effect, either in a positive or in a negative manner. These customers are the *Sure Things*, who buy anyway, and the *Lost Causes*, who will never buy. The optimal uplift model does not distinguish between these two groups because the uplift for both groups is the same and equal to zero. The response rate in this group is different from zero because we have the *Sure Things*, who respond, and is different from 100% because we also have the *Lost Causes*, who do not respond. Note that the response rate level shown in Figure 4.7 for the combined group of *Sure Things* and *Lost Causes* was arbitrarily set at approximately 50%, assuming this group consists evenly of *Sure Things* and *Lost Causes*. Of course, the proportion of *Persuadables, Sure Things, Lost Causes* and *Do-Not-Disturbs* depends on the nature of the application. Therefore, the cutoff points on the x-axis shown on the curve for the optimal model in Figure 4.7 are also arbitrary.

Finally, the model ranks the customers for whom the treatment has a negative effect, that is, the *Do-Not-Disturbs*. Because these customers respond when not treated, we observe a response rate equal to 100% in the control group. Conversely, a response rate of zero is observed in the treatment group for these customers because they do not respond if treated.

Note that in Figure 4.6, the uplift in the top deciles is rather low and even negative in the third decile. The largest uplift is situated in the bottom deciles, corresponding to the customers who have been assigned a low score or uplift by the uplift model! Therefore, we can conclude that the uplift model yielding the uplift by decile graph in Figure 4.6 is not performing well and has limited practical value. In Figure 4.8, an uplift by decile curve of a *good* (i.e., accurate) uplift model is shown. A large uplift is achieved for the customers receiving the highest uplift scores, whereas negative uplift is observed for the customers assigned the lowest scores. Note that this curve is closer to the optimal shape of the curve, as shown in Figure 4.7.

An important final remark concerns the actual values of the estimated uplift, which are less relevant. Although calibrated uplift estimates that are exact in an *absolute* manner could be useful, the ranking of customers, or the *relative* scores, are more important.

Cumulative Uplift or Qini Curve

The performance of an uplift model can alternatively be visualized by plotting the cumulative difference in response rate between treatment and control groups in the test set as a function of a selected

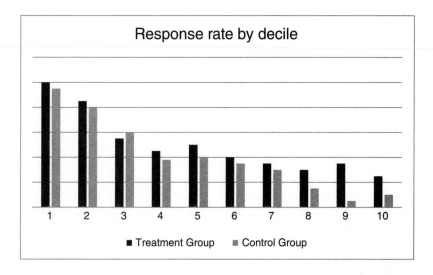

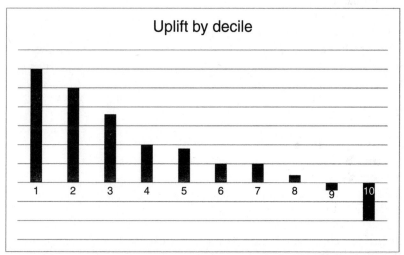

Figure 4.8 Uplift by decile curve of an accurate uplift model.

fraction *x* of the customers as ranked by the uplift model from high to low uplift. This curve is called the cumulative uplift, cumulative incremental gains, or Qini curve (Radcliffe 2007). The cumulative difference in response rate is measured as the absolute or relative number of additional responders, that is, respectively expressed as the additional number as an amount of responders or as a fraction of the total population. Note that performance is again evaluated by comparing groups of observations rather than individual observations.

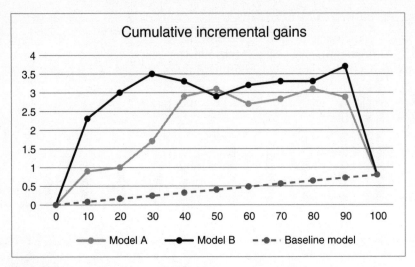

Figure 4.9 Cumulative incremental gains charts or Qini curves for two uplift models and the baseline model.

Figure 4.9 displays a Qini curve for an uplift model that can be benchmarked to the diagonal representing the Qini curve of a baseline random model. The cumulative incremental gains achieved by the random model are purely due to the treatment effect, and there is no additional gain by using the model to select customers. A *good* uplift model therefore should have a Qini curve that is well above the diagonal, thus further increasing the effect of the treatment as measured in terms of response.

Note that in Figure 4.9, the cumulative incremental gains on the *y*-axis could be expressed relative to the overall uplift effect, or increase in response rate, that is achieved by the treatment when comparing the full treatment and control group response rates. The overall uplift effect is equal to the cumulative incremental gain for treating 100% of the population. The Qini curves of the two uplift models shown in Figure 4.9 have not been normalized, and, as seen in the figure, the overall uplift effect of the treatment is approximately 0.8%. Moreover, the uplift effect is greater than 0.8% when selecting a smaller fraction of customers because the cumulative incremental gains for fractions below 100% are well above the diagonal. Because the distribution of treatment and control group customers along the uplift score range are generally not identical, a correction might be applied when plotting the Qini curve.

Performance Metrics

Performance metrics assess the quality of uplift models by summarizing the accuracy of the predictions made by the model in a single number. Although such metrics are less apt to provide detailed insight in the fine granular results, they do have the advantage of allowing easy comparison between different models. Often, alternative models are developed, and subsequently, they need to be compared. Likewise, for pruning decision trees, a performance metric is also required. In addition to helping identify the best model, performance metrics may serve as the objective function when building an uplift model (Naranjo 2012). This is outside the scope of this chapter but will be discussed in the next chapter on profit-driven analytics.

When adopting the visual evaluation approaches discussed above for comparing different models, one may find inconclusive results because performance is a function of the targeting depth, i.e., the fraction of customers that is treated. For example, in Figure 4.9, the Qini curves of two models are plotted. It can be seen that the black curve of uplift model B tops the gray curve of uplift model A for most values x, representing the fraction of customers that are treated. However, for $x = 50\%$, that is, when approximately half of the customers are treated, it appears from the curves that model A performs better than model B. Thus, the plotted Qini curves do not offer a conclusive answer to the question of which of these two models performs best (although indeed one may be inclined to select model B).

Although metrics are clearly of great practical use, it is challenging to develop an adapted and intuitive measure for uplift model evaluation. In this section, we will discuss two measures proposed in the literature that are directly related to the visual evaluation approaches introduced in the previous section: quantile uplift and Qini measures.

Quantile Uplift Measures

In many studies on uplift modeling, performance is evaluated by reporting the uplift obtained when treating a specific quantile or proportion of the population. For instance, the top decile uplift is often used as a metric. Note that this value can directly be observed in the uplift by deciles graph discussed above, which additionally provides the uplift for other deciles. Accordingly, little added value is provided using quantile uplift values, although they do facilitate the communication, reporting, and comparison of model performance. They also may be directly linked to the actual usage of the uplift model when in practice the top decile will be effectively selected and targeted in a campaign. Note that top decile uplift relates to the uplift by decile graph in a manner very similar to how the top decile lift relates to the lift curve, as discussed in Chapter 2.

Somewhat more refined and informative are **quantile uplift ratio measures,** such as the ratio of the uplift achieved in a quantile over the overall or baseline uplift (Radcliffe and Surry 2011). For instance, the ratio of the uplift in the top decile over the baseline uplift can be used, which again reminds us of the top-decile lift measure discussed in Chapter 2 in terms of providing an indication of how much improvement the model offers over randomly selecting a treatment group.

One alternative ratio measure that provides an indication of the ability of a model to rank customers accurately in terms of the resorted effect of the treatment is the ratio of an upper quantile uplift value and a bottom quantile uplift value. For instance, the ratio of the top decile uplift and the bottom decile uplift provides an indication of how well *Persuadables* receive a high uplift score and *Do-Not-Disturbs* a low uplift score.

Note that quantile uplift based measures may be highly sensitive to the selected quantile or cutoff value of the uplift score and therefore can lead to ineffective conclusions when they are used for model comparison. As indicated by Radcliffe and Surry (2011), *"Changing the value of the cutoff may change or reverse the results of a comparison."* The Qini measure discussed next provides an alternative that does not depend on the cutoff score, thus greatly improving the quantile uplift measures in this respect.

Qini Measure

The Qini measure, introduced by Radcliffe (2007) and equivalent to the AUUC (Rzepakowski, Piotr; Jaroszewicz 2010), is adapted from the well-known Gini measure to evaluate binary classification models. The Gini measure (also called the accuracy ratio) is related to the Gini curve (also called the cumulative gains, cumulative percentage captured, or cumulative accuracy profile curve), which plots the fraction of captured positive class observations as a function of increasing cutoff score or selected fraction of the population as ranked by the model, and is related to the AUC measure as discussed in Chapter 2.

The Qini measure is defined in relation to the cumulative incremental gains, cumulative uplift, or Qini curve discussed above. It measures the area between the Qini curve of the uplift model and the Qini curve of the baseline random model—that is, the diagonal in Figure 4.9.

Note that the Qini measure is different from the Gini measure in the sense that it is *unscaled* and not limited between zero and one. The Gini measure takes the ratio of the area between the diagonal and the Gini curve of the model and the area between the diagonal and the optimal curve of the perfect classification model. Similarly, one could think of taking the ratio of the unscaled Qini of a model and the unscaled Qini of a perfect model, which is the area between the diagonal and the optimal Qini curve. One obvious question is what the optimal curve would look like. Indeed, this curve relates to the optimal non-cumulative uplift curve, which is shown in Figure 4.7 and stems from the optimal response curves for the treatment and control group, also shown in Figure 4.7. The cumulative version of this optimal uplift curve is the optimal cumulative uplift or Qini curve.

The issue with the optimal Qini curve is that the cutoff points are unknown since we cannot know (because of the FPCI) how many *Persuadables, Sure Things, Lost Causes,* and *Do-Not-Disturbs* there are in the population. Thus, the denominator required to scale or normalize the unscaled Qini measure in a manner similar to that of the Gini measure cannot be determined. In Radcliffe and Surry (2011), a simplified optimal Qini curve is proposed. This optimal curve ignores downlift and characterizes the optimal uplift model as fully achieving the observed overall uplift $\bar{u}$ in the treatment over the control group by selecting the proportion $\bar{u}$ of highest-ranked or -scored customers. This enables the calculation of an unscaled Qini metric for the optimal model and the scaling of the Qini metric so its value is between zero and one.

Although facilitating a comparison of uplift models and often used in the academic literature on uplift modeling, the unscaled Qini has limited practical use because it does not offer a benchmark value that allows easy interpretation, and on a related note, it is application dependent. This means that Qini values of models developed on different datasets, for different treatments, etc., cannot be compared. This is exactly what is valuable about measures such as AUC and R^2, which allow data scientists to interpret the performance of a model by comparing it to other models.

Thus, the scaled Qini effectively improves on the unscaled Qini in the sense that it facilitates interpretation and comparison.

Nonetheless, an additional drawback of the Qini measure that remains when scaling concerns the assessment of the full ranking made by the Qini measure. Because the Qini measure (similar to the AUC or Gini measure) evaluates model performance across all possible cutoff scores, it accounts for how well the model ranks every entity in the population, whether that entity has a very low, low, medium, high, or very high uplift score.

Typically, treating the full customer base is not optimal in terms of profitability, as will be further elaborated in Chapter 6. Thus, in many practical settings, we are interested only in how well the model performs on a fraction of the population. More specifically, we are concerned about how well the model performs on the customers that will effectively be treated. Often this concerns only a small fraction of customers (i.e., those with the highest uplift scores).

As will be discussed in the Chapter 6, to maximize the payoff of running a marketing campaign, the selected fraction of customers to be treated needs to be optimized as a function of the power or accuracy of the model (Verbeke et al. 2012; Verbraken et al. 2013). It will be shown that the optimal fraction should be used as a cutoff score to evaluate the performance of a model for reaching valid conclusions. A similar procedure could be developed for evaluating uplift models but may be too complex to elaborate in detail. Thus, there may be a sufficient, simplified version that sets a cutoff score close or equal to the operating point, as discussed for the quantile uplift measures. Such a cutoff score could then be used for calculating a quantile Qini measure—for instance, the top decile Qini, which is equal to the area between the Qini curve and the diagonal over the interval $x \in [0,0.1]$, with x representing the selected fraction of customers.

PRACTICAL GUIDELINES

Two-Step Approach for Developing Uplift Models

Various approaches for uplift modeling have been discussed in this chapter, hence an important question that may arise is which technique you should adopt for practically developing an uplift model. Although heavily dependent on the available time for developing the model, on specific requirements that hold within the application setting and personal preferences, as well as on the available skill and experience of the involved data scientist(s), we present the following guidelines and two-step approach for developing uplift models:

1. *Select a subset of good candidate techniques from the various approaches that are available.* Good can be defined with respect to the above-mentioned factors:

   a. *Available development time:* if little time is available, a small number or even just a single approach can be selected, preferably approaches the data scientist is experienced with or at least understands well, and which require little time to implement and apply. Recommendable approaches here are the two-model approaches and regression approaches, including Lo's, Lai's, and the generalized Lai method. When more time is available a more extensive set can be selected, or alternatively, promising but new (to the data scientist) techniques can be tested such as uplift random forests or bagging.

   b. *Available skill and experience:* when the data scientist has great skill and experience in applying logistic regression, it makes sense to adopt the two-model or Lo's approach, or alternatively Lai's or the generalized Lai method, before testing tree-based approaches. Conversely, when the data scientist has often used decision trees and ensembles before, then tree-based and ensemble approaches may be preferred and selected as candidate techniques.

   c. *Specific requirements and personal preferences:* for instance, when the interpretability of the resulting model is important (see analytical evaluation criteria as discussed in Chapter 1), then *good* candidate techniques are regression- and tree-based approaches, which allow to gain insight in the extracted patterns and selected predictors variables. Personal preferences of the data scientist may lead to selecting, for example, tree-based approaches instead of regression-based techniques.

   In addition to these considerations, it is recommended to include at least one technique from each of the various groups of uplift modeling approaches discussed in this chapter. Given the substantial variability in terms of performance that is observed in experimental evaluations of these techniques, as such we ensure not to miss out on a substantially better uplift model by excluding a priori certain groups of approaches that may be better fit to the particular problem characteristics.

2. *Implement and experimentally evaluate the selected uplift modeling approaches in terms of the appropriate evaluation measures.* Prior to implementation and evaluation, an order in which the selected techniques are to be developed should be established. In a first step, one may apply a *simpler* approach so as to gain insight in the data and problem characteristics, as well as to establish a baseline model to which subsequent models can be compared. Recommendable candidate baseline techniques are the two-model approach and Lo's approach. These have the advantage of allowing data scientists to reuse standard analytical techniques that they might be experienced with, such as logistic regression and decision trees, although as well neural networks or ensembles can be adopted if preferred or appropriate. The order in which the remaining selected techniques are applied can be decided on in function of both the expected performance and the required time and difficulty to implement the approaches. Clearly, an approach that is expected to yield good performance at low implementation cost should be tested before spending resources on implementing experimental, risky approaches.

Purely from a performance perspective, experimental evaluations indicate ensemble-based approaches to yield overall the best performance in terms of Qini measure as well as quantile uplift measures (Kane et al., 2014; Soltys et al. 2015). Experiments that we conducted ourselves indicate uplift random forests overall to be a powerful approach, but at the same time we find a two-model approach, as well as Lo's and the generalized Lai method to perform well. However, substantial variation is observed in terms of performance across applications, and often, alternative approaches do better for a specific dataset. Also, the base response rate and the fraction of customers that will eventually be treated have an important impact and should be acknowledged in adopting the most appropriate approach in a particular setting. Therefore, the second step in the two-step approach—the experimental evaluation of the selected candidate techniques—is of critical importance in selecting the optimal solution.

Implementations and Software

All of the ensemble uplift modeling approaches discussed in this section have been implemented in the open source Uplift Modeling R package published and maintained by Leo Guelman, which can be found online at https://CRAN.R-project.org/package=uplift and which seamlessly integrates within the open source statistical software R (R Core team 2015). The SBUT and DBUT uplift decision tree techniques have been implemented in this package as base learners that can be selected in combination with the uplift random forests, uplift bagging, or causal conditional inference forests meta-learning schemes.

The two-model and regression-based approaches can be implemented in a straightforward manner in standard analytics software. Lo's approach requires including the treatment and treatment interaction effects in the set of candidate predictor variables when developing a binary prediction model, whereas Lai's method and the generalized Lai method require a transformation of the target variable as illustrated in Table 4.4 and Table 4.5.

Elaborated example applications, including data and code to develop uplift models, are published on the accompanying book website: www.profit-analytics.com.

CONCLUSION

Uplift modeling essentially allows us to distill and estimate the net effect of a treatment on an individual entity (e.g., the change in a customer's purchasing or churning behavior resulting from targeting that customer in a response or retention campaign). The main challenge in uplift modeling is the fundamental problem of causal inference. Essentially, the FPCI concerns the impossibility of simultaneously observing the effect of multiple different treatments on the same entity. For instance, a customer cannot be targeted with a response campaign while being excluded from that campaign. If this were possible, we would be able to observe or measure the exact difference in behavior because of the treatment, but clearly, we cannot. Therefore, uplift modeling contrasts and analyzes the behavior of groups of entities receiving different treatments to indirectly learn the effect of a treatment as a function of an entity's characteristics.

For the specific purpose of uplift modeling, a relatively elaborate experimental design needs to be established to gather the required data, as extensively discussed in this chapter. Various modeling approaches have been introduced for estimating uplift, ranging from simple yet intuitive approaches to complex but more powerful techniques. Evaluating the obtained uplift models is not a trivial task: again, due to the FPCI, it is impossible to simply compare predictions and outcomes. Therefore, to provide detailed insight in uplift model performance, specialized plots and measures such as uplift curves and the Qini measure are needed.

REVIEW QUESTIONS

Multiple Choice Questions

Question 1

Treatment responders are either:

    a. Sure Things or Do-Not-Disturbs
    b. Lost Causes or Persuadables
    c. Persuadables or Sure Things
    d. Lost Causes or Do-Not-Disturbs

Question 2

Treatment nonresponders are either:

    a. Sure Things or Do-Not-Disturbs
    b. Lost Causes or Persuadables
    c. Persuadables or Sure Things
    d. Lost Causes or Do-Not-Disturbs

Question 3

Control responders are either:

    a. Sure Things or Do-Not-Disturbs
    b. Lost Causes or Persuadables
    c. Persuadables or Sure Things
    d. Lost Causes or Do-Not-Disturbs

Question 4

Control nonresponders are either:

    a. Sure Things or Do-Not-Disturbs
    b. Lost Causes or Persuadables
    c. Persuadables or Sure Things
    d. Lost Causes or Do-Not-Disturbs

Question 5

What is the formula of true lift?

    a. true Lift $= (R_{M,T} - R_{M,C}) - (R_{R,T} - R_{R,C})$
    b. true Lift $= (R_{M,C} - R_{M,T}) - (R_{R,T} - R_{R,C})$
    c. true Lift $= (R_{M,T} - R_{M,C}) - (R_{R,C} - R_{R,T})$
    d. true Lift $= (R_{M,C} - R_{M,T}) - (R_{R,C} - R_{R,T})$

Question 6

Given model A yielding $R_{M,T} = 7.1\%, R_{M,C} = 2.8\% R_{R,T} = 6.4\% R_{R,C} = 2.9\%$, and model B yielding $R_{M,T} = 13.1\%, R_{M,C} = 8.8\% R_{R,T} = 10.5\% R_{R,C} = 6.8\%$, which is the best model according to the true lift evaluation criterion?

a. Model A
b. Model B
c. Model A and Model B perform equally well.
d. There is not enough information provided allowing to calculate the true lift evaluation criterion

Question 7

What is the lift score following Lai's method and the Generalized Lai method for a customer with the following probability scores: $p(TR|x) = 0.14, p(TN|x) = 0.04, p(CR|x) = 0.48,$ and $p(CN|x) = 0.24$.

a. Lai $= -0.62$ and generalized Lai $= 0.08$
b. Lai $= 0.08$ and generalized Lai $= 0.28$
c. Lai $= -0.14$ and generalized Lai $= 0.22$
d. Lai $= 0.25$ and generalized Lai $= -0.19$

Question 8

What is the Kullback-Leibler divergence gain for the following split?

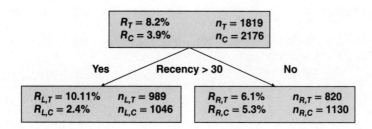

a. 0.0008
b. 0.0231
c. 0.0278
d. 0.0179

Question 9

Which is not a visual evaluation approach for assessing the performance of an uplift model?

    a. Cumulative accuracy profile curve
    b. Uplift by decile graph
    c. Response rate by decile graph
    d. Qini curve

Question 10

Which is not an appropriate evaluation metric for assessing the performance of an uplift model?

    a. AUUC
    b. Top-decile uplift
    c. AUC
    d. Qini

Open Questions

Question 1

Discuss the experimental design to collect the required data for uplift modeling and the differences with a traditional setup for applying analytics.

Question 2

Explain, in your own words, what interaction effects are and why these are explicitly included in Lo's method.

Question 3

Explain why and how the target variable in Lai's method is being redefined.

Question 4

Explain which uplift modeling approaches can be applied for uplift regression modeling and which cannot be applied.

Question 5

Define and discuss the area under the uplift curve as an evaluation metric for uplift models.

NOTE

1. https://CRAN.R-project.org/package=uplift.

REFERENCES

Baesens B., D. Roesch, and H. Scheule. 2016. *Credit Risk Analytics—Measurement Techniques, Applications and Examples in SAS*. Hoboken, NJ: John Wiley and Sons.

Breiman, L. 1996. "Bagging Predictors." *Machine Learning* 24 (2):123–140.

Breiman, L., J. H. Friedman, R. Olshen, C. J. Stone, and R. A. Olsen. 1984. *Classification and Regression Trees*. Monterey, CA: Wadsworth and Brooks.

Chickering, D. M., and D. Heckerman. (2000, June). "A Decision Theoretic Approach to Targeted Advertising." In *Proceedings of the Sixteenth conference on Uncertainty in artificial intelligence* (pp. 82–88). Morgan Kaufmann Publishers Inc.,

Collett, D. 2015. *Modelling survival data in medical research*. CRC press.

Csiszar, I., and P. C. Shields. 2004. "Information Theory and Statistics: A Tutorial." *Foundations and Trends in Communications and Information Theory* 1: 417–528.

Dejaeger, K., W. Verbeke, D. Martens, and B. Baesens. 2012. "Data Mining Techniques for Software Effort Estimation: A Comparative Study." *Software Engineering, IEEE Transactions* 38 (2): 375–397.

Goetghebeur, E., and K. Lapp. 1997. "The Effect of Treatment Compliance in a Placebo-Controlled Trial: Regression with Unpaired Data." *Journal of the Royal Statistical Society: Series C (Applied Statistics)* 46 (3): 351–364.

Guelman, L., M. Guillén, and A. M. Pérez-Marín. 2012. "Random Forests for Uplift Modeling: An Insurance Customer Retention Case." Lecture Notes in Business Information Processing 115 LNBIP, 123–133.

Guelman, L., M. Guillén, and A. M. Pérez-Marín. 2014. "Optimal Personalized Treatment Rules for Marketing Interventions: A Review of Methods, a New Proposal, and an Insurance Case Study." (working paper) Retrieved from http://diposit.ub.edu/dspace/bitstream/2445/98449/1/Risk14-06_Guelman.pdf.

Guelman, L., M. Guillén, and A. M. Pérez-Marín. 2015. "A Decision Support Framework to Implement Optimal Personalized Marketing Interventions." *Decision Support Systems* 72: 24–32.

Hansotia, B., and B. Rukstales. 2002a. "Direct Marketing for Multichannel Retailers: Issues, Challenges and Solutions." *Journal of Database Marketing* 9 (3): 259–266.

Hansotia, B., and B. Rukstales. 2002b. "Incremental Value Modeling." *Journal of Interactive Marketing* 16 (3): 35–46.

Holland, P. W. 1986. "Statistics and Causal Inference." *Journal of the American Statistical Association* 81 (396): 945.

Holmgren, E., and Koch, G. 1997. "Statistical Modeling of Dose-Response Relationships in Clinical Trials—A Case Study." *Journal of Biopharmaceutical Statistics* 7 (2): 301–311.

Issenberg, S. 2012. "How President Obama's Campaign Used Big Data to Rally Individual Voters." *MIT Technology Review.*

Kane, K., V. S. Y. Lo, and J. Zheng. 2014. "Mining for the Truly Responsive Customers and Prospects Using True-Lift Modeling: Comparison of New and Existing Methods." *Journal of Marketing Analytics* 2 (4): 218–238.

Kass, G. V. 1980. "An Exploratory Technique for Investigating Large Quantities of Categorical Data." *Applied Statistics* 29: 119–127.

Kohavi, R., and R. Longbotham. 2015. "Online Controlled Experiments and A/B Tests." *Encyclopedia of Machine Learning and Data Mining* (Ries 2011), 1–11.

Lai, L. Y.-T. 2006. *Influential Marketing: A New Direct Marketing Strategy Addressing the Existence of Voluntary Buyers.* Simon Fraser University.

Lai, Y. T., K. Wang, D. Ling, H. Shi, and J. Zhang. 2006. "Direct Marketing When There Are Voluntary Buyers." In Proceedings of the IEEE International Conference on Data Mining, ICDM, 922–927.

Lee, L. 1999. "Measures of Distributional Similarity." In Proceedings of the 37th Annual Meeting of the Association for Computational Linguistics, College Park, Maryland, USA, 25–32.

Lo, V. S. Y. 2002. "The True Lift Model: A Novel Data Mining Approach to Response Modeling in Database Marketing." *ACM SIGKDD Explorations Newsletter* 4 (2): 78–86.

Naranjo, O. M. 2012. "Testing a New Metric for Uplift Models" (August). Retrieved from http://www.maths.ed.ac.uk/~mthdat25/uplift/Mesalles NaranjoOscar-1.

Quinlan, J. R. 1993. *C4.5: Programs for Machine Learning.* San Francisco: Morgan Kaufmann Publishers Inc.

R Core team. 2015. "R: A Language and Environment for Statistical Computing. R Foundation for Statistical Computing." Vienna, Austria. Retrieved from http://www.r-project.org/.

Radcliffe, N. J. 2007. "Using Control Groups to Target on Predicted Lift: Building and Assessing Uplift Model." *Direct Marketing Analytics Journal* 3:14–21.

Radcliffe, N. J., and P. D. Surry. 1999. "Differential Response Analysis: Modeling True Responses by Isolating the Effect of a Single Action." *In Credit Scoring and Credit Control VI.*

Radcliffe, N. J., and P. D. Surry. 2011. "Real-World Uplift Modeling with Significance-Based Uplift Trees." White Paper TR-2011-1, Stochastic Solutions, (section 6). Retrieved from http://www.stochasticsolutions.com/pdf/sig-based-up-trees.pdf.

Russek-Cohen, E., and R. M. Simon. 1997. "Evaluating Treatments When a Gender by Treatment Interaction May Exist." *Statistics in Medicine* 16 (4): 455–464.

Rzepakowski, P., and S. Jaroszewicz. 2010. "Decision Trees for Uplift Modeling." In *Data Mining (ICDM), 2010 IEEE 10th International Conference on* (pp. 441–450). IEEE.

Rzepakowski, P., and S. Jaroszewicz. 2012. "Decision Trees for Uplift Modeling with Single and Multiple Treatments." *Knowledge and Information Systems*, 32 (2): 303–327.

Siegel, E. 2011. "Uplift Modeling: Predictive Analytics Can't Optimize Marketing Decisions Without It." *Prediction Impact white paper sponsored by Pitney Bowes Business Insight.*

Soltys, M., S., Jaroszewicz, S., and P. Rzepakowski. 2015. "Ensemble Methods for Uplift Modeling." *Data Mining and Knowledge Discovery* 29 (6): 1531–1559.

Su, X., D. M. Nickerson, C.-L. Tsai, H. Wang, and B. Li. 2009. "Subgroup Analysis via Recursive Partitioning." *Journal of Machine Learning Research* 10: 141–158.

Verbeke, W., K. Dejaeger, D. Martens, J. Hur, and B. Baesens. 2012. "New Insights into Churn Prediction in the Telecommunication Sector: A Profit Driven Data MiningApproach." *European Journal of Operational Research* 218: 211–229.

Verbraken, T., Verbeke, W., and Baesens, B. 2013. "A Novel Profit Maximizing Metric for Measuring Classification Performance of Customer Churn Prediction Models." *IEEE Transactions on Knowledge and Data Engineering* 25: 961–973.

CHAPTER **5**

Profit-Driven
Analytical
Techniques

INTRODUCTION

In Chapter 4, uplift modeling was introduced as a means to further optimize marketing campaigns by estimating the net effect of a campaign on customer behavior. More generally, uplift modeling allows users to optimize decision making by estimating the net effect of operational decisions. When applied for developing retention campaigns, uplift modeling allows to select only those would-be churners that can effectively be retained, as well as to customize the campaign so as to maximize the probability for individual would-be churners to be retained by the campaign. The returns of such a campaign can even be further optimized by accounting for customer value and by adopting profit-driven analytics as introduced in this chapter. Customers with a high CLV that are about to churn may be given a stronger incentive to remain loyal, and are more important to be detected when about to churn than a customer with a low CLV. Acknowledging customer value when developing predictive and descriptive analytical models, as well as when making decisions based on these models, is what profit-driven analytics are about.

In this chapter, we introduce various profit-driven analytical techniques. The first section of this chapter motivates the use of profit-driven predictive analytics and discusses a number of key concepts, such as the cost matrix and the cost-sensitive classification cutoff.

Next, a cost-sensitive classification framework is introduced that structures the discussion of cost-sensitive classification techniques in the subsequent section. In the third section, we then discuss cost-sensitive regression approaches for continuous target variable estimation such as demand.

Additionally, profitability can also be considered when developing descriptive analytical models. In the second part of this chapter, we discuss profit-driven customer segmentation and market basket analysis, which are profit-oriented extensions to standard clustering and association rule mining approaches as introduced in Chapter 2.

PROFIT-DRIVEN PREDICTIVE ANALYTICS

The Case for Profit-Driven Predictive Analytics

Cost-sensitive analytical techniques account for the costs and benefits of business decisions based on predictions made by the resulting analytical model. These costs and benefits typically depend on various characteristics of the error that is made, such as the type of misclassification (e.g., false positive versus false negative) or the size of the error, the true value of the target variable and (possibly) as well additional characteristics of the entity for which the prediction is made.

For instance, as discussed in Chapter 3, many organizations optimize their retention efforts by predicting customer churn. A customer churn prediction model that accurately identifies customers that are about to churn allows an organization to target those customers with a marketing campaign that incentivizes them to remain loyal. The predictive strength of the churn prediction model clearly is of crucial importance, as will be discussed further in Chapter 6, and depending on the predictive strength, more (or fewer) customers will be targeted to maximize the returns of the retention campaign. When the customer churn prediction model wrongly identifies a customer as a churner, this customer will be included in the retention campaign and offered an incentive. Here, the misclassification costs are those attributable to contacting the customer and the cost of the incentive. This cost is relatively low compared to that of incorrectly classifying a churner as a nonchurner since this customer will therefore not be targeted, and thus will not be retained. Accordingly, the misclassification cost for this type of error roughly equals the customer's lifetime value, which is typically much larger than the cost of misclassifying a nonchurner as a churner.

Hence, when developing a customer churn prediction model, these different kinds of misclassification costs are ideally considered in the sense that we *prefer* one type of error over the other type. However, the statistical perspective adopted in the standard design of classification techniques (as discussed in Chapter 2) does not account for imbalanced misclassification costs and weighs each incorrect classification equally *while* learning, as do standard evaluation measures such as AUC *after* learning when assessing the predictive strength of the model.

We strongly believe that in a business setting, it is essential to acknowledge costs and benefits to learn *better* models, with *better* meaning cost-optimal. Accounting for imbalanced costs and benefits may be done when evaluating a model, as will be discussed extensively in the next chapter. Or alternatively, as will be discussed in this chapter, we already take the resulting use and profitability of the model into account while learning the model. In the first part of this chapter, we therefore introduce and illustrate a selection of cost-sensitive classification techniques; later on, we will also introduce cost-sensitive learning approaches for regression.

Cost-sensitive classification techniques optimize the predictions made by the resulting model by letting the user specify the costs and benefits that result from making either a correct or an incorrect classification for either possible class in terms of a cost matrix. Because benefits are negative costs (or, vice versa, costs are negative benefits), we can use the term cost to refer both to benefits and costs. In line with the convention in the academic literature, henceforth in this chapter and book we will consistently and only be speaking of costs, which cost-sensitive classification techniques aim to minimize.

In the following section, we will first introduce a number of essential concepts to cost-sensitive classification, after which a selected number of cost-sensitive classification techniques are introduced.

Cost Matrix

Table 5.1 resumes the confusion matrix for binary classification defined in Chapter 2 as a two-by-two matrix summarizing the number of correct and incorrect predictions for both the positive and negative class. The rows represent the predictions that are made, and the columns represent the actual outcomes or vice versa (Powers 2007).

Table 5.1 Confusion Matrix

	Actual Negative	Actual Positive
Predicted Negative	True negatives (TN)	False negatives (TN)
Predicted Positive	False positives (TP)	True positives (TP)

The *true negatives* and *true positives* are the correctly classified observations for the negative and positive class, respectively, whereas the *false negatives* and *false positives* represent the incorrectly classified cases of the positive and negative class, respectively. As such, FN and FP represent the errors of the classification model. In many, if not most, settings, these errors have different implications and importance, meaning that a false positive error has a different cost than a false negative error.

In many business applications (e.g., credit risk modeling, customer churn prediction, fraud detection, etc.) and non-business-oriented applications (e.g., cancer detection, machine component failure prediction, etc.), the misclassification costs associated with false positives and false negatives are typically imbalanced.

For instance, in credit risk modeling, incorrectly classifying a bad applicant (which we define as a positive observation) as a good applicant (which we define as a negative observation) is costlier than erroneously predicting a good applicant to be a defaulter. In other words, the cost of a false negative is significantly higher than the cost of a false positive. In the first case, a loss will be incurred from giving a loan to a customer who will not be able to repay some fraction of the loan, whereas in the second case, the cost involves the opportunity cost of missed revenues and profit.

In the first case, such an opportunity cost may also have to be added because when granting a loan to a defaulter, the financial institution missed revenues and profits from not granting a loan to a good payer. In the second case, and when a fixed number or total amount of loans is given, one may argue that the real cost of a false positive additionally depends on the alternative decision, meaning that it depends on whether the applicant receiving a loan instead of the incorrectly classified applicant eventually defaulted or not. If not, then the cost is zero, whereas in the event of default, the cost is much higher. However, one probably cannot say which applicant was given a loan instead, and therefore, it is necessary to use some aggregate average measure.

The discussion on the involved costs in this example illustrates the challenge of establishing the *precise* costs and benefits associated with each cell in the confusion matrix. This certainly is the case when a top-ranked fraction of customers is selected for further *treatment* based on the predictions made by the classification model. For instance, this occurs when only a subgroup of the customers is selected:

- To be targeted in a campaign
- To be granted a loan
- To be included in a marketing campaign
- To be inspected for fraud

In these cases, the misclassification costs also depend on the ratio of positives versus negatives in the non-selected fraction of observations. To specify the exact involved costs, deep insight in the specifications of the business application is typically required, along with detailed accounting figures.

The existence of imbalanced misclassification costs is not the exact same problem as the existence of an imbalanced class distribution, although many solutions that are being applied for resolving the class imbalance problem can be adopted for addressing unequal misclassification costs, as will be elaborated in the following sections.

Table 5.2 represents the *cost matrix C* for a binary classification problem and having a fixed misclassification cost for each possible outcome.

In the cost matrix, the elements $C(0,0)$ and $C(1,1)$ represent the cost of a true negative (TN) and a true positive (TP) prediction, respectively. In other words, these elements represent the cost of correctly predicting a negative observation to be negative and a positive observation to be positive. Typically $C(0,0)$ and $C(1,1)$ are negative or zero and therefore represent a benefit or zero cost. Hence, the shorthand notation b_0 and b_1, respectively, as will also be adopted in the next chapter, and the negation since the benefit is the negative cost, or vice versa. Indeed, correctly detecting (for instance) a fraudulent credit-card transaction to be malicious or a nonfraudulent transaction to be legitimate generates a benefit.

On the other hand, the elements $C(0,1)$ and $C(1,0)$ (which will be represented in shorthand notation as c_1 and c_1, respectively) represent the costs associated with incorrectly classifying a positive observation to be negative (i.e., a false negative (FN)), and a negative observation to be positive (i.e., a false positive (FP)), respectively. Misclassifications will effectively lead to costs. Not detecting a fraudulent credit-card transaction yields a loss because the amount of the transaction is typically reimbursed to the credit-card owner, even when no recoveries are made.

Blocking a legitimate transaction also generates costs in terms of missed income to both the merchant and the credit-card company, with the latter typically charging a fixed amount or a small fraction of the

Table 5.2 Cost Matrix for a Binary Classification Problem

	Actual Negative	Actual Positive
Predicted Negative	$C(0,0) = -b_0$	$C(0,1) = c_1$
Predicted Positive	$C(1,0) = c_0$	$C(1,1) = -b_1$

transaction value to the merchant. Costs do not necessarily have to be monetary in nature in the sense that they also may represent time, energy consumption, distance, and so on.

The publicly available and often-cited *German Credit Data*, published at the UCI Machine Learning Repository website[1] (Bache and Lichman 2013), contains observations for a financial institution's customers and includes a number of predictor variables and a target variable indicating whether the customer defaulted. The original problem formulation suggests the use of the cost matrix in Table 5.3.

In Table 5.3, *bad* means default ($y = 1$) and *good* ($y = 0$) means no default. How the publisher of the data arrived at this exact cost matrix is undocumented. Although these values may appear unrealistic at first sight, we note that in a practical setting it is often a challenge to obtain sensible values. In addition, as we will demonstrate later, it is the proportion of the misclassification costs in the cost matrix, not absolute values, that truly matters.

As an alternative to calculating the values in the cost matrix, those values may roughly be approximated as follows. Often, when the misclassification costs are imbalanced the class distribution is also imbalanced, as will be elaborated on in the final section of this chapter. When no further information on misclassification costs is available, they can be assumed to be inversely proportional to the class distribution (Japkowicz and Stephen, 2002). For instance, in the case of German Credit Data, the proportion of *bads* to *goods* is 30% to 70%. One may then approximate the cost of misclassifying a *bad* customer as *good* to be proportional to 1:30 and the misclassification cost of predicting a *good* customer as *bad* to be proportional to 1:70. These values can be multiplied with a constant value without altering their relative proportion. It is effectively the relative proportion, which is important here, not the absolute values of the misclassification costs as will be discussed below. When multiplying with the proportion of majority class observations, we always reach a misclassification cost of one for majority class observations, and in this setup, we reach a misclassification cost of $2.33 = (1/0.33) \cdot 0.70$ for the minority class observations—that is, for the *bad* observations. Note the significant difference with the provided cost matrix above, which more than doubles the misclassification cost for the minority class.

Table 5.3 Example Cost Matrix for the German Credit Data

	Actual *Good*	Actual *Bad*
Predicted *Good*	$C(0,0) = 0$	$C(0,1) = 5$
Predicted *Bad*	$C(1,0) = 1$	$C(1,1) = 0$

Misclassification costs may also be estimated by an expert in an intuitive manner based on business knowledge and experience. Although such an estimate obviously is less exact in nature, this approach will require much less effort when no useful information is readily available to determine these values and permit us to make straightforward use of cost-sensitive learning for building a classification model with improved performance.

To structure and formalize the estimation of the cost matrix using expert knowledge, the following approach, called planning poker, for estimating project time and costs used by software development teams may be adopted (Mahnič and Hovelja 2012; Moløkken-Østvold, Haugen, and Benestad 2008). Software development costs are typically difficult to project and therefore are estimated by domain experts with many years of experience. To structure the estimation process and therefore to achieve more accurate and reliable estimates, a group of experts is assembled and provided with a list of well-specified functionalities that are to be developed, along with a set of playing cards, each of which has a relative value—or in other words, is worth some points. These points have no meaning but allow the experts to rank functionalities in terms of the expected amount of effort that will be required to elaborate them by assigning to each functionality points in a relative way. In rounds, and without having discussed these issues initially, the experts must simultaneously play one card per functionality. Accordingly, each expert provides an *independent* estimate. These estimates may then be discussed, and a final estimate is to be agreed on by the group. Alternatively, the average value may be adopted as a final score for a functionality. (Note, the strong resemblance to the underlying setup of ensemble methods introduced in Chapter 2.) The final cost of the software development project is then calculated by multiplying the numbers of points assigned to each functionality with a cost per point based on historical accounting information, resemblances with similar past projects, and domain expert input.

In a similar way, the relative costs of misclassifications could be estimated by a group of experts by having them rank or assign points to a set of randomly selected observations or observations pertaining to the different cells in the confusion and cost matrices.

Additionally, it is useful to test the sensitivity of the resulting cost-sensitive classifier to the exact values in the cost matrix by varying the cost values in an experimental setup and monitoring the model's resulting performance in terms of the appropriate performance measures for evaluating the model. The sensitivity of the results may be high or low, depending on which factors have an impact. When sensitivity is low, the exact values of the cost matrix are not very important, and the conclusions and results obtained are insensitive to the cost matrix. When sensitivity is high, the conclusions and results are highly dependent on the cost matrix and are therefore not robust. In that situation, it is recommended both to further investigate the root causes of the instability and to establish trustworthy values for the cost matrix so that the final results will be reliable and can be acted on to maximize profitability.

Finally, one may and possibly should adopt an opportunistic approach to establishing the cost matrix in the sense that the cost matrix adopted when learning a model not necessarily should represent *actual* costs. Instead, the cost matrix that maximizes performance in terms of the applicable evaluation measure should be used, and as such, the cost matrix can be approached as if it is a parameter of the classification technique. Indeed, a sensitivity analysis is to be performed for various cost matrices to see the impact on the performance, subsequently allowing selection of the optimal cost matrix for developing the final model. Note that the sensitivity analysis and tuning of the cost matrix needs to be performed on the training data, excluding the test data, just as in any parameter tuning setup.

In addition, also in multiclass and ordinal classification problems a confusion matrix and a cost matrix can be specified, with the cost matrix C determining the costs associated with correct and incorrect classifications. So, a cost matrix C specifies values $C(j, k)$ which represent the cost of classifying an observation as class j when the true class is k. When J classes exist, a J-by-J confusion and cost matrix emerges with a cell for each pair of predicted and true classes.

In the event of an ordinal classification problem, one may expect the confusion matrix to be diagonally dominant, meaning that the values of the cells in the matrix are higher the closer they are to the diagonal. This signifies that the predictive model succeeds in making exact estimates, or when the estimate is not exact, larger errors are more unlikely than smaller errors.

Conversely, the cost matrix associated with an ordinal classification problem may be expected to be inverse diagonally dominant, meaning that misclassification costs increase when the error becomes larger. For instance, when building a credit rating model (Berteloot et al. 2013), to *overrate* an obligor by two notches (i.e., two classes up) is much more severe than to overrate it by one notch. Simultaneously, the matrix may be asymmetric; depending on one's perspective, underrating is more conservative in terms of estimating the involved credit risk and therefore has a smaller impact. For example, the cost matrix in Table 5.4 applies to an ordinal credit rating estimation setting, reflects the above reasoning, and adds severe punishment for missing defaults.

Table 5.4　Cost Matrix for an Ordinal Classification Problem

		Actual rating						
		A	B	C	D	E	F	Default
Predicted rating	A	0	2	4	8	16	32	100
	B	1	0	2	4	8	16	100
	C	2	1	0	2	4	8	100
	D	3	2	1	0	2	4	100
	E	4	3	2	1	0	2	100
	F	5	4	3	2	1	0	100
	Default	6	5	4	3	2	1	0

Cost-Sensitive Decision Making with Cost-Insensitive Classification Models

We start from a classification model producing conditional probability estimates $p(j|x) = p_j$ for an observation x belonging to class j. In a binary classification problems, with $j = 1$ representing the positive class and $j = 0$ the negative class, we have the following:

$$p(1|x) = p_1$$
$$p(0|x) = p_0 = 1 - p_1$$

An observation could be classified as positive if $p_1 > p_0$ or equivalently if $p_1 > 0.5$. Such a classification decision is cost-insensitive in the sense that it does not account for misclassification costs, as discussed in the previous paragraph, when assigning a class label to an observation.

Alternatively, when a cost matrix is specified that provides costs for correct and incorrect predictions, a cost-sensitive classification decision, such as described by Elkan (2001), assigns the class label that results in the lowest **expected loss**. The expected loss $\ell(x, j)$ associated with predicting class j for an observation x can be computed using the conditional probability estimates p_1 and p_0 from the classification model $f(x)$ and the cost matrix C defined in the previous section as follows:

$$\ell(x, j) = \sum_k p(k|x) \cdot C(j, k),$$

With $\ell(x, j)$ the expected loss for classifying an observation x as class j, and $C(j, k)$ the cost of classifying an observation as class j when the true class is k. Note that the formula for the expected loss can also be applied for calculating the expected loss in a multiclass classification problem. In that situation, k runs from 1 to J, with J the number of classes. At the end of this section, an example is provided on the calculation of the expected losses for the German Credit Data example, using the cost matrix introduced in the previous section.

In the binary case, using the concept of expected loss leads to classifying observation x as a positive observation if the expected loss for classifying it as a positive observation is smaller than the expected loss for classifying it as a negative observation; i.e., if $\ell(x, 1) < \ell(x, 0)$. When inserting the formula for the expected loss defined above, we obtain:

$$p_0 \cdot C(1,0) + p_1 \cdot C(1,1) < p_0 \cdot C(0,0) + p_1 \cdot C(0,1),$$

which is equivalent to:

$$p_0 \cdot (C(1,0) - C(0,0)) < p_1 \cdot (C(0,1) - C(1,1)).$$

If $\ell(x, 1) > \ell(x, 0)$, then the optimal classification is to label observation x as a negative observation. If $p_1 = T_{CS}$, with T_{CS} the cost-sensitive cutoff value, then $\ell(x, 1) = \ell(x, 0)$. This means that either class label is cost-optimal since classifying the observation either as a positive observation or as a negative observation leads to the same minimum expected loss. This is equivalent to having $p_1 = p_0 = 0.5$ in the cost-insensitive setting.

T_{CS} is calculated from the above equation by setting the left-hand side equal to the right-hand side, replacing p_0 with $1 - p_1$ and reworking the formula to obtain the following expression for $p_1 = T_{CS}$ (Ling and Sheng 2008):

$$T_{CS} = \frac{C(1,0) - C(0,0)}{C(1,0) - C(0,0) + C(0,1) - C(1,1)}.$$

The cost-sensitive cutoff value T_{CS} therefore expresses the minimum value of p_1 for the cost-optimal class to be the positive class. When p_1 is smaller than T_{CS}, the negative class label is cost-optimal. Thus, for cost-sensitive decision making using a cost-insensitive classification model producing conditional probability estimates, it is sufficient to adjust the cutoff value for classifying observations as positive or negative from 0.5, which indeed can be interpreted as a cost-insensitive cutoff value T_{CIS}, to the cost-sensitive cutoff value T_{CS}. Note that in the above equation for calculating T_{CS}, one may assume that the denominator is different from zero, which will be the case when misclassification costs are higher than costs related to correct predictions. This is a reasonable condition that will always be satisfied in practical settings, since the latter are typically negative because representing a benefit.

When taking a constant term and either adding it to or subtracting it from the upper and lower cells in for either or both the left- and the right-hand side column, the predicted class of an observation will not change. Indeed, this results from adding these constant terms to both the expected loss $\ell(x, 1)$ and $\ell(x, 0)$ in the left- and the right-hand side of the inequality above. These constant terms may be taken as equal to the cost of a true negative for the left-hand column in the cost matrix and to the cost of a true positive within the right-hand column in the cost matrix, leading to the equivalent, yet simpler cost matrix in Table 5.5.

In the cost matrix of Table 5.5, no costs are associated with classifying an observation correctly, which arguably allows for an easier intuitive interpretation. When $C'(1,0) = C'(0,1)$, the classification problem is cost-insensitive. The more imbalanced the misclassification costs, the stronger the case for applying cost-sensitive classification approaches and the higher the potential benefits from adopting cost-sensitive classification techniques.

When adopting the simpler cost matrix of Table 5.5, the expression for the cost-sensitive cutoff T_{CS} above also reduces to a simpler form without impacting the actual resulting value:

$$T_{CS} = \frac{C'(1,0)}{C'(1,0) + (0,1)}.$$

Dividing finally both the numerator and denominator by $C'(1, 0)$ leads to the following equation:

$$T_{CS} = \frac{1}{1 + \dfrac{C'(0,1)}{C'(1,0)}}.$$

From this equation we see that it is the ratio of $C'(1, 0)$ and $C'(0, 1)$ that determines the cost-sensitive cutoff—that is, the relative and not the absolute values as indicated before.

Although the approach for making cost-sensitive decisions by adjusting the classification cutoff is simple, sensible, and importantly from a practical perspective, requires very little effort to implement, this approach appears overly simplistic in practice because it leads to

Table 5.5 Simplified Cost Matrix

	Actual Negative	Actual Positive
Predicted Negative	0	$C'(0,1) = C(0,1) - C(1,1)$
Predicted Positive	$C'(1,0) = C(1,0) - C(0,0)$	0

suboptimal results in terms of making the model truly cost-sensitive and maximizing profitability (Petrides and Verbeke 2017)..A series of more advanced and powerful approaches for obtaining a cost-sensitive classification model will be discussed in the next section.

■ EXAMPLE

We may calculate the cost-sensitive cutoff T_{CS} for the cost matrix provided in the above section for the German Credit Data as follows:

$$T_{CS} = \frac{C'(1,0)}{C'(1,0) + C'(0,1)} = \frac{1}{1+5} = \frac{1}{6} = 0.1667.$$

Hence, if a cost-insensitive classifier $f(x)$ predicts a probability $p(1|x) = 0.22$, then applying the cost-sensitive cutoff $T_{CS} = 0.1667$ leads to assigning class 1 (*bad*), whereas applying the cost-insensitive cutoff $T_{CIS} = 0.5$ leads to assigning class 0 (*good*).

The associated expected losses for both classes are calculated as follows:

$$\ell(x,0) = \sum_{j} p(j|x) \cdot C(0,j) = 0.22 \cdot 5 = 1.10.$$

$$\ell(x,1) = \sum_{j} p(j|x) \cdot C(1,j) = 0.78 \cdot 1 = 0.78.$$

Clearly, the expected loss for assigning class one is smaller than for assigning class zero, which corresponds to the classification that is obtained when using the cost-sensitive cutoff. When the probability $p(1|x) = T_{CS} = 0.1667$, the expected losses for assigning class labels 0 and 1 become respectively equal to:

$$\ell(x,0) = \sum_{j} p(j|x) \cdot C(0,j) = 0.1667 \cdot 5 = 0.8333.$$

$$\ell(x,1) = \sum_{j} p(j|x) \cdot C(1,j) = 0.8333 \cdot 1 = 0.8333.$$

Cost-Sensitive Classification Framework

There is an overwhelming amount of literature on cost-sensitive learning, with many approaches that have been proposed, adapted, combined, and so forth (Ling and Sheng, 2008; Lomax and Vadera, 2011; Nikolaou et al. 2016). Case studies and experimental evaluations report conflicting results on the actual performance of these approaches. In this section, we present three perspectives that allow us to frame, compare, and categorize the various cost-sensitive approaches, offering deeper insight in the nature of cost-sensitive learning.

Class-Dependent and Observation-Dependent Cost-Sensitive Learning

The misclassification costs specified in the cost matrix **C** introduced in the previous section are assumed to be constant across observations. In many settings, however, they are not. For instance, when detecting fraudulent credit-card transactions the cost of missing a fraudulent transaction depends on the amount involved, which is different for each transaction. Therefore, the misclassification costs are observation-dependent.[2] Often, in such cases the average misclassification cost is calculated for specifying the cost matrix **C**, which serves as input to a first type of cost-sensitive classification techniques that will be discussed in this chapter and referred to as the **class-dependent cost-sensitive learning (CCS)** techniques.

Alternatively, for each observation in the dataset, the exact costs may be considered when building a classification model. A second class of techniques that will be discussed is referred to as the **observation-dependent cost-sensitive learning (OCS)** techniques and allows us to account individually for the specific costs involved for each observation in the data (Zadrozny and Elkan 2001; Brefeld, Geibel, and Wysotzki 2003; Aodha and Brostow 2013; Bahnsen, Aouada, and Ottersten 2015).

Rather than focusing on the costs of observations, there are also techniques that focus on the costs of predictor variables and minimizing the cost of the model in terms of the total cost of the adopted predictor variables. These techniques will not be discussed in this chapter. For more information, see Maldonado and Crone (2016).

Pre-, During-, or Post-Training Approaches

Both CCS and OCS learning approaches can be categorized depending on the stage in the analytics process model in which costs are introduced and accounted for. A first group of approaches aims to make the resulting predictive model cost-sensitive by manipulating the data in a pre-processing step. A second group of approaches concern techniques that have been designed to account for costs at the time of estimating the model. A third group concerns post-processing approaches that make cost-sensitive decisions based on cost-insensitive predictions. The first of these post-processing methods has already been discussed in this chapter when introducing the cost-sensitive decision-making approach and the cost-sensitive classification cutoff T_{CS} proposed by Elkan (2001).

Whereas the first group of approaches adopts a relatively simple strategy for arriving at cost-sensitive classification models (and therefore, such approaches are significantly simpler to implement), the second group of approaches, which accounts for costs during model building, includes approaches that are more complex in nature since these techniques' inner learning algorithm is adapted.

The third group of approaches, the post-processing approaches, are somewhat related to the profit measures that will be discussed in the next chapter in terms of the underlying reasoning. From a practitioner's perspective, these approaches are also simpler to implement because it is not necessary to alter the internal mechanism for learning a model.

Experiments learn that all three groups may but do not always result in improved classification models compared to adopting traditional (i.e., cost-insensitive) learning approaches, at least when making comparisons in terms of total costs and benefits (i.e., in terms of the profit resulting from operating the resulting models). Clearly, we need to adopt cost-sensitive evaluation measures when developing cost-sensitive predictive models. If not, improvements in terms of reduced costs or increased profit may go unnoticed since cost-insensitive evaluation measures simply cannot detect them.

Direct Methods versus Meta-Learning Methods

In addition to the two dimensions already discussed, according to Ling and Sheng, (2008), cost-sensitive learning approaches may also be grouped in *direct methods* and *meta-learning* or *wrapper* approaches. Direct methods adapt the learning algorithm to take costs into account during model building, whereas wrapper approaches can be combined with any cost-insensitive learning algorithm to account for imbalanced misclassification costs.

Examples of direct methods include ICET (Turney 1995) and cost-sensitive decision trees (Drummond and Holte 2000), whereas the group of meta-learning approaches includes the subgroup of thresholding methods such as MetaCost (Domingos 1999), cost-sensitive naïve Bayes (Chai et al. 2004), and empirical thresholding (Sheng and Ling 2006), and the subgroup of sampling approaches, such as the weighting approach (Ting 2002) and the costing method (Zadrozny et al. 2003). Several of these methods, along with others, will be discussed more in detail in the section below.

Table 5.6 provides a structured overview of the cost-sensitive classification approaches that will be discussed in this chapter, adopting

Table 5.6 Structured Overview of the Cost-Sensitive Classification Approaches Discussed in This Chapter

	Pre-Training	During	Post-Training
Direct methods	Data sampling ■ Oversampling ■ Undersampling ■ SMOTE Weighting methods ■ C4.5CS ■ C4.50CS ■ Weighted logistic regression ■ Cost-sensitive logistic regression ■ Observation-dependent cost-sensitive logistic regression	Decision tree modification ■ Cost-sensitive pruning ■ Decision trees with minimal costs ■ Cost-sensitive decision trees	Direct cost-sensitive decision making
Meta-learning methods	Weighting methods ■ Naïve cost-sensitive AdaBoost ■ Naïve observation-dependent cost-sensitive AdaBoost ■ Weighted random forests ■ Cost-sensitive random forests ■ Example-dependent cost-sensitive random forests Rebalancing ensemble methods ■ SMOTEBoost ■ EasyEnsemble ■ RUSBoost ■ Cost-sensitive random forests	AdaBoost variants ■ CSB0 ■ CSB1 ■ CSB2 ■ AdaCost ■ AdaC1 ■ AdaC2 ■ AdaC3	MetaCost

both the grouping in pre-, during-, and post-training approaches as well as the grouping in direct and meta-learning approaches.

COST-SENSITIVE CLASSIFICATION

Because many cost-sensitive learning techniques have been developed, in this section, we will introduce only a selected subset of approaches.

The presented approaches have been selected based on their popularity and usability with regards to the intended purpose, and most importantly, based on their potential to increase performance in terms of cost reduction, as reported in the literature. In structuring this section, we use the framework introduced in Table 5.6 to categorize approaches to pre-, during-, and post-training methods.

Pre-Training Methods

Within the pre-training methods, three subgroups of approaches can be identified:

1. A first set of methods adapt the distribution of the data and are called *data sampling* or **rebalancing methods**.

2. Rebalancing methods can be applied in combination with any classifier, but given their natural fit, they have often been combined with ensemble approaches for cost-sensitive classification. Such combined setups are called **rebalancing ensemble methods**, and given their popularity, they will be separately discussed in this section.

3. Pre-training methods assigning weights that are proportional to the involved misclassification costs to all observations in a dataset are called **weighting methods**. Weighting observations essentially has the same purpose as sampling, but from a technical perspective, they require the selected base classifier to be able to account for weights when learning a classification model. Weights are determined by a **frequency variable** in the dataset, which has a value for each observation expressing the relative prevalence or importance of an observation.

In the following sections, we look more closely at these three groups of approaches.

Rebalancing Methods

The class distribution φ is defined as the ratio of the number of positive observations n_1 over the number of negative observations n_0 in a dataset:

$$\varphi = \frac{n_1}{n_0}.$$

The basic premise of data sampling is that by altering the class distribution of the dataset that is used to learn a classification model, any classification technique may be *tuned* so that it inherently applies the cost-sensitive cutoff T_{CS}, implicitly determined by the cost matrix, instead of the default cost-insensitive classification cutoff $T_{CIS} = 0.5$ (Elkan 2001).

The cutoff T_{CS} is incorporated by resampling the dataset so that the ratio of the number of positive observations n_1 over the number of negative observations n_0 in the training data becomes equal to:

$$\varphi_{CS} = \varphi \cdot \frac{(1 - T_{CS})}{T_{CS}} = \frac{n_1}{n_0} \cdot \frac{(1 - T_{CS})}{T_{CS}}.$$

Note that when resampling after the above equation, using a cost-insensitive cutoff $T_{CIS} = 0.5$ is equivalent to adopting a cost-sensitive cutoff T_{CS} with the original class distribution φ. As can be deduced from the above equation, the class distribution φ_{CS} may be obtained by resampling so the number of positive observations n_1 becomes equal to n_1':

$$n_1' = n_1 \cdot \frac{(1 - T_{CS})}{T_{CS}}.$$

Reworking this formula leads to a more interpretable expression, since:

$$\frac{(1 - T_{CS})}{T_{CS}} = \frac{C'(0,1)}{C'(1,0)},$$

we obtain:

$$n_1' = n_1 \cdot \frac{C'(0,1)}{C'(1,0)},$$

which means that the new number of positives is equal to the original number of positives times the ratio of the cost of a false negative over the cost of a false positive. Because the positive class typically represents the *class of interest* (e.g., default, churn, fraud, etc.), a false negative is typically costlier than a false positive. In other words, missing a defaulter, for instance, is costlier than incorrectly classifying a good customer. This means that the ratio of $C'(0, 1)$ over $C'(1, 0)$ is larger than one, and thus, $n_1' > n_1$. Therefore, the number of observations of the positive class is to be increased, which may be achieved by oversampling as will be illustrated in the next section. Because typically the class of interest (i.e., the positive class) is the minority class, it makes sense that the number of positive observations must be increased. This indeed may be expected to result in more importance being attached to the positive class observations, which are costlier to miss, thus indirectly leading to a predictive model that accounts for the misclassification costs.

As an alternative approach to oversampling the positive class to achieve the cost-sensitive class distribution φ_{CS}, one could undersample the negative class. From the equation to calculate φ_{CS} above, we see that the cost-sensitive distribution is also achieved when resampling the number of negative observations from n_0 to n_0':

$$n_0' = n_0 \cdot \frac{T_{CS}}{(1 - T_{CS})} = n_0 \cdot \frac{C'(1,0)}{C'(0,1)}.$$

Because $C'(1,0) < C'(0,1)$, as explained earlier, the number of negative observations is to be decreased, which may be achieved by undersampling, as explained in the following section. The negative class is typically the majority class; therefore, it makes sense to reduce the number of negative observations in the dataset. Again, this can be expected to result in the positive class observations becoming more dominant and (importantly) accurately classified.

EXAMPLE

Building on the previous example, we calculate the cost-sensitive class distribution for the *German Credit Data* containing 1,000 observations, of which 700 are *good* ($y = 0$) and 300 are *bad* ($y = 1$) customers: $n_0 = 700$ and $n_1 = 300$. The class distribution φ can be calculated as follows:

$$\varphi = \frac{n_1}{n_0} = \frac{300}{700} = 0.4286.$$

Given the cost-sensitive cutoff $T_{CS} = 0.1667$ as calculated before, we calculate the cost-sensitive class distribution φ_{CS} following the formula discussed above:

$$\varphi_{CS} = \frac{n_1}{n_0} \cdot \frac{(1 - T_{CS})}{T_{CS}} = \frac{300}{700} \cdot \frac{(1 - 0.1667)}{0 \cdot 1667} = 2.14.$$

The cost-sensitive class distribution φ_{CS} may be achieved by oversampling the number of positive observations n_1 to n_1':

$$n_1' = n_1 \cdot \frac{(1 - T_{CS})}{T_{CS}} = n_1 \cdot \frac{C'(0,1)}{C'(1,0)} = 300 \cdot \frac{5}{1} = 1,500.$$

One may check whether the cost-sensitive class distribution is obtained by calculating the ratio of n_1' over n_0:

$$\varphi' = \frac{n_1'}{n_0} = \frac{1,500}{700} = 2.14 = \varphi_{CS}.$$

Alternatively, we can undersample the negative class so the number of negative observations becomes equal to n'_0:

$$n'_0 = n_0 \cdot \frac{T_{CS}}{(1 - T_{CS})} = n_0 \cdot \frac{C'(1,0)}{C'(0,1)} = 700 \cdot \frac{1}{5} = 140.$$

We again check whether the cost-sensitive class distribution is achieved by calculating the ratio of n_1 over n'_0:

$$\varphi' = \frac{n_1}{n'_0} = \frac{300}{140} = 2.14 = \varphi_{CS}.$$

Over- and Undersampling

Oversampling is illustrated in Figure 5.1. Observations of the positive class (e.g., fraudulent credit-card transactions) are simply duplicated. When applying oversampling for cost-sensitive classification, each positive observation is duplicated as many times as required for the total number of positive observations to become equal to n'_1 —that is, the original number n_1 times the ratio of $C'(0, 1)$ over $C'(1, 0)$ as discussed and illustrated above. In the example of Figure 5.1, observations 1 and 4, which are both fraudulent transactions, have been duplicated to achieve the required number of observations of the positive class n'_1.

Original data

	ID	Variables	Class
Train	1	...	Fraud
	2	...	No Fraud
	3	...	No Fraud
	4	...	Fraud
	5	...	No Fraud
	6	...	No Fraud
Test	7	...	No Fraud
	8	...	No Fraud
	9	...	Fraud
	10	...	No Fraud

Oversampled data

	ID	Variables	Class
Train	1	...	Fraud
	1	...	Fraud
	2	...	No Fraud
	3	...	No Fraud
	4	...	Fraud
	4	...	Fraud
	5	...	No Fraud
	6	...	No Fraud
Test	7	...	No Fraud
	8	...	No Fraud
	9	...	Fraud
	10	...	No Fraud

Figure 5.1 Oversampling the fraudsters.

| Original data | | | | Undersampled data | | |

Original data

	ID	Variables	Class
Train	1	...	Fraud
	2	...	No Fraud
	3	...	No Fraud
	4	...	Fraud
	5	...	No Fraud
	6	...	No Fraud
Test	7	...	No Fraud
	8	...	No Fraud
	9	...	Fraud
	10	...	No Fraud

Undersampled data

	ID	Variables	Class
Train	1	...	Fraud
	3	...	No Fraud
	4	...	Fraud
	6	...	No Fraud
Test	7	...	No Fraud
	8	...	No Fraud
	9	...	Fraud
	10	...	No Fraud

Figure 5.2 Undersampling the nonfraudsters.

Undersampling is illustrated in Figure 5.2. The observations with IDs 2 and 5, which both concern nonfraudulent transactions, have been omitted to create a training set with the required number of observations of the negative class and to achieve the cost-sensitive class distribution φ_{CS}. The observations that are removed can be selected randomly. Under- and oversampling can also be combined for achieving the cost-sensitive class distribution φ_{CS} specified in the previous section. It is important to note that both oversampling and undersampling should be conducted on the training data and not on the test data. Remember, as discussed in Chapter 2, to obtain an unbiased view of model performance, the latter should remain untouched during model development.

Synthetic Minority Oversampling Technique (SMOTE)

As an alternative to undersampling and oversampling, and to achieve the cost-sensitive class distribution φ_{CS}, alternative sampling approaches may be used. One such alternative sampling approach is SMOTE, which is an acronym for synthetic minority oversampling technique.

Rather than simply duplicating observations, as in standard oversampling, SMOTE creates additional *synthetic* observations based on the existing minority or positive observations (Chawla et al. 2002). SMOTE is illustrated in Figure 5.3, in which the circles represent the negative observations, and the squares represent the positive observations. For each positive observation, SMOTE calculates the k nearest neighbors, with k being a parameter that can be set or tuned by the user. Assume

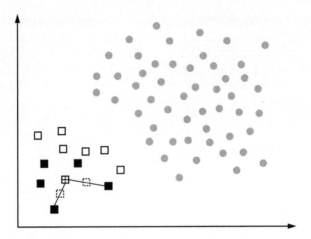

Figure 5.3 Synthetic minority oversampling technique (SMOTE).

we consider the positive observation represented by the crossed square, and pick the five nearest neighbors, which are represented by the black squares. Depending on the amount of additional minority class observations needed, one or more of the nearest neighbors are then selected to create additional, synthetic positive observations.

For instance, if the required cost-sensitive distribution is equal to three times the original class distribution, then we need three times the original number of positive observations. Thus, we need to add two observations per original observation and therefore a random two of the k nearest neighbors are selected (alternatively, the two nearest neighbors can be selected, i.e., k can be set equal to two). The next step is to randomly create two synthetic observations along the line connecting the observation under investigation (crossed square) with the two random nearest neighbors.

These two synthetic observations are represented by the dashed squares in the figure. For example, consider an observation with characteristics (e.g., age and income) of 30 and 1,000 and its nearest neighbor with corresponding characteristics 62 and 3,200. We generate a random number between 0 and 1—say, 0.75. The synthetic observation then has age $30 + 0.75 \cdot (62 - 30)$, which is equal to 54, and income $1,000 + 0.75 \cdot (3,200 - 1,000) = 2,650$.

Alternatively, SMOTE may combine the synthetic oversampling of the positive class with undersampling the negative class to achieve the required class distribution. Note that in their original paper, Chawla et al. (2002) also developed an extension of SMOTE to work with categorical variables. Empirical evidence has shown that SMOTE usually works better than either under- or oversampling. For instance, in the field of fraud detection SMOTE has proven a valuable tool that effectively improves detection power (Van Vlasselaer, Eliassi-Rad, Akoglu, Snoeck, and Baesens, 2015). Finally, note that sampling is an approach that may also be adopted for solving the **imbalanced class distribution problem,** as will be discussed more in detail later in this chapter.

Rebalancing Ensemble Methods

The literature has proposed numerous cost-sensitive ensemble-based approaches that essentially combine a rebalancing and an ensemble method, possibly with additional adjustments. Combining undersampling, oversampling, or SMOTE with bagging, boosting, or random forests, as discussed in Chapter 2, leads to a series of combined setups. Some of these setups have been effectively tested and reported on in the literature. Additionally, one may vary the base learners in these ensemble methods, allowing for even more combinations and thus cost-sensitive learning approaches. Table 5.7 provides an overview of rebalancing ensemble methods for cost-sensitive learning that have been proposed and evaluated in the literature.

As an alternative to applying an ensemble in combination with a sampling method that alters the class distribution, any classification technique can be adopted instead of an ensemble method. This leads to many additional possible combinations and cost-sensitive learning approaches. All are essentially instances of the discussed rebalancing approach.

Although the setup of rebalancing methods is relatively straightforward and intuitive, such methods may perform well in terms of making the classifier cost-sensitive and therefore increase performance as measured in terms of profitability. Sampling approaches also allow reuse of *traditional* approaches such as logistic regression or decision trees, and thus do not require complex adaptations of the operational analytics processes. Therefore, they also facilitate the development of interpretable models, which in many settings is an imperative requirement. Note that the interpretability of the model depends on the selected classification approach and that a black-box model will be obtained when using an ensemble approach as the approaches in Table 5.7 do. However, it must be stressed that these approaches do not necessarily and may not always lead to good results. As always, cautious evaluation and experimentation is advised. More advanced during-training methods discussed later in this chapter not only increase complexity but also may further improve the performance.

Table 5.7 Overview of Sampling Based Ensemble Approaches for Cost-Sensitive Learning

Name *Reference*	Description
SMOTEBoost *(Chawla, Lazarevic, Hall, and Bowyer, 2003)*	Modifies the weight of each observation in AdaBoost as discussed in Chapter 2 using the SMOTE sampling approach discussed in this section. Note here that SMOTEBoost has been proposed by the developer of SMOTE.
EasyEnsemble *(Liu, Wu, and Zhou 2009)*	Combines random undersampling and Bagging, and replaces CART as a base learner by AdaBoost, leading to a complex yet flexible (and therefore, a potentially powerful) setup.
RUSBoost *(Seiffert et al. 2010)*	Replaces SMOTE in the SMOTEBoost approach by a random undersampling scheme.
Cost-Sensitive Random Forests *(Petrides and Verbeke 2017)*	Similar to the balanced random forests approach for dealing with imbalanced class distributions (Chen, Liaw, and Breiman 2004), this approach samples equally sized sets from the training set, each with a cost-sensitive class distribution φ_{CS}. The adopted sampling approach may be oversampling, undersampling, SMOTE, or any other sampling approach that allows alteration of the class distribution accordingly.

Weighting Methods

An approach that is similar to sampling is weighting. Weighting approaches achieve the cost-sensitive class distribution φ_{CS} by assigning weights to observations in the training set. Weights are typically determined by a **frequency variable** in the dataset, which specifies a weight for each observation expressing the relative prevalence or importance of the observation. These weights are subsequently accounted for by the learning method that is applied.

Accordingly, weighting is more complex than sampling in the sense that the actual learning technique must be adapted to accommodate the use of weights. However, once a technique has been adapted and implemented, the application is straightforward, and indeed, the user may not necessarily need to know exactly how the learning method was adapted. Weighting approaches essentially are extended versions of classification techniques, accommodating the use of weights and procedures for setting the values of these weights. Table 5.8 provides a dense overview of some such approaches proposed in the literature.

Table 5.8 Overview of Weighting Approaches for Cost-Sensitive Learning

Name Reference	Description
C4.5CS (Ting 2002)	Extends the classic C4.5 decision-tree learning technique discussed in Chapter 2 to allow for incorporating weights in the learning process, aiming at learning cost-sensitive decision trees. The weights of positive and negative class observations are set to: $$w_1 = \frac{C'(0,1)}{C'(0,1) \cdot n_1 + C'(1,0) \cdot n_0},$$ $$w_0 = \frac{C'(1,0)}{C'(0,1) \cdot n_1 + C'(1,0) \cdot n_0}.$$ The sum of all weights equals one. The fractions used in calculating the entropy and gain measure for deciding which split to make at node t are replaced by weighted fractions calculated as follows: $$p_{w_{1,t}} = \frac{n_{1,t} \cdot w_1}{n_{1,t} \cdot w_1 + n_{0,t} \cdot w_0},$$ and $p_{w_{0,t}} = 1 - p_{w_{1,t}}$. For pruning, minimum weight is considered instead of minimum error, and a new observation is classified as positive if at leaf node t: $$n_{1,t} \cdot w_1 > n_{0,t} \cdot w_0.$$ Note that an elaborated example is provided below in Table 5.8.
C4.5OCS (Petrides and Verbeke 2017)	Note that the above approach can be extended in a straightforward manner to consider observation-dependent misclassification costs instead of class-dependent misclassification costs. For instance, if $C'(0, 1)$ is observation-dependent, then the weight $w_{1,i}$ for a positive observation i, assuming $C'(1, 0)$ constant, can be calculated as follows: $$w_{1,i} = \frac{C'(0,1)_i}{\left(\sum_{i=1}^{n_1} C'(0,1)_i\right) + C'(1,0) \cdot n_0}.$$

(continued)

Table 5.8 (Continued)

Name Reference	Description
	The weights of negative observations remain constant and equal to: $$w_0 = \frac{C'(1,0)}{\left(\sum_{i=1}^{n_1} C'(0,1)_i\right) + C'(1,0) \cdot n_0}.$$ Other steps in C4.5CS are to be adjusted accordingly, accounting for the example dependent weights in calculating entropy measures for splits and when pruning.
Naïve Cost-Sensitive AdaBoost (NCSA) *(Masnadi-Shirazi and Vasconcelos 2011; Viola and Jones 2001)* Naïve Observation-Dependent Cost-Sensitive AdaBoost (NECSA) *(Petrides and Verbeke 2017)*	This approach is identical to AdaBoost, except for the initialization of the weights, which occurs in a cost-sensitive manner, i.e., each positive observation w_1 and each negative observation is assigned a weight w_0 using the above definitions for w_1 and w_0 provided for the C4.5CS approach, so that all weights sum up to one. Alternatively, observation-dependent weights w_i can be used as defined above (see C4.5OCS), leading to an observation-dependent cost-sensitive boosting approach.
Weighted Random Forests (WRF) *(Chen et al. 2004)* Cost-Sensitive Random Forests (CSRF) Observation-dependent Cost-Sensitive Random Forests (OCSRF) *(Petrides and Verbeke 2017)*	A weighted random forest is a variant of the random forests algorithm allowing the use of weighted observations. By adopting the class w_1 for positive and weights w_0 for negative observations as defined for C4.5CS, the basic random forests approach introduced in Chapter 2 is rendered cost-sensitive. Alternatively, observation-dependent weights w_i can be used as defined above (see C4.5OCS), leading to an observation-dependent cost-sensitive random forest.
Weighted Logistic Regression (WLR) *(King and Zeng 2001)* Cost-Sensitive Logistic Regression (CSLR) Observation-Dependent Cost-Sensitive Logistic Regression (OCSLR) *(Petrides and Verbeke 2017)*	The maximum likelihood approach for estimating a logistic regression model can be extended straightforward to accommodate the use of weights associated with observations by formulating the weighted likelihood L_w as follows: $$L_w(\beta\|y) = \prod_{i=1}^{n} (w_1 \cdot p_{1,i})^{y_i} \cdot (w_0 \cdot (1 - p_{1,i}))^{(1-y_i)}.$$ Fitting the logistic regression then involves finding the set of coefficients β that maximizes the weighted likelihood L_w instead of the unweighted likelihood, as in standard, unweighted logistic regression (see Chapter 2). By setting

Table 5.8 (Continued)

Name Reference	Description
	the weights of positive and negative observations as discussed above (see C4.5CS), a cost-sensitive logistic regression model is obtained. By adopting observation-dependent weights in the weighted likelihood function, an observation-dependent cost-sensitive logistic regression model can be estimated: $$L_{ew}(\beta\|y) = \prod_{i=1}^{n} (w_i \cdot p_{1,i})^{y_i} \cdot (w_i \cdot (1 - p_{1,i}))^{(1-y_i)}$$ where L_{ew} is the observation-dependent weighted likelihood, which is to be maximized.

Given the definitions of the weighted likelihood and the observation-dependent weighted likelihood, which extend standard likelihood to account for a frequency variable and therefore allowing weighting, essentially any technique that accommodates a maximum likelihood approach for estimating the model parameters can be made class-dependent and observation-dependent cost-sensitive, respectively.

The extension of a decision-tree learning algorithm to include weights in the splitting, stopping, and assignment decisions enables the induction of both cost-sensitive decision trees and cost-sensitive ensembles by using the weighted decision-tree learner as a base learner.

EXAMPLE

Elaborating on the German Credit Data example introduced above, we can calculate the gain measure for a candidate split S following the C4.5CS (Ting 2002) approach.

The weights to be used for positive observations, *bads* ($y = 1$), can be calculated as defined in Table 5.8:

$$w_1 = \frac{C'(0,1)}{C'(0,1) \cdot n_1 + C'(1,0) \cdot n_0} = \frac{5}{5 \cdot 300 + 1 \cdot 700} = 0.0023.$$

The weights to be used for negative observations, *goods* ($y = 0$), are equal to

$$w_0 = \frac{C'(1,0)}{C'(0,1) \cdot n_1 + C'(1,0) \cdot n_0} = \frac{1}{5 \cdot 300 + 1 \cdot 700} = 4.5455\text{e-}04.$$

Then, assume the following candidate split S:

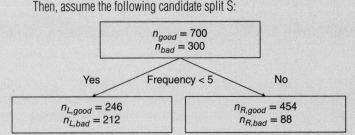

The *weighted fractions* to be used for calculating the entropy and gain measure for the parent, left and right child node are calculated as

$$p_{W_1,\text{parent}} = \frac{n_{1,\text{parent}} \cdot W_1}{n_{1,\text{parent}} \cdot W_1 + n_{0,\text{parent}} \cdot W_0} = \frac{300 \cdot 0.0023}{300 \cdot 0.0023 + 700 \cdot 4.5455e\text{-}04}$$
$$= 0.6844$$

$$p_{W_0,\text{parent}} = 1 - p_{W_1,\text{parent}} = 0.3156,$$

$$p_{W_1,\text{left}} = \frac{212 \cdot 0.0023}{212 \cdot 0.0023 + 246 \cdot 4.5455e\text{-}04} = 0.8135,$$

$$p_{W_0,\text{left}} = 1 - p_{W_1,\text{left}} = 0.1865,$$

$$p_{W_1,\text{right}} = \frac{88 \cdot 0.0023}{88 \cdot 0.0023 + 454 \cdot 4.5455e\text{-}04} = 0.4951,$$

$$p_{W_0,\text{right}} = 1 - p_{W_1,\text{right}} = 0.5049.$$

Plugging in these weighted fractions into the formula to calculate the entropy in the parent, the left, and the right child node,

$$E(S)_{\text{parent}} = -p_{W_0,\text{parent}} \cdot \log_2(p_{W_0,\text{parent}}) - p_{W_1,\text{parent}} \cdot \log_2(p_{W_1,\text{parent}})$$
$$E(S)_{\text{parent}} = -0.3156 \cdot \log_2(0.1356) - 0.6844 \cdot \log_2(0.6844) = 0.8995,$$
$$E(S)_{\text{left}} = -0.1865 \cdot \log_2(0.1865) - 0.8135 \cdot \log_2(0.8135) = 0.6941,$$
$$E(S)_{\text{right}} = -0.5049 \cdot \log_2(0.5049) - 0.4951 \cdot \log_2(0.4951) = 0.9999.$$

Then, for calculating the gain measure we need to calculate the weighted fractions of observations in the left and the right child node as follows:

$$p_{W_\text{left}} = \frac{212 \cdot 0.0023 + 246 \cdot 4.5455e\text{-}04}{300 \cdot 0.0023 + 700 \cdot 4.5455e\text{-}04} = 0.7063,$$

$$p_{W_1,\text{right}} = 1 - p_{W_\text{left}} = 0.2937.$$

This allows us to calculate the cost-sensitive gain value for this candidate split:

$$\text{Gain} = E(S)_{\text{parent}} - p_{W_\text{left}} \cdot E(S)_{\text{left}} - p_{W_1,\text{right}} \cdot E(S)_{\text{right}},$$
$$\text{Gain} = 0.8995 - 0.7063 \cdot 0.6941 - 0.2937 \cdot 0.9999 = 0.1156.$$

During-Training Methods

A second group of cost-sensitive classification techniques adjusts the learning process to directly account for misclassification costs when training the classification model. In this section, we mainly focus on decision-tree-based techniques, which naturally can be extended to account for costs. The main difference with the weighting approaches discussed before, which require an extension of the learning mechanism to account for weights, is that during-training methods alter the inner learning mechanism instead of extending it to accommodate for weights.

Decision Tree Modification

Standard, i.e., cost-insensitive, decision tree algorithms were introduced in Chapter 2 and will be adapted to account for imbalanced misclassification costs in this chapter. Two such adaptations can be envisaged for making trees cost-sensitive:

1. The impurity measure used by decision tree algorithms to make the splitting decision, for instance, entropy as used by C4.5 or Gini as used by CART, can be replaced by a *cost measure*. The aim of splitting a node is then to reduce the overall misclassification cost instead of reducing the overall impurity in terms of class membership.

2. Alternatively, or additionally, one can use a cost measure to replace the evaluation measure used for tree pruning, tuning the tree for simultaneously achieving generalization power and minimizing overall misclassification costs on a validation set.

Table 5.9 presents a selection of cost-sensitive decision-tree approaches proposed in the literature, making one or both of the above general adaptations to standard classification-tree-learning algorithms.

A recent preprint by the developers of CSDT (Bahnsen et al. 2016) introduces an ensemble of cost-sensitive decision trees (OCSDT) (Bahnsen, Aouada, and Ottersten 2016), essentially combining several CSDTs (as discussed in Table 5.9) with an additional *cost-sensitive voting system*. Similar to the OCSDT approach, other cost-sensitive decision tree approaches could be used as base learners to be combined with any ensemble approach, resulting in a cost-sensitive classifier.

Generally, many more combinations and variations could be conceived. Many such combinations have already been defined,

Table 5.9 Overview of Cost-Sensitive Decision-Tree Approaches

Name *Reference*	Description
Cost-sensitive pruning *(Bradford et al. 1998)*	Pruning can be straightforwardly made cost-sensitive by minimizing the expected loss, $\ell(\mathbf{x}, i)$, as defined earlier in this chapter, instead of the expected error or misclassification rate, as explained in Chapter 2 (see Figure 2.13 in Chapter 2). Note that nodes are labeled to result in the lowest misclassification cost. Misclassification costs can be summed over child nodes to monitor total misclassification costs as a function of the size of the tree, to decide about optimal tree size.
Decision trees with minimal costs (DTMC) *(Ling et al. 2004)*	DTMCs perform cost-minimizing splitting and labeling, but do not apply cost-sensitive pruning. The split selected in a node is the split that instead of maximizing the *information gain* value maximizes the *overall misclassification cost reduction*, which is measured as follows: $$\text{Cost reduction} = C_t - \sum_{i=1}^{k} C_{t_i},$$ Where C_t are the costs at node t, equal to $n_{1,t} \cdot C'(0,1)$ if the node is labeled as negative and $n_{0,t} \cdot C'(1,0)$ when labeled positive, and C_{t_1} to C_{t_k} are the costs at the child nodes of node t, calculated in the same way as C_t. During tree growing, a node t is labeled positive if $p_{1,t} > T_{CS}$, meaning that the cost-sensitive cutoff is applied as discussed in the introduction of this chapter. Note that an elaborated example is provided in Table 5.9.
Cost-sensitive decision trees (CSDT) *(Bahnsen et al. 2015)*	CSDTs apply the same cost-minimizing splitting and labeling method as DTMCs, but include observation-dependent costs. Accordingly, CSDT is an observation-dependent cost-sensitive classification approach. Additionally, cost-sensitive pruning is applied in the same way as discussed above (Bradford et al. 1998) but again taking into account observation-dependent instead of average class-dependent misclassification costs.

implemented, experimentally evaluated, and reported on in the literature, which addresses a variety of problems and cases. Hence, gaining insight and selecting the optimal approach when elaborating a practical application represents a challenge, given the vast amount of papers and approaches constituting the field of cost-sensitive learning.

EXAMPLE

Let us resume the previous example to illustrate the cost reduction criterion, as adopted in decision trees with minimal costs and defined in Table 5.9, to evaluate the following candidate split S:

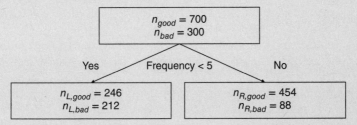

First, we need to calculate the costs C_t at the various nodes t, equal to $n_{1,t} \cdot C'(0,1)$ if the node is labeled *good* and $n_{0,t} \cdot C'(1,0)$ when the node is labeled *bad*. Note that a node t is labeled *bad* if $p_{1,t} > T_{CS}$ and is labeled *good* if $p_{1,t} < T_{CS}$.

For the parent, left and right child node we have

$$p_{1,\text{parent}} = \frac{300}{1,000} = 0.3,$$

$$p_{1,\text{left}} = \frac{212}{212 + 246} = 0.4629,$$

$$p_{1,\text{right}} = \frac{88}{88 + 454} = 0.1624.$$

As elaborated above, we have the cost-sensitive cutoff $T_{CS} = 0.1667$, and therefore, since $p_{1\text{parent}} > T_{CS}$ and $p_{1,\text{left}} > T_{CS}$, the parent node and the left child node are labeled positive, that is, *bad*, whereas the right child node is labeled *good*. Then, the costs C_t are calculated as follows:

$$C_{\text{parent}} = n_{0,\text{parent}} \cdot C'(1,0) = 700 \cdot 1 = 700;$$

$$C_{\text{left}} = n_{0,\text{left}} \cdot C'(1,0) = 246 \cdot 1 = 246;$$

$$C_{\text{right}} = n_{0,\text{right}} \cdot C'(0,1) = 88 \cdot 5 = 440.$$

Note that if we invert the labels in the nodes, then the costs for each node are higher and respectively equal $C_{\text{parent}} = 300 \cdot 5 = 1500$, $C_{\text{left}} = 212 \cdot 5 = 1060$, and $C_{\text{right}} = 454 \cdot 1 = 454$. The cost reduction can then be calculated for split S as follows:

$$\text{Cost reduction} = C_t - \sum_{i=1}^{k} C_{t_i} = 700 - (246 + 440) = 14.$$

> By calculating the obtained cost reduction across all possible splits, the best split can be iteratively selected in growing a tree. Subsequently, standard (cost-insensitive) pruning can be applied.

AdaBoost Variants

Many adaptations of the boosting meta-learning approach (AdaBoost), as discussed in Chapter 2, have been proposed in the literature on cost-sensitive learning. A selected number of these approaches have been summarized in Table 5.10. Note that in Table 5.10, only the steps that are different from the original AdaBoost algorithm are discussed.

As discussed in Chapter 2, the original AdaBoost algorithm assigns to each observation an initial weight $w = \frac{1}{n}$ and then builds a model on the weighted observations. The predicted outcome $h \in \{-1,1\}$ is subsequently compared with the true label $y \in \{-1,1\}$ for determining the updated weight for each observation using the formula:

$$w' = \frac{w \cdot e^{-\alpha y h}}{Z},$$

with Z a normalizing factor making the sum of all weights equal to one and α a function of the error rate ε of the model, calculated as follows:

$$\alpha = \frac{1}{2} \ln \left(\frac{1-\varepsilon}{\varepsilon} \right).$$

Essentially, all of the methods in Table 5.10 update the weights of observations in the training data differently, depending on the class label of the observation and accounting for the misclassification costs specified in the cost matrix. In other words, various **cost-sensitive weight update functions** have been proposed in the literature, each of which adapts the weights of the observations after each iteration in a slightly different way.

In the formulas in Table 5.10, as in the original AdaBoost setup, the total error ε of the model is the sum of the weights of all misclassified observations, y is the true class label of an observation, and Z is the normalizing factor that makes the sum of all weights equal to one.

Several more AdaBoost variations adopting cost-sensitive weight update functions other than the approaches discussed in Table 5.10 have been proposed in the literature, including AdaUBoost (Karakoulas and Shawe-Taylor 1999), Asymmetric AdaBoost (Viola and Jones 2001), and Cost-Sensitive AdaBoost (Masnadi-Shirazi and Vasconcelos 2011). However, these variations have only seldom been applied

Table 5.10 Overview of Cost-Sensitive Boosting Based Approaches

Name Reference	Description
CSB0, CSB1, CSB2 *(Ting 2000)*	As in the NCSA approach discussed in Table 5.8, weights are initialized by assigning to each positive observation a weight w_1 and to each negative observation a weight w_0, so that all weights sum up to one. In addition to the cost-sensitive initialization, the weights are updated in a cost-sensitive manner after each iteration, i.e., after constructing each tree in the ensemble, as in the original AdaBoost approach. For method CSB j, weights are updated as a function of parameter α_j with $j = 0, 1$, or 2. CSB0 and CSB1 use a fixed parameter α, respectively $\alpha_0 = 0$ and $\alpha_1 = 1$. CSB2 uses a parameter α which is a function of the error ε: $$\alpha = \frac{1}{2} \cdot \ln\left(\frac{1-\varepsilon}{\varepsilon}\right),$$ with ε the overall error of the tree. Subsequently, the weights w of correctly classified observations, both positive and negative, are updated as follows: $$w' = \frac{w \cdot e^{-\alpha_j}}{Z}.$$ The weights of positive and negative misclassified observations are updated respectively as follows: $$w_1' = \frac{C'(0,1) \cdot w_1 \cdot e^{\alpha_j}}{Z}$$ $$w_0' = \frac{C'(1,0) \cdot w_0 \cdot e^{\alpha_j}}{Z}.$$ Note that if $C'(0,1) = C'(1,0) = 1$, then the misclassification costs are equal and $w_1' = w_0'$, and CSB2 reduces to the original AdaBoost approach.
AdaCost *(Fan, Stolfo, Zhang, and Chan 1999)*	AdaCost increases the weight of misclassified observations proportionally with the cost and reduces the weights inversely proportional with the cost when correctly classified. Initialization of the weights occurs as in the CSB j approaches above. Subsequently, the weight of an observation is updated as follows: $$w' = \frac{w \cdot e^{-\alpha y h \beta}}{Z},$$ where α is equal to: $$\alpha = \frac{1}{2} \cdot \ln\left(\frac{1-r}{1+r}\right),$$ with $r = \sum w \cdot y \cdot h \cdot \beta$.

(continued)

Table 5.10 *(Continued)*

Name Reference	Description
	β is the cost adjustment function and is defined as: $$\beta = 0.5(1 - C_+),$$ $$\beta = 0.5(1 - C_-),$$ for a correctly classified positive and negative observation, respectively, and by $$\beta = 0.5(1 + C_+),$$ $$\beta = 0.5(1 + C_-),$$ for incorrectly classified positive and negative observation, respectively, with C_+ and C_- scaled or standardized values of $C'(0, 1)$ and $C'(1, 0)$ within the interval $(0, 1]$.
AdaC1 (Sun, Kamel, Wong, and Wang 2007)	AdaC1 includes costs in the exponent in the weight-updating formula of the original AdaBoost approach. The weights of positive and negative misclassified observations, respectively, are updated as follows: $$w_1' = \frac{w_1 \cdot e^{-\alpha h C'(0,1)}}{Z},$$ $$w_0' = \frac{w_0 \cdot e^{\alpha h C'(1,0)}}{Z},$$ where α is equal to $$\alpha = \frac{1}{2} \cdot \ln\left(\frac{1 + r_t - r_f}{1 - r_t - r_f}\right),$$ with $$r_t = \sum_{y=h} w_1 \cdot C'(0,1) + \sum_{y=h} w_0 \cdot C'(1,0),$$ $$r_f = \sum_{y \neq h} w_1 \cdot C'(0,1) + \sum_{y \neq h} w_0 \cdot C'(1,0).$$
AdaC2 (Sun et al. 2007)	Compared to AdaC1, AdaC2 includes costs outside the exponent in the weight-updating formula of the original AdaBoost approach. Weights are updated as follows: $$w_1' = \frac{C'(0,1) \cdot w_1 \cdot e^{-\alpha h}}{Z},$$ $$w_0' = \frac{C'(1,0) \cdot w_0 \cdot e^{\alpha h}}{Z},$$ where $$\alpha = \frac{1}{2} \cdot \ln\left(\frac{r_t}{r_f}\right),$$ and r_t and r_f are defined as above in AdaC1.

Table 5.10 *(Continued)*

Name Reference	Description
AdaC3 (Sun et al. *2007*)	AdaC3 includes costs both inside and outside the exponent and therefore combines the AdaC1 and AdaC2 approaches. Observations are updated as follows: $$w_1' = \frac{C'(0,1) \cdot w_1 \cdot e^{-\alpha h C'(0,1)}}{Z},$$ $$w_0' = \frac{C'(1,0) \cdot w_0 \cdot e^{\alpha h C'(1,0)}}{Z},$$ where $$\alpha = \frac{1}{2} \cdot \ln \left(\frac{r_t + r_f + r_{2t} - r_{2f}}{r_t + r_f - r_{2t} + r_{2f}} \right),$$ with r_t and r_f as above in AdaC1 and AdaC2, and with $$r_{2t} = \sum_{y=h} w_1 \cdot C'(0,1)^2 + \sum_{y=h} w_0 \cdot C'(1,0)^2,$$ $$r_f = \sum_{y \neq h} w_1 \cdot C'(0,1)^2 + \sum_{y \neq h} w_0 \cdot C'(1,0)^2.$$

in practice and from experiments it appears they do not provide any significant advantages over the discussed approaches.

An additional step in AdaBoost and the discussed variations is to obtain for each observation a class label by applying the cost-sensitive cutoff T_{CS}, as discussed above. The cutoff can be applied either to obtain a final prediction or during the ensemble learning after estimating each tree for calculating a cost-sensitive error, which can then be used for weighting observations.

Post-Training Methods

Two post-training methods have been identified in the literature—direct cost-sensitive decision making (which applies the cost-sensitive cutoff T_{CS} discussed above) and MetaCost.

Direct Cost-Sensitive Decision Making

As discussed in the introduction section of this chapter, a cost-sensitive cutoff T_{CS} can be adopted to consider misclassification costs when turning probability estimates into class labels. Any classifier producing probability estimates therefore can be transformed into a cost-sensitive classifier.

However, classification models in business are often constructed for ranking entities instead of labeling them. For instance, when building a customer churn prediction model, the aim is to rank customers as accurately as possible from high to low risk of churning. This allows subsequently selecting a certain top fraction of customers that are most likely to churn for inclusion in a retention campaign. As will be discussed in Chapter 6, the exact fraction is to be optimized to maximize the campaign's return. When customers are ranked instead of labeled, the flexibility offered by a ranking in setting the cutoff score for including customers in a retention campaign is lost, leading to a significant reduced practical use. Other applications, such as credit scoring and fraud detection, as well require accurate ranking instead of labeling. In all of these settings, the direct cost-sensitive decision-making approach has little to no value, and a pre-training or during-training approach is preferred instead. Alternatively, MetaCost may be employed as discussed next.

MetaCost

Because of its simplicity and flexibility, MetaCost, introduced by Domingos (1999), is one of the most popular approaches for estimating a cost-sensitive classification model. MetaCost develops a cost-sensitive classification model in three steps:

1. In a first step, MetaCost obtains for each observation probability estimates to belong to either class by applying an ensemble method.

2. In the second step, the cost-sensitive cutoff T_{CS} defined in the first section of this chapter is adopted for classifying and relabeling each observation based on the predicted probabilities by the ensemble in the first step.

3. In the third and final step, a single classifier is trained on the relabeled training dataset.

Table 5.11 illustrates the MetaCost approach. In the original formulation, MetaCost adopts bagging for developing an ensemble in the first step of the approach. However, alternative meta-learning schemes such as boosting or random forests may also be adopted instead. In the final step of the MetaCost approach, essentially any classification technique, as discussed in Chapter 2, can be applied for developing a cost-sensitive classification model. Therefore, one main advantage of this approach is the possibility of estimating an intuitively interpretable model by constructing a logistic regression model, a decision

Table 5.11 Example of the MetaCost Approach

MetaCost		
Step #	**Description**	**Input Data**
Step 1	The original dataset is used to learn an ensemble model predicting the original target variable, i.e., *Churn*.	<table><tr><th>ID</th><th>Recency</th><th>Frequency</th><th>Monetary</th><th>Churn</th></tr><tr><td>C1</td><td>26</td><td>4.2</td><td>126</td><td>Yes</td></tr><tr><td>C2</td><td>37</td><td>2.1</td><td>59</td><td>No</td></tr><tr><td>C3</td><td>2</td><td>8.5</td><td>256</td><td>No</td></tr><tr><td>C4</td><td>18</td><td>6.2</td><td>89</td><td>No</td></tr><tr><td>C5</td><td>46</td><td>1.1</td><td>37</td><td>Yes</td></tr><tr><td>...</td><td>...</td><td>...</td><td>...</td><td>...</td></tr></table>
Step 2	The cost-sensitive cutoff $T_{CS} = 0.23$ is applied in a second step to the *Ensemble model estimates*, obtaining *Ensemble class labels*.	<table><tr><th>ID</th><th>Recency</th><th>Frequency</th><th>Monetary</th><th>Ensemble estimate</th></tr><tr><td>C1</td><td>26</td><td>4.2</td><td>126</td><td>0.42</td></tr><tr><td>C2</td><td>37</td><td>2.1</td><td>59</td><td>0.27</td></tr><tr><td>C3</td><td>2</td><td>8.5</td><td>256</td><td>0.04</td></tr><tr><td>C4</td><td>18</td><td>6.2</td><td>89</td><td>0.15</td></tr><tr><td>C5</td><td>46</td><td>1.1</td><td>37</td><td>0.21</td></tr><tr><td>...</td><td>...</td><td>...</td><td>...</td><td>...</td></tr></table>
Step 3	In a third step a classification model is learned using a standard classification approach with the *Ensemble class labels* as the target variable.	<table><tr><th>ID</th><th>Recency</th><th>Frequency</th><th>Monetary</th><th>Ensemble label</th></tr><tr><td>C1</td><td>26</td><td>4.2</td><td>126</td><td>Yes</td></tr><tr><td>C2</td><td>37</td><td>2.1</td><td>59</td><td>Yes</td></tr><tr><td>C3</td><td>2</td><td>8.5</td><td>256</td><td>No</td></tr><tr><td>C4</td><td>18</td><td>6.2</td><td>89</td><td>No</td></tr><tr><td>C5</td><td>46</td><td>1.1</td><td>37</td><td>No</td></tr><tr><td>...</td><td>...</td><td>...</td><td>...</td><td>...</td></tr></table>

tree, or any other interpretable classification model in the final step. MetaCost offers a simple approach to making any operational model cost-sensitive by adding two steps to the current operational analytics process—the first two steps of the MetaCost approach.

Evaluation of Cost-Sensitive Classification Models

In addition to the standard performance measures discussed in Chapter 2, Chapter 6 will provide an extended introduction to profit-driven and cost-sensitive evaluation measures. Compared to evaluating classification models from a purely statistical perspective, adopting a profit-driven perspective will be shown to impact model selection and parameter tuning, eventually increasing (from a business perspective) the profitability of implementing and operating an analytical model.

When building a cost-sensitive classification model, it clearly makes sense to adopt cost-sensitive evaluation measures as will be introduced in Chapter 6 for model performance evaluation instead of merely relying on standard cost-insensitive performance measures such as AUC, Gini, and KS-distance. Of course, these measures still have use and do provide insight with respect to certain characteristics of the model, but they are unable to accurately account for imbalanced misclassification costs. Thus, cost-sensitive measures are required when evaluating cost-sensitive predictive models so as to provide complementary insight. As always, it is highly recommendable to assess model performance using multiple measures to cover different dimensions related to model performance.

Imbalanced Class Distribution

Cost-sensitive classification approaches may also be used to address the related but somewhat different challenge of imbalanced class distributions, meaning that observations of one class are much more prevalent than observations of the other class or classes. In many business applications, the class distribution appears to be heavily imbalanced:

- In customer churn prediction, typically only a small fraction of customers are churners—possibly even less than 1%, depending on the setting and time horizon over which churn is recorded (Verbeke et al. 2012).

- In credit risk modeling only a minority of the customers defaults, which in some credit portfolios amounts to only a few or even none at all; such portfolios are called low-default portfolios and are both important and of particular interest to financial institutions (Pluto and Tasche 2006).

- In many fraud-detection applications, a strongly imbalanced class distribution is observed. For instance, only a minority of credit-card transactions are fraudulent, only a small number of citizens and corporations do not pay their taxes correctly, etc. (Van Vlasselaer et al. 2015).

Additionally, in response modeling, human resources analytics, machine failure prediction, health analytics, and many other domains there are typically far fewer observations of one class or group. In all of these applications, the minority class is usually designated the positive class.

Although having imbalanced misclassification costs often results in an imbalanced class distribution, this is not automatically the case. Nor does an imbalanced class distribution necessarily lead to imbalanced misclassification costs. However, in most settings both problem characteristics effectively appear to manifest simultaneously, as in the above-provided examples. Intuitively, it makes sense that something rare is more precious or costly to miss, or vice versa—that something precious is rarer.

The class imbalance problem may cause classification algorithms to yield poor predictive performance because of the availability of insufficient training data to learn powerful predictive patterns. Cost-sensitive learning approaches are typically adopted to address this issue. Given their simplicity, weighting approaches are often used (see, e.g., Verbeke et al. 2012). By making the minority class more prevalent—for instance, by oversampling the minority class or undersampling the majority class in the training data and therefore by balancing the class distribution, the learning process is impacted. Incorrect classifications for minority or positive class observations will become more important, and therefore, the resulting model will be more focused on correctly classifying these observations. The objective is to find and include predictive patterns for the minority class in the model and to therefore make the classification model more accurate in predicting minority class observations.

When the aim of sampling is to address poor predictive performance due to a highly skewed class distribution, the sampling rate or the sampled class distribution is to be determined by the data scientist. Experimental studies are inconclusive as to the optimal sampling rate and thus do not come up with concrete guidelines or rules of thumb. The impact of sampling is likely dependent on both the nature of the given classification problem and the classification technique that is adopted. Therefore, the only trustworthy guideline that can be provided is to consider the sampled class distribution as a parameter of the model, which can be tuned to optimize performance.

The literature has shown that undersampling usually results in better classifiers than oversampling (Chawla et al. 2002). However, large experimental benchmarking studies cannot establish a statistically significant difference in performance across different applications when undersampling or oversampling (Verbeke et al. 2012). Although in particular cases, meaning for a specific dataset, sampling does appear to improve classification performance, the impact also appears to depend on the classification technique that is used.

When applying sampling or weighting for addressing the class imbalance problem, it must be noted that the resulting model will not produce well-calibrated probability estimates that represent a *true*, absolute estimate of the chance for the outcome to be positive. This is a consequence of the sampling process. For instance, when the fraction of positive observations in the dataset is increased from 1% to 5% by applying a sampling procedure, a classification model that is trained on these data will (for a test dataset that was randomly sampled from the overall dataset and as such is identically distributed as the original, unsampled training set) on average predict a 5% probability for the outcome to be positive, instead of 1%, which is the *true* positive rate in the test set.

When calibrated probability estimates are required instead of a score, the estimates produced by a classification model trained on sampled data need to be adjusted. A simple adjustment procedure has been proposed (Saerens, Latinne, and Decaestecker 2002):

$$p(y_i|x) \frac{\frac{p(y_i)}{p_S(y_i)} p_S(y_i|x)}{\sum_{j=1}^{J} \frac{p(y_j)}{p_S(y_j)} p_S(y_j|x)},$$

where y_j represents class $j = 1 \ldots J$, with J the number of classes, $p_S(y_i|x)$ is the probability of class y_i estimated for observation x on the over- or undersampled training dataset, $p(y_i|x)$ is the adjusted probability estimate, $p_S(y_i)$ is the prior probability of class y_i on the over- or undersampled training dataset, and $p(y_i)$ represents the original prior of class y_i.

EXAMPLE

To illustrate this formula, let us resume the above example, with the original binary class distribution to be 1% positive versus 99% negative observations and the oversampled class distribution to be 5% positive versus 95% negative observations. Then, an observation x predicted to have a 5% probability of being positive by a classification model trained on the oversampled data has an adjusted probability of being positive following the above formula, which is equal to

$$p(1|x) = \frac{\frac{1\%}{5\%} 5\%}{\frac{99\%}{95\%} 95\% + \frac{1\%}{5\%} 5\%} = 1.$$

This appears to be a logical result since 5% is the average prior probability of having a positive outcome in the oversampled training set, which should correspond to an adjusted probability equal to the prior probability of having a positive outcome in the original dataset.

Implementations

The cost-sensitive classification approaches discussed in this chapter will be published in 2018 by George Petrides and Wouter Verbeke as an open-source R package on https://cran.r-project.org/web/packages/.

Elaborated example applications, including data and code to learn cost-sensitive classification models, are published on the book's companion website: www.profit-analytics.com.

COST-SENSITIVE REGRESSION

The Case for Profit-Driven Regression

In this section, we focus on cost-sensitive regression, which allows users to explicitly account for the *true costs* associated with errors on estimates made by a regression model. Cost-insensitive regression approaches typically assume the cost to be a quadratic function of the size of the error, independent of the sign of the error and the characteristics of the entity for which the estimate is produced. However, the true costs in a business setting that result from prediction errors on an estimate produced by a regression model are typically much more complex in nature and heavily depend on the precise application properties. Similar to cost-sensitive classification, ignoring the true costs will most likely lead to suboptimal model performance from a profit perspective.

For instance, when customer demand is predicted for optimizing the production planning and supply chain in a business context, it is obvious that different costs are involved when overestimating and underestimating future demand. Figure 5.4 compares a quadratic cost function and an illustrative true cost function in demand forecasting. Overestimation leads to overstock, which comes as of a certain level with stepwise increasing inventory costs. Underestimation on the other hand leads to out-of-stock situations, and therefore, possibly, missed sales revenues. To some level, overstock is preferred since leading to lower costs, which should be considered when developing a predictive model and is the motivation for applying cost-sensitive regression.

Clearly, there is a relationship with the field of cost-sensitive classification; this relationship will briefly be explored later in this chapter. However, whereas cost-sensitive learning for classification has received a great amount of attention in recent years from both scientists and practitioners, with many approaches that have been developed and are readily available for use, cost-sensitive regression appears to be a relatively underexplored field, with only a limited number of papers and cases documented in the literature.

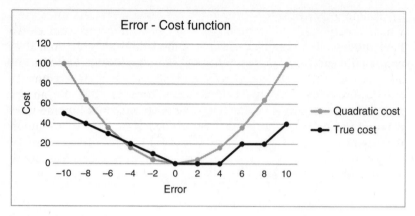

Figure 5.4 Quadratic cost versus true cost as a function of the prediction error.

COST-SENSITIVE LEARNING FOR REGRESSION

During Training Methods

Approaches to the cost-sensitive *learning* of regression models allow the adoption of alternative, nonsymmetric cost functions during model learning. These methods are complex, and few experimental evaluations indicating the strength of these approaches can be found. Thus, in this chapter we merely provide a dense overview of these approaches.

Crone, Lessmann, and Stahlbock (2005) focus on cost-sensitive learning for time series regression with asymmetric losses for under- versus overestimation by specifying adapted objective functions for training neural network predictors. The aim is to maximize the utility resulting from the predictions made by the regression model. The authors firmly stress the need to evaluate a forecast by measuring monetary costs arising out of suboptimal decisions based on imprecise predictions—for instance, future demand by customers that leads to overstock or out-of-stock situations. In inventory management, these two types of errors are associated with very different costs, which are certainly not quadratic and frequently nonsymmetric. A linear non- or asymmetric cost function as introduced by Granger (1969) is adopted as the objective function in training a neural network forecasting model. The authors indicate the possible use of a dynamic or variable cost function for neural network training as developed by Haiqin, Irwin, and Chan (2002) for support vector regression (SVR), allowing for varying or heteroscedastic training objectives—that is, allowing the consideration of a nonuniform cost function over the domain of the target variable.

Haiqin et al. (2002) focus on predicting financial time series, which are typically nonstationary and noisy in nature and clearly have different costs associated with under- and overestimation. Their approach adapts the margins of the epsilon-insensitive loss function adopted in SVR to the problem specifications, allowing asymmetric and nonfixed (i.e., nonuniform) margins to be used in training an SVR model. Interestingly, to assess model performance and provide more detailed insight, they calculate both the MAD as well as the upside mean absolute deviation (UMAD) and downside mean absolute deviation (DMAD) to distinguish and separately measure the upside and downside risk when over- or underestimating the true value.

$$\text{UMAD} = \frac{1}{n}\sum_{i=1}^{n}|y_i - \hat{y}_i| \text{ for } \hat{y}_i > y_i,$$

$$\text{DMAD} = \frac{1}{n}\sum_{i=1}^{n}|y_i - \hat{y}_i| \text{ for } \hat{y}_i < y_i.$$

Granger (1969) is the earliest retrieved source reporting the inappropriateness of a quadratic loss function and the existence of nonsymmetric cost functions in the field of economics and management. The consequences of using a generalized cost function and distribution of the target variable are studied to assess the suitability and possible bias of a linear predictor of the target variable in terms of both the predictor variables and a bias term. Christoffersen and Diebold (1996, 1997) further discuss prediction under asymmetric loss and provide methods for approximating the optimal predictor under more general loss functions via series expansion.

Post-Training Methods

A simple yet elegant tuning approach to cost-sensitive regression was introduced in Bansal, Sinha, and Zhao (2008). Similar to the post-training methods discussed for cost-sensitive classification, the proposed approach tunes a regression method by modifying the predictions for the resulting outcomes to be cost-optimal. The main advantage of the approach, which in the literature is denoted *BSZ* as an acronym of the surnames of the developers, is its flexibility in allowing the adoption (without modifications) of any regression method for learning the base regression model that is tuned.

One important component of the tuning method is the **average misprediction cost (AMC)** evaluation metric for assessing the performance of a regression model in a cost-sensitive way. Assuming a prediction error e to yield a cost characterized by a cost function $C(e)$ then the AMC of a regression model f is defined as follows:

$$AMC = \frac{1}{n} \sum_{i=1}^{n} C(e_i) = \frac{1}{n} \sum_{i=1}^{n} C(y_i - \hat{y}_i).$$

As already discussed, the AMC should be measured over an independent test set. Some of the required properties of the cost function C are as follows:

1. $C(e) \geq 0$;
2. $C(0) = 0$;
3. $|e_1| < |e_2| \wedge e_1 e_2 \rightarrow C(e_1) < C(e_1)$.

The first two properties essentially express that the cost function respectively should be nonnegative and equal to zero when a prediction is exact—that is, when the error is zero. The third property requires the cost function to be monotonic both for positive and negative errors. As a result, the cost function is convex. The cost function C is problem dependent in the sense that it needs to reflect the actual costs experienced in the business setting in which the regression model is operated. The cost function is similar to the profit function that will be defined in Chapter 6 for evaluating classification models from a profit perspective.

Rather than optimizing a cost-sensitive objective function during model learning, the proposed method aims to minimize the associated cost of a regression model after it is learned by tuning the predictions of the regression model. In Bansal et al. (2008), a simple tuning procedure is proposed to shift the predictions by adding an adjustment factor δ. In other words, an adjusted model $f' = f + \delta$ is fitted by finding the optimal value for δ that minimizes the AMC (as defined above) over the training data. The AMC of the adjusted model is the following function of δ:

$$AMC = \frac{1}{n} \sum_{i=1}^{n} C(y_i - f'(x_i)) = \frac{1}{n} \sum_{i=1}^{n} C(y_i - f(x_i) + \delta).$$

Thus, some flexibility is added to the model allowing predictions to shift such that lower average misprediction costs can be achieved. The parameter δ can be fitted by applying any suitable optimization approach to minimize the above objective function. However, because the cost function is convex, an efficient hill-climbing algorithm is designed (Bansal et al. 2008), as detailed in Algorithm 5.1.

Algorithm 5.1 BSZ Performance-Tuning Algorithm

Inputs:

Γ: A base regression method (e.g., linear regression)

S: A training dataset, $S = \{(\mathbf{x}_i, \mathbf{y}_i)\}_{i=1}^{n}$

C: A cost function

p: A given precision of adjustment ($p > 0$)

1: Train a regression model f using Γ based on S

2: **if** AMC(p) < AMC(0)

3:         $d = 1$ (with d the direction of adjustment)

4: **else if** AMC(p) > AMC(0)

5:         $d = 1$

6: **else**

8:         Return f

9: **end if**

10: $\delta_{prev} = 0$

11: **loop**

12:         $s = 1$ (with s the hill-climbing stride)

13:         $\delta = \delta_{prev}$

14:         **Loop**

15:                 $\delta_{prev} = \delta$

16:                 $\delta = \delta + s \cdot d \cdot p$

17:                 $s = s \cdot 2$

18:                 $\delta_{next} = \delta + s \cdot d \cdot p$

19:         **until** AMC(δ_{next}) > AMC(δ)

20: **until** $s \leq 2$

21: Return adjusted regression model $f' = f + \delta$

EXAMPLE

Several papers in the literature on cost-sensitive regression are applied to predict loan charge-off (Bansal et al. 2008; Czajkowski, Czerwonka, and Kretowski 2015; Zhao, Sinha, and Bansal 2011). Assume we have a dataset S allowing the estimation of a linear regression model f to predict the loan charge-off amount using Ordinary Least Squares, as discussed in Chapter 2. Note that OLS assumes a symmetric and quadratic error function. However, as discussed extensively in Bansal et al. (2008), a *linlin* cost function $C_{linlin}(e)$

(as illustrated in Figure 5.5) better reflects the *true* costs associated with errors on the predicted amounts. A ratio of 1:5 of the cost per unit for underestimation c_u versus overestimation c_o is adopted. The *linlin* cost function is generally defined as follows:

$$C_{linlin}(e) = \begin{cases} c_u|y - \widehat{y}| & \text{for } \widehat{y} < y \\ 0 & \text{for } \widehat{y} = y \\ c_o|y - \widehat{y}| & \text{for } \widehat{y} > y \end{cases}$$

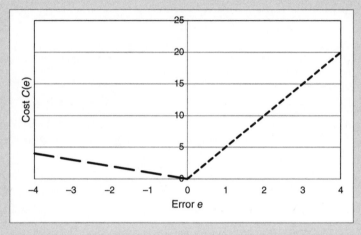

Figure 5.5 Linlin cost function C_{linlin} in function of the prediction error e.

Next, we can go through the steps of Algorithm 5.1. In the first step, a linear regression model f is estimated. Suppose this model is associated with the relation between the AMC and the adjustment factor δ, as shown in Figure 5.6. Note that we do not directly obtain this function, but can calculate AMC for any value of δ using the formula introduced above. The aim of Algorithm 5.1 is to efficiently arrive at the adjustment factor δ that minimizes the AMC without having to exhaustively calculate this function.

In step 2 of Algorithm 5.1, the direction of adjusting the model f is determined. The aim is to minimize the AMC, so in step 2, it is checked whether AMC decreases when δ is positive. The precision of adjustment p is set in this example to 0.1 and represents the step size that is used in

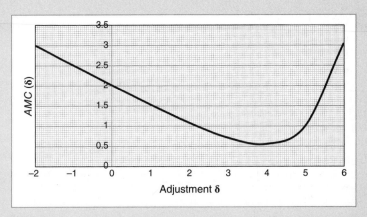

Figure 5.6 Average misprediction cost in function of the adjustment δ.

increasing or decreasing the adjustment. Because $AMC(0) = 2.01$ and $AMC(p) = AMC(0.1) = 1.96$, in step 2, we find that $AMC(p) < AMC(0)$. Thus, the direction of adjustment d is set to 1 in step 3, meaning that by increasing δ, the AMC will decrease.

Subsequently, the algorithm jumps to step 10, in which the adjustment value δ_{prev} is initialized to 0. Two loops then implement a hill-climbing (or a hill-descent) approach to finding the optimal adjustment factor δ. The basic idea is simply to arrive at the optimal value in an accelerated stepwise manner, which is facilitated by the convexity of the cost and thus, the AMC function. In the inner loop, in each iteration the adjustment factor δ is approximately doubled since in each iteration, the parameter s is doubled, which together with the precision parameter p controls the step size—that is, the growth or increase of δ. The inner loop ends when the AMC of the new or next δ is larger than that of the current δ. The outer loop then sets δ to a previous value and again attempts to approach the optimal value by restarting the inner loop. The parameter s is reinitialized to enable a more refined approximation. When s in the last iteration of the inner loop equals 1 or 2, then this means that δ in the last iteration was close or equal to the optimal value, and the outer loop ends. Table 5.12 elaborates some iterations to illustrate how the algorithm arrives at finding the optimal adjustment δ. Eventually, the algorithm will converge to a value near 3.91, as shown in Figure 5.6.

Table 5.12 Elaborated Example of Algorithm 5.1

loop iteration		1					2	...
s = 1	s	1					1	...
$\delta = \delta_{prev}$	δ	0					1.5	...
loop Iteration		1.1	1.2	1.3	1.4	1.5	2.1	...
$\delta_{prev} = \delta$	δ_{prev}	0	0.1	0.3	0.7	1.5	1.5	...
$\delta = \delta+s*d*p$	δ	0.1	0.3	0.7	1.5	3.1	1.6	...
s = s*2	s	2	4	8	16	32	2	...
$\delta_{next} = \delta+s*d*p$	δ_{next}	0.3	0.7	1.5	3.1	6.3	1.8	...
until AMC(δ_{next})>AMC(δ)	AMC(δ_{next})> or <AMC(δ)	1.86						

<1.96	1.67
<1.86	1.29
<1.67	0.67
<1.29	4.30
>0.67	1.16
<1.25	...
until $s \leq 2$	...

An extension of the above-introduced tuning method was proposed by the same authors in Zhao et al. (2011). Whereas the basic tuning method simply shifts the predictions of the original regression model by adding a constant adjustment factor δ, the extended version enables the fitting of a more general function—that is, a polynomial function of degree m, which takes the original regression model f as the input variable to produce a cost-sensitive estimate for the target variable:

$$f'(x) = g(f(x)) = \sum_{j=1}^{m} \beta_j f(x)^j.$$

Note that although $f(x)^0 = 1$, when setting m equal to one, we do not exactly arrive at the basic tuning method. Since for $m = 1$ we get $f' = \beta_0 + \beta_1 f$, which is different from $f' = \delta + f$ as adopted in the basic tuning method, given that the extended tuning approach multiplies the base regression model f with a coefficient β_1.

We refer to Zhao et al. (2011) for the full details on the extended hill-climbing algorithm for finding both the optimal parameters β_j and the polynomial degree m to minimize the AMC. However, from the experimental evaluations reported in both Zhao et al. (2011) and Czajkowski et al. (2015), it seems that only a relatively small improvement in further reducing misprediction costs is achieved from extending the tuning method, and the simple approach achieves the bulk of potential gains. Nonetheless, even a small reduction in average cost per prediction may represent a significant overall cost reduction when aggregating over a large population, such as a customer base.

PROFIT-DRIVEN DESCRIPTIVE ANALYTICS

In the second part of this chapter, we focus on profit-driven descriptive analytics. We first adopt a profit-oriented perspective toward segmentation and subsequently toward association rules, extending the standard clustering and association rule mining approaches discussed in Chapter 2.

Profit-Driven Segmentation

Direct Profit-Driven Segmentation

A direct approach to segment customers in a profit-driven manner is to group customers based on their lifetime value, as discussed in Chapter 3. The definition of CLV that is adopted for segmenting customers may either be backward or forward looking, or a combination of both. Backward- and forward-looking CLV, respectively, indicate the net revenues that have been generated by a customer in the past or that will be in the future, transformed to current monetary value.

Throughout this section, we will elaborate a case study and apply the discussed approaches on a synthetic CLV example dataset containing information on 1,000 customers, including CLV as well as RFM and cost of service (CoS) information. The example dataset can be obtained from the book's companion website. We start the analysis by plotting the distribution of the customer lifetime value for the observations in the dataset, as shown in Figure 5.7.

The distribution in Figure 5.7 allows us to segment the customer base in terms of CLV in an intuitive manner.

Doing so, we arrive, for instance, at the three customer segments shown in Figure 5.8 and reported on in Table 5.13:

- The first group, which is denoted the *Bronze* segment in line with an often adopted marketing approach to characterize customer segments, is bringing heavy losses.
- The second group (i.e., the *Silver* segment), is the category containing most customers with most of them bringing positive revenue, although some of them yield negative returns.
- The *Gold* segment finally only contains customers that bring a significant profit to the company.

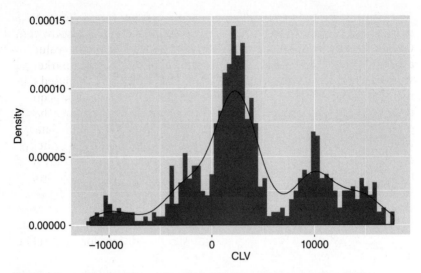

Figure 5.7 Customer lifetime value distribution for a dataset containing 1,000 customers.

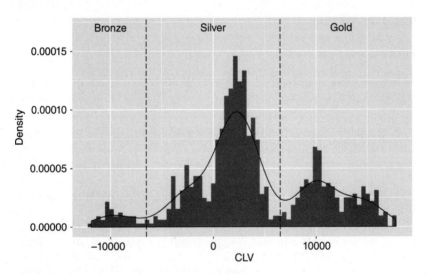

Figure 5.8 Three-cut strategy for CLV segmentation.

Table 5.13 Average CLV and Fraction of Observations per Segment

Segment	CLV (€)	% Cases
Bronze	−9,545	5%
Silver	1225	65%
Gold	115,79	30%

A correct customer segmentation is of key importance toward the marketing processes of an organization. Stahl et al. (2012) show that CLV is directly related to brand equity (i.e., the economic value of a brand). Hence, the essential importance of developing marketing strategies and campaigns that account for CLV. Defining CLV-based segments supports the development of, for example, retention or acquisition campaigns that focus on high-value customers. For instance, based on insights provided by the segmentation of the CLV example dataset, we may decide that customers in the Bronze segment should either be targeted in an upsell or cross-sell campaign. Alternatively, we may seek to actively end the relation (which is called forced churn) with Bronze segment customers, or if this is not possible or desirable, at least we should make sure never to target these customers in a retention campaign to prevent them from churning. Gold segment customers, on the other hand, would be very expensive to lose and therefore should be more rapidly included in retention campaigns.

The direct, intuitive segmentation approach adopted in the previous example, however, is not based on data and therefore arbitrary and possibly suboptimal. As an alternative, K-means and SOMs may be adopted to define profit-driven segments.

K-Means for Profit-Driven Segmentation

A very popular segmentation approach in the industry is K-means clustering, as explained in Chapter 2. K-means clustering can be used for performing a profit analysis by revealing how key profit-driving variables relate to different segments of customers. A typical application of K-means in a profit-driven environment characterizes clusters according to the average CLV of the customers in the resulting segments. Note that the CLV is typically not taken into account in the segmentation step for finding similar customers, but is only used in a post-processing step to analyze the obtained segments.

We will elaborate this approach for the previously introduced CLV example dataset. We can start by constructing three segments to allow comparison with the previous analysis. Therefore, we have applied the K-means procedure with $K = 3$ on the observations in the CLV dataset, excluding the CLV variable, leading to the three segments shown in Figure 5.9. In this figure, we used principal component analysis as discussed in Chapter 2 to visualize the three resulting segments. The idea of using PCA for cluster visualization is to create a plot with the first two or three principal components, for 2D or 3D graphs, respectively, and then overlaying the cluster boundaries. In a simple dataset, such as this one, the clustering procedure gives neatly packed results, but

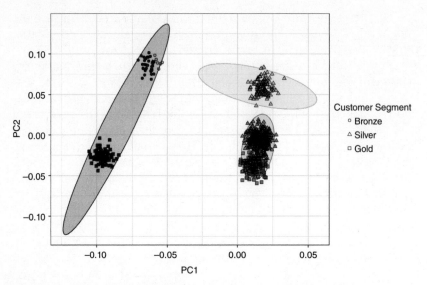

Figure 5.9 Three-group customer segmentation.

in a real-life dataset the observations can be spread across the graph in a less apparent order. PCA can help in visualizing clusters, but we need to carefully consider how much variance is represented by the principal components that are plotted. If the first two or three principal components do not capture a large part of the variance within the dataset, then the visualization could be misleading.

From Figure 5.9, we see that three groups are not sufficient to appropriately segment the customer base. The left cluster in fact consists of two groups of customers. Therefore, we have re-run the K-means clustering procedure with $K = 4$ to group the customer base into four segments by splitting the left-most cluster as shown in Figure 5.10a.

Comparing the results of the K-means clustering to the direct segmentation in terms of Bronze, Silver, and Gold customers, leads to the following findings:

■ Most Bronze customers are in the upper left segment.

■ The upper right cluster only exclusively contains Silver customers.

■ There are at least four, and possibly even five segments, instead of three.

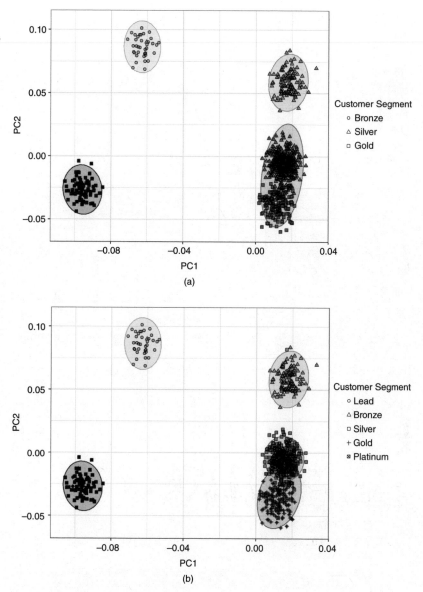

Figure 5.10 Plot of the first two principal components following a *K*-means clustering of the CLV example dataset.

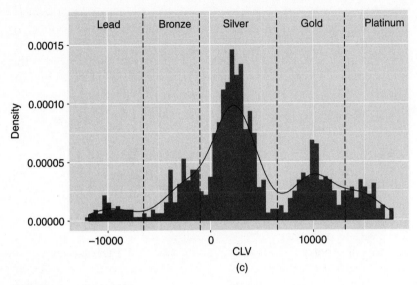

Figure 5.10 *(Continued)*

When looking at the lowest-right cluster in Figure 5.10a, which is composed mostly of Gold customers, it appears to be appropriate to further split this segment into two segments. Doing so leads to the five segments characterized in Table 5.14, which allows us to decide about the appropriateness of creating five segments by analyzing the average values of the variables (CLV, RFM, CoS) in the dataset for the resulting five segments. In general, if the average values overall are sufficiently different, then it is meaningful to create separate segments. Whereas if we find the average values to be similar (e.g., for the two segments making up the lower-right cluster in Figure 5.10a), then it might be preferable to merge these segments.

Table 5.14 Average CLV, RFM Variables and Cost of Service for the Observations in the Five *K*-means Clusters

Segment	CLV	Recency	Frequency	Monetary	CoS
Platinum	14,952	3	89	2,392	2,552
Gold	9,989	17	18	9,809	8,974
Silver	2,360	31	17	9,462	8,605
Bronze	−2,829	56	13	6,903	9,530
Lead	−9,555	58	48	2,607	3,615

For the five resulting segments in Table 5.14, comparing the average CLV indicates that five appears to be an appropriate number of segments. The average CLV varies significantly across the segments, and also the average RFM and CoS values vary significantly across the five segments, which therefore are concluded to effectively represent five different groups of customers that can be identified in the customer base.

The resulting five customer segments, as shown in Figures 5.10b and 5.10c, can then be analyzed and characterized by interpreting the average values reported in Table 5.14. For instance, the platinum segment can be described as high-value customers that appear to buy often, as indicated, respectively, by the high average CLV and the low average recency and high average frequency that is observed for this segment. Note that the high frequency compensates for the relatively low average monetary value of purchases, which, combined with a low cost of service, explains the high average CLV that is observed for this segment. Customers in the Silver segment, on the other hand, spend large amounts of money, but their purchases come at a high cost of service. Silver customers also purchase quite often, overall making them valuable customers. Similar, and even more detailed analyses can be made for the other segments, providing insight and allowing us to develop tailored campaigns and strategies for increasing the overall profitability.

Self-Organizing Maps for Profit-Driven Segmentation

Self-organizing maps, introduced in Chapter 2, can be adopted to visualize datasets in a profit-oriented manner and to find the optimal number of segments to create. We elaborate the approach again using the CLV example dataset introduced before. The objective now is to obtain a 2D visualization of this dataset—for instance, by using heatmaps to visualize the U-matrix and the component planes, and to design a clustering strategy over the neurons in the map to obtain meaningful and useful segments.

The first step in developing an SOM is to decide on the variables that will be included in the analysis. In our example, we include the RFM and CoS variables. The second step involves the design of the map, and more specifically, the topology and the size of the map. In general, a hexagonal topology can be recommended, with the appropriate size of the map depending on the size and the complexity of the dataset. Kohonen (2014) has recommended that the size of the map should be determined by trial and error. This can be done by comparing maps of different sizes in terms of the resulting *density* and the resolution of the resulting image. Both should be *sufficient*, as will be explained next.

The density of a map refers to the number of observations represented by each neuron in the map, in other words, the number of observations for which a neuron is the best matching unit (see Chapter 2). A sufficient density is typically defined as about 30 observations per neuron, minimum. Since the CLV dataset contains 1,000 observations, the map should therefore have at most about $\frac{1,000}{30} \cong 33$ neurons. The resolution of a map refers to the ability to provide refined, detailed insight in variations across the observations. If a map is made up of a single neuron, representing the average observation, no insight at all in variations or distributions is provided, and the resolution is therefore zero. The more neurons we use, the higher the resolution of the map will be. But as a consequence of using more neurons, the density will become lower. Therefore, deciding on the size of a map is about finding the optimal trade-off between density and resolution.

The observations in the dataset should be distributed across the SOM, with some variability in terms of the density acceptable and to be expected. When the dataset tends to have naturally occurring clusters of observations, then it can even be expected (and acceptable) that some regions of the map represent only few, if any, observations (Kangas, Kohonen, and Laaksonen, 1990).

For the CLV example, we have trained maps[3] on the dataset of size 4-by-4, 5-by-5, and 6-by-6. The resulting density maps are shown in Figure 5.11. Density maps are heatmaps indicating the number of observations that are represented by the neurons in the map by means of color coding. A dark color indicates that a neuron is the best matching unit for many observations, whereas a light color indicates few observations to be represented by a neuron. Note that the map of size 6-by-6 in total contains 36 neurons, which is more than the maximum number of 33 neurons as calculated before following the minimum density guideline, but only slightly so possibly still acceptable.

The first conclusion that can be drawn from Figure 5.11 is that the 4-by-4 map is too densely packed, with a minimum observation density of 50 and a maximum of 150, or 15% of the observations in the dataset. This is too much. The map does not represent the topology of the variable space with a sufficient resolution, and therefore it is discarded. The 6-by-6 map, on the other hand, has a density that appears to be too low. Note that the color coding for the 6-by-6 map is different from the other maps, with dark colors representing values of 50. Several neurons and even regions in this map do not represent a sufficient number of observations, falling to around 20 observations per

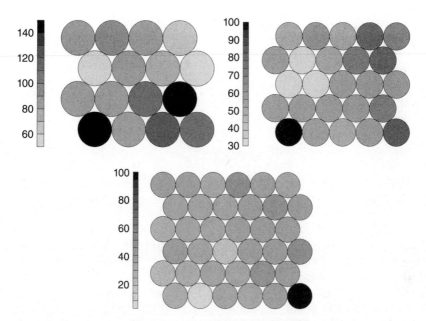

Figure 5.11 Density maps of CLV example dataset SOMs of different sizes.

neuron in the less-dense parts of the map. Although looking promising at first sight, the 6-by-6 map does not necessarily represent the shape of the dataset reliably. Note that the number of neurons in the 6-by-6 map is above the maximum number of neurons calculated following the minimum density guideline, as indicated before, and therefore was expected possibly to be of too low resolution.

The 5-by-5 map, finally, has a mixture of neurons with between 35 and 100 observations per neuron. There is one neuron with 100 observations, which is a lot. However, later analyses will show this is not an issue but related to a particular characteristic of the dataset. We could extend the analysis for determining the appropriate size to an asymmetric map of 5-by-6. However, for elaborating this example, we are satisfied with the 5-by-5 map.

Another visualization of the selected 5-by-5 SOM that may help in understanding the multidimensional structure of the example CLV dataset is a distance map, shown in Figure 5.12. A distance map basically visualizes the U-matrix, as defined in Chapter 2, as a heatmap. The color coding indicates the average distance between a neuron and neighboring neurons in terms of the connecting weights. In Figure 5.12, dark colors indicate a large distance and therefore can be interpreted as cluster boundaries.

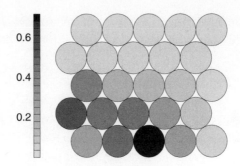

Figure 5.12 Distance map of the CLV example dataset SOM.

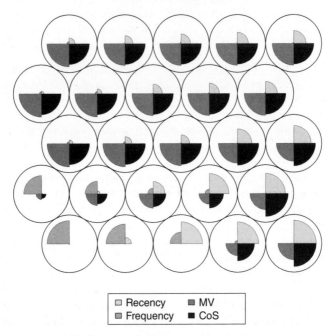

Figure 5.13 Codebook vector graph of the CLV example dataset SOM.

For a small number of variables (four or five at most) the codebook vector graph is an excellent visualization of the contribution to the map of each variable. A codebook vector graph combines basically different component planes, as introduced in Chapter 2, in a single visualization. The codebook for the 5-by-5 SOM that was trained on the CLV example dataset is shown in Figure 5.13.

A codebook shows the relative importance of variables for each neuron in the map, by visualizing the relative sizes of the weights of the connections between each neuron and the input neurons (i.e., the variables). A codebook can provide insight in the composition of the dataset in terms of segments as well as variations in the variables that define these segments. An indication regarding segments in the example CLV dataset can be obtained from the codebook in Figure 5.13 as follows:

- The lower right region of the map appears to represent a segment of customers with a relatively high cost of service (CoS), low monetary value (MV), and high recency. Along the diagonal, recency seems to be the characteristic with higher variation.

- The lower-left region of the map appears to represent a segment of customers with a very high frequency. These will appear to be the platinum customers that were defined before.

Note that interpreting a SOM using codebooks (as well as using density-, distance- or heatmaps) requires some skill, insight, and experience, which come with practice.

When there are many variables in the dataset, it makes sense to study component planes of variables instead of a codebook graph. Component planes have been introduced in Chapter 2 and can be visualized as well using heatmaps, adopting again a color-coding scheme to indicate the distribution of a selected variable across the neurons in the map.

The heatmaps shown in Figure 5.14 provide additional insight and allow us to gain a clear picture of the different segments in the dataset. The variables in the dataset have been normalized to the [0, 1] range, so the color scale can be compared across the heatmaps of different variables. From Figure 5.14 it appears that the monetary value and cost of service are spread across opposite sections of the map (i.e., the upper-left region versus the lower-right region), whereas frequency and cost of service seem to be almost tied together. These heatmaps can help in creating meaningful clusters, but preferably we use the neurons of the SOM to create statistically valid segments, as we will explain next.

In Chapter 2, we showed how hierarchical clustering can be used to create fine-tuned segments when there are few observations in the dataset. A self-organizing map in fact could be regarded as a small dataset of prototype observations, since that is what neurons are. A hierarchical clustering algorithm can be applied to these observations to find groups of similar neurons. Each resulting group composes a segment in the underlying dataset, consisting of the observations represented by the neurons in the group. The average

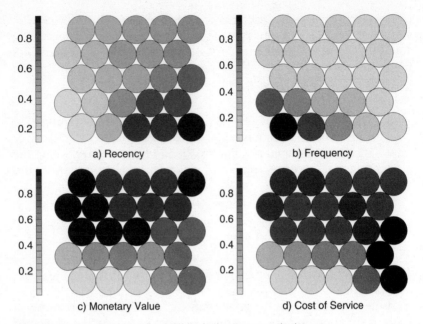

Figure 5.14 Heatmaps for the variables in the CLV example dataset.

observations over the resulting clusters of prototype observations are then representative for these segments and facilitate interpretation, in a similar manner as Table 5.13 and Table 5.14. Figure 5.15 shows the dendrogram resulting from applying a hierarchical clustering procedure using single linkage on the 5-by-5 SOM.

It can be seen from the dendrogram in Figure 5.15 that a relatively large group of neurons is found to be very similar. These are grouped in cluster C4. The other clusters that we define by setting the maximum intra-group distance at 0.75, are clusters C1, C2, C3, and C5, as shown in Figure 5.15. These clusters include fewer neurons, which as well appear to be less alike. The resulting clusters have been plotted on the codebook vector graph of the SOM, as shown in Figure 5.16.

The plot in Figure 5.16 allows us to interpret the resulting customer segments by analyzing their behavior in terms of the RFM and CoS variables. Customers in cluster C2, situated in the lower-left part of the SOM, appear to have a relatively high value for frequency, but a low value for cost of service, recency, and monetary value. These are the Platinum customers we defined before when discussing the K-means and direct profit-driven segmentation approaches. The Gold customers are in cluster C1, right next to the platinum customers in the self organizing map, with a higher recency, but still with a comparatively high frequency. The customers in cluster C5 in the lower right part of the

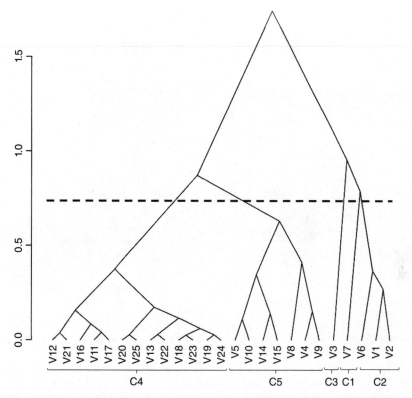

Figure 5.15 Dendrogram plot of the hierarchical clustering procedure using single linkage.

map are the loss-inducing customers, with a high cost of service but a low monetary value and frequency. These were grouped in the Lead segment before.

Looking back at the heatmaps shown in Figure 5.14, we arrive at the same insights. The bread-and-butter Silver customers, representing the large majority of customers, are grouped in cluster C4 at the top of the map. The remaining cluster C3, finally, contains the mixed-bags customers, with a mixture of different values and centered in one isolated neuron, which appears to be rather different from its neighboring nodes, as can be observed as well from the distance map shown in Figure 5.12.

The running example that has been elaborated in this section illustrates the potential power of self-organizing maps to provide an insightful and profit-oriented visualization of a complex dataset, and how it can be used to create representative, value-centric customer

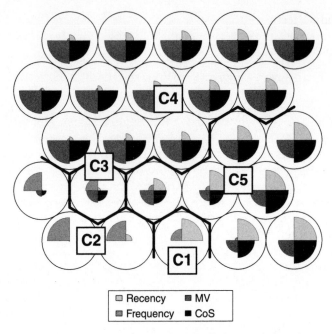

Figure 5.16 Codebook vector graph with clustering limits superimposed.

segments and profiles. As a hierarchical clustering procedure was used to generate the final clusters, nothing is stopping us from using more or less groups. This flexibility allows us, for instance, to align the number of clusters with a company's general marketing strategy or business processes. Even individual neurons can be used as clusters, when a very detailed segmentation of the customers is required. New customers can be quickly assigned to such a detailed customer segment simply by finding the best matching unit in the self-organizing map.

Profit-Driven Association Rules

In Chapter 2, we discussed how association rules can be extracted from a transactional database. Remember, an association rule can be characterized by means of its support, confidence, and lift. These three measures are statistical performance measures but convey no information about the profit impact, which is from a business perspective obviously more relevant. In fact, the statistical strength of an association rule can be orthogonal to its economic relevance. For example, it could perfectly be that the association rules detected only account for a small portion of the overall profit. Consider the following two examples of association rules for a luxury foods shop:

Champagne → Caviar (Support = 1%; Confidence = 72%)

Champagne → Olives (Support = 10%; Confidence = 78%)

Although the second rule has a higher statistical support and confidence, the first one may be more valuable from a profit perspective. Typically, high profit items such as caviar will occur more rarely, which implies that the minimum support threshold should be lowered in order to detect them. Unfortunately, this will lead to a combinatorial explosion of association rules and thus a more intensive post-processing step. Since these high-profit items often occur more rarely, another option is to define a constraint (e.g., price is > €100), which can then be explicitly taken into account in the algorithm generating the association rules (Han and Kamber 2011).

Let's now reconsider our two example association rules discussed above. Suppose we know a customer bought champagne. Should we recommend the most likely item—say, olives, or the most profitable item, say caviar? The inverse relationship between the likelihood to buy and the amount to spend further complicates this choice (Wang et al. 2002). A better strategy would be to calculate the expected profit (EP) as follows (Kitts et al. 2000):

$$EP(X \rightarrow Y) = Confidence(X \rightarrow Y) \sum_i Profit(Y_i),$$

where the summation ranges over all items in item set Y. The EP basically measures the expected profit of buying items Y_i once a customer has bought the items in X. As such, it measures the recommendation value of itemset Y and can be used to recommend the itemset Y with the biggest EP instead of the highest confidence. A key drawback of the EP is that it does not factor in the baseline or prior probability $P(Y)$ of buying the items Y. For items that are frequently purchased anyway (and thus have high $P(Y)$ values), it may not make much sense to recommend them. The incremental profit (IP) accounts for this and is defined similar to lift except that it subtracts $P(Y)$ instead of dividing by it as follows (Kitts et al. 2000):

$$IP(X \rightarrow Y) = (Confidence(X \rightarrow Y) - P(Y)) \sum_i Profit(Y_i).$$

Hence, once a customer has bought items X, the items Y with maximal $IP(X \rightarrow Y)$ can be recommended.

EXAMPLE

Consider the following transactions database:

Transaction ID	Items
T001	stella, hoegaarden, diapers, baby food, pizza
T002	coke, stella, diapers
T003	cigarettes, diapers, baby food, pizza
T004	chocolates, diapers, hoegaarden, apples
T005	tomatoes, water, leffe, stella, pizza
T006	spaghetti, diapers, baby food, stella, pizza
T007	water, stella, baby food, pizza
T008	diapers, baby food, spaghetti
T009	baby food, stella, diapers, hoegaarden, pizza
T010	apples, chimay, baby food

The association rule baby food, diapers → stella, pizza has a support of 30% and a confidence of 60%.

Let us now assume that the profits for baby food, diapers, stella, and pizza are 2, 3, 1, and 4, respectively. The EP then becomes:

$$EP = 0.6 \cdot (1 + 4) = 3,$$

and the IP, given the a-priori probability of the itemset $Y = \{$stella, pizza$\}$ being bought equal to 50%, i.e., $P(Y) = 0.5$:

$$IP = (0.6 - 0.5) \cdot (1 + 4) = 0.5.$$

The above example tacitly made two simplifications. First, it assumed that all products were bought in the same quantities. Second, it did not factor in any price discounts or promotions on the target items (i.e., stella and pizza) to help convince customers to make the purchase. Since both these factors have an impact on the profit, we will elaborate on them in what follows.

Quantitative association rules take into account the quantity of the items. A straightforward approach to extract quantitative association rules is by discretizing quantitative items into intervals and treat them as nominal variables in the transaction database (Srikant and Agrawal 1996). Instead of having items like stella, tomatoes, etc., we will now have items such as stella:3..6 (denoting the purchase of between 3 and 6 bottles of stella), tomatoes:6+ (denoting the purchase of more than

6 tomatoes), and so on. The discretization can be done using concept hierarchies provided by business experts or by using the quantity distribution of the items. Obviously, a more fine granular discretization implies a lower support to find associations (Han and Kamber 2011).

Wang et al. (2002) introduced the idea of profit mining to take into account promotion codes when mining and using association rules. They recoded transactions by making an explicit distinction between the items to be recommended (target items) and the others (nontarget items). Moreover, every transaction also includes the promotion code and quantity of each item purchased. Profit mining then aims at recommending a target item and promotion code to future customers whenever they buy nontarget items.

Other attempts have been made as well to combine profit or other business objectives with association rules. Brijs et al. (1999) introduced the PROFSET model, which integrates the discovery of frequent itemsets with a model for product selection using integer programming. PROFSET stands for PROFitability per SET, since the model includes the profitability per frequent itemset so as to maximize the cross-selling effects between products. By using sensitivity analysis, they were able to quantitatively assess the profitability impact of product assortment decisions. Tao, Murtagh, and Farid (2003) introduce a new algorithm called WARM (Weighted Association Rule Mining), which integrates item weights (based on, e.g., profit) in the association rule mining process. Choi, Ahn, and Kim (2005) characterized the business value of association rules by considering their recency, frequency, and monetary (RFM) properties. The recency refers to the time trend of an association rule and can be quantified by calculating the degree of change in support. Rules with a strong increasing support might indicate emerging patterns and corresponding business opportunities. The frequency refers to the statistical significance and can be measured by the support, confidence, and lift. Finally, the monetary value reflects on the profitability of a rule as discussed earlier.

CONCLUSION

In this chapter, we have introduced a range of profit-driven analytical techniques. Profit-driven predictive analytics aim at maximizing the profits resulting from the predictions made by an analytical model when operated in a business setting. To maximize profitability, the costs of errors can be explicitly accounted for either in a pre-processing step, during training, or in a post-processing step. The involved errors are either misclassification errors in a classification context or regression errors when developing a regression model. We have discussed and illustrated various cost-sensitive classification approaches and cost-sensitive regression approaches that can be applied in these three stages. The complexity of the discussed techniques ranges from relatively low to very high. Clearly, the involved complexity may impact the practical use of these approaches in terms of the interpretability and the required effort to develop and implement cost-sensitive analytical models. On the other hand, a successful adoption of profit-driven predictive analytics can generate significant gains in terms of profits and lead to an important competitive advantage.

Profit-driven descriptive analytics are excellent tools to explore and understand data prior to (or in parallel with) applying predictive analytics, with a key focus on profitability. Customers can be segmented, for instance, following a direct profit-driven segmentation approach to analyze the distribution of the customer lifetime value across the customer base. If a company has additional customer data, then a proper clustering algorithm can be used to create more refined segments. RFM and socio-demographic variables can be added to the analysis, allowing a clustering approach such as K-means to create both meaningful and useful groups. A more advanced analysis, which is especially useful when there is even more data, is to train a self-organizing map. Self-organizing maps can, quite literally, paint a clear picture of the structure of the data and as such provide useful insights in the profit distribution across customer segments, as extensively illustrated in this chapter. Finally, we also discussed profit-driven association rules, which extends the standard approach introduced in Chapter 2 by adding a profitability layer to the analysis, as such generating association rules that are optimal from a business perspective.

To support the adoption by practitioners of the approaches discussed in this chapter, example datasets and implementations have been published on the book's companion website: www.profit-analytics.com.

REVIEW QUESTIONS

Multiple Choice Questions

Assume a dataset containing 8,663 negative and 2,337 positive observations, and the following cost matrix:

	Actual Negative	Actual Positive
Predicted Negative	$C(0,0) = 0$	$C(0,1) = 7$
Predicted Positive	$C(1,0) = 2$	$C(1,1) = 0$

Question 1

What is the class distribution φ?

   a. 0.27
   b. 0.22
   c. 3.50
   d. 0.29

Question 2

What is the cost-sensitive cutoff T_{CS}?

   a. 0.27
   b. 0.22
   c. 3.50
   d. 0.29

Question 3

If a cost-insensitive classifier $f(x)$ predicts a probability $p(1|x) = 0.22$, then what are the expected losses for both classes?

   a. $\ell(x,0) = 5.46$ and $\ell(x,0) = 0.44$
   b. $\ell(x,0) = 0.50$ and $\ell(x,0) = 0.50$
   c. $\ell(x,0) = 0.44$ and $\ell(x,0) = 5.46$
   d. $\ell(x,0) = 1.54$ and $\ell(x,1) = 1.56$

Question 4

What is the cost-sensitive distribution φ_{CS}?

   a. 0.96
   b. 0.78
   c. 12.41
   d. 0.08

Question 5

To achieve the above cost-sensitive distribution (rounded to two decimals, as in the answer on question 4), what is the required resampled number of negatives?

   a. 6757
   b. 8316
   c. 8180
   d. 8286

Question 6

To achieve the above cost-sensitive distribution (rounded to two decimals, as in the answer on question 4), what is the required resampled number of positives?

   a. 2443
   b. 2475
   c. 2244
   d. 2434

Question 7

What are the weights to be used in the C4.5CS approach for positive and negative observations?

   a. $w_0 = 2.0781e - 04$ and $w_1 = 5.9374e - 05$
   b. $w_0 = 0.2222$ and $w_1 = 0.7778$
   c. $w_0 = 0.7778$ and $w_1 = 0.2222$
   d. $w_0 = 5.9374e - 05$ and $w_1 = 2.0781e - 04$

Question 8

Calculate the cost-sensitive gain value as adopted in the C4.5CS approach for the following candidate split:

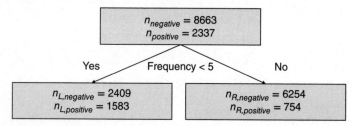

   a. 0.0245
   b. 0.4321
   c. 0.0245
   d. 0.0341

Question 9

What is the meaning or effect of the factor δ in the BSZ cost-sensitive regression approach?

   a. This factor determines the step size in the hill-climbing optimization procedure of the BSZ approach.

b. This factor is added to the estimates of a regression model to make the estimates cost-optimal.

c. The factor δ determines the direction of adapting the estimates by the regression model that is post-processed.

d. The factor δ is the decay parameter in the exponential weighting function adopted by the BSZ approach.

Question 10

Consider the following statements on constructing CLV-based customer segments using the CLV distribution:

    I. Profits are not considered, as no RFM variables are used.

    II. The distribution must be studied to create segments based on distributional peaks.

    III. It might be insufficient to use just CLV as the distribution might not be clear-cut.

Which of these statements are true?

a. I and II
b. Just I
c. II and III
d. I, II, and III

Question 12

Consider the following statements regarding K-means clustering for segmentation:

    I. Only RFM variables are relevant; no other variables should be included.

    II. The centroids of the clusters give the average description of each group.

    III. The number of clusters must be determined using trial and error.

    IV. Graphical analyses must be complemented by tables and numerical analyses.

Which of these statements are true?

a. I and III
b. II and III
c. II and IV
d. III and IV

Question 13

Consider the following statements regarding self-organizing maps:

   I. They are a type of neural networks.

   II. They require a hierarchical clustering procedure to obtain the final number of clusters.

   III. They are trained using the competitive learning paradigm.

   IV. They can be used for clustering on its own or in parallel with other clustering techniques.

Which of these statements are true?

a. I and III
b. I, II, and III
c. I, III, and IV
d. Just I

Question 14

When defining a self-organizing map topology, which statement is not correct?

a. The number of neurons must be statistically significant.
b. The number of prototypes can be determined by trial and error.
c. Hexagonal shapes tend to represent the original topology of the space better than rectangular shapes.
d. A density graph helps in studying if the chosen shape and size are adequate.

Question 15

Consider the following statements regarding visualizations of self-organizing maps:

   I. A codebook is only relevant when there are few variables in the dataset.

   II. A heatmap can be used to see the distribution of all variables across the prototype vectors.

   III. The distance graph allows a quick view of potential clusters by detecting isolated groups.

   IV. Superimposing the cluster boundaries over the heatmap allows seeing the characteristics of the clusters.

Which of these statements are true?

a. I, II, and III
b. I, III, and IV
c. II and III
d. I, II, III, and IV

Question 16

Which statement is not correct?

a. The support, confidence, and lift of an association rule convey no information about the profit impact of the rule.
b. The expected profit (EP) of an association rule takes into account the prior probability of buying an item.
c. Quantitative association rules consider the quantity of the items.
d. Association rules with a strong increasing support might indicate emerging patterns and corresponding business opportunities.

Open Questions

Question 1

Explain the difference between profit-driven predictive analytics and standard predictive analytics discussed in Chapter 2, and illustrate the need for profit-driven predictive analytics in a business setting.

Question 2

Discuss the difference between pre-training, during-training, and post-training cost-sensitive classification approaches and the impact thereof in terms of practical use in a business setting such as customer churn prediction.

Question 3

Explain in your own words why it is important to adopt cost-sensitive evaluation measures when developing cost-sensitive classification models.

Question 4

Discuss the two basic adaptations that are made to standard decision-tree approaches to make them cost-sensitive.

Question 5

Explain the basic workings of the BSZ cost-sensitive regression approach.

Question 6

Discuss the limitations of the standard loss functions used to train and evaluate regression models in a business setting, such as demand estimation.

Question 7

In the example application that was discussed throughout the section on profit-driven descriptive analytics, the CLV variable was used to analyze the results from K-means and SOM, but was not included in the calculations of the clustering procedure itself. Repeat the analyses, including the variable and answer the following questions.

    a. Does including the variable contribute to each clustering algorithm? Why or why not?

    b. Do you think that it should be included in general, more complex datasets?

    c. Is the same number of neurons required to correctly describe the resulting SOM?

    d. What graphical differences can you see in the component plane heatmaps for each variable? Why do these differences occur?

NOTES

1. https://archive.ics.uci.edu/ml/index.html.
2. In this book, we consistently adopt the term observation, as discussed in Chapter 1, and therefore as well the term observation-dependent. Whereas in the literature, often the term example-dependent is used as a synonym (Aodha and Brostow 2013), as well as instance-varying or example-specific.
3. All SOMs were created using the Kohonen R package (Wehrens and Buydens 2007).

REFERENCES

Aodha, O. Mac, and G. J. Brostow. 2013. "Revisiting Example Dependent Cost-Sensitive Learning with Decision Trees." *Proceedings of the IEEE International Conference on Computer Vision*, 193–200.

Bache, K., and M. Lichman. 2013. "UCI Machine Learning Repository." *University of California Irvine School of Information*. Retrieved from http://www.ics.uci.edu/~mlearn/MLRepository.html.

Bahnsen, A. C., D. Aouada, and B. Ottersten. 2015. "Example-Dependent Cost-Sensitive Decision Trees." *Expert Systems with Applications* 42(19): 6609–6619.

Bahnsen, A. C., D. Aouada, and B. Ottersten. 2016. *Ensemble of Example-Dependent Cost-Sensitive Decision Trees*. Retrieved from http://arxiv.org/abs/1505.04637.

Bansal, G., A. P. Sinha, and H. Zhao. 2008. "Tuning Data Mining Methods for Cost-Sensitive Regression: A Study in Loan Charge-Off Forecasting." *Journal of Management Information Systems*, 25(3), 315–336.

Berteloot, K., W. Verbeke, G. Castermans, T. Van Gestel, D. Martens, and B. Baesens. 2013. "A Novel Credit Rating Migration Modeling Approach Using Macroeconomic Indicators." *Journal of Forecasting*, 32: 654–672.

Bradford, J. P., C. Kunz, R. Kohavi, C. Brunk, and C. E. Brodley. (1998, April). "Pruning Decision Trees with Misclassification Costs." In *European Conference on Machine Learning* (pp. 131–136). Springer, Berlin, Heidelberg.

Brefeld, U., P. Geibel, and F. Wysotzki. 2003. "Support Vector Machines with Example Dependent Costs." *Proceedings of the European Conference on Machine Learning*, 23–34.

Brijs, T., G. Swinnen, K. Vanhoof, and G. Wets. 1999. "Using Association Rules for Product Assortment Decisions." *Proceedings of the Fifth ACM SIGKDD International Conference on Knowledge Discovery and Data Mining - KDD '99*, 254–260.

Chai, X. C. X., L. D. L. Deng, Q. Y. Q. Yang, and C. X. Ling. 2004. "Test-Cost Sensitive Naive Bayes Classification." *Fourth IEEE International Conference on Data Mining (ICDM2004)*, 51–58.

Chawla, N. V, K. W. Bowyer, L. O. Hall, and W. P. Kegelmeyer. 2002. "SMOTE: Synthetic Minority Over-Sampling Technique." *Journal of Artificial Intelligence Research*, 16(1): 321–357.

Chawla, N. V, A. Lazarevic, L. O. Hall, and K. Bowyer. 2003. "SMOTEBoost: Improving Prediction of the Minority Class in Boosting." *Principles of Knowledge Discovery in Databases, PKDD-2003*, 107–119.

Chen, C., A. Liaw, and L. Breiman. 2004. "Using Random Forest to Learn Imbalanced Data." *University of California, Berkeley*, 110.

Choi, D. H., B. S. Ahn, and S. H. Kim. 2005. "Prioritization of Association Rules in Data Mining: Multiple Criteria Decision Approach." *Expert Systems with Applications* 29(4): 867–878.

Christoffersen, P. F., and F. X. Diebold. 1996. "Further Results on Forecasting and Model Selection under Asymmetric Loss." *Journal of Applied Econometrics* 11(5): 561–571.

Christoffersen, P. F., and F. X. Diebold. 1997. "Optimal Prediction Under Asymmetric Loss." *Econometric Theory* 13(6): 808–817.

Crone, S. F., S. Lessmann, and R. Stahlbock. 2005. "Utility-Based Data Mining for Time Series Analysis—Cost-Sensitive Learning for Neural Network Predictors." *UBDM '05 Proceedings of the 1st International Workshop on Utility-Based Data Mining*, 59–68.

Czajkowski, M., M. Czerwonka, and M. Kretowski. 2015. "Cost-Sensitive Global Model Trees Applied to Loan Charge-Off Forecasting." *Decision Support Systems*, 74, 57–66.

Domingos, P. 1999. "MetaCost: A General Method for Making Classifiers Cost-Sensitive." In *Proceedings of the Fifth ACM SIGKDD International Conference on Knowledge Discovery and Data Mining KDD'99* (pp. 155–164).

Drummond, C., and R. C. Holte. 2000. "Exploiting the Cost (In)sensitivity of Decisions Tree Splitting Criteria." *International Conference on Machine Learning* 1(1): 239–246.

Elkan, C. 2001. "The Foundations of Cost-Sensitive Learning." In *Proceedings of the Seventeenth International Joint Conference on Artificial Intelligence (IJCAI'01)*.

Fan, W., S. J. Stolfo, J. Zhang, and P. K. Chan. 1999. "AdaCost: Misclassification Cost-Sensitive Boosting." In *Proceedings of the 16th International Conference on Machine Learning, Morgan Kaufmann, San Francisco, CA* (pp. 97–105).

Granger, C. W. J. 1969. "Prediction with a Generalized Cost of Error Function." *Journal of the Operational Research Society* 20(2): 199–207.

Haiqin, Y., K. Irwin, and L. Chan. 2002. "Non-fixed and Asymmetrical Margin Approach to Stock Market Prediction Using Support Vector Regression." In *Proceedings of ICONIP 2002* (pp. 1–5). Singapore.

Han, J., and M. Kamber. 2011. *Data Mining: Concepts and Techniques*. Elsevier.

Japkowicz, N., and S. Stephen. 2002. "The Class Imbalance Problem: A Systematic Study." *Intelligent Data Analysis* 6(5): 429–449.

Kangas, J. A., T. K. Kohonen, and J. T. Laaksonen. 1990. "Variants of Self-Organizing Maps." *IEEE Transactions on Neural Networks*, 1(1), 93–99.

Karakoulas, G., and J. Shawe-Taylor. 1999. "Optimizing Classifiers for Imbalanced Training Sets." *Neural Information Processing Systems* 11: 253–259.

King, G., and Zeng, L. 2001. "Logistic Regression in Rare Events Data." *Political Analysis*, 9(2): 137–163.

Kohonen, T. 2014. "MATLAB Implementations and Applications of the Self-Organizing Map." Helsinki: Unigrafia.

Ling, C. X., and V. S. Sheng. 2008. "Cost-Sensitive Learning and the Class Imbalance Problem." In *Encyclopedia of Machine Learning*.

Ling, C. X., Q. Yang, J. Wang, and S. Zhang. 2004. "Decision Trees with Minimal Costs." *Twenty-First International Conference on Machine Learning (ICML2004)*, 69.

Liu, X.-Y., J. Wu, and Z.-H. Zhou. 2009. "Exploratory Undersampling for Class Imbalance Learning." *IEEE Transactions on Systems, Man and Cybernetics*, 39(2): 539–550.

Lomax, S., and S. Vadera. 2011. "An Empirical Comparison of Cost-Sensitive Decision Tree Induction Algorithms." *Expert Systems* 28(3): 227–268.

Mahnič, V., and T. Hovelja. 2012. "On Using Planning Poker for Estimating User Stories." *Journal of Systems and Software* 85: 2086–2095.

Maldonado, S., and S. F. Crone. 2016. "Time Series Feature Selection with SVR." Poznan, Poland: EURO2016.

Masnadi-Shirazi, H., and N. Vasconcelos. 2011. "Cost-Sensitive Boosting." *IEEE Transactions on Pattern Analysis and Machine Intelligence* 33(2): 294–309.

Moløkken-Østvold, K., N. C. Haugen, and H. C. Benestad. 2008. "Using Planning Poker for Combining Expert Estimates in Software Projects." *Journal of Systems and Software*, 81(12): 2106–2117.

Nikolaou, N., N. Edakunni, M. Kull, P. Flach, and G. Brown. 2016. "Cost-Sensitive Boosting Algorithms: Do We Really Need Them?" *Machine Learning* 104(2–3): 359–384.

Petrides, G., and W. Verbeke. 2017. "Cost-Sensitive Learning for Binary Imbalanced Datasets Using Decision Trees Ensembles." *Machine Learning*, Submitted.

Pluto, K., and D. Tasche. 2006. "Estimating Probabilities of Default for Low Default Portfolios." In *The Basel II Risk Parameters: Estimation, Validation, and Stress Testing* (pp. 79–103).

Powers, D. M. W. 2007. "Evaluation: From Precision, Recall and F-Factor to ROC, Informedness, Markedness and Correlation." School of Informatics and Engineering, Flinders University Adelaide Australia, Technical Report SIE-07-001 (December).

Saerens, M., P. Latinne, P., and C. Decaestecker. 2002. "Adjusting the Outputs of a Classifier to New a Priori Probabilities: A Simple Procedure." *Neural Computation* 14(1): 21–41.

Seiffert, C., T. M. Khoshgoftaar, J. Van Hulse, and A. Napolitano. 2010. "RUS-Boost: A Hybrid Approach to Alleviating Class Imbalance." *IEEE Transactions on Systems, Man, and Cybernetics Part A: Systems and Humans* 40(1): 185–197.

Sheng, V., and C. Ling. 2006. "Thresholding for Making Classifiers Cost-Sensitive." *Proceedings of the National Conference on Artificial Intelligence*, 476–481.

Srikant, R., and R. Agrawal. 1996. "Mining Quantitative Association Rules in Large Relational Tables." *ACM SIGMOD Record* 25(2): 1–12.

Stahl, F., M. Heitmann, D. R. Lehmann, and S. A. Neslin. 2012. "The Impact of Brand Equity on Customer Acquisition, Retention, and Profit Margin." *Journal of Marketing* 76(4): 44–63.

Sun, Y., M. S. Kamel, A. K. C. Wong, and Y. Wang. 2007. "Cost-Sensitive Boosting for Classification of Imbalanced Data." *Pattern Recognition* 40(12): 3358–3378.

Tao, F., F. Murtagh, and M. Farid. 2003. "Weighted Association Rule Mining Using Weighted Support and Significance Framework." *KDD 2003 Proceedings of the Ninth ACM SIGKDD International Conference on Knowledge Discovery and Data Mining*, 661–666.

Ting, K. M. 2000. "A Comparative Study of Cost-Sensitive Boosting." In *Proceedings of the 17th International Conference on Machine Learning*.

Ting, K. M. 2002. "An Instance-Weighting Method to Induce Cost-Sensitive Trees." *IEEE Transactions on Knowledge and Data Engineering* 14(3): 659–665.

Turney, P. 1995. "Cost-Sensitive Classification: Empirical Evaluation of a Hybrid Genetic Decision Tree Induction Algorithm." *Journal of Artificial Intelligence Research* 2: 369–409.

Van Vlasselaer, V., T. Eliassi-Rad, L. Akoglu, M. Snoeck, and B. Baesens. 2016. "Gotcha! Network-based Fraud Detection for Social Security Fraud." *Management Science*, forthcoming.

Verbeke, W., K. Dejaeger, D. Martens, J. Hur, and B. Baesens. 2012. "New Insights into Churn Prediction in the Telecommunication Sector: A Profit-Driven Data Mining Approach." *European Journal of Operational Research* 218(1): 211–229.

Viola, P. A, and M. J. Jones. 2001. "Fast and Robust Classification Using Asymmetric AdaBoost and a Detector Cascade." *Proc. NIPS* (December), 1311–1318.

Wang, K., S. Zhou, and J. Han. 2002. "Profit Mining: From Patterns to Actions." *Advances in Database Technology, EDBT 2002, Lecture Notes in Computer Science* 2287: 70–87.

Wehrens, R., and L. M. C. Buydens. 2007. "Self- and Super-Organizing Maps in R: The Kohonen Package." *Journal of Statistical Software* 21(5): 1–19.

Zadrozny, B., and C. Elkan. 2001. "Learning and Making Decisions When Costs and Probabilities Are Both Unknown." In *Proceedings of the Seventh ACM SIGKDD International Conference on Knowledge Discovery and Data Mining - KDD '01* (pp. 204–213).

Zadrozny, B., J. Langford, and N. Abe. 2003. "Cost-Sensitive Learning by Cost-Proportionate Example Weighting." *ICDM '03 Proceedings of the Third IEEE International Conference on Data Mining*.

Zhao, H., A. P. Sinha, and G. Bansal. 2011. "An Extended Tuning Method for Cost-Sensitive Regression and Forecasting." *Decision Support Systems* 51(3): 372–383.

CHAPTER **6**

Profit-Driven Model Evaluation and Implementation

INTRODUCTION

As an alternative to adopting profit-driven analytical techniques, as discussed in the previous chapter, we may implement a profit-driven analytics strategy by looking at the profitability of analytical models in the evaluation step. This omits the use of complex modeling techniques and may therefore be of preference. We do want to warn the reader, however, that the process of developing and applying an appropriate and accurate profit-sensitive evaluation may turn out to be challenging. In this chapter, we support the development of such evaluation by discussing a series of advanced measures for profit-driven performance assessment of classification and regression models. We aim to provide deeper insight in the basic principles underlying these measures, and from these discussions we will as well arrive at some key guidelines regarding the operational implementation of these measures.

In the first part of this chapter, we will focus on classification models. We will start by discussing the most straightforward and intuitive profit-based evaluation approach, i.e., calculating the average misclassification cost. Related to this is the selection of a classification cutoff score, which can be tuned using the average misclassification cost to optimize the resulting profitability of the model. Consequently, the evaluation of a classification model has practical and important implications towards the implementation of the model. This is followed by a study of a series of receiver operating characteristic (ROC)-based measures for profit-driven evaluation: First, we will develop the H-measure and discuss problems related to using the area under the receiver operating characteristic curve (AUC) when misclassification costs are imbalanced, after which we introduce the more complex maximum profit (MP) and expected maximum profit (EMP) measures. Both the MP and EMP measure allow users to account for specific and complex cost-benefit distributions, which we will exemplify for the case of customer churn prediction and credit scoring. The first part of this chapter is concluded with an explanation of the ROCIV measure, which allows users to account for observation-dependent costs in evaluating a classification model. All these measures will be illustrated by means of a case study, which is developed throughout the first part of the chapter using a synthetic dataset on microfinance loans provided on the book's companion website, www.profit-analytics.com.

Whereas the average misclassification cost approach, introduced in the first section of this chapter, is intuitive and straightforward (but nonetheless does offer valuable insight and practical use), the discussions on the ROC-based profit-driven evaluation measures in this chapter are more advanced and technical in nature, requiring the reader to possess advanced background knowledge. References will be provided to assist the reader in acquiring this background knowledge, if lacking.

The main takeaway of the first part of this chapter is that ROC analysis or standard statistical evaluation measures as discussed in Chapter 2 might not be sufficient to appropriately evaluate analytical models when profits are involved, which is typically the case in a business setting. The good news is that there is an array of metrics available to support an appropriate evaluation in such cases. The bad news is that an important challenge remains to be addressed by the data scientist, which is to select the right measure and to possibly adapt it to the specific characteristics of the application setting. The discussions and examples in this chapter should help the reader in addressing this challenge.

In the second part of this chapter, we will focus on the evaluation of regression models. In the previous chapter, the need for profit-driven regression models, and therefore as well the need for profit-driven evaluation measures to assess the performance of regression models, has been thoroughly motivated. Also, the extensive number of examples illustrating the need for such measures in a classification context is indicative for a similar need to exist in a regression context. However, whereas powerful profit-driven evaluation approaches have been developed for classification models, the available number of such approaches for evaluating regression models is limited. Nonetheless, two interesting measures have been recently developed which will be discussed and illustrated in this chapter. Following an extensive discussion of loss functions and standard error-based evaluation measures, in the final section of this chapter we introduce REC curves and REC surfaces. REC surfaces provide a certain flexibility to adapt to specific application characteristics. More specifically, they can account for the specific cost-benefit structure that is involved, and provide an accurate indication of the profitability of the model, complementing thereby standard evaluation measures such as R^2 or MSE.

PROFIT-DRIVEN EVALUATION OF CLASSIFICATION MODELS

A straightforward and intuitive method for evaluating a classification model in a profit-driven manner is to measure the total or average misclassification cost associated with the prediction errors that are made by a classification model. This approach will be explained and illustrated with a case study in the next section. More advanced measures, all of them related to the ROC curve (see Chapter 2), have been actively developed in recent years. The first of these measures, Hand's H-Measure, is based on the concept of the expected value of a cost distribution. Verbeke et al. (2012) and Verbraken et al. (2014), introducing the maximum profit (MP) and expected maximum profit (EMP) measure, respectively, extended the same idea to more general situations, including settings where both costs and benefits are uncertain or stochastic. All these measures focus on cases where we have imbalanced, class-dependent misclassification costs; alternatively, the observations themselves may involve variable misclassification costs (i.e., observation-dependent misclassification costs), for which case Fawcett (2006b) developed the concept of the ROCIV curves.

Average Misclassification Cost

Calculating the average misclassification cost (i.e., the average mis-prediction cost introduced in Chapter 5) is the most straightforward and intuitive approach to analyze the performance of a classification model from a profit-driven perspective. Note that the average misclassification cost is independent of the number of observations in the test set, and therefore could be more convenient to use than the total misclassification cost. In what follows, we discuss how to calculate the average misclassification cost for evaluating a classification model and study the pitfalls we might encounter.

In Chapter 2, a model was generally defined as a function $f: X \rightarrow Y$, where X corresponds to the set of all predictor variables and Y corresponds to the target variable that we aim to estimate as a function of the predictor variables. When the target variable only has two possible outcomes (e.g., a credit applicant is either good or bad), then we have a binary classification problem and $Y = \{0,1\}$. When the target variable has more than two, but still a discrete and limited number of possible outcomes, then $Y = \{1,\dots,J\}$, with J the number of classes. Both in business and beyond, binary classification problems are far more common than multiclass problems. Moreover, multiclass problems can always be mapped to a set of binary classification problems using, for example, One-versus-One or One-versus-All coding (Baesens 2014). In a classification problem, the modeled function f approximates the class probabilities $p(j|x_i)$, i.e., the probabilities for an observation i with characteristics x_i, which in short we refer to as observation x_i, to belong to the various classes j and $\sum_j p(j|x_i) = 1$.

In the previous chapter, we extensively discussed the cost matrix C as introduced by Dominguez (1999) to characterize and account for imbalanced costs in classification problems. The elements of the cost matrix C are associated with the elements of the confusion matrix as introduced in Chapter 2. Element $C(j,k)$ of the cost matrix represents the cost of predicting an observation to belong to class j, whereas the actual class is k. Remember that as discussed before in Chapter 5, when a cost is negative, it represents a benefit. For the binary case, the cost matrix looks as in Table 6.1 below.

Note that we can simplify the cost matrix by subtracting the values of $C(0,0)$ and $C(1,1)$ from the values in the first and second column, respectively, leading to cost matrix C' with $C'(0,0)$ and $C'(1,1)$ equal to zero. It is the ratio of the values $C'(0,1)$ and $C'(1,0)$ in the simplified cost matrix C' that eventually matters, as discussed in Chapter 5. Several application-specific cost matrices will be discussed throughout this chapter.

The cost matrix allows to calculate the average misclassification cost of predictions of a classification model over a test set

Table 6.1 Cost Matrix for a Binary Classification Problem

	Actual Negative	Actual Positive
Predicted Negative	$C(0,0)$	$C(0,1)$
Predicted Positive	$C(1,0)$	$C(1,1)$

(see Chapter 2), as we know the actual class label for each observation in the test set. There are two approaches that can be adopted for calculating the average misclassification cost:

1. A first approach simply compares for each observation in the test set the class that is predicted by the classification model and the actual class. The involved costs for correct and incorrect classifications for positive and negative observations are averaged, yielding the average misclassification cost. When the classification model produces conditional class probabilities, then the estimated class label for observation x_i can either be obtained as:

   a. the class label with the highest conditional class probability $p(j|x_i)$, i.e., $\hat{y}_i = argmax_j\{p(j|x_i)\}$;

   b. the class label resulting in the lowest expected loss $\ell(x_i, k)$, as discussed in the previous chapter.

   These two approaches correspond, respectively, to using a cost-insensitive or cost-sensitive cutoff (see Chapter 5) for turning class probabilities into class labels. In fact, we may use any cutoff for turning class probabilities into class labels. As will be illustrated in a following case study on cutoff point tuning in credit scoring, varying the adopted cutoff typically gives rise to a variable average misclassification cost.

   The cost $C(x_i)$ of predicting a class label $\hat{y}_i$ for observation x_i is equal to the element $C(\hat{y}, y_i)$ of the (simplified) cost matrix that corresponds with the pair of the predicted class label $\hat{y}_i$ and the actual class label y_i. Then the average misclassification cost, calculated over the observations in the test set, corresponds to:

$$AMC = \frac{1}{n}\sum_i C(\hat{y}_i, y_i).$$

2. Instead of predicted class labels, an alternative approach uses the conditional class probabilities $p(j|x_i)$ estimated by the classification model to calculate the *expected* average misclassification cost, E-AMC, of using the model (Elkan 2001). For an observation x_i of class k, the misclassification cost $C(x_i)$ is calculated as follows:

$$C(x_i) = \sum_j p(j|x_i)C(j, k).$$

   Note the similarity between the above equation of the expected misclassification cost and the equation of the expected loss $\ell(x_i, j)$ of an observation x_i with class label k predicted to be of class j, as defined in the previous chapter:

$$\ell(x_i, j) = \sum_k p(k|x_i) \cdot C(j,k).$$

The expected loss is calculated for a predicted class j, which is fixed, by multiplying the class probabilities estimated by the classification model with the associated costs, $C(j,k)$ and summing across the actual class labels k. The expected cost, however, is different from the expected loss since it is calculated from the perspective of the actual class k, which is fixed, by multiplying the class probabilities estimated by the classification model with the associated costs, $C(j,k)$, and summing across the predicted classes j. Calculating the expected loss for all possible classes j, allows a cost-optimal prediction for an observation x_i, as discussed in Chapter 5. Calculating the expected misclassification cost is only meaningful to do for the actual class that is observed for an observation. A practical example, elaborating and comparing the calculation and interpretation of the expected loss and expected misclassification cost, is provided below.

The expected average misclassification cost, which we will denote $E\text{-}AMC$ to distinguish from the approach previously discussed, is calculated by averaging the expected misclassification costs of the observations in the test set:

$$E\text{-}AMC = \frac{1}{n}\sum_i C(x_i).$$

The average misclassification cost measures allow users to evaluate a classification model in a sensible and intuitive profit-driven manner. They provide an interpretable indication of performance in terms of cost or benefit and can be used for comparing alternative classification models. Also, as will be elaborated in the case study on cutoff point tuning below, the average misclassification cost allows users to compare the profitability of a classification model across classification cutoffs.

EXAMPLE

The *German Credit Data* example dataset introduced in the previous chapter comes with the cost matrix defined in Table 6.2, with *bad* meaning default and *good* meaning no default. Bad is the positive class ($y = 1$) and good the negative class ($y = 0$).

In the previous chapter, we calculated the expected loss for classifying an observation x either as good or bad, with the conditional class probabilities estimated by a classifier $f(x)$ equal to $p(1|x) = 0.22$ and accordingly,

Table 6.2 Cost Matrix for the German Credit Data Example Dataset

	Actual *good*	Actual *bad*
Predicted good	$C(0,0) = 0$	$C(0,1) = 5$
Predicted bad	$C(1,0) = 1$	$C(1,1) = 0$

$p(0|\mathbf{x}) = 1 - p(1|\mathbf{x}) = 1 - 0.22 = 0.78$. Then the expected loss for classifying $\mathbf{x}$ either as good or bad equals:

$$\ell(\mathbf{x}, 0) = \sum_k p(k|\mathbf{x}) \cdot C(0, k) = 0.78 \cdot 0 + 0.22 \cdot 5 = 1.10,$$
$$\ell(\mathbf{x}, 1) = \sum_k p(k|\mathbf{x}) \cdot C(1, k) = 0.78 \cdot 1 + 0.22 \cdot 0 = 0.78.$$

The expected loss for classifying $\mathbf{x}$ as bad is smaller than for classifying $\mathbf{x}$ as good, leading to classifying the observation as bad, $\widehat{y} = 1$.

When the actual class of the observation is good, $y = 0$, then we can calculate the (expected) misclassification cost $C(\mathbf{x})$ for observation $\mathbf{x}$ using the above introduced two approaches, as follows:

1. Using the predicted class label:

$$C(\mathbf{x}) = C(\widehat{y}, y) = C(1,0) = 1.$$

2. Using the conditional class probability estimates:

$$C(\mathbf{x}) = \sum_j p(j|\mathbf{x}) \cdot C(j, 0) = 0.78 \cdot 0 + 0.22 \cdot 1 = 0.22.$$

Assume we have an alternative classification model, $f'(\mathbf{x})$, which produces for the same observation the conditional probability estimates $p(1|\mathbf{x}) = 0.12$ and $p(0|\mathbf{x}) = 0.88$, then following the calculation of the expected loss the observation is classified as good. Following the two approaches for calculating the average misclassification cost, we obtain $C(\mathbf{x}) = 0$ and $C(\mathbf{x}) = 0.12$, respectively. Note that these are lower than for the first classification model, which makes sense since the alternative model $f'(\mathbf{x})$ correctly predicts the class of the observation to be good.

The classification model yielding the lowest (expected) average misclassification cost could be considered the *best* model from a profitability perspective. In general, the estimation of the average misclassification cost can be robust in the short term and provide a trustworthy indication of the future performance of the model. The average misclassification cost, however, is more susceptible to changes in the distribution of the observations along the conditional class probability estimates than measures that have been specifically designed to estimate the profitability across the distribution of the observations directly, such as the MP and EMP measures, which will be discussed in subsequent sections of this chapter.

The average misclassification cost approach can be extended in a straightforward manner to accommodate a time-dependent or observation-dependent (see Chapter 5) cost matrix, as follows:

- When the cost matrix is time-dependent, a set of matrices $\{C_t(j, k)\}_t$ can be used to calculate the average misclassification cost as in the above equations, associating each observation to a time frame t such that each observation i has an associated time frame t_i. The expected misclassification cost for an observation x_i of class k, then corresponds to:

$$C(x_i) = \sum_j p(j \mid x_i) C_{t_i}(j, k).$$

This approach can be useful in fast-changing environments where costs depend on external effects, such as the price of a market asset, or in long-term models where inflation could make the comparison of nominal profits misleading.

- When the cost matrix is observation-dependent, again a set of matrices $\{C_i(j,k)\}_i$ is to be used for calculating the average misclassification cost, following the expression provided above for the time-dependent cost matrix. Care should be taken here, since the average misclassification cost may not accurately indicate future profitability of a classification model when the distribution of the observations shifts in time. A sophisticated extension to the AUC measure developed by Fawcett (2007) that allows users to analyze the performance of a classification model with observation-dependent costs will be discussed in a later section in this chapter.

Cutoff Point Tuning

This section briefly discusses cutoff point tuning, which is a widely used approach allowing analysis of profitability when evaluating a classification model and related to the average misclassification cost discussed in the previous section. Cutoff point tuning is related to the ROC-based measures discussed later in this chapter, and of specific interest in application settings with observation-dependent misclassification costs.

To correctly evaluate the performance of a model in a profit-oriented environment, it is necessary to simulate the real conditions in which the model will operate. Most classification models estimate conditional class probabilities, but usually clear-cut decisions are to be made, requiring a class label to be estimated. For instance, in application credit scoring, a decision needs to be made about accepting or rejecting a loan application based on the estimated conditional probability of the applicant to default.

Class labels can be derived from class probability estimates in various manners—for instance, by adopting a cost-sensitive or cost-insensitive cutoff as already discussed. When the problem is binary and when the objective is to maximize the future profit of adopting and implementing the model, the decision boils down to setting a cutoff T, which will maximize the future profitability, or equivalently, minimize the future losses. An appropriate model evaluation in a profit-driven environment must then include a profit-oriented decision regarding this optimal cutoff. This is called **cutoff point tuning,** which allows users to make profit-sensitive decisions with profit-insensitive classification models.

The average misclassification cost approaches discussed in the previous section assume a constant cost matrix C. However, in application settings with observation-dependent misclassification costs, the average misclassification cost will depend on the cutoff that is chosen, or more precisely, the average misclassification cost will have different values across the probability distribution over the observations induced by the model. This occurs in credit scoring, for example, where higher value loans typically involve higher risk and higher misclassification costs. We will study approaches that explicitly include this effect and which take as input the ROC curve, and provide a measure that considers the effect of the distribution of the profits across the probability estimates. Before doing so, however, we elaborate a case study, illustrating how the average misclassification cost evaluation approach can be used to make decisions in a practical case study.

CASE STUDY

In this case study, we adopt the average misclassification cost as discussed in the above section to decide about setting a cutoff point, which is a crucial decision that heavily impacts the profitability of a credit risk model, as extensively discussed in Chapter 3.
A cutoff point is needed for deciding about accepting or rejecting an application based on the estimated probability for the applicant to default. We will make use of the MicroCredit dataset in this case study, which is a simulation of real credit data on microloans.
The MicroCredit dataset can be downloaded freely from the book's companion website. More information on this dataset is provided in the open questions section at the end of this chapter (see also Bravo et al. 2013).

The MicroCredit dataset contains 10,000 observations and was randomly split in a training and a test set containing respectively 70% and 30% of the observations. A logistic regression model was estimated on the training set and evaluated on the test set. For a variable cutoff point T, which is used to turn the conditional class probabilities into estimated class labels $\hat{y}$, Table 6.3 reports:

- The fraction of observations classified as good applications and which consequently would be accepted—that is, the percentage of observations x_i with $p(1|x_i) < T$ ($y = 1$ represents a bad observation);

- The accuracy for the goods (i.e., the specificity), for the bads (i.e., the sensitivity), as well as the overall accuracy; the accuracy evaluation measure has been defined in Chapter 2 as the percentage correctly classified observations;

- The average actual cost per misclassified observation at cutoff T for the goods and the bads; these can be interpreted as approximations for the elements $C(1, 0)$ and $C(0, 1)$, respectively, of the cost matrix in a setting with observation-dependent costs; remark that these values are not equal to the average misclassification cost as defined earlier, since calculated as the average value of the actual misclassification cost *over the misclassified goods and bads* in the test set, whereas the AMC is calculated *over all (both misclassified and correctly classified) goods and bads* in the test set;

- The average misclassification cost for each class individually, as well as over all observations in test set.

Table 6.3 Cutoff Points, Accuracies, and Costs. The cutoff with the best accuracy is 0.90, and the one with the lowest average misclassification cost is 0.55.

Cutoff (T)	Accepted (%)	Accuracies (%)			Cost (€)		AMC (€)		
		Good	Bad	Overall	Good	Bad	Good	Bad	Overall
0.40	16.50%	19.20%	91.00%	38.10%	256	1789	206.57	56.95	194.46
0.45	24.40%	28.00%	85.60%	43.10%	238	1614	171.34	82.68	187.46
0.50	34.20%	38.70%	78.30%	49.10%	220	1402	134.66	107.84	178.94
0.55	45.30%	50.50%	69.10%	55.30%	207	1226	102.65	134.62	175.11
0.60	57.00%	62.10%	57.20%	60.80%	196	1102	74.15	167.52	178.34
0.65	68.30%	72.80%	44.30%	65.40%	184	1009	49.97	199.43	184.04
0.70	79.40%	83.00%	30.60%	69.30%	170	941	28.89	232	192.54
0.75	89.00%	91.40%	17.70%	72.10%	152	886	13.03	258.92	200.69
0.80	95.70%	96.70%	7.30%	73.30%	130	848	4.24	279.02	209.02
0.85	99.10%	99.30%	1.40%	73.60%	94	820	0.66	287.04	212.3
0.90	99.90%	99.90%	0.10%	73.80%	64	813	0.03	288.52	212.93

The cutoff T allows to label every observation in the test set and to calculate the AMC for the goods and the bads, as reported in Table 6.3, by taking the ratio of the summed misclassification costs for all incorrectly classified goods and bads over the total number of goods and bads, respectively. The AMC for the goods decreases when the cutoff increases, since the number of misclassified goods decreases, as indicated by the increasing specificity (i.e., the accuracy for the goods) for higher values of T. Therefore, also the total sum of misclassification costs and as such the AMC for the goods will decrease for an increasing value of the cutoff. The AMC of the bads, on the other hand, increases for an increasing cutoff, since the total number of misclassified bads rises as indicated by the increasing sensitivity (i.e., the accuracy of the bads). Therefore, the total sum of misclassification costs and the AMC for the bads increases for higher values of the cutoff.

The observation-dependent misclassification costs in the MicroCredit case context are estimated as follows:

- The cost of classifying an actual good applicant as a defaulter—that is, the cost $C_i(1,0)$ of predicting observation i to be positive whereas it is actually negative—equals the expected return on investment of the loan, ROI_i, times the loan amount, A_i:

$$C_i(1,0) = ROI_i \cdot A_i.$$

- The cost of classifying an actual defaulter as a good applicant—that is, the cost $C_i(0,1)$ of predicting observation i to be negative whereas it is actually positive—equals the monetary loss that is incurred because of the default; the loss is calculated as the fraction of the exposure at default which has not been recovered after all collection actions have been exhausted (see Chapter 3):

$$C_i(0,1) = LGD_i \cdot EAD_i.$$

This leads to the observation-dependent cost matrix $\boldsymbol{C}_i$:

$$\boldsymbol{C}_i = \begin{bmatrix} 0 & LGD_i \cdot EAD_i \\ ROI_i \cdot A_i & 0 \end{bmatrix}.$$

The observation-dependent misclassification costs have been averaged over the misclassified goods and bads and reported in Table 6.3. From this table, we see that the average cost of misclassified goods, as well as bads, strongly depends on the cutoff T! This dependency can be explained by the fact that risk (as indicated by the credit score) and returns (as indicated by the average cost) are not independent. In other words, the distribution of the observation-dependent costs is not independent from the credit score distribution.

The explanation of this effect is specific to the microfinance business, where applicants having a low probability to default can take larger loans and have to provide less collateral (where collateral can be collected by the microlender to reduce the loss when an obligor defaults). Nonrejected applicants having a relatively high probability to default, on the other hand, will only be granted loans involving a smaller amount and will be required to provide more collateral, relative to the loan amount. Additionally, in micro-lending typically the interest rate that is charged is approximately the same for all customers and independent of the creditworthiness of the applicant.[1] So, the returns on a microloan are only determined by the loan amount and not the interest rate. Finally, it is important to know that the probability to be bad as estimated at the time of application is strongly correlated with the probability to be bad as estimated by the model we are currently developing.

When the cutoff is low, the misclassified bads typically concern observations that were scored high in terms of creditworthiness at the time of application, and therefore involve high loan amounts and low collateral amounts or quality. The involved cost for these misclassified bads will consequently be high. When the cutoff is high, on the other hand, the misclassified bads concern both applications that were scored high and low in terms of creditworthiness. On average, the involved cost in misclassified bads therefore is lower than when the cutoff is low.

The same reasoning applies to the goods. When the cutoff is high, the misclassified goods concern observations which at the time of application were scored low in terms of creditworthiness. Hence, the involved loan amount is small and the amount of collateral is high, leading to a low average cost for the misclassified goods when the cutoff is high. On the other hand, when the cutoff is low, also goods that at the time of application were scored high will be misclassified. These involve larger loan amounts and possible as well lower collateral amounts. This will lead to a larger average cost associated with the misclassified goods when we set a low cutoff value.

Because the average cost of misclassified goods and bads depends on the cutoff score, it is inappropriate to use the average cost matrix and to use the cost-sensitive classification cutoff T_{CS}, as introduced in the previous chapter, for classifying customers as good or bad and to decide about which customers to accept and reject. Therefore, in this setting, an analysis as shown in Table 6.3 is indispensable to arrive at a profit-optimal decision regarding the cutoff score to implement for accepting or rejecting loan applications.

Another important issue in this case concerns the heavily imbalanced class distribution, with the ratio of goods to bads equal to 73.8% to 26.2%. In a typical retail bank, it is to be expected that a portfolio of loans consists of more good than bad borrowers, but the cost of accepting a defaulter is far greater than the cost of rejecting a good applicant. This leaves the data scientist with a tough choice—to either maximize the overall accuracy and accept many defaulters by implementing a high cutoff, $T = 0.9$, thus losing a million euro on new defaulters, or to minimize the average misclassification cost by setting the cutoff at $T = 0.55$, as such restraining the acceptance rate to 34%.

An alternative solution in this case could be to use a committee. If we accept that models in general are not sufficiently accurate over *a certain* score range, then why leave the decision for observations with a score in that range to the model? A sensible alternative would be to make use of human expert judgment in making the final decision for these observations. This leads to a two-cutoff-point strategy, classifying applicants per the following rules:

- Applicants having a score below the first cutoff (e.g., $T_1 = 0.55$) are in the immediate acceptance range. Applications in this range are automatically approved. An offer can be made without further credit risk analysis required, and an express process for loan granting is available involving minimum hassle. In this preapproved range, the model has a very high accuracy over the bad applicants, meaning there are few bads with a score below the first cutoff, so the involved costs are low.

- Scores above the second cutoff (e.g., $T_2 = 0.90$) are in the immediate rejection range. In this range, many applicants are defaulters and no applications are accepted.

- Scores in between the two cutoffs (e.g., between 0.55 and 0.90) are in the committee range and further analyzed by a credit officer. More information may be requested from the applicant to allow a thorough risk analysis to be made. For example, more recent information on the current salary may be requested, additional collateral or guarantors may be required, or external information from a credit bureau can be purchased with the aim to allow an accurate human-based evaluation.

Figure 6.1 illustrates the two-cutoff-point strategy. In line with Table 6.3, the graph in Figure 6.1 shows both the defaulter accuracy (i.e., the sensitivity) and the total cost of using the model, which is equal to the average misclassification cost times the number of observations. The first cutoff can be installed at a score above which insufficient certainty is provided by the model in terms of the probability of the applicant to be bad. The second cutoff can be set at a score where the risk and expected cost when accepting is certain to be too high since the sensitivity is too low.

Alternatively, the second cutoff score could be set at 0.85. This would only marginally affect the potential profits, but does notably reduce the committee range. This significantly reduces the number of applications that are to be inspected by the

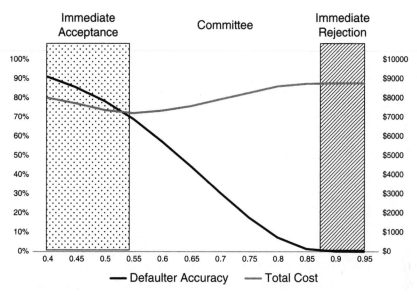

Figure 6.1   Illustration of the two-cutoff point strategy.

committee, which represents a cost that has not been assessed explicitly in this analysis, but could be substantial.

The evaluation strategy could be further tweaked by including in the analysis the cost of the evaluation by a committee and the capacity of the financial institution to have a committee decide about applications. In the example, approximately half the applicants would be sent to a committee, which likely is too much. Typical values range in between 25% to 35%. Ultimately, this decision is not a statistical one, but a commercial one, depending on the strategy that the user of the model wants to follow given the business objectives and budgets of the organization.

In this case study, we have illustrated cutoff point tuning and the use of the simplest profit-driven measure we have at our disposal: the average misclassification cost. Many assumptions are made when using this measure, the most important of these being the fact that the average values will remain relatively constant in time over the different portfolios. This assumption likely does not hold in a changing and competitive environment, requiring us to turn to more sophisticated approaches. One popular approach is to adapt the ROC curve in order to simultaneously analyze multiple cutoff points and find the one that is the best performing in terms of profits.

ROC Curve-Based Measures

In Chapter 2, the concept of the *area under the receiver operating characteristic curve* (AUROC or AUC, for short) was introduced. This measure is born from the ROC curve, which is constructed from the pairs (1 – Specificity, Sensitivity) calculated over the observations in a test set, or a segmentation of it when there are many cutoff points. Figure 6.2 resumes the example ROC curve discussed in Chapter 2. Note that the use of an ROC curve to evaluate the performance of a classification model is equivalent to plotting the performance for a large selection of cutoff points. ROC analysis has been the standard approach for model evaluation in business analytics for a long time. The characteristics and behavior of ROC curves have been studied in depth for analyzing its appropriateness to evaluate classification models, as well as to identify and address possible shortcomings. Flach (2011) explains that the ROC curve can be used to identify in which regions of the cutoff range one classifier outperforms another, in which regions a classifier performs worse than chance and, more importantly from the perspective of this book, to determine a cutoff point that minimizes the (expected) error rate or some given misclassification costs, when the cost distributions are known.

An ROC curve is usually paired with the analysis of the area under the curve, the AUC, which can be interpreted as the average sensitivity considering all possible specificities. More formally, assuming a score function $s(x) = p(1|x)$, with cumulative distributions $F_0(s)$ and $F_1(s)$ for

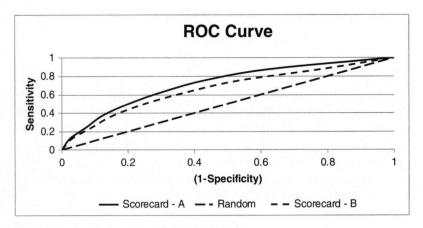

Figure 6.2 Receiver operating characteristic curve.

the negative and positive observations, respectively, associated with densities $f_0(s)$ and $f_1(s)$, then the AUC can be expressed as:

$$AUC = \int\limits_{-\infty}^{\infty} (1 - F_1(s))f_0(s)ds.$$

This means that the AUC naturally considers all errors as equally costly, which evidently goes against the objective of performing a profit-sensitive analysis. This characteristic of the AUC can cause problems in real-world applications. For example, in fraud detection, the performance of the model on transactions at the *bottom of the ranking* (i.e., at the *right on the ROC curve* for values of 1 − Specificity close to 1, reflecting the sensitivity of the model for transactions that are indicated by the model to have a very small probability of being fraudulent) will be of little practical use and importance. This, in fact, relates to earlier discussions in Chapters 4 and 5, where we indicated that in most business applications the aim is to rank entities in order to allow a small fraction of entities with a high probability to be positive (e.g., to be fraudulent) to be selected for further treatment (e.g., a fraud investigation). Hence, it is the *top fraction*, rather than the bottom fraction with low probabilities to be positive, which is of practical importance. The performance of the model at the *top of the ranking* (i.e., at the *left on the ROC curve* for values of 1 − Specificity close to zero) requires an evaluation for high cutoff scores—in fact, only for high cutoff scores, since low cutoff scores relate to the performance at the bottom of the ranking.

Therefore, some modifications of the ROC curve and the AUC have been proposed which allow to account for these implications of the practical use of the model on the relevance of the ROC curve and the AUC, by calculating *partial* curves that are better suited for such specific applications (Dodd and Pepe 2003; McClish 1989). The drawback of these modified ROC curves is the loss of the *objectivity* of the AUC. Some *subjectivity* enters the model evaluation, in terms of the selected range of cutoff points that is selected. The data scientist implementing the model might decide that the relevant range of cutoff scores, which directly relates to the potential fraction of entities labeled positive and selected for further treatment, is in between 0.3 and 0.6. Another data scientist, however, could deem the range to be in between 0.2 and 0.7, potentially leading to substantially different conclusions, for instance, in terms of model selection. There are no general guidelines to decide about the appropriate range of cutoff scores to be used, since the appropriate range depends on the very exact characteristics of the business application and the organization that develops and implements the model.

There is another critical problem in using the AUC as an evaluation measure, as identified by Hand (2009):

> The AUC is equivalent to averaging the misclassification loss over a cost-ratio distribution that depends on the score distributions..." and "...using the AUC is equivalent to measuring classifier performance using an instrument which varies from classifier to classifier.

It is possible to derive the AUC measure from the integration of the losses that come from choosing an optimal cutoff. This cutoff is obtained by minimizing the loss over the mixture of the scores arising from the classifier. In simpler terms, the AUC will compare different classifiers from distributions that come from the classifiers themselves, so might give inconsistent results. This problem is particularly severe when comparing classifiers over different test sets, and it is now accepted that the measure cannot be used in these settings.

To overcome these problems, two related measures have been proposed in recent years, both modifying the use of the distribution of the scores in favor of the distribution of the costs. These measures, both applicable to binary classification problems, are the **H-measure** and the **(expected) maximum profit measure**. We study both measures in detail in the next sections.

H–Measure

The H-measure, as introduced by Hand (2009), is a first ROC curve-based measure that *explicitly* assesses the impact of costs in the evaluation of a classification model. In deriving the H-measure, we start by defining the prior probabilities of belonging to the positive class ($y = 1$), π_1, or the negative class ($y = 0$), π_0, such that $\pi_1 + \pi_0 = 1$.

An observation will be classified as positive if the score $s(x)$, with $s(x)$ equal to or a monotonic transformation of the probability $p(1|x)$ of an observation x to be positive estimated by the classification model $f(x)$, is greater than the cutoff T that is adopted—that is, if $s(x) > T$ then $\hat{y} = 1$, and classified as negative otherwise, if $s(x) \leq T$ then $\hat{y} = 0$. An additional input to the analyses here is the cost matrix C, as introduced in the previous chapter. To simplify the derivation of the H-measure, we either adopt the simplified cost matrix or assume that correct classifications incur no cost, leading to

$C(0,0) = C(1,1) = 0$. For notational convenience, we will also adopt the following shorthand notation for the misclassification costs: $C(1,0) = c_0$, the cost of misclassifying a negative class observation, and $C(0,1) = c_1$, the cost of misclassifying a positive class observation. Remember from Chapter 5 that it may be challenging to accurately estimate the values c_0 and c_1, as these often depend on complex market interactions or on the specific business application and setting where the model is operated. Nonetheless, we find that in most applications it is possible to roughly estimate the distribution of these costs. Some approaches for this have already been discussed in the previous chapter. Alternatively, the cost distribution can arise from a graph analysis, as we will illustrate in the case study below. The idea here is to fit a parametric distribution to the observed costs.

The H-measure adopts a *one-size-fits-all* approach across various applications in terms of the specification of the distribution of the costs, whereas the MP and EMP measures, which will be discussed in a later section, are more flexible in terms of the specification of the cost distribution. This turns out to be an advantage of the MP and EMP measures, since it is possible to tune these measures exactly to the specific business setting where the model will be operated, but as well a disadvantage, since they require formulating a profit equation that fits the application. This could be challenging. Vice versa, the H-measure has the advantage of being more user-friendly and easier to apply, but then again, is less flexible in fitting the *true* cost distribution and therefore possibly not fully adapted to the specific application characteristics. This could lead to the H-measure being less accurate or correct.

Following the discussion in Hand (2009), for a cutoff T, the overall misclassification loss, Q, is given by the following function:

$$Q(T; c_0, c_1) \triangleq c_0 \pi_0 (1 - F_0(T)) + c_1 \pi_1 F_1(T).$$

The optimal value of the cutoff, i.e., T, which minimizes the loss, is then defined as the following function of c_0 and c_1:

$$T(c_0, c_1) \triangleq \arg \min_T \{ c_0 \pi_0 (1 - F_0(T)) + c_1 \pi_1 F_1(T) \}.$$

Since the optimal cutoff will only depend on the ratio of the misclassification costs, as argued in the previous chapter, it is convenient to transform the pair (c_0, c_1) to the pair (b, c), defined by $b = c_0 + c_1$ and $c = \frac{c_1}{(c_0 + c_1)}$, so that we only have one parameter, c, which depends on the ratio of the costs and as such determines the optimal cutoff. Then the argument of the optimal cutoff T^* yielding minimum loss, simplifies to a function of c:

$$T^*(c) = \arg \min_T \{ (1 - c) \pi_0 (1 - F_0(T)) + c \pi_1 F_1(T) \}.$$

The overall misclassification cost, Q, for any value of the cutoff, can then be written as:

$$Q(T; b, c) \triangleq \{(1 - c)\pi_0(1 - F_0(T)) + c\pi_1 F_1(T)\}b.$$

If the score distributions $F_0(T)$ and $F_1(T)$ are differentiable, then by differentiating the above equation we can find the optimal cutoff T^* that satisfies the equation:

$$(1 - c)\pi_0 f_0(T) = c\pi_1 f_1(T).$$

and $\frac{d^2Q}{dt^2} > 0$. Ensuring that the score distributions are concave for the optimal cutoff to be unique, is a first step in the development of the H-Measure. The concavity of the ROC curve has been shown to be an important property of AUC analysis since, if the curve is nonconcave—as is usually the case when constructed empirically—then the resulting AUC is unlikely to generalize to other datasets (Flach 2011). Instead of using the AUC value derived from the empirical ROC curve, better is to consider the use of the **convex hull**[2] of the ROC curve, given by:

1. $(1 - F_0(T),\ 1 - F_1(T))$, for all T values satisfying $\arg \min_{T'} Q(T; b,c)$ for some c as c ranges over the interval $[0, 1]$. Values of T having no c over the interval $[0,1]$ making T the optimal cutoff, minimizing the loss, $Q(T; b,c)$, concern the nonconcave sections of the ROC.

2. For these nonconcave sections of the ROC, the convex hull is given by the points on the line interval connecting points $(1 - F_0(T_L), 1 - F_1(T_L))$ and $(1 - F_0(T_U),\ 1 - F_1(T_U))$, and with T_L and T_U the cutoffs yielding the upper and lower end points on the curve that bound the nonconcave sections.

Figure 6.3 shows an example of the convex hull for an empirically constructed, nonconcave, ROC curve. Provost and Fawcett (1999), as well as Flach (2003), highlight the benefits of using the convex hull. If a point falls on the convex hull, then the classifier represented by that point will be optimal under any distributional assumptions of the underlying data. That makes it optimal for comparing multiple models and test sets. The H-measure is calculated over the convex hull of the ROC curve, which is a piecewise concave function and will therefore yield a unique optimal value for the cutoff.

A second step in the derivation of the H-measure, next to ensuring the optimal cutoff to be unique, concerns an assumption which is to be made regarding the applicable cost ratio distribution. Such an assumption is made *explicitly* in the H-measure, rather than implicitly as in

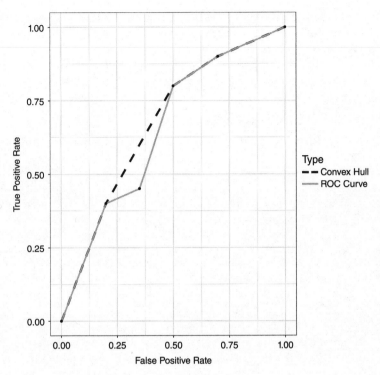

Figure 6.3 Convex hull for a nonconcave ROC curve.

the AUC measure. Hand (2009) proves there is a cost ratio distribution implicitly being used by the AUC, which depends on the score distribution and hence varies from classifier to classifier. This is of course nonsensical. The H-measure instead explicitly adopts a distribution for the ratio of the misclassification costs, as captured by the parameter $c = \frac{c_1}{(c_0 + c_1)} = \left(1 + \frac{c_0}{c_1}\right)^{-1}$. Since the misclassification costs c_0 and c_1 are often hard to estimate exactly, or since they may be stochastic in nature, Hand (2009) proposes to adopt a function $u(c)$ which describes the uncertainty regarding the true cost ratio. This function, which is a probability density function, is used to calculate the *expected* loss over the convex hull of the ROC curve, given by:

$$L = \int Q(T(c); c) \cdot u(c) dc. \tag{1}$$

The third and final step in the derivation of the H-measure is then to choose an appropriate distribution for the parameter c, and as such, for the ratio of the misclassification costs. Hand (2009) proposes to use a beta distribution for this purpose, given its versatility. The functional form of the beta distribution is equal to:

$$h(x; \alpha, \beta) = \frac{\Gamma(\alpha + \beta)}{\Gamma(\alpha)\Gamma(\beta)} x^{\alpha-1}(1 - x)^{\beta-1},$$

with α and β shape parameters and $\Gamma(x) = \int_0^{\infty} x^{z-1} e^{-x} dx$, the gamma function, which is the extension of the factorial operator for continuous values.

The beta distribution can take many shapes, and thus can be adapted to many different distributions. Figure 6.4 shows different shapes for the beta function for variable values of the parameters α and β. In general, these parameters can be estimated to fit the distribution of a stochastic variable x (here, the cost ratio parameter c) using the method of moments, as the following relationships hold:

$$\mu = \frac{\alpha}{\alpha + \beta},$$

$$\sigma^2 = \frac{\alpha\beta}{(\alpha + \beta)^2(\alpha + \beta + 1)}.$$

Replacing the values of μ and σ^2 by their unbiased estimators, the sample mean and sample variance of the objective variable, and solving the system of equations, leads to an approximation of the values of a and β, which result in a shape of the beta distribution that fits the objective variable x. Alternatively, the value of the parameters α and β can be obtained following a maximum likelihood estimation

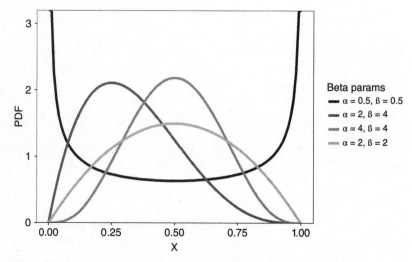

Figure 6.4 Beta distribution for different values of the parameters α and β.

(Griffiths 1973; Paolino 2001; Smithson and Verkuilen 2006), which could provide more robust values.

Hand (2009), in fact, does not recommend using the method of moments or maximum likelihood estimation to obtain the parameters α and β, but to choose (somewhat arbitrarily) a distribution by setting values for α and β that represents the uncertainty on the cost balance between negative and positive events and that is either observed in the data or expected to occur in the future. For example, choosing $\alpha = 2$ and $\beta = 4$ leads to a unimodal distribution with mean 1:3, which arguably could be a good fit for the case where $c_1 > c_0$. Similarly, an argument can be made for choosing $\alpha = 4$ and $\beta = 4$ when it is expected that $c_1 \approx c_0$, or $\alpha = 2$ and $\beta = 2$ when there is no knowledge on the cost distribution on beforehand. Figure 6.4 shows the resulting distributions for these different sets of values of α and β.

The argument for moving from the proven arbitrariness of using AUC curves (given the implicit use of a cost distribution depending on the score distribution of a classifier) to compare classifier performance, to the somewhat challenging and possibly arbitrary choice of a distribution for $u(c)$, is to make the underlying assumptions transparent and explicit, as such allowing a correct comparison between classifiers. Whereas the AUC measure hides the assumed cost structure in the distributions of the scores, the H-measure explicitly forces the data scientist to make a conscious choice regarding the functional form of the cost distribution $u(c)$. Once a distribution has been chosen, all comparisons between multiple classifiers and across datasets should be coherent.

The final form of the H-measure integrates the distribution $u(c)$ to the expression of the minimal loss, which is a function of c, as expressed by Equation 1. Assuming a beta distribution for $u(c)$, it is possible to estimate the maximum loss, which occurs when the ROC curve is a perfect straight line:

$$L_{\max} = \pi_0 \int_0^{\pi_1} (1 - c) \cdot u(c)dc + \pi_1 \int_{\pi_1}^1 c \cdot u(c)dc. \tag{2}$$

The general H-measure, as defined in Equation 3, is then calculated as one minus the ratio of the expected loss as expressed by Equation 1 and the maximum loss as expressed by Equation 2. Consequently, a higher value of the H-measure indicates a better performance, with $H = 0$, similar to $AUC = 0.5$, representing the performance of a random model yielding an arbitrary score distribution:

$$H = 1 - \frac{L}{L_{\max}} = 1 - \frac{\int Q(T(c); c) \cdot u(c)dc}{\pi_0 \int_0^{\pi_1} (1 - c) \cdot u(c)dc + \pi_1 \int_{\pi_1}^1 c \cdot u(c)dc}. \tag{3}$$

CASE STUDY

Throughout this chapter, we elaborate a case study using the MicroCredit example dataset introduced in the previous case study. We will illustrate the use of the various performance measures that are discussed in this chapter by evaluating and comparing the performance of five classification models developed on this dataset. We will show how to correctly estimate the parameters of the performance measures, such as the α and β parameters of the H-measure. The case will first highlight the limitations of the AUC measure when adopted in a context of profit-driven model evaluation. The shortcomings of the AUC measure motivate the development and adoption of more advanced performance metrics such as the H-measure and the maximum profit measures, which will be discussed in a subsequent section. The adoption of these measures in this case will be shown to lead to selecting the *best* model, with best meaning profit-optimal. The MicroCredit dataset, as well as snippets of code to estimate basic as well as advanced performance measures, are available for the reader to experiment with from the book's companion website.

The case involves the selection of a classification model that is to be implemented and operated by a microlender. A consultant was hired by the microlender and provided the MicroCredit dataset. The consultant developed five logistic regression models to estimate the probability of a microloan applicant to default, using a random training set containing 70% of the observations. Since all models involve equal deployment costs, the choice concerns which model will perform *best* on future applications, which we will evaluate using the test set containing 30% of the observations. How *best* is defined, in fact, follows from the evaluation measure that we adopt. A first and typical approach to compare the performance of classification models is to analyze the ROC curves, plotted in Figure 6.5 for all five models.

From Figure 6.5, we can immediately see that the curves intersect across the range of the false positive rate on the *x*-axis. No curve is above all others over the entire range—in other words, no curve presents *stochastic dominance*. As a result, no model can be concluded to be superior to the others and we have to extend our analysis to reach a solution.

At this point, we might simply calculate basic performance metrics in order to decide about which model to select. Table 6.4 presents the values of two such performance measures which are often used in practice to this end: the accuracy, for a cutoff $T = 0.50$, as well as the AUC. Based on the reported accuracies and AUC values in Table 6.4, we are inclined to select Model 5, which yields both the highest accuracy and AUC. The accuracy of Model 5 is 70.8% versus 70.6% for both Model 3 and 4, which in terms of accuracy are both the next best. The AUC of Model 5 is 0.620 versus 0.618 for Model 3, the next best.

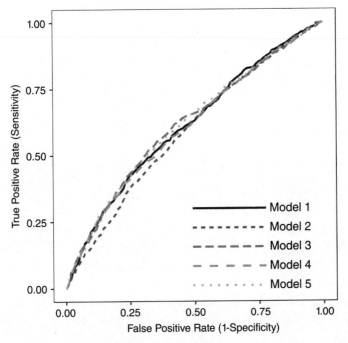

Figure 6.5 ROC curves for five credit risk models.

Table 6.4 Accuracy and AUC for the Five Candidate Models

Model	Accuracy	AUC
Model 1	70.3%	0.614
Model 2	70.1%	0.591
Model 3	70.6%	0.618
Model 4	70.6%	0.608
Model 5	70.8%	0.620

However, from a profit perspective, selecting Model 5 would be a suboptimal decision. A warning sign for this comes from the ROC curves. The curves cross each other multiple times across the range of the false positive rate. This means that no model is always the *best* model and that different models could represent the best choice, depending on the cutoff point and the involved cost distribution. A first proof of Model 5 being suboptimal arises from calculating the AUC of the convex hull of the ROC curves of the five models, as reported in Table 6.5. Looking at Table 6.5 and analyzing the performance of the five models using the AUC of the convex hull, we see that Model 3 instead of Model 5 is the best performing model.[3]

Table 6.5 AUC and AUC of the Convex Hull for the Five Candidate Models

Model	AUC	AUC Convex Hull
Model 1	0.614	0.622
Model 2	0.591	0.599
Model 3	0.618	0.627
Model 4	0.608	0.615
Model 5	0.620	0.625

The AUC of the convex hull has been discussed in this chapter to be more robust and to more accurately indicate the true performance of a model over the population distribution than the AUC. Nonetheless, the AUC of the convex hull still ignores the true cost distribution. Given that in this business setting costs do matter, we can turn to the H-measure for arriving at a profit optimal model selection.

In this case study, we calculate the H-measure as implemented in the *hmeasure* R package, which does not require the user to specify values for the α and β parameters of the beta distribution (which, if preferred, of course can still be done), and only requires the user to provide a value for the severity ratio, SR, as defined above:

$$SR = \frac{c}{1 - c} = \frac{c_1}{c_0}.$$

The severity ratio should provide an indication on the expected or average value of the cost ratio. A distribution $u(c)$ is then fitted, similar to the unimodal distribution shown in Figure 6.4 with $\alpha = 2$ and $\beta = 4$. By default, the procedure sets $\alpha = 2$, and calculates β so as the mode of the fitted distribution to reflect the expected, average cost ratio as expressed by the severity ratio. For more details on the underlying approach, one may refer to the package documentation (Anagnostopoulos and Hand 2012). In line with the discussion in the previous case study on cutoff point tuning, the severity ratio can be estimated based on the following assumptions regarding the involved misclassification costs:

- The cost of misclassifying a good applicant as a bad applicant, c_0, has been defined before as the total return on a loan, which is equal to the return on investment of the loan times the loan amount. The ROI of a loan equals the ratio of the total interest that is paid, discounted by an appropriate discount rate to account for the time value of money, and the loan amount. Following Bravo et al. (2013), in this case study the average value of the ROI is taken equal to 26.44% of the loan amount. Financial institutions can be expected to know the average ROI of a loan, which is usually calculated as part of the balanced scorecard of the organization or as part of the economic capital estimates. As the H-measure accounts for the average misclassification cost and not the observation-dependent misclassification costs, we estimate the average return over the training set observations using the average ROI of 26.44%. Multiplied with the average loan amount, we arrive at an average cost of misclassifying a good applicant, c_0 = €290.10 per loan.[4]

■ Misclassifying a bad applicant as a good applicant, c_1, will yield a monetary loss equal to the loss given default, the percentage lost after collections actions, of the loan times the exposure at default, the amount that the borrower owed when default occurred, of the loan. The MicroCredit dataset provides LGD and EAD values for the bad observations (since good applicants have not defaulted, no LGD and EAD has been observed), allowing us to calculate the average cost of misclassifying a bad applicant over the training set as the multiplication of the average LGD and the average EAD. This results in c_1 = €82.50 per loan.

This leads to the following cost matrix:

$$C = \begin{bmatrix} 0 & c_1 \\ c_0 & 0 \end{bmatrix} = \begin{bmatrix} 0 & LGD \cdot EAD \\ ROI \cdot A & 0 \end{bmatrix} = \begin{bmatrix} 0 & 82.50 \\ 290.10 & 0 \end{bmatrix}.$$

Using these average misclassification costs, we can calculate the severity ratio as follows:

$$SR = \frac{c_1}{c_0} = \frac{82.50}{290.10} = 0.2844.$$

The value of the severity ratio subsequently allows us to calculate the H-measure for the five candidate models, as reported in Table 6.6. As can be seen from Table 6.6, Model 3 achieves the highest value for the H-measure. There is even a more solid indication now that Model 3 should be selected, profitability being the main objective of developing and implementing the model.

Table 6.6 H-Measure for the Five Candidate Models. Model 3 is the selected one, not Model 5.

Model	H-Measure
Model 1	0.064
Model 2	0.043
Model 3	0.071
Model 4	0.060
Model 5	0.068

Maximum Profit Measures

Two alternative metrics toward evaluating classification models in a profit-driven manner are presented by the maximum profit framework. A first metric that extends the H-measure is the maximum profit measure as proposed by Verbeke et al. (2012). The MP measure allows us to account for a more complex but deterministic cost and benefit structure. A second metric that will be discussed in this section, the expected maximum profit measure, extends the MP framework to problems with stochastic cost and benefit structures.

Both methodologies can be adapted to practically any business problem, and are geared toward more advanced organizations possessing a mature analytics skillset. The requirement to develop a deeper insight in the cost-benefit structure of the company for adapting these measures to the specific business problem they are applied to might be off-putting for data scientists who have not conducted such a profound analysis as this before or who have limited insight in classification model evaluation. Luckily, these generic measures have standard definitions that are readily available for use for evaluating customer churn prediction models and credit scoring models.

MP Measure

The maximum profit framework, proposed by Verbeke et al. (2012) and extended by Verbraken et al. (2013), provides additional flexibility compared to the H-measure by taking into account the costs and benefits resulting from incorrect and correct classifications, respectively, as well as the uncertainty regarding these costs and benefits, for arriving at an accurate indication of the expected future profitability of a classification model.

In line with the formal notation conventions adopted before, the MP measure is developed from a set n of observations, with a fraction π_0 of negative class observations (e.g., nonfraudsters, good payers, nonchurners), a fraction π_1 of positive class observations (e.g., fraudsters, defaulters, churners), and a model that induces cumulative distributions $F_0(T)$ and $F_1(T)$, describing, respectively, the fractions of negative and positive observations with conditional positive class probabilities below the cutoff T. Note that the fractions π_0 and π_1 are the prior class probabilities of belonging to the negative and positive class, respectively. This leads to the confusion matrix, as already defined in Chapter 2 before and shown in Table 6.7. The confusion matrix expresses the numbers of observations of both the negative

Table 6.7 Confusion Matrix for a Binary Classification Problem

	Actual Negative	Actual Positive
Predicted Negative	$\pi_0 F_0(T)n$	$\pi_0(1 - F_0(T))n$
Predicted Positive	$\pi_1 F_1(T)n$	$\pi_1(1 - F_1(T))n$

and positive class that have been correctly and incorrectly classified by a classification model in function of the cutoff T (i.e., the number of true negatives, true positives, false negatives, and false positives, respectively).

In elaborating the MP measures, the following shorthand notation and convention regarding the sign for the elements of the cost matrix will be adopted:

$$C = \begin{bmatrix} C(0,0) & C(0,1) \\ C(1,0) & C(1,1) \end{bmatrix} = \begin{bmatrix} -b_0 & c_1 \\ c_0 & -b_1 \end{bmatrix}.$$

The benefits b_0 and b_1 are obtained from correctly identifying an observation of, respectively, the negative and the positive class, whereas the misclassification costs c_0 and c_1 result from, respectively, misclassifying a negative observation as a positive observation and vice versa. The values b_0, c_0, b_1, and c_1 are positive, unless explicitly stated otherwise. Note that b_0 and b_1 as such have the opposite sign of the equivalent elements $C(0,0)$ and $C(1,1)$ in the cost matrix, respectively. Remember that we explained in the previous chapter that the elements in the cost matrix are to be interpreted as costs, with negative costs in fact being benefits.

In contrast with previous approaches, the MP framework explicitly makes use of the benefits related to classifying entities correctly, leading to the calculation of profit from the point of view of the business implementing the classification model as the net difference between total benefits and total costs, rather than loss as the total costs. The profit be can calculated by first multiplying the elements in the confusion matrix provided in Table 6.7 with the related elements in the cost-benefit matrix, and then summing the resulting values. Dividing by the number of observations n then yields the average classification profit, P, per observation in function of the classification cutoff T:

$$\begin{aligned} P(T; b_0, c_0, b_1, c_1) &= b_0\pi_0 F_0(T) + b_1\pi_1(1 - F_1(T)) \\ &\quad - c_0\pi_0(1 - F_0(T)) - c_1\pi_1 F_1(T) \\ &= (b_0 + c_0)\pi_0 F_0(T) - (b_1 + c_1)\pi_1 F_1(T) b_1\pi_1 - c_0\pi_0. \end{aligned}$$

Maximizing the average profit in function of the cutoff value, T, leads to the **maximum profit (MP)** measure (Verbeke et al. 2012) defined as follows:

$$MP = \max_{\forall T} P(T; b_0, c_0, b_1, c_1) = P(T^*; b_0, c_0, b_1, c_1),$$

with T the optimal cutoff under the given cost-benefit distribution:

$$T^* = \arg \max_{\forall T} P(T; b_0, c_0, b_1, c_1).$$

The optimal cutoff value T satisfies the first order condition for maximizing the average profit:

$$\frac{f_0(T)}{f_1(T)} = \frac{\pi_1(b_1 + c_1)}{\pi_0(b_0 + c_0)} = \frac{\pi_1}{\pi_0}\theta,$$

where $\theta = \frac{(b_1 + c_1)}{b_0 + c_0}$ is introduced for notational convenience and is called the **cost-benefit ratio** in line with the cost ratio defined before. The cost-benefit ratio indicates that the optimal cutoff and the maximum profit depends on a ratio of costs and benefits, and thus is not dependent on the measurement scale, again in line with previous discussions on the cost ratio. Since all parameters (b_0, c_0, b_1, c_1) are positive, the value of θ ranges from zero to plus infinity.

Note that the right-hand side of the first order condition equation only contains the prior class probabilities and cost and benefit parameters. The left-hand side of the equation is the ratio of the probability density functions evaluated at a cutoff T, and corresponds to a certain slope on the ROC curve. Thus, varying θ from zero to infinity corresponds to a translation over the ROC curve (Verbraken et al. 2013). In this case, the optimal cutoff is clearly defined and the optimal fraction of the entities that should be selected for further treatment to maximize the profit equals:

$$\bar{\eta}_{MP} = 1 - (\pi_0 F_0(T^*) + \pi_1 F_1(T^*)).$$

The MP measure presents a flexible, interpretable, and business-oriented alternative for profit-sensitive evaluation of classification models when the costs and profits are deterministic and known, as well as stable in time. When there is uncertainty regarding the exact costs and benefits that will result from implementing the classification model, it makes sense to acknowledge that uncertainty and to take the intrinsic stochastic nature of the costs and benefits explicitly into account. The EMP framework, as such, extends the MP approach, by taking into account distributions of costs and benefits in estimating the expected maximum profit.

EMP Measure

Verbeke et al. (2012) argue that the MP measure by itself can be used to make decisions. This is indeed true in scenarios where the cost-and-benefit parameters are stable across all different cutoff points T and across the time horizon. This might be the case in some business applications, such as an insured portfolio of bonds, where each defaulted loan comes with a fixed cost in the form of an excess and the profit is a fixed amount. However, in many situations, the costs and benefits are uncertain. To deal with this, Verbraken et al. (2013) developed the concept of the expected maximum profit (EMP).

The EMP measure assumes that the cost and benefit parameters, b_0, c_0, b_1 and c_1, are not always exactly known or may vary following a joint probability distribution $h(b_0, c_0, b_1, c_1)$. When this is the case, the measure can be estimated as the expected value of the MP measure, as expressed by the following equation:

$$EMP = \int_{b_0}\int_{c_0}\int_{b_1}\int_{c_1} P(T^*(\theta); b_0, c_0, b_1, c_1) \cdot h(b_0, c_0, b_1, c_1) db_0 dc_0 db_1 dc_1.$$

The developers showed that the EMP corresponds to an integration over a range of the ROC curve, and that it represents an upper bound to the profit a company can achieve by applying the classification model. Again, it is possible to estimate the optimal fraction, $\overline{\eta}_{EMP}$, of entities to classify as positives and to select for further treatment (e.g., the fraction of customers to classify as churners and to target in a retention campaign or the fraction of credit-card transactions to flag as suspicious and to further investigate):

$$\overline{\eta}_{EMP} = \int_{b_0}\int_{c_0}\int_{b_1}\int_{c_1} [\pi_0(1 - F_0(T^*)) + \pi_1(1 - F_1(T^*))]$$
$$\cdot h(b_0, c_0, b_1, c_1) db_0 dc_0 db_1 dc_1.$$

The EMP measure requires a functional form to be selected for the joint probability density function of the cost and benefit parameters, $h(b_0, c_0, b_1, c_1)$. Verbraken et al. (2013) proposed a functional form to adopt for evaluating customer churn prediction models, whereas Verbraken et al. (2014) estimated the functional form to use in credit scoring. We will present the resulting EMP measures in the next sections, and illustrate the use of the EMP measure for credit scoring by extending the MicroCredit case study.

MP and EMP for Customer Churn Prediction

Customer churn prediction, as introduced in Chapter 3, is one of the best-known applications of analytics in marketing. Verbeke et al. (2011) define the models used for customer churn prediction as the ones aimed at detecting customers with a high propensity to attrite within a given time frame. Its usefulness is apparent, as it is discussed in Chapter 3 that it is far more expensive to attract new customers than it is to retain existing customers. Neslin et al. (2006) posit that the cost of mismanaging churn prediction by using a model with low predictive accuracy can amount to hundreds of thousands of dollars and therefore conclude that practitioners should always be on the lookout for better approaches.

One direct improvement could be to incorporate the costs and benefits of the approach into the model selection phase, as proposed by Verbeke et al. (2012) and Verbraken et al. (2013). These two publications adapt, respectively, the MP and EMP measures to the problem of customer churn prediction, studying the cost-and-benefit structure of customer churn management.

The customer churn management process, as explained in Neslin et al. (2006), is illustrated in Figure 6.6. In a typical company, churn management is a regular (e.g., monthly) activity where the existing customer base of n customers is segmented into a group of would-be churners and a group of nonchurners. For the purpose of this segmentation, a classification model is applied to predict future churners. The segment of the would-be churners consists of a fraction η of the customers. These are included in a retention campaign with the obvious aim to retain them, at a cost of contact, f, and a fixed *administrative cost* of running the campaign, A. Additionally, the selected customers are offered an incentive to stay (e.g., a 12-month discount over their

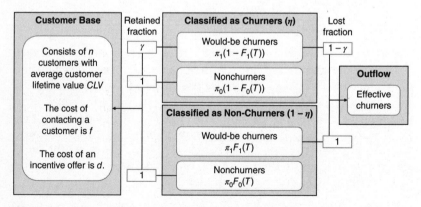

Figure 6.6 Customer churn management process. Adapted from Verbraken et al. (2013).

mobile telco plan is offered), which if the customer effectively stays comes at a cost to the organization, d. Customers in the nonchurner segment (a fraction $1 - \eta$) are not targeted and not offered an incentive, so do not involve a direct cost to the company.

Intrinsically, prior to the marketing campaign is launched, there are two groups of customers: there is a fraction π_0 of the customers that have no intention to leave the company—that is, actual nonchurners, and there is a fraction $\pi_1 = 1 - \pi_0$ of customers that do have the intention of leaving, that is, actual would-be churners. These two intrinsic groups do not fully coincide with the segments of churners and nonchurners as predicted by the customer churn prediction model. Since the model will not be 100% accurate, there will be actual would-be churners and actual nonchurners both within the segment of predicted churners and predicted nonchurners.

Customers in the segment of predicted nonchurners are not targeted and consequently will not change their intention. Consequently, actual would-be churners in this segment will churn since not offered an incentive to remain loyal, and actual nonchurners will not churn. The behavior of customers that have been included in the campaign, on the other hand, may change because of contacting them, and because of the incentive that is offered, but not always it does so:

- The nonchurners that receive the offer take it and do not churn (these are *Sure Things*, as defined in Chapter 4). In addition to the contacting cost, f, a cost d related to the incentive that is offered is assumed to be incurred for all of them.

- The churners that receive the offer do not all take the offer, however. It is typically assumed that only a fraction γ of the actual would-be churners takes the offer and does not churn (these are *Persuadables*, see Chapter 4), whereas the rest $(1 - \gamma)$ reject the offer and do churn (these are *Lost Causes*, see Chapter 4).

In this setup, we do not consider *Do-Not-Disturbs* to exist, as discussed in Chapter 4, which are customers that react adversely to marketing actions; for instance, nonchurners that do churn when they are targeted in a retention campaign. Such customers may effectively represent an important issue in churn modeling, particularly when the offers that are made are not attractive. However, under normal conditions the fraction of *Do-Not-Disturbs* can be expected to be small in customer churn prediction, which allows us to simplify the problem and assume the fraction of *Do-Not-Disturbs* to be zero.

Considering that each customer represents an average $CLV = \sum_i^n \frac{CLV_i}{n}$ to the company, the total profit of conducting a retention campaign for the company can be calculated as follows:

$$\text{Profit} = n\eta[(\gamma CLV + d(1 - \gamma))\pi_1 \lambda - d - f] - A.$$

The value of λ corresponds to the *lift coefficient* (see Chapter 2) and will be the key in determining the parameters for the MP and the EMP specifications. Given a predictive model producing the score distributions $F_0(T)$ and $F_1(T)$, the lift depends on the cutoff T that is used to segment the customer base and is defined as the ratio of the churn rate in the segment of predicted churners and the overall churn rate in the customer base:

$$\lambda(T) = \frac{1 - F_1(T)}{\eta(T)},$$

with

$$\eta(T) = 1 - (\pi_0 F_0(T) + \pi_1 F_1(T)).$$

To adapt the above profit formula to the maximum profit framework, we assume that the administrative cost is small in comparison with the variable costs and can be discarded ($A = 0$). Introducing two dimensionless parameters $\delta = \frac{d}{CLV}$ and $\phi = \frac{f}{CLV}$ for notational convenience, we arrive at the following equation for the average classification profit, P^{CCP}, of a classifier for customer churn:

$$\begin{aligned}
P^{CCP}&(T; \gamma, CLV, \delta, \phi) \\
&= CLV(\delta + \phi) \cdot \pi_0 F_0(T) - (CLV(\gamma(1 - \delta) - \phi)) \cdot \pi_1 F_1(T) \\
&\quad + (CLV(\gamma(1 - \delta) - \phi)) \cdot \pi_1 - CLV(\delta + \phi) \cdot \pi_0.
\end{aligned}$$

This equation matches with the general definition of the average classification profit, P defined above, with the following cost and benefit parameters:

$$b_1 = CLV(\gamma(1 - \delta) - \phi),$$
$$c_0 = CLV(\delta + \phi).$$

Note that b_0 and c_1 in this case are equal to zero since the profit of a customer retention campaign will only be determined by the costs and benefits related to the segment of predicted churners, if we compare with the baseline situation of running no campaign at all. No costs or benefits from running the campaign then result from the predicted nonchurner segment. The maximum profit measure to evaluate a customer churn prediction model then is defined (Verbeke et al. 2012):

$$MP^{CCP} = \max_{\forall T} P^{CCP}(T; \gamma, CLV, \delta, \phi).$$

The MP measure is based on the concept of assessing the performance at the optimal cutoff, rather than selecting an arbitrary cutoff and report on the lift at that cutoff (e.g., the top-decile lift), as often used in the industry as well as the academic literature. From the previous equations, we can estimate the optimal fraction of customers to be contacted as follows. First, we find the optimal cutoff point, which is equal to the cutoff that maximizes the average profit per customer in the customer base:

$$T^* = \arg\max_T P^{CCP}(T; \gamma, CLV, \delta, \phi).$$

This allows us subsequently to calculate the optimal fraction of customers to target in the retention campaign, which equals:

$$\bar{\eta}_{MP}^{CCP} = 1 - (\pi_0 F_0(T^*) + \pi_1 F_1(T^*)).$$

When the cost and benefit parameters are uncertain, we can still apply the framework by using the EMP measure. Verbraken et al. (2013) argue that the contact cost f and the cost of the incentive d can be reliably estimated since flowing from the design of the retention campaign, as well as the customer lifetime value (see Chapter 3). However, the fraction of customers taking the offer, γ, is much less certain. Therefore, a distribution $h(\gamma)$ reflecting the uncertainty on the value of the retention rate can be assumed, allowing to derive the expected maximum profit from the average classification profit equation as:

$$EMP^{CCP} = \int_\gamma P^{CCP}(T(\gamma); \gamma, CLV, \delta, \phi)h(\gamma)d\gamma,$$

with $T(\gamma)$ the optimal cutoff for a given γ, and $h(\gamma)$ the probability density function reflecting the uncertainty on the actual value of the parameter γ. The functional form of the distribution $h(\gamma)$ is up for discussion, but in line with the H-measure, Verbraken et al. (2013) argue that the beta distribution is appropriate to use in this setting. The parameters α and β are to be determined by an expert, so as to reflect the expected value for the retention rate γ (i.e., μ) and the uncertainty (i.e., σ^2) regarding this estimate, using the method of moments.

EMP for Credit Scoring

To apply the general EMP framework to the case of credit scoring, the conditions to determine the optimal cutoff value have to be adapted. This requires specifying the parameters b_0, c_0, b_1 and c_1, as well as the probability distribution $h(b_0, c_0, b_1, c_1)$. The methodology developed by Bravo et al. (2013) is followed to determine these parameters. Note that, similar to the customer churn prediction setting, we calculate the profitability of the credit scoring model by comparing to a baseline situation where we accept all applications. Therefore, no benefit or cost is involved in classifying an observation as negative, meaning good and leading to acceptance of the application. Hence, b_0 and c_1 are equal to zero. The profit formula underlying the EMP measure for credit scoring only takes into account the average benefit and cost of, respectively, correctly or incorrectly labeling an obligor as bad. Both b_1 and c_0 are expressed relative to the loan amount, A; as such, the profit is expressed per unit loan amount, allowing more easily to fit a probability density function expressing the uncertainty on these parameters. In fact, we have defined b_1 and c_0 already before, in the MicroCredit case study, as follows:

- The benefit of correctly identifying a defaulter, b_1, corresponds to the loss following default, which equals the unrecovered part of the exposure at time of default, i.e., $LGD \cdot EAD$. The loss is then divided by the loan amount, A, to arrive at the loss fraction relative to the loan amount, λ:

$$b_1 = \frac{LGD \cdot EAD}{A} = \lambda.$$

  Note the difference between the LGD and the loss fraction, expressing the loss relative to the exposure at default and the loan amount, respectively. The distribution of the loss fraction is uncertain. Similar to LGD, it can be assumed to follow a three-part distribution with two point-masses, p_0 and p_1, corresponding to the probabilities of 0% loss rate and 100% loss rate, respectively. Figure 6.7 in the following case study shows this functional form. The remaining part of the distribution can be assumed to correspond to a uniform distribution over the interval (0, 1) with the density expressed as

$$h(\lambda) = 1 - p_0 - p_1.$$

- The cost of incorrectly classifying a nondefaulter as a defaulter, c_0, is equal to the return on investment (ROI) of the loan, where the investment equals the loan amount, A. It can be argued that in contrast to the LGD, interest rates vary much less, so the parameter c_0 can be considered constant. In a real application, the average over the portfolio can be used to approximate the value, as was shown in the cutoff point tuning case study previously discussed in this chapter.

This leads to the following cost matrix, with ROI and λ average values:

$$C = \begin{bmatrix} -b_0 & c_1 \\ c_0 & -b_1 \end{bmatrix} = \begin{bmatrix} 0 & 0 \\ ROI & \lambda \end{bmatrix}.$$

Note, as explained in the previous chapter, that this cost matrix can be simplified to the equivalent cost matrix

$$C' = \begin{bmatrix} 0 & c_1 + b_1 \\ c_0 + b_0 & 0 \end{bmatrix} = \begin{bmatrix} 0 & \lambda \\ ROI & 0 \end{bmatrix}.$$

which was previously adopted in the MicroCredit case study, with both ROI and λ multiplied with the average loan amount to arrive at the average misclassification costs.

As the credit evaluation is a mandatory part of the loan-granting process, a fixed cost involved in evaluating an application is incurred for all applications. Therefore, it is discarded from the further profit analysis. Following these assumptions, the EMP measure for credit scoring is expressed by:

$$EMP^{CS} = \int_0^1 P(T(\theta); \lambda, ROI) \cdot h(\lambda) d\lambda,$$

with

$$P(T; \lambda, ROI) = \lambda \cdot \pi_1 (1 - F_1(T)) - ROI \cdot \pi_0 (1 - F_0(T)),$$

and $\theta = \lambda/ROI$ (since b_0 and c_1 are zero). The factor $\lambda \cdot \pi_1 (1 - F_1(T))$ in the above profit formula represents the total benefit of the true positives—that is, actual bads that have been detected—whereas the part $-ROI \cdot \pi_0 (1 - F_0(T))$ represents the total cost of the false positives—that is, goods have been deemed bad and consequently rejected.

The EMP measure presents an interesting alternative approach for evaluating classification models in challenging situations where the profit expression needs to incorporate uncertainties regarding the business line under scrutiny. The works by Verbraken et al. (2013, 2014) provide valid approaches for customer churn prediction and credit scoring applications. Given the required knowledge of the underlying profit structure, the EMP measure can be extended to other settings as well.

Implementations

Several implementations of the H-measure are readily available for use, such as the *hmeasure* R package (Anagnostopoulos and Hand 2012) as used in the MicroCredit case study, which as well allows to calculate the AUC, the AUC of the convex hull, and several standard performance measures. Implementations of the MP and EMP measure for evaluating customer churn prediction models and credit scoring models are freely available through the open-source R package EMP (Bravo et al. 2015), which can be obtained through the package manager CRAN or from the book's companion website.

● CASE STUDY

We illustrate once again the application of the EMP measure in credit scoring continuing the MicroCredit case study. In our previous analysis, neither the AUC of the convex hull nor the H-measure has taken into account the distribution of profits or the cutoff point that maximizes the profit. Here is where the EMP measure can provide the final piece of information. For the credit scoring version of the EMP measure, we need the estimate the parameters p_0 and p_1, that is, the proportion of observations at $LGD = 0\%$ and $LGD = 100\%$. We can study the histogram of the distribution of the LGD variable to get an idea of the distribution.

Figure 6.7 shows the distribution of the LGD variable, both as a histogram and as a table. We can see that most observations fall either in the 0 to 0.1 group or in the 0.9 to 1 group, and that between 0.1 and 0.9 the distribution of the LGD follows a quasi-uniform distribution. The functional form given by the EMP for credit scoring assumes this shape. This is, of course, not fortuitous; this functional form seems to fit this problem very well. Some examples of LGD distributions, many with this shape, can be seen in Loterman et al. (2012). We can now define the parameters of the LGD for the EMP distribution as follows: $p_0 = 0.72$ and $p_1 = 0.10$. Calculating the EMP using these parameters leads to the EMP values and optimal fractions to be selected, as reported in Table 6.8.

From Table 6.8 we can see that following the EMP measure, again Model 3 is to be selected over Model 5. Now we are certain that from profitability point-of-view, Model 3 is

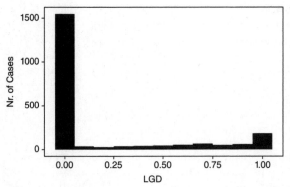

Group	Percentage
0.0–0.1	72%
0.1–0.2	2%
0.2–0.3	1%
0.3–0.4	2%
0.4–0.5	8%
0.5–0.6	2%
0.6–0.7	3%
0.7–0.8	3%
0.8–0.9	2%
0.9–1.0	10%

Figure 6.7 LGD histogram and percentage of observations per score group.

Table 6.8 EMP and Selected
Fraction per Model

Model	EMP	Fraction η
Model 1	0.0174	0.141
Model 2	0.0166	0.158
Model 3	0.0174	0.146
Model 4	0.0170	0.155
Model 5	0.0173	0.141

the optimal choice. Furthermore, the measure suggests that we reject 14.6% of the total number of applications. We can use the independent test set to apply the model under these conditions and estimate the total profit from the total benefits and losses that are achieved following this strategy, as reported in Table 6.9. As can be seen from this table, Model 3 generates almost 5% more profits than the second best competing model (i.e., Model 5).

Table 6.9 Benefits, Costs, and Profits for the
Test Set. Model 3 gives the better performance,
as expected.

Model	Benefits (€)	Costs (€)	Profits (€)
Model 3	571.061	−111.560	459.501
Model 5	555.190	−127.431	427.759

In this case study, we have clearly shown the limitations of supporting only on the AUC measure to select a candidate model when misclassification costs are imbalanced. Moreover, we have illustrated the use and merits of adopting recently developed profit-based measures.

A key takeaway is that for developing profit-driven business analytical models, it is essential to identify situations when the convex hull of the AUC curve, cost-driven or profit-driven, measures are to be preferred over using the standard AUC measure to evaluate and select classification models. Such situations typically occur:

- When the classification problem involves imbalanced costs and benefits per class;
- When the ROC curves of the models that are being compared intersect, i.e., when there is no stochastic dominance of one model over the others;
- When the comparisons need to be carried out across different test sets.

In all these cases, the AUC of the convex hull, but preferably the H-measure or alternatively the MP or EMP measures, should be used for making a profit-optimal decision as to which classification model to select and effectively implement. Additionally, the use of the MP and/or EMP measure provides an indication of the optimal cutoff and the optimal fraction of entities to select.

Profit-Driven Evaluation with Observation-Dependent Costs

Fawcett (2006a) studies the advantages and limitations of the use of ROC curves across variable environments and applications in terms of the actual cost structure, as well as for different degrees of imbalanced class distributions (see Chapter 5). Fawcett (2006b) additionally analyzes the use of the ROC curve in applications where the cost matrix is variable across observations (i.e., when the cost matrix is observation-dependent[5] as discussed in the previous chapter).

An observation-dependent cost matrix naturally arises in business settings. For example, in the MicroCredit case study, so far we have mainly used a class-dependent cost matrix, whereas in fact the cost matrix is observation-dependent, as discussed in the cutoff point tuning case study. In line with previous discussions, Table 6.10 shows the applicable observation-dependent cost matrix, providing the loan-specific misclassification costs for loan i involving a loan amount A_i, an exposure at default EAD_i, a loss given default LGD_i, and a return on investment ROI_i, as per Verbraken et al. (2014). The analysis presented so far in the MicroCredit case study calculated the average over the distribution of the values in the observation-dependent cost matrix. Fawcett (2006b) proposes a more refined approach than averaging the observation-dependent cost matrix to obtain a class-dependent cost matrix. The proposed approach extends the analysis of the ROC curve and therefore is dubbed ROCIV, as an acronym for ROC with instance-varying costs.

The first step in the ROCIV analysis is to transform the cost matrix in Table 6.10 into a matrix that compares the cost or benefit of adopting a classification model with a baseline model or baseline

Table 6.10 Observation-Dependent Cost Matrix for Credit Scoring

	Actual Good	Actual Bad
Predicted Good	0	$LGD_i \cdot EAD_i$
Predicted Bad	$ROI_i \cdot A_i$	0

situation. Remember that as well in specifying the cost and benefit parameters of the MP and EMP measures for evaluating customer churn prediction and credit scoring models, we compared against a baseline situation—in customer churn prediction the baseline situation was not running any retention campaigns (all customers predicted to be nonchurners), and in credit scoring the baseline situation was defined as accepting all applications (all applications predicted good). The baseline model in general is defined here as a model that classifies all observations as negative.

Formally and in line with the conventions adopted elsewhere in this book, we define the positive class observations to have a value one for the target variable ($y = 1$), the negative class observations a value zero ($y = 0$), and the cost matrix C_i for each observation i with elements $C_i(\hat{y}, y)$ such that:

$$C_i = \begin{bmatrix} C_i(0,0) & C_i(0,1) \\ C_i(1,0) & C_i(0,1) \end{bmatrix}.$$

Then the transformed matrix C_i^* which is used in ROCIV analysis is obtained by subtracting for each observation the first row from both the first and second row. Additionally, in Fawcett (2006b), the sign of element $C_i^*(1,1)$ is inverted, facilitating the interpretation by turning the cost matrix into a cost-benefit matrix with element $C_i^*(1,1)$ now to be interpreted as a benefit instead of a cost and having a positive value. A similar approach was adopted in the MP framework discussed before. Inverting the sign of the element $C_i^*(1,1)$ yields a negative cost value, which as discussed before as such represents a benefit. Correctly predicting a positive observation should indeed yield a benefit or a negative cost.

The transformed cost matrix represents the involved cost and benefit in function of the actual class, compared to labeling every observation to be a member of the negative class (e.g., in the credit scoring example, predicting all applicants to be good):

$$C_i^* = \begin{bmatrix} 0 & 0 \\ C_i(1,0) - C_i(0,0) & -1 \cdot (C_i(1,1) - C_i(0,1)) \end{bmatrix} = \begin{bmatrix} 0 & 0 \\ c_{i,0} & b_{i,1} \end{bmatrix}.$$

For notational convenience, we introduce the following shorthand notation for the nonzero values in the transformed cost matrix: $C_i^*(0,0) = c_{i,b}$ and $C_i^*(0,1) = b_{i,1}$. In the credit scoring example, the cost matrix of Table 6.10 then becomes the following transformed cost-benefit matrix:

$$C_i^* = \begin{bmatrix} 0 & 0 \\ ROI_i \cdot A_i & LGD_i \cdot EAD_i \end{bmatrix}.$$

When using the transformed observation-dependent cost-benefit matrix to calculate the total cost over the predictions made by a model, we basically calculate the profit of using the model compared to the baseline model.

The baseline model in a credit scoring context classifies all observations as good, leading to all applications being accepted. When the model classifies an applicant as good, there is no difference with the prediction made by the baseline model. Hence, the cost or benefit of classifying an observation as good in the transformed cost matrix equals zero, both for the actual class being good or bad. There will only be a difference when the prediction of the model is different from the prediction that is made by the baseline model—when the model predicts an applicant to be bad. When the observation effectively concerns a bad application, then a benefit equal to the loss that would have been incurred is achieved. When the observation is actually good, then compared to the baseline model, a cost is incurred, equal to the return that the loan would have generated.

The ROCIV curve is then constructed as follows. In a first step, the total potential false positive cost from using the model is calculated, by aggregating the observation-dependent costs for all the negative class observations. The total potential false positive cost is incurred if a model classifies all negative observations as positive—for instance, in the credit scoring example, if all goods are predicted to be bad. Similarly, the total potential true positive benefit is calculated by aggregating the observation-dependent benefits for all the positive class observations, which indicates the maximum profit that could be achieved by using the model. The maximum benefit would be achieved if the model classifies all positives as positives—for example, predicts all bads to be bad.

The total potential false positive cost and true positive benefit are used to scale the realized false positive cost and true positive benefit, which depend on the cutoff that is used to classify observations based on the predicted conditional class probabilities by the model. Then for all possible cutoffs, we can calculate the pair of the false positive cost and true positive benefit, relative to the total potential false positive cost and the total potential true positive benefit, respectively. The resulting set of pairs constitutes the ROCIV curve. Algorithm 6.1 provides a description of the procedure to construct the ROCIV curve.

The area under the ROCIV curve is called the AUCIV and allows to evaluate of a classification model taking into account an

Algorithm 6.1 ROCIV

Inputs:

1. Observations i in dataset D. n_0 of the negative class and n_1 of the positive class ($n_0 + n_1 = n$).

2. $p_i = p(1|x_i)$: Probability estimate of belonging to the positive class for $x_i \in D$, ranked from high to low in a list D_0.

3. Costs $c_{i,0}$ and benefit $b_{i,1}$ for each observation i with true label y_i.

1: **For** $i \in D$:

2:   **if** $y_i = 1$: $Pos_{Total} = Pos_{Total} + b_{i,1}$

3:   **else** $Neg_{Total} = Neg_{Total} + c_{i,0}$

4:   $FP_{cost} = 0, TP_{benefit} = 0, ROCIV = \{ \quad \}, p_{prev} = -1$

5: **While** $i \leq n$

6:   **if** $p_i \neq p_{prev}$

7:     $ROCIV = ROCIV \cup \left(\dfrac{FP_{cost}}{Neg_{Total}}, \dfrac{TP_{benefit}}{Pos_{Total}} \right)$

8:     $p_{prev} = p_i$

9:   **if** $y_i = 1$: $TP_{benefit} = TP_{benefit} + b_{i,1}$

10:   **else** $FP_{cost} = FP_{cost} + c_{i,0}$

11:   $k = k + 1$

12:   $ROCIV = ROCIV \cup \left(\dfrac{FP_{cost}}{Neg_{Total}}, \dfrac{TP_{benefit}}{Pos_{Total}} \right)$

observation-dependent cost matrix. There is an intuitive interpretation of the area under the ROCIV curve: the AUCIV corresponds to the probability that the classification model will rank a randomly chosen positive class observation above a randomly chosen negative class observation, with the probability of both the positive and negative class observations to be chosen proportional to their cost. This is an extension of the intuitive interpretation of the AUC, which is the same probability, but with each (positive or negative) observation having the same probability to be chosen.

The AUCIV is a generally applicable measure that allows us to include observation-dependent costs and benefits into ROC analysis, and complements the other measures we have discussed in this chapter.

PROFIT-DRIVEN EVALUATION OF REGRESSION MODELS

In Chapter 2, regression was defined as a type of predictive analytics that concerns the study of relationships between observable variables, and more specifically between a target variable y and a set of predictor variables $\mathbf{x}$. The target variable in a regression context is quantitative and continuous in nature (e.g., demand), whereas in a classification context, the target variable is qualitative and discrete in nature, assuming values in a finite set. In a forecasting context, the relation between a target variable and time is explicitly assessed. Supervised learning refers to classification and regression, including forecasting, as a group of tasks that are similar in nature.

In supervised learning, the target variable is modeled as a function of the predictor variables based on a set of historical observations (i.e., a model is fitted to data containing simultaneous measurements of the target and predictor variables). The aim of estimating such a model is to establish the relation or detect dependencies between the predictor variables and the target variable, which may generally serve two main purposes—either to *explain* the observed variability or behavior or to *predict* the often unobserved or future value of the target variable (Breiman 2001; Shmueli and Koppius 2011) as a function of the predictor variables. The discussion in this chapter is primarily situated in the field of supervised learning for prediction, although it may also have practical use when building regression models for explaining observed behavior.

For either purpose, it is typically essential to assess the *quality* of a model before adopting it. Quality may be evaluated using various criteria as discussed in Chapter 1, depending on the exact problem setting or application at hand, user requirements, and managerial preferences. Important quality criteria concern statistical performance or prediction error, generalization behavior, economic cost and benefit, model significance, complexity and stability, comprehensibility and justifiability, operational efficiency, regulatory compliance, and relevance. These quality criteria have already been extensively discussed in Chapters 1, 2, and 3 (Martens et al. 2010).

Statistical performance is typically of primary importance in assessing model quality when the goal of the model is to predict, although usually it is not the only criterion that is adopted. In the first part of this chapter, we have extended the standard performance measures for classification models, as presented in an introductory section on model evaluation in Chapter 2. We have discussed in detail how performance evaluation can account for the actual costs and benefits (or in an aggregated manner the profitability) associated with adopting and implementing a classification model in an operational setting to provide a more tangible and optimal indication of performance tuned to the application's characteristics. In this section, we likewise will further expand upon the discussion on performance measures in the context of regression, extending upon the discussion on cost-sensitive regression approaches in Chapter 5.

Loss Functions and Error-Based Evaluation Measures

Formally, a regression function is defined as a general function $f(x)$, $f : X \to Y$, with $X \subset \mathbb{R}^V$ and $Y \in \mathbb{O}$, with $\mathbb{O}$ the output space and $\mathbb{O} \subset \mathbb{R}$. A regression function is fitted to estimate observed outputs $Y \in \mathbb{O}$ using a sample of observations $D \subset X$ and $D = \{x_i, y_i\}_{i=1}^{n}$. For each observation x of the sample D, an error $e(x)$ can be calculated equal to the difference between the estimated and observed target value, $e(x) = Y - f(x)$, $e : E \subset \mathbb{R} \to \mathbb{R}$, $\forall x \in D$. A *loss* or *cost* function $\ell(Y, f(x))$ determines the penalty or severity assigned to an error e (Hastie, Tibshirani, and Friedman 2001; Provost and Fawcett 2013) in evaluating the generalization performance of regression models. Typical choices for the loss function are squared error and absolute error loss functions:

$$\ell(Y, f(\mathbf{x})) = (Y - f(x))^2,$$
$$\ell(Y, f(\mathbf{x})) = |Y - f(x)|.$$

Squaring the errors expresses a quadratically increasing (i.e., more than proportional) importance assigned to larger errors. Absolute loss assigns an equal importance to each unit of error. Regression evaluation measures subsequently aggregate the *individual* losses or error terms (i.e., on all observations in the test set) to yield a single value that indicates the quality of the regression model in terms of approximating the observed output values.

A number of traditional, widely adopted evaluation measures have been summarized in Table 6.11. These measures were discussed in Chapter 2. In penalizing and aggregating individual errors, these measures make (implicit) assumptions about the relative importance of the individual errors, as will be discussed in detail below. Note that the MSE and MAD performance measures in Table 6.11 are expressed in a certain unit and on a certain scale, whereas R^2 and Pearson correlation are not. The unit and scale of the mean absolute deviation measure are the same as the unit and scale of the target variable, and the unit and scale of the mean squared error are the squared unit and scale of the target variable, respectively. Conversely, the R^2 and Pearson correlation measures are independent of the unit and scale of the target variable.

Table 6.11 Overview of Standard Regression Evaluation Measures

Measure	Acronym	Formula
Mean squared error	MSE	$\frac{1}{n}\sum_{i=1}^{n}(y_i - \widehat{y}_i)^2$
Mean absolute deviation	MAD	$\frac{1}{n}\sum_{i=1}^{n}|y_i - \widehat{y}_i|$
Coefficient of determination	R^2	$1 - \dfrac{\sum_{i=1}^{n}(y_i - \widehat{y}_i)^2}{\sum_{i=1}^{n}(y_i - \bar{y}_i)^2}$
Pearson correlation coefficient	ρ	$\dfrac{\sum_{i=1}^{n}(\widehat{y}_i - \bar{\widehat{y}})(y_i - \bar{y}_i)}{s(\widehat{y})s(y)}$

They are unitless and take a value in the range of zero to one and minus one to one, enabling comparison across different applications.

Regression models are being adopted for practical estimation purposes in a multitude of application fields ranging from the prediction of customer demand in supply-chain management, over the estimation of required software development effort for cost assessment and pricing, to loss given default prediction in a credit-risk modeling setting (Dejaeger et al. 2012; Loterman et al. 2012). The purely statistical perspective (introduced above) toward the generalization performance of a regression model makes perfect sense within a statistical framework, that is, when evaluating performance in a generalized, abstract manner.

However, from an applied perspective, the statistical measures introduced in the above section do not provide an insightful or customized assessment of a regression model since they do not consider the actual use or practical purpose of the model. Indeed, and even worse, statistical measures make important assumptions about the relative importance of individual errors. These assumptions are typically inappropriate for particular problem settings and lead to an impertinent assessment and a suboptimal model selection. Essentially, goodness of fit from a statistical perspective is not the same as goodness of fit from an applied perspective.

As indicated by several authors (Christoffersen and Diebold 1996, 1997; Crone, Lessmann, and Stahlbock 2005; Granger 1969; Luis Torgo and Ribeiro 2007), wrongful predictions of a continuous target variable in real-world applications such as finance, fraud detection, supply chain management, meteorology, or ecology, may come with asymmetric costs—for example, they may differ depending on both the sign of the error—and nonuniform costs (i.e., costs that depend on the actual value of the target variable). Note that the MSE and MAD loss functions defined above as the squared and absolute difference between the actual and predicted value, as well as the other evaluation measures defined in Table 6.11, assume symmetrical and uniform costs. The sign of the error is ignored, and a uniform penalty is assigned to errors across the domain of the target variable. To address these shortcomings, a limited number of alternative approaches have been developed to generalize the loss function. Two of these measures—REC curves and surfaces—provide practical use and allow us to evaluate regression models in a profit-oriented manner.

REC Curve and Surface

In Luís Torgo (2005), regression error characteristic (REC) curves as introduced by Bi and Bennett (2003) are extended to REC surfaces by adding the distribution of the errors across the domain of the target variable. REC curves visualize the cumulative distribution of the errors and therefore characterize the predictive performance of a regression model in a fashion similar to that of receiver operating characteristic curves (ROC) which characterize binary classification models. A REC curve plots the error tolerance on the x-axis versus the percentage of points predicted within the tolerance on the y-axis. The resulting curve estimates the cumulative distribution function of the error. The error on the x-axis can be defined as the squared error $(y_i - \hat{y}_i)^2$ or the absolute deviation $|y_i - \hat{y}_i|$. Just as with the ROC curve, the perfect model is situated in the upper-left corner. Hence, the quicker the curve approaches this point, the better the model. The area above the curve then represents an overall error measure that should preferably be as small as possible. As an example, consider the data represented in Table 6.12. The corresponding REC curve is depicted in Figure 6.8.

REC surfaces extend REC curves by plotting the cumulative distribution of the error as a function of both the error size and the value of the target variable, and as such provide additional information

Table 6.12 Data for REC Curve

Tolerance (MAD)	Predictions within Tolerance	Cumulative Accuracy
0	60	30%
0.05	118	59%
0.1	164	82%
0.2	182	91%
0.5	200	100%

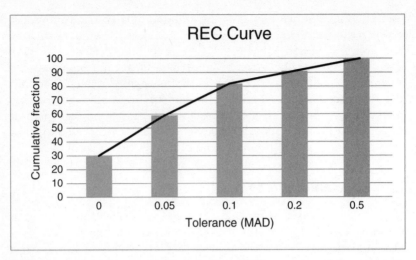

Figure 6.8 Regression error characteristic (REC) curve.

about the performance of the model. When non-uniform costs are associated with errors as a function of the actual value of the target variable, improved model assessment may result from the provision of additional insight in the distribution of the errors. The introduction of REC surfaces (Luís Torgo 2005) is driven by applications in which the cost of an error strongly depends on the actual value of the target variable, and more specifically, settings in which small errors are preferred when the target value is large such as outlier or extreme value prediction. Figure 6.9 provides an example of a REC surface, extending the REC curve provided in Figure 6.8 by adding the target variable as a dimension to the plot and facilitating more detailed analysis of the performance of the regression model. Note that the target variable in this example has only four possible outcomes.

As an alternative to the overall REC surface, parts of the surface can be further analyzed, e.g., for the range of target values that are most of interest, i.e., most valuable to accurately predict.

A more elaborate utility-based evaluation framework has also been proposed, allowing for differentiated scores to be assigned to predictions of a regression model that accounted for costs and benefits conforming to application preference biases (Ribeiro and Torgo 2008; Luis Torgo and Ribeiro 2007). The presented approach again focuses on nonuniform costs across the domain of the target variable, and although not explicitly stated nor elaborated as such, it may be extended to accommodate a problem setting with asymmetric costs and benefits across the error distribution.

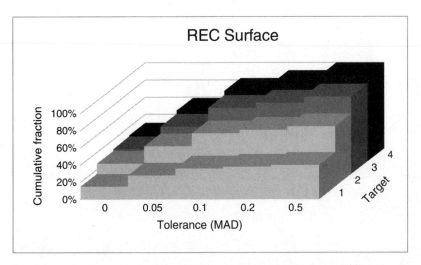

Figure 6.9 Regression error characteristic surface following the data in Table 6.13.

Table 6.13 Data for REC Surface

		Tolerance (MAD)				
		0	0.05	0.1	0.2	0.5
Target	1	15%	28%	36%	38%	40%
	2	27%	47%	62%	66%	70%
	3	29%	55%	77%	83%	90%
	4	15%	28%	36%	38%	40%

For arriving at a utility function $U(\hat{Y}, Y)$, which assigns a utility value to any pair of an estimate $\hat{y}$ when the actual target value is y, two functions are defined:

1. A relevance function $\phi(Y) : \mathbb{R} \to 0..1$, that maps the domain of the target variable into a $0..1$ scale of relevance, whereby 1 represents maximum relevance; $\phi(Y)$ expresses the relative importance of the value of the target variable across the domain of the target variable, allowing the consideration of nonuniform costs across the domain of the target variable. No functional shape is assumed for $\phi(Y)$, which is expected to be specified by the user using his/her domain knowledge. The developers indicate that specifying the relevance function is the most challenging step in the process, requiring insight in

the application and mathematical skills to map an appropriate function to express the relevance. In Torgo and Ribeiro (2007), a function that is inversely proportional to the probability density function of the target variable is adopted since relevance is assumed to be related to rarity. The more seldom a value, the more relevant it is to accurately predict. This is the case in outlier prediction, such as extreme weather conditions, highly profitable customers, or high variations of stock prices.

2. A function $\zeta : \mathbb{R}_0^+ \to [-B, B]$, specifying the utility associated with a certain error, which indeed is a loss function assigning an importance to an error as a function of the size of the error.

$$\zeta(L(\hat{Y}, Y)) = \text{sgn}(t - L(\hat{Y}, Y)) \cdot B \cdot (1 - e^{-\eta \cdot |t - L(\hat{Y}, Y)|}).$$

The function ζ smoothly decreases the utility of a prediction $\hat{y}$ from the maximum utility B, which is to be specified by the user, for an error zero, to the minimum benefit $-B$. In addition to the value of B, two more parameters need to be specified for fixing the function ζ, which is prespecified as a negative exponential relation between error and utility:

1. A decay parameter η;

2. A cutoff value T, stipulating the cutoff value above which an error will yield negative utility and below which it will yield positive utility; in other words, T is the admissible error amplitude.

The final utility function $U(\hat{Y}, Y)$ of a prediction $\hat{y}$ for an actual value y extends the above defined utility function ζ by additionally taking into consideration the relevance of both $\hat{y}$ and y as expressed by the relevance function $\phi(Y)$. The final utility value depends on whether a positive benefit $(L(\hat{Y}, Y) \leq T)$ or negative benefit $(L(\hat{Y}, Y) > T)$ is achieved, which is, respectively, the case when the error is below or above the admissible error amplitude T, as described by the function:

$$U(\hat{Y}, Y) = \begin{cases} min\{\phi(Y), \phi(\hat{Y})\} \cdot \zeta(L(\hat{Y}, Y)) & \text{for } L(\hat{Y}, Y) \leq T \\ ((1 - p) \cdot \phi(\hat{Y}) + p \cdot \phi(Y)) \cdot \zeta(L(\hat{Y}, Y)) & \text{for } L(\hat{Y}, Y) > T \end{cases}$$

In the first case, for $L(\hat{Y}, Y) \leq T$, the error is deemed admissible since it is below the cutoff T and the estimate sufficiently accurate. The utility then is proportional to the smallest relevance of $\hat{y}$ and y, as expressed by the function ϕ defined above. The idea here is that the smallest of these two determines the eventual utility or amount of benefit that we get from the prediction.

In the second case, for $L(\hat{Y}, Y) > T$, the error is considered substantial and causing a negative benefit to be achieved since it is above the cutoff T. The related cost we incur then is proportional to the weighted average of the relevances of both $\hat{y}$ and y as expressed by the relevance function ϕ, with the weight p setting the relative importance of two types of errors, false alarms versus missed events. An event in the case of outlier detection for instance being an extreme value of the target variable.

The function $U(\hat{Y}, Y)$ defines a utility surface over all combinations of the predicted and actual values of the target variable and can be considered as a continuous and smooth version of a cost matrix. Indeed, this function is a two-dimensional loss function penalizing errors as a function of the actual and predicted value of the target variable for a test observation. Averaging the individual utilities over all observations in the test set, similar to the calculation of MSE and MAD but with a different underlying loss function, leads to an evaluation measure expressing the average utility per test case.

This average utility measure identifies and allows nonuniformity over the domain of the target variable as an important dimension to be taken into account both in specifying a loss function and in defining a conceptually useful evaluation measure in terms of average utility generated. However, the presented approach may pose practical difficulties both in setting the various parameters and in elaborating a customized relevance and utility function to the problem at hand. However, any approach that aims to consider the exact cost and benefit structure of the regression problem will have to address the challenge of explicitly specifying this relation. Moreover, although these measures are appropriate in extreme value prediction, which was the main application in the work that introduced this approach (Ribeiro and Torgo 2008), many regression problems do not come with a binary misclassification structure as specified by the cutoff value T; instead, they are continuous in nature.

CONCLUSION

Profit-driven model evaluation is probably the most straightforward approach towards developing profit-driven analytical models. A diversity of measures has been developed and can be used by practitioners in various problem settings. A well-informed data scientist, such as the readers of this book, will be able to leverage the measures discussed in this chapter for performance assessments that are application-oriented and that are more effective in analyzing model performance from a business perspective.

The most straightforward way to evaluate a model in a profit-driven manner is to estimate the values of the benefits and costs for each customer or event being analyzed (not necessarily an easy task) and then calculate the average misclassification cost of the model. This average will represent the mean value of the profit when using the model over the long run, assuming the sample that is originally used to develop the model is representative for the population and that the population is stable in the long run.

The average misclassification approach is probably too simple a measure for assessing performance in a more complex business setting. The ROC-based profit measures are a natural extension to ROC analysis, which incorporate costs and benefits explicitly rather than implicitly, and can help deal with distributional issues regarding costs and benefits. Among these measures, the H-measure is one of the most recognized approaches. The H-measure weights the ROC curve by a beta distribution allowing it to fit diverse cost structures. Even though the measure does not include benefits explicitly, if the joint distribution of the costs and benefits are known, then the problem can be reduced. Thus, this measure can be very flexible and is a starting point for a profit-sensitive analysis.

When benefits and costs are more complex, then measures such as the MP or EMP measure may offer additional flexibility to account for specific problem characteristics. The stochastic nature of the EMP measure, allowing complex cost distributions to be assessed, can support profit-driven analysis in most business scenarios. This comes at the cost of having to study the distribution of profits in detail, which might be difficult and costly to small organizations.

Finally, a dedicated section in this chapter introduced profit-driven measures for evaluating regression models. REC curves and REC surfaces may complement standard evaluation measures and provide additional insight with regards to the performance and profitability of a regression model. In summary, many options are available to conduct profit-driven evaluation of predictive analytics models. An organization with a profit-driven objective for modeling should study and deploy the most appropriate methodology for its business processes. Proper model evaluation is bound to bring tangible monetary improvements, which, in turn, will result in an increased ROI for the whole business line, as will be discussed in Chapter 7.

REVIEW QUESTIONS

Multiple Choice Questions

Question 1

Which of the below statements is true?

   a. An average misclassification cost measure is only appropriate for binary problems.
   b. The optimum cutoff of a problem depends only on the distribution of the scores for binary problems.
   c. The average profit derived from a chosen model is the only value needed to calculate the EMP measure.
   d. The profits of a model must be estimated and decided by the data scientist, not by the model.

Question 2

Consider the following statements on setting the cutoff point of a model using the average misclassification cost:

   I. It is important to estimate the costs and benefits for each cutoff.

   II. The coverage (number of observations that receive an action) should be included in the analysis.

   III. The best cutoff will always be the one with minimum average misclassification cost.

   IV. A large training set is required so it allows users to calculate the true average misclassification cost.

   Which of these statements are true?

   a. I, III, IV
   b. I, II, IV
   c. II, IIII, IV
   d. I, II, III, IV

Question 3

Which statement is not true regarding a committee-based two-cutoff-point strategy?

   a. It will give more flexibility to the company when deciding the cutoff.

b. It can generate savings, as the cost of the committee will be off-set by the losses avoided.

c. It requires a sophisticated analysis team to make better-informed decisions.

d. It only requires knowledge of the profit structure of the process.

Question 4

The MP value is different from the H-measure because:

a. The MP measure is based on profits, the H-measure on costs.
b. The H-measure does not minimize costs along the curve.
c. The MP does not consider any variability in profits.
d. The MP measure does not use the ROC curve.

Question 5

Which one of the following statements is not true regarding EMP?

a. It considers the general distribution of profits, thus making it appropriate for changing environments.
b. It is calculated over the upper convex hull of the ROC curve.
c. It is an extension of the H-measure and the MP measure.
d. It can only be applied for churn and credit scoring.

Question 6

The ROC-based measures all use the upper convex hull of the ROC curve because:

a. It is easier to calculate the convex hull of the ROC curve instead of the ROC curve itself.
b. The upper convex hull will be the same for all test sets, so now they are comparable (as opposed to the AUC measure).
c. A minimum cost or maximum profit value can be obtained at each segment of the ROC curve given the concavity of the convex hull.
d. It is easier to calculate the AUC of the convex hull than the AUC of the ROC curve.

Question 7

When defining the profits of the application of a credit scoring model, which statement is not true?

a. The benefits can be estimated using the ROI of the loans.
b. The losses are the most relevant factor.
c. The distribution of losses tends to follow a beta distribution.
d. The balance of the number of good observations, their profits, and the number of defaulters and their losses must be leveraged.
e. The defaulters are usually more expensive than the non-defaulters.

Question 8

When thinking about profit-driven evaluation of a churn model:

a. The cost structure will depend only on the customers that churn during a period.
b. The cost of contacting the customers is usually higher than the cost of losing a customer.
c. It is expected that the retention actions are successful for potential churners, so they need to be well designed.
d. It is usually not convenient to conduct retention actions, as the cost tends to be too high.

Question 9

The AUC measure does not give adequate results when comparing different datasets on the test set. This occurs because:

a. The ROC curve is different for each model.
b. The integral that defines the AUC cannot be estimated with different datasets.
c. The AUC is estimated using the score distribution of each test set.
d. The test sets have different sizes, therefore different cost proportions.

Question 10

Consider the following statements regarding the ROCIV measure:

I. It allows us to calculate an equivalent of the AUC measure when costs vary per observation.
II. It is a maximum profit measure.
III. It is relevant for environments where the distributions of costs are not known.

IV. It requires greater insight regarding the behavior of the subjects under analysis than a distribution-based measure does.

Which of these statements are true?

a. I and II
b. I and III
c. I and IV
d. II and III

Open Questions

The MicroCredit example dataset is to be used for solving the below questions. It is freely downloadable from the book's companion website. The dataset consists of simulated examples derived from a real Micro Credit dataset used in Bravo et al. (2013), and has the following variables:

- Amount: The amount in euro of the loan.
- Term: The term of the loan.
- Age: The age of the applicant at the time of application.
- Region: The region of the country the applicant lives in at the time of application.
- Econ_Sector: A grouping of the economic sector the applicant operates in at the time of borrowing.
- Target: The objective variable, if the applicant defaulted within the first 12 months of the loan.
- EAD: The exposure at the time of default.
- LGD: Loss given default of the loan.

The first five variables can be used to build a model with the data. In what follows, we assume that the ROI of the nondefaulters is equal to 30% of the amount of the loan.

Question 1

Train a logistic regression model. Report the following measures:

a. Accuracy
b. AUC
c. H-measure
d. EMP for credit scoring

What can you say about your model? How well does it discriminate?

Question 2

Build a cutoff point table for the model developed in Question 1 and decide on the following:

a. A minimum-cost cutoff.
b. A maximum-profit cutoff
c. A maximum accuracy cutoff

Compare each cutoff and discuss the business implications of each.

Question 3

Design a two-cutoff-point strategy from your results in Question 2. Assume that each committee runs at a cost of € 100 per evaluated loan. How does your strategy change? Is it worth it to have a committee in this case?

Question 4

For credit scoring datasets, an alternative view is that each observation has a different cost of misclassification (in addition to each class). For the MicroCredit dataset (and in general for most loan applications) the nondefaulters incorrectly predicted will involve a cost of $ROI_i \cdot A_i$ and the defaulters involve a misclassification cost of $LGD_i \cdot EAD_i$.

Implement the ROCIV strategy by Fawcett (2007) and evaluate your model. Do your results change? Would you make different decisions by evaluating this model on a case-by-case basis? Discuss when it could be relevant to choose AUCIV versus another profit-based or cost-based analysis. Are the results of AUCIV comparable when using different test datasets?

NOTES

1. The reason for charging the same interest rate to all customers is the social objective of microfinance, which aims to give access to banking services to people who, e.g., would never get a loan with a traditional credit institution. This allows, for instance, entrepreneurs to start-up a small scale business, helping them to improve their situation.

2. Note that the words convex and concave are used in opposite manners by mathematicians, who developed the concept of the convex hull, and the machine learning community, for which the convex hull makes the ROC curve concave (Hand 2008).

3. The AUC analysis can be further extended by bootstrapping the models, allowing to estimate the AUC and AUC over the convex hull with confidence intervals and to compare the obtained values using robust statistical tests.

4. Remark that both the average cost of misclassifying a good applicant and a bad applicant is relatively low, since the example dataset concerns microloans, which typically involve small loan amounts, and as such small returns or losses.

5. Observation-dependent is also referred to in the literature as instance-varying, example-specific or example-dependent.

REFERENCES

Anagnostopoulos, C., and D. J. Hand. 2012. "hmeasure: The H-measure and Other Scalar Classification Performance Metrics." R Package version 1.0. Available Online https://cran.r-project.org/web/packages/hmeasure/index.html.

Baesens, B. 2014. *Analytics in a Big Data World: The Essential Guide to Data Science and its Applications*. Hoboken, NJ: Wiley and SAS Business.

Baesens, B., D. Roesch, and H. Scheule. 2016. *Credit Risk Analytics: Measurement Techniques, Applications, and Examples in SAS*. Hoboken, NJ: Wiley and SAS Business.

Bravo, C., S. Maldonado, and R. Weber. 2013. "Granting and Managing Loans for Micro-Entrepreneurs: New Developments and Practical Experiences." *European Journal of Operational Research*, 227, 2: 358–366.

Bravo, C. and Vanden Broucke, S. and Verbraken, T. 2015. EMP: Expected Maximum Profit Classification Performance Measure. R package version 3.0.0. Available Online: http://cran.r-project.org/web/packages/EMP/index.html.

Dodd, L. E., and M. S. Pepe. 2003. "Partial AUC Estimation and Regression." *Biometrics* 59: 614–623.

Domingos, P. 1999. "MetaCost: A General Method for Making Classifiers Cost-Sensitive." Proceedings of the Fifth ACM SIGKDD International Conference on Knowledge Discovery and Data Mining, 155–164. San Diego, California, August 15–18.

Dragos D. M., and T. G. Dietterich. 2000. "Bootstrap Methods for the Cost-Sensitive Evaluation of Classifiers." In Proceedings of the Seventeenth International Conference on Machine Learning (ICML '00), Pat Langley (Ed.). San Francisco: Morgan Kaufmann Publishers Inc., 583–590.

Drummond, C., and R. C. Holte. 2000. "Explicitly Representing Expected Cost: An Alternative to ROC Representation." In Proceedings of the Sixth ACM SIGKDD International Conference on Knowledge Discovery and Data Mining (KDD '00). ACM, New York, 198–207.

Fawcett, T. 2006a. "An Introduction to ROC Analysis." *Pattern Recognition Letters* 27 (8): 861–874.

Fawcett, T. 2006b. "ROC Graphs with Instance Varying Costs." *Pattern Recognition Letters* 27 (8): 882–891.

Flach, P. A. 2003, January. "The Geometry of ROC Space: Understanding Machine Learning Metrics through ROC Isometrics." In *Proceedings of the Twentieth International Conference on Machine Learning*, 194–201. Washington, DC.

Flach, P. A. 2011. "ROC Analysis." In *Encyclopedia of Machine Learning*. New York: Springer, pp. 869–875.

Griffiths, D. A. 1973. "Maximum Likelihood Estimation for the Beta-Binomial Distribution and an Application to the Household Distribution of the Total Number of Cases of a Disease." *Biometrics* 29 (4): 637–648.

Hand, D. 2009. "Measuring Classifier Performance: A Coherent Alternative to the Area under the ROC Curve." *Machine Learning* 77: 103–123.

Loterman, G., I. Brown, D. Martens, C. Mues, and B. Baesens. 2012. "Benchmarking Regression Algorithms for Loss Given Default Modeling." *International Journal of Forecasting* 28 (1): 161–170.

McClish, D. K. 1989. "Analyzing a Portion of the ROC Curve." *Medical Decision Making* 9, 190–195.

Neslin, S. A., S. Gupta, W. Kamakura, J. Lu, and C. H. Mason. 2006. "Defection Detection: Measuring and Understanding the Predictive Accuracy of Customer Churn Models." *Journal of Marketing Research* 43 (2): 204–211.

Paolino, P. 2001. "Maximum Likelihood Estimation of Models with Beta-Distributed Dependent Variables." *Political Analysis* 9 (4): 325–346.

Provost, F. J., and T. Fawcett. 1997, August. "Analysis and Visualization of Classifier Performance: Comparison under Imprecise Class and Cost Distributions." *In* KDD, Vol. 97, pp. 43–48.

Smithson, M., and J. Verkuilen. 2006. "A Better Lemon Squeezer? Maximum-Likelihood Regression with Beta-Distributed Dependent Variables." *Psychological Methods* 11(1): 54.

Sullivan Pepe, M., and T. Cai. 2004. "The Analysis of Placement Values for Evaluating Discriminatory Measures." *Biometrics* 60 (2): 528–535.

Verbeke, W., D. Martens, C. Mues, and B. Baesens. 2011. "Building Comprehensible Customer Churn Prediction Models with Advanced Rule Induction Techniques." *Expert Systems with Applications* 38 (3): 2354–2364.

Verbeke, W., K. Dejaeger, D. Martens, J. Hur, and B. Baesens. 2012. "New Insights into Churn Prediction in the Telecommunication Sector: A Profit Driven Data Mining Approach." *European Journal of Operational Research* 218 (1): 211–229.

Verbraken, T., W. Verbeke, and B. Baesens. 2013. "A Novel Profit Maximizing Metric for Measuring Classification Performance of Customer Churn Prediction Models." *IEEE Transactions on Knowledge and Data Engineering* 25 (5): 961–973.

Verbraken, T., C. Bravo, R. Weber, and B. Baesens. 2014. "Development and Application of Consumer Credit Scoring Models Using Profit-Based Classification Measures." *European Journal of Operational Research* 238 (2): 505–513.

CHAPTER 7

Economic Impact

INTRODUCTION

The investment in big data and analytics entails various economic challenges, which we address in this chapter. First we elaborate on the economic value of both technologies by zooming into the total cost of ownership (TCO) and return on investment (ROI). It will be clear that in the current setting it is difficult to accurately quantify these two key investments. Next, we review key economic considerations such as in-sourcing versus outsourcing, on-premise versus in the cloud, and open-source versus commercial software solutions. Obviously, selecting from among these options should be done with due diligence given the impact thereof on the TCO and ROI. The chapter concludes by giving some recommendations about how to improve the ROI by considering new sources of data, improving data quality, involving senior management, choosing the right organization format, and establishing cross-fertilization between business units.

ECONOMIC VALUE OF BIG DATA AND ANALYTICS

Total Cost of Ownership (TCO)

The total cost of ownership (TCO) of an analytical model refers to the cost of owning and operating the analytical model over its expected lifetime, from inception to retirement. It should consider both quantitative and qualitative costs and is a key input to make strategic decisions about how to optimally invest in analytics. The costs involved can be decomposed into acquisition costs, ownership and operation costs, and post-ownership costs, as illustrated with some examples in Table 7.1.

The goal of TCO analysis is to get a comprehensive view of all costs involved. From an economic perspective, this should also include the timing of the costs through proper discounting using, for example, the weighted average cost of capital (WACC) as the discount factor. Furthermore, it should help identify any potential hidden and/or sunk costs. In many analytical projects, the combined cost of hardware and software is subordinate to the human resources cost that comes with the development and usage of the models such as training, employment, and management costs (Lismont et al. 2017). The high share of personnel cost can be attributed to three phenomena: an increase in the number of data scientists; a higher use of open-source tools (see below); and cheaper data storage and sharing solutions.

TCO analysis allows cost problems to be pinpointed before they become material. For example, the change management costs to migrate from a legacy model to a new analytical model are often largely underestimated. TCO analysis is a key input for strategic decisions such as vendor selection, in-sourcing versus outsourcing, on-premise versus in the cloud solutions, overall budgeting, and capital calculation. Note that when making these investment decisions, it is also very important to include the benefits in the analysis, since TCO only considers the cost perspective.

Table 7.1 Example Costs for Calculating Total Cost of Ownership (TCO)

Acquisition Costs	Ownership and Operation Costs	Post-Ownership Costs
■ Software costs, including initial purchase, upgrade, intellectual property, and licensing fees ■ Hardware costs, including initial purchase price and maintenance ■ Network and security costs ■ Data costs, including costs for purchasing external data ■ Model developer costs such as salaries and training	■ Model migration and change management costs ■ Model setup costs ■ Model execution costs ■ Model monitoring costs ■ Support costs (troubleshooting, helpdesk,...) ■ Insurance costs ■ Model staffing costs such as salaries and training ■ Model upgrade costs ■ Model downtime costs	■ De-installation and disposal costs ■ Replacement costs ■ Archiving cost

Return on Investment (ROI)

Return on investment (ROI) is defined as the ratio of the net benefits or net profits over the investment of resources that generated this return. The latter essentially comprises the total cost of ownership (see above) and all follow-up expenses such as costs of marketing campaigns, fraud handling, bad debt collection, and others. ROI analysis is an essential input to any financial investment decision; it offers a common firm-wide language to compare multiple investment opportunities and decide which one(s) to go for.

For companies like Facebook, Amazon, Netflix, Uber, and Google, a positive ROI is obvious since they essentially thrive on data and analytics. Hence, they continuously invest in new analytical technologies since even a small incremental new insight can translate into competitive advantage and significant profits. The Netflix competition is a nice illustration of this whereby Netflix provided an anonymized dataset of user ratings for films and awarded $1 million for any team of data scientists that could beat its own recommender system with at least a 10% increase in performance.

For traditional firms in the financial services, manufacturing, healthcare and pharmaceutics sectors, among others, the ROI of big data and analytics may be less clear-cut and harder to determine. Although the cost component is usually not that difficult to approximate, the benefits are much harder to precisely quantify. One of the reasons is that the benefits may be spread over time (short term, medium term, long term) and across the various business units of the organization. Analytical models offer these benefits:

- Increase sales (e.g., as a result of a response modeling or up/cross-selling campaign).
- Reduce fraud losses (e.g., as a result of a fraud detection model).
- Reduce credit defaults (e.g., as a result of a credit scoring model).
- Identify new customer needs and opportunities (e.g., as a result of a customer segmentation model).
- Automate or enhance human decision making (e.g., as a result of a recommender system).
- Develop new data-driven services and business models (e.g., data poolers that gather data and sell the results of analyses).

When fully automating human decision making, the elimination of current and future employees allows the resultant benefits to be quantitatively assessed. However, when it comes to merely enhancing human performance, the benefits are less compelling and thus harder to quantify. In fact, many analytical models yield intangible benefits, which are hard to include, yet substantial, in an ROI analysis. Think about social networks. Analytically modeling word-of-mouth effects (e.g., in a churn or response setting) can have material economic impact but the precise value thereof is hard to quantify. The benefits may also be spread across multiple products, channels, and in time. Think about a response model for mortgages. The effect of successfully attracting a mortgage customer could create cross-selling effects toward other bank products (e.g., checking account, credit-card, insurance). Furthermore, since a mortgage is a long-term engagement, the partnership may be further deepened in time hereby contributing to the customer's CLV. Disentangling all these profit contributions is clearly a challenging task, complicating the calculation of the ROI of the original mortgage response model.

A vast majority of implementations of big data and analytics have reported significant returns. A study by Nucleus research[1] in 2014 found that organizations obtained returns of $13.01 for every dollar invested which increased from just $10.66 in 2011. PredictiveanalyticsToday.com[2] conducted a poll from February 2015 to March 2015 with 96 valid responses. The results are displayed in Figure 7.1. From the pie chart, it can be concluded that only a minority (10%) reported no ROI of bit data and analytics. Other studies have also reported strong positive returns, although the ranges typically vary.

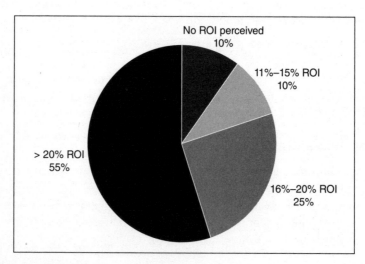

Figure 7.1 ROI of big data and analytics.
(PredictiveanalyticsToday.com 2015).

Critical voices have been heard as well, even questioning positive returns of investing in big data and analytics. The reasons often boil down to the lack of good-quality data, management support, and a company-wide data-driven decision culture, as we discuss in a later section.

Profit-Driven Business Analytics

ROI is defined in the previous section as the ratio of the net benefits or net profits over the investment of resources that generated this return. The investment of resources basically equals the total cost of ownership discussed before in this chapter. To increase ROI, indeed opportunities exist to lower the TCO, for example, by outsourcing and adopting cloud or open-source solutions as will be discussed in detail in the following sections. However, to our belief, the largest potential for boosting ROI hides in tuning the analytical models that are being developed for maximizing the net benefits or net profits. Providing approaches and guidance for doing so is exactly the main objective of this book. As explicitly stated in the introductory chapter, we aim to facilitate and support the adoption of a profit-driven perspective toward the use of analytics in business. To this end, a range of value-centric approaches have been discussed which allow to explicitly account for and maximize the profitability of the eventual analytical model, throughout the subsequent steps in the analytics process model as discussed in Chapter 1. Several illustrative examples have been provided in this book, and many more on the accompanying website,[3] of how these profit-driven approaches can be applied in real-life cases, with an illustration of the difference in terms of the resulting profit that is achieved when compared to the standard analytical approaches currently in use.

KEY ECONOMIC CONSIDERATIONS

In-Sourcing versus Outsourcing

The growing interest and need for big data and analytics combined with the shortage of skilled talent and data scientists in Western Europe and the United States has triggered the question of whether to outsource analytical activities. This need is further amplified by competitive pressure on reduced time to market and lower costs. Companies need to choose between in-sourcing or building the analytical skillset internally, either at the corporate level or business line level, outsource all analytical activities, or go for an intermediate solution whereby only part of the analytical activities are outsourced. The dominant players in the outsourcing analytics market are India, China, and Eastern Europe, with some other countries (e.g., Philippines, Russia, South Africa) gaining ground as well.

Various analytical activities can be considered for outsourcing ranging from the heavy-lifting grunt work (e.g., data collection, cleaning, and preprocessing), set-up of analytical platforms (hardware and software), training and education, to the more complex analytical model development, visualization, evaluation, monitoring, and maintenance. Companies may choose to grow conservatively and start by outsourcing the analytical activities step by step, or immediately go for the full package of analytical services. It speaks for itself that the latter strategy is more inherently risky and should thus be more carefully and critically evaluated.

Despite the benefits of outsourcing analytics, it should be approached with a clear strategic vision and critical reflection with awareness of all risks involved. First of all, the difference between outsourcing analytics and traditional ICT services is that analytics concerns a company's front-end strategy, whereas many ICT services are part of a company's back-end operations. Another important risk is the exchange of confidential information. Intellectual property (IP) rights and data security issues should be clearly investigated, addressed, and agreed on. Moreover, all companies have access to the same analytical techniques, so they are only differentiated by the data they provide. Hence, an outsourcer should provide clear guidelines and guarantees about how intellectual property and data will be managed and protected (using, e.g., encryption techniques and firewalls), particularly if the outsourcer also collaborates with other companies in the same industry sector. Another important risk concerns the continuity of the partnership. Offshore outsourcing companies are often subject to mergers and acquisitions, not seldom with other outsourcing companies collaborating with the competition, hereby diluting any competitive advantage realized. Furthermore, many of these outsourcers face high employee turnover due to intensive work schedules, the boredom of performing low-level activities on a daily basis, and aggressive headhunters chasing these hard-to-find data science profiles. This attrition problem seriously inhibits a long-term thorough understanding of a customer's analytical business processes and needs. Another often-cited complexity concerns the cultural mismatch (e.g., time management, different languages, local versus global issues) between the buyer and outsourcer. Exit strategies should also be clearly agreed on. Many analytical outsourcing contracts have a maturity of three to four years. When these contracts expire, it should be clearly stipulated how the analytical models and knowledge can be transferred to the buyer thereof to ensure business continuity. Finally, the shortage of data scientists in the United States and Western Europe will also be a constraint, and might even be worse, in the countries providing outsourcing services. These countries typically have universities with good statistical education and training programs, but their graduates lack the necessary business skills, insights, and experience to make a strategic contribution with analytics.

Given these considerations, many firms are quite skeptical about outsourcing and prefer to keep all big data and analytics in house. Others adopt a partial outsourcing strategy, whereby baseline, operational analytical activities such as query and reporting, multi-dimensional data analysis, and OLAP are outsourced, whereas the advanced descriptive, predictive, and social network analytical skills are developed and managed internally.

On Premise versus the Cloud

Most firms started to develop their first analytical models using on-premise architectures, platforms, and solutions. However, given the significant amount of investment in installing, configuring, upgrading, and maintaining these environments, many companies have started looking at cloud-based solutions as a budget-friendly alternative to further boost the ROI. In what follows, we elaborate on the costs and other implications of deploying big data and analytics in the cloud.

An often-cited advantage of on-premise analytics is that you keep your data in-house, as such giving you full control over it. However, this is a double-edged sword since it also requires firms to continuously invest in high-end security solutions to thwart data breach attacks by hackers, which are becoming ever more sophisticated. It is precisely because of this security concern that many companies have started looking at the cloud. Another driver concerns the scalability and economies of scale offered by cloud providers, since they pledge to provide customers with state-of-the-art platforms and software solutions. The computation power needed can in fact be entirely tailored to the customer, whether it is a Fortune 500 firm or a small- or medium-sized enterprise (SME). More capacity (e.g., servers) can be added on the fly whenever needed. On-premise solutions need to carefully anticipate the computational resources needed and invest accordingly, whereby the risk of over-investment or under-investment significantly jeopardizes the ROI of analytical projects. In other words, upsizing or downsizing scalability on premise is a lot more tedious and cost consuming.

Another key advantage relates to the maintenance of the analytical environment. Average on-premise maintenance cycles typically range around 18 months. These can get quite costly and create business continuity problems because of backward compatibility issues, new features added, old features removed, and new integration efforts needed, among others. When using cloud-based solutions, all these issues are taken care of and maintenance or upgrade projects may even go unnoticed.

The low footprint access to data management and analytics capabilities will also positively impact the time to value and accessibility. As mentioned, there is no need to set up expensive infrastructure (e.g., hardware, operating systems, databases, analytical solutions), upload and clean data, or integrate data. Using the cloud, everything is readily accessible. It significantly lowers the entry barrier to experiment with analytics, try out new approaches and models, and combine various data sources in a transparent way. All of this contributes to the economic value of analytical modeling and also facilitates serendipitous discovery of interesting patterns.

Cloud-based solutions catalyze improved collaboration across business departments and geographical locations. Many on-premise systems are loosely coupled or not integrated at all, thereby seriously inhibiting any firm-wide sharing of experiences, insights, and findings. The resulting amount of duplication efforts negatively impacts the ROI at corporate level.

From the above discussion, it becomes clear that cloud-based solutions have a substantial impact in terms of TCO and ROI of your analytical projects. However, as with any new technology, it is advised to approach it with a thoughtful strategic vision and the necessary caution. That is why most firms have started adopting a mixed approach by gently migrating some of their analytical models to the cloud so as to get their toes wet and see what the potential but also caveats are of this technology. It can, however, be expected that given the many (cost) advantages offered, cloud-based big data and analytics will continue to grow.

Open-Source versus Commercial Software

The popularity of open-source analytical software such as R and Python has sparked the debate about the added value of commercial tools such as SAS, SPSS, and Matlab, among others. In fact, commercial and open-source software each has its merits, which should be thoroughly evaluated before any software investment decision is made. Note that they can, of course, also be combined in a mixed setup.

First of all, the key advantage of open-source software is that it is obviously available for free, which significantly lowers the entry barrier to its use. This may be particularly relevant to smaller firms that wish to kick off with analytics without making investments that are too big. However, this clearly poses a danger as well, since anyone can contribute to open source without any quality assurance or extensive prior testing. In heavily regulated environments such as credit risk (the Basel Accord), insurance (the Solvency Accord), and pharmaceutics (the FDA regulation), the analytical models are subject to external supervisory review because of their strategic impact on society—which is now bigger than ever before. Hence, in these settings, many firms prefer to rely on mature commercial solutions that have been thoroughly engineered and extensively tested, validated, and completely documented. Many of these solutions also include automatic reporting facilities to generate compliant reports in each of the settings mentioned. Open-source software solutions come without any kind of quality control or warranty, which increases the risk of using them in a regulated environment.

Another key advantage of commercial solutions is that the software offered is no longer centered on dedicated analytical workbenches—for example, data preprocessing and data mining—but on well-engineered business-focused solutions which automate the end-to-end activities. As an example, consider credit risk analytics which starts from initially framing the business problem, to data preprocessing, analytical model development, model monitoring, stress testing and regulatory capital calculation (Baesens et al. 2016). To automate this entire chain of activities using open source would require various scripts, likely originating from heterogeneous sources, to be matched and connected, resulting in a melting pot of software, whereby the overall functionality can become unstable and unclear.

Contrary to open-source software, commercial software vendors also offer extensive help facilities such as FAQs, technical support hot lines, newsletters, and professional training courses, to name some. Another key advantage of commercial software vendors is business continuity. More specifically, the availability of centralized R&D teams (as opposed to worldwide loosely connected open-source developers), which closely follow up on new analytical and regulatory developments provides a better guarantee that new software upgrades will provide the facilities required. In an open-source environment, you need to rely on the community to voluntarily contribute, which provides less of a guarantee.

A disadvantage of commercial software is that it usually comes in prepackaged, black-box routines, which, although extensively tested and documented, cannot be inspected by the more sophisticated data scientist. This is in contrast to open-source solutions, which provide full access to the source code of each of the scripts contributed.

Given the previous discussion, it is clear that both commercial and open-source software have strengths and weaknesses. Hence, it is likely that both will continue to coexist, and interfaces should be provided for both to collaborate, as is the case for SAS and R/Python, for example.

IMPROVING THE ROI OF BIG DATA AND ANALYTICS

New Sources of Data

The ROI of an analytical model is directly related to its predictive and/or statistical power, as extensively discussed in Chapters 4 to 7 of this book. The better an analytical model can predict or describe customer behavior, the better the effectiveness and the higher the profitability of the resulting actions. In addition to adopting profit-driven analytical approaches, one way to further boost ROI is by investing in new sources of data, which can help to further unravel complex customer behavior and improve key analytical insights. In what follows, we briefly explore various types of data sources that could be worthwhile pursuing in order to squeeze more economic value out of analytical models.

A first option concerns the exploration of network data by carefully studying relationships between customers. These relationships can be explicit or implicit. Examples of explicit networks are calls between customers, shared board members between firms, and social connections (e.g., family or friends). Explicit networks can be readily distilled from underlying data sources (e.g., call logs), and their key characteristics can then be summarized using featurization procedures, as discussed in Chapter 2. In our previous research (Verbeke et al. 2014; Van Vlasselaer et al. 2017), we found network data to be highly predictive for both customer churn prediction and fraud detection. Implicit networks or pseudo networks are a lot more challenging to define and featurize.

Martens and Provost (2016) built a network of customers where links were defined based on which customers transferred money to the same entities (e.g., retailers) using data from a major bank. When combined with non-network data, this innovative way of defining a network based on similarity instead of explicit social connections gave a better lift and generated more profit for almost any targeting budget. In another, award-winning study they built a geosimilarity network among users based on location-visitation data in a mobile environment (Provost et al. 2015). More specifically, two devices are considered similar, and thus connected, when they share at least one visited location. They are more similar if they have more shared locations and as these are visited by fewer people. This implicit network can then be leveraged to target advertisements to the same user on different devices or to users with similar tastes, or to improve online interactions by selecting users with similar tastes. Both of these examples clearly illustrate the potential of implicit networks as an important data source. A key challenge here is to creatively think about how to define these networks based on the goal of the analysis.

Data are often branded as the new oil. Hence, data-pooling firms capitalize on this by gathering various types of data, analyzing them in innovative and creative ways, and selling the results thereof. Popular examples are Equifax, Experian, Moody's, S&P, Nielsen, and Dun & Bradstreet, among many others. These firms consolidate publically available data, data scraped from websites or social media, survey data, and data contributed by other firms. By doing so, they can perform all kinds of aggregated analyses (e.g., geographical distribution of credit default rates in a country, average churn rates across industry sectors), build generic scores (e.g., the FICO in the United States), and sell these to interested parties. Because of the low entry barrier in terms of investment, externally purchased analytical models are sometimes adopted by smaller firms (e.g., SMEs) to take their first steps in analytics. Besides commercially available external data, open data can also be a valuable source of external information. Examples are industry and government data, weather data, news data, and search data (e.g., Google Trends). Both commercial and open external data can significantly boost the performance and thus economic return of an analytical model.

Macroeconomic data are another valuable source of information. Many analytical models are developed using a snapshot of data at a particular moment in time. This is obviously conditional on the external environment at that moment. Macroeconomic up- or downturns can have a significant impact on the performance and thus ROI of the model. The state of the macroeconomy can be summarized using measures such as gross domestic product (GDP), inflation, and unemployment. Incorporating these effects will allow us to further improve the performance of analytical models and make them more robust against external influences.

Textual data are also an interesting type of data to consider. Examples are product reviews, Facebook posts, Twitter tweets, book recommendations, complaints, and legislation. Textual data are difficult to process analytically since they are unstructured and cannot be directly represented into a matrix format. Moreover, these data depend on the linguistic structure (e.g., type of language, relationship between words, negations, etc.) and are typically quite noisy data due to grammatical or spelling errors, synonyms, and homographs. However, they can contain very relevant information for your analytical modeling exercise. Just as with network data, it will be important to find ways to featurize text documents and combine it with your other structured data. A popular way of doing this is by using a document term matrix indicating what terms (similar to variables) appear and how frequently in which documents (similar to observations). It is clear that this matrix will be large and sparse. Dimension reduction will thus be very important, as the following activities illustrate:

- Represent every term in lower case (e.g., PRODUCT, Product, product become product).
- Remove terms that are uninformative, such as stop words and articles (e.g., the product, a product, this product become product).
- Use synonym lists to map synonym terms to one single term (product, item, article become product).
- Stem all terms to their root (products, product become product).
- Remove terms that only occur in a single document.

Even after the above activities have been performed, the number of dimensions may still be too big for practical analysis. Singular Value Decomposition (SVD) offers a more advanced way to do dimension reduction (Meyer 2000). SVD works similar to principal component analysis (PCA) and summarizes the document term matrix into a set of singular vectors (also called latent concepts), which are linear combinations of the original terms. These reduced dimensions can then be added as new features to your existing, structured dataset.

Besides textual data, other types of unstructured data such as audio, images, videos, fingerprint, GPS, and RFID data can be considered as well. To successfully leverage these types of data in your analytical models, it is of key importance to carefully think about creative ways of featurizing them. When doing so, it is recommended that any accompanying metadata are taken into account; for example, not only the image itself might be relevant, but also who took it, where, and at what time. This information could be very useful for fraud detection.

Data Quality

Besides volume and variety, the veracity of the data is also a critical success factor to generate competitive advantage and economic value from data. Quality of data is key to the success of any analytical exercise since it has a direct and measurable impact on the quality of the analytical model and hence its economic value. The importance of data quality is nicely captured by the well-known *GIGO* or *garbage in, garbage out* principle: Bad data yield bad analytical models (see Chapter 2).

Data quality is often defined as fitness for use, which illustrates the relative nature of the concept (Wang et al. 1996). Data with quality for one use may not be appropriate for another use. For example, the extent to which data are required to be accurate and complete for fraud detection may not be required for response modeling. More generally, data that are of acceptable quality in one application may be perceived to be of poor quality in another application, even by the same users. This is mainly because data quality is a multidimensional concept in which each dimension represents a single construct and also comprises both objective and subjective elements. Therefore, it is useful to define data quality in terms of its dimensions as illustrated in Table 7.2 (Wang et al. 1996).

Most organizations are becoming aware of the importance of data quality and are looking at ways to improve it. However, this often turns out to be harder than expected, more costly than budgeted, and definitely not a one-off project but a continuous challenge. The causes of data quality issues are often deeply rooted within the core organizational processes and culture, as well as in the IT infrastructure and architecture.

Whereas often only data scientists are directly confronted with the consequences of poor data quality, resolving these issues and, importantly, their causes typically requires cooperation and commitment from almost every level and department within the organization. It most definitely requires support and sponsorship from senior executive management in order to increase awareness and set up data governance programs to tackle data quality in a sustainable and effective manner, as well as to create incentives for everyone in the organization to take their responsibilities.

Table 7.2 Data Quality Dimensions (Wang et al. 1996)

Category	Dimension	Definition: the extent to which...
Intrinsic	Accuracy	Data are regarded as correct.
	Believability	Data are accepted or regarded as true, real, and credible.
	Objectivity	Data are unbiased and impartial.
	Reputation	Data are trusted or highly regarded in terms of their source and content.
Contextual	Value-added	Data are beneficial and provide advantages for their use.
	Completeness	Data values are present.
	Relevancy	Data are applicable and useful for the task at hand.
	Timeliness	Data are available at the right moment for the task at hand.
	Appropriate amount of data	The quantity or volume of available data is appropriate.
Representational	Interpretability	Data are in appropriate language and unit and the data definitions are clear.
	Representational consistency	Data are represented in a consistent way.
	Concise representation	Data are represented in a compact way.
	Ease of understanding	Data are clear without ambiguity and easily comprehended.
Accessibility	Accessibility	Data are available or can be easily and quickly retrieved.
	Security	Access to data can be restricted and hence kept secure.

Data preprocessing activities such as handling missing values, duplicate data, or outliers (see Chapter 2) are corrective measures for dealing with data quality issues. These are, however, short-term remedies with relatively low cost and moderate return. Data scientists will have to keep applying these fixes until the root causes of the issues are resolved in a structural way. In order to do so, data quality programs need to be developed that aim at detecting the key problems. This will include a thorough investigation of where the problems originate from, in order to find and resolve them at their very origin by introducing preventive actions as a complement to corrective measures. This obviously requires more substantial investments and a strong belief in the added value and return thereof. Ideally, a data governance program should be put in place assigning clear roles and responsibilities with respect to data quality. Two roles that are essential in rolling out such a program are data stewards and data owners.

Data stewards are the data quality experts who are in charge of assessing data quality by performing extensive and regular data quality checks. They are responsible for initiating remedial actions whenever needed. A first type of action to be considered is the application of short-term corrective measures as already discussed. Data stewards are, however, not in charge of correcting the data themselves: This is the task of the data owner. Every data field in every database of the organization should be owned by a data owner, who is able to enter or update its value. In other words, the data owner has knowledge about the meaning of each data field and can look up its current correct value (e.g., by contacting a customer, by looking into a file). Data stewards can request data owners to check or complete the value of a field, as such correcting the issue. A second type of action to be initiated by a data steward concerns a deeper investigation into the root causes of the data quality issues that were detected. Understanding these causes may allow the designing of preventive measures that aim at eradicating data quality issues. Preventive measures typically start by carefully inspecting the operational information systems from which the data originate. Based on this inspection, various actions can be undertaken, such as making certain data fields mandatory (e.g., social security number), providing drop-down lists of possible values (e.g., dates), rationalizing or simplifying the interface, and defining validation rules (e.g., age should be between 18 and 100). Implementing such preventive measures will require close involvement of the IT department in charge of the application. Although designing and implementing preventive measures will require more efforts in terms of investment, commitment, and involvement than applying corrective measures would, they are the only type of action that will improve data quality in a sustainable manner, and as such secure the long-term return on investment in analytics and big data!

Management Support

To fully capitalize on big data and analytics, it should conquer a seat in the board of directors. This can be achieved in various ways. Either an existing chief-level executive (e.g., the CIO) takes the responsibility or a new CXO function is defined such as chief analytics officer (CAO) or chief data officer (CDO). To guarantee maximum independence and organizational impact, it is important that the latter directly reports to the CEO instead of another C-level executive. A top-down, data-driven culture where the CEO and his subordinates make decisions inspired by data combined with business acumen will catalyze a trickledown effect of data-based decision making throughout the entire organization.

The board of directors and senior management should be actively involved in the analytical model building, implementation, and monitoring processes. Of course, one cannot expect them to understand all underlying technical details, but they should be responsible for sound governance of the analytical models. Without appropriate management support, analytical models are doomed to fail. Hence, the board and senior management should have a general understanding of the analytical models. They should demonstrate active involvement on an ongoing basis, assign clear responsibilities, and put into place organizational procedures and policies that will allow the proper and sound development, implementation, and monitoring of the analytical models. The outcome of the model monitoring exercise must be communicated to senior management and, if needed, accompanied by appropriate (strategic) response. Obviously, this requires a careful rethinking of how to optimally embed big data and analytics in the organization.

Organizational Aspects

In 2010, Davenport, Harris, and Morison wrote:

> There may be no single right answer to how to organize your analysts, but there are many wrong ones.

As mentioned before, investments in big data and analytics only bear fruit when a company-wide data culture is in place to actually do something with all these new data-driven insights. If you would put a team of data scientists in a room and feed them with data and analytical software, then the chances are pretty small that their analytical models and insights will add economic value to the firm. A first hurdle concerns the data, which are not always readily available. A well-articulated data governance program is a good starting point (see above). Once the data are available, any data scientist will be able to derive a statistically meaningful analytical model from it. However, this does not necessarily imply that the model adds economic value, since it may not be in sync with the business objectives (see Chapter 3). And suppose it was in sync, how do we sell it to our business people such that they understand it, trust it, and actually start using it in their decision making? This implies delivering insights in a way that is easy to understand and use by representing them in, for example, simple language or intuitive graphics.

Given the corporate-wide impact of big data and analytics, it is important that both gradually permeate into a company's culture and decision-making processes, as such becoming part of a company's DNA. This requires a significant investment in terms of awareness and trust that should be initiated top-down from the executive level as discussed above. In other words, companies need to thoroughly think about how they embed big data and analytics in their organization in order to successfully compete using both technologies.

Lismont et al. (2017) conducted a worldwide, cross-industry survey of senior-level executives to investigate modern trends in the organization of analytics. They observed various formats used by companies to organize their analytics. Two extreme approaches are centralized, where a central department of data scientists handles all analytics requests, and decentralized where all data scientists are directly assigned to the respective business units. Most companies opt for a mixed approach combining a centrally coordinated center of analytical excellence with analytics organized at business unit level. The center of excellence provides firm-wide analytical services and implements universal guidelines in terms of model development, model design, model implementation, model documentation, model monitoring, and privacy. Decentralized teams of one to five data scientists are then added to each of the business units for maximum impact. A suggested practice is to rotationally deploy the data scientists across the business units and center so as to foster cross-fertilization opportunities between the different teams and applications.

Cross-Fertilization

Big data and analytics have matured differently across the various business units of an organization. Triggered by the introduction of regulatory guidelines (e.g., Basel II/III, Solvency II) as well as driven by significant returns/profits, many firms (particularly financial institutions) have invested in big data and analytics for risk management for quite some time now. Years of analytical experience and perfecting contributed to very sophisticated models for insurance risk, credit risk, operational risk, market risk, and fraud risk. The most advanced analytical techniques such as survival analysis, random forests, neural networks, and (social) network learning have been used in these applications. Furthermore, these analytical models have been complemented with powerful model monitoring frameworks and stress testing procedures to fully leverage their potential.

Marketing analytics is less mature, with many firms starting to deploy their first models for churn prediction, response modeling, or customer segmentation. These are typically based on simpler analytical techniques such as logistic regression, decision trees or K-means clustering. Other application areas such as HR and supply chain analytics start to gain traction although not many successful case studies have been reported yet.

The disparity in maturity creates a tremendous potential for cross-fertilization of model development and monitoring experiences. After all, classifying whether a customer is creditworthy in risk management is analytically the same as classifying a customer as a responder, or not, in marketing analytics, or classifying an employee as a churner, or not, in HR analytics. The data preprocessing issues (e.g., missing values, outliers, categorization), classification techniques (e.g., logistic regression, decision trees, random forests) and evaluation measures (e.g., AUC, lift curves) are all similar. Only the interpretation and usage of the models will be different. Additionally, there is some tuning/adaptation in the setup and in gathering the "right" data—what characteristics are predictive for employee churn? How do we define employee churn? How much time on beforehand do we have to/can we predict? The cross-fertilization also applies to model monitoring, since most of the challenges and approaches are essentially the same. Finally, gauging the effect of macroeconomic scenarios using stress testing (which is a common practice in credit risk analytics) could be another example of sharing useful experiences across applications.

To summarize, less mature analytical applications (e.g., marketing, HR and supply chain analytics) can substantially benefit from many of the lessons learned by more mature applications (e.g., risk management) as such avoiding many rookie mistakes and expensive beginner traps. Hence, the importance of rotational deployment (as discussed in the previous section) to generate maximum economic value and return is clear.

CONCLUSION

In this chapter, we zoomed into the economic impact of analytical models. We first provided a perspective on the economic value of big data and analytics by discussing total cost of ownership (TCO), return on investment (ROI), and profit-driven business analytics. We elaborated on some key economic considerations, such as in-sourcing versus outsourcing, on-premise versus in the cloud configurations, and open-source versus commercial software. We also gave some recommendations about how to improve the ROI of big data and analytics by exploring new sources of data, safeguarding data quality and management support, careful embedding of big data and analytics in the organization, and fostering cross-fertilization opportunities.

REVIEW QUESTIONS

Multiple Choice Questions

Question 1

Which of the following costs should be included in a total cost of ownership (TCO) analysis?

a. acquisition costs
b. ownership and operation costs
c. post-ownership costs
d. all of the above

Question 2

Which of the following statements is not correct?

a. ROI analysis offers a common firm-wide language to compare multiple investment opportunities and decide which one(s) to go for.
b. For companies like Facebook, Amazon, Netflix, and Google, a positive ROI is obvious since they essentially thrive on data and analytics.
c. Although the benefit component is usually not that difficult to approximate, the costs are much harder to precisely quantify.
d. Negative ROI of big data and analytics often boils down to the lack of good quality data, management support, and a company-wide data driven decision culture.

Question 3

Which of the following is not a risk when outsourcing big data and analytics?

a. need for all analytical activities to be outsourced
b. exchange of confidential information

    c. continuity of the partnership
    d. dilution of competitive advantage due to, for example, mergers and acquisitions

Question 4

Which of the following is not an advantage of open-source software for analytics?

    a. It is available for free.
    b. A worldwide network of developers can work on it.
    c. It has been thoroughly engineered and extensively tested, validated, and completely documented.
    d. It can be used in combination with commercial software.

Question 5

Which of the following statements is correct?

    a. When using on-premise solutions, maintenance or upgrade projects may even go by unnoticed.
    b. An important advantage of cloud-based solutions concerns the scalability and economies of scale offered. More capacity (e.g., servers) can be added on the fly whenever needed.
    c. The big footprint access to data management and analytics capabilities is a serious drawback of cloud-based solutions.
    d. On-premise solutions catalyze improved collaboration across business departments and geographical locations.

Question 6

Which of the following are interesting data sources to consider to boost the performance of your analytical models?

    a. network data
    b. external data
    c. unstructured data such as text data and multimedia data
    d. all of the above

Question 7

Which of the following statements is correct?

    a. Data quality is a multidimensional concept in which each dimension represents a single construct and also comprises both objective and subjective elements.

b. Data preprocessing activities such as handling missing values, duplicate data, or outliers are preventive measures for dealing with data quality issues.

c. Data owners are the data quality experts who are in charge of assessing data quality by performing extensive and regular data quality checks.

d. Data stewards can request data scientists to check or complete the value of a field, as such correcting the issue.

Question 8

To guarantee maximum independence and organizational impact of analytics, it is important that

a. The chief data officer (CDO) or chief analytics officer (CAO) reports to the CIO or CFO.

b. The CIO takes care of all analytical responsibilities.

c. A chief data officer or chief analytics officer is added to the executive committee, who directly reports to the CEO.

d. Analytics is supervised only locally in the business units.

Question 9

What is the correct ranking of the following analytics applications in terms of maturity?

a. marketing analytics (most mature), risk analytics (medium mature), HR analytics (least mature)

b. risk analytics (most mature), marketing analytics (medium mature), HR analytics (least mature)

c. risk analytics (most mature), HR analytics (medium mature), marketing analytics (least mature)

d. HR analytics (most mature), marketing analytics (medium mature), risk analytics (least mature)

Question 10

Which of the following activities could be considered to boost the ROI of big data and analytics?

a. investing in new sources of data

b. improving data quality

c. involving senior management

d. choosing the right organization format

e. establishing cross-fertilization between business units

f. all of the above

Open Questions

Question 1

Conduct a SWOT analysis for the following investment decisions:

a. In- versus outsourcing analytical activities
b. On-premise versus in the cloud analytical platforms
c. Open-source versus commercial analytical software

Question 2

Give examples of analytical applications where the following external data can be useful:

a. macroeconomic data (e.g., GDP, inflation, unemployment)
b. weather data
c. news data
d. Google Trends search data

Question 3

Discuss the importance of data quality. What are the key dimensions? How can data quality issues be dealt with in the short term and the long term?

Question 4

How can management support and organizational format contribute to the success of big data and analytics? Discuss ways to generate cross-fertilization effects.

Question 5

Read the following article: B. Baesens, S. De Winne, and L. Sels, "Is Your Company Ready for HR Analytics?" *MIT Sloan Management Review* (Winter 2017). See mitsmr.com/2greOYb.

a. Summarize important cross-fertilization opportunities between customer and HR analytics.
b. Which techniques from customer churn prediction could be useful for employee churn prediction?
c. What about customer segmentation?

d. Which model requirements are different in HR analytics compared to customer analytics?
e. Illustrate with examples.

NOTES

1. http://nucleusresearch.com/research/single/analytics-pays-back-13-01-for-every-dollar-spent/.
2. http://www.predictiveanalyticstoday.com/return-of-investment-from-predictive-analytics/.
3. www.profit-analytics.com.

REFERENCES

Ariker M., A. Diaz, C. Moorman, and M. Westover. 2015. "Quantifying the Impact of Marketing Analytics." *Harvard Business Review* (November).

Baesens B., D. Roesch, and H. Scheule. 2016. *Credit Risk Analytics—Measurement Techniques, Applications and Examples in SAS*. Hoboken, NJ: John Wiley & Sons.

Davenport T. H., J. G. Harris, and R. Morison. 2010. *Analytics at Work: Smarter Decisions, Better Results*. Boston: Harvard Business Review Press.

Lismont, J., J. Vanthienen, B. Baesens, and W. Lemahieu. 2017. "Defining Analytics Maturity Indicators: A Survey Approach." submitted for publication.

Martens D., F. Provost. 2016. "Mining Massive Fine-Grained Behavior Data to Improve Predictive Analytics." *MIS Quarterly* 40 (4): 869–888.

Meyer, C. D. 2000. *Matrix Analysis and Applied Linear Algebra*. Philadelphia: SIAM.

Provost F., D. Martens, and A. Murray. 2015. "Finding Similar Mobile Consumers with a Privacy-Friendly Geosocial Design." *Information Systems Research* 26 (2): 243–265.

Van Vlasselaer, V., T. Eliassi-Rad, L. Akoglu, M. Snoeck, and B. Baesens. 2017. "GOTCHA! Network-based Fraud Detection for Security Fraud." *Management Science*, forthcoming.

Verbeke, W., D. Martens, and B. Baesens. 2014. "Social Network Analysis for Customer Churn Prediction." *Applied Soft Computing* 14: 341–446.

Wang R. Y., and D. M. Strong. 1996. "Beyond Accuracy: What Data Quality Means to Data Consumers." *Journal of Management Information Systems* 12 (4): 5–34.

About the Authors

Wouter Verbeke, PhD, is assistant professor of business informatics and data analytics at Vrije Universiteit Brussel (Belgium). He graduated in 2007 as a civil engineer and obtained a PhD in applied economics at KU Leuven (Belgium) in 2012. His research is mainly situated in the field of predictive, prescriptive, and network analytics, and is driven by real-life business problems, including applications in customer relationship, credit risk, fraud, supply chain, and human resources management. Specifically, his research focuses on taking into account costs and benefits in developing and evaluating business analytics applications. Wouter teaches several courses on information systems and advanced modeling for decision making to business students and provides training to business practitioners on customer analytics, credit risk modeling, and fraud analytics. His work has been published in established international scientific journals such as *IEEE Transactions on Knowledge and Data Engineering, European Journal of Operational Research,* and *Decision Support Systems.* He is also author of the book *Fraud Analytics Using Descriptive, Predictive & Social Network Techniques—The Essential Guide to Data Science for Fraud Detection,* published by Wiley in 2015. In 2014, he won the EURO award for best article published in the *European Journal of Operational Research* in the category "Innovative Applications of O.R."

Bart Baesens, PhD, is a professor at KU Leuven (Belgium) and a lecturer at the University of Southampton (United Kingdom). He has done extensive research on big data and analytics, fraud detection, customer relationship management, Web analytics, and credit risk management. His findings have been published in well-known international journals (e.g., *Machine Learning, Management Science, IEEE Transactions on Neural Networks, IEEE Transactions on Knowledge and Data Engineering, IEEE Transactions on Evolutionary Computation, Journal of Machine Learning Research,* and more) and he has presented at international top conferences. He is also author of the books *Credit Risk Management: Basic Concepts* (http://goo.gl/T6FNOn), published by Oxford University Press in 2008; *Analytics in a Big Data World* (http://goo.gl/k3kBrB), published by Wiley in 2014; *Fraud Analytics using Descriptive, Predictive and Social Network Techniques* (http://goo.gl/P1cYqe)

published by Wiley in 2015; and *Beginning Java Programming: The Object-Oriented Approach* (http://goo.gl/qHXmk1) published by Wiley in 2015. He also offers e-learning courses on credit risk modeling (see http://goo.gl/cmC2So) and advanced analytics in a big data world (see https://goo.gl/2xA19U). His research is summarized at www.dataminingapps.com. He also regularly tutors, advises, and provides consulting support to international firms with respect to their big data and analytics strategy.

Cristián Bravo, PhD, is lecturer (assistant professor) in business analytics at the Department of Decision Analytics and Risk, University of Southampton. Previously he served as Research Fellow at KU Leuven, Belgium; and as research director at the Finance Centre, Universidad de Chile. His research focuses on the development and application of predictive, descriptive, and prescriptive analytics to the problem of credit risk in micro, small, and medium enterprises. His work covers diverse topics and methodologies, such as semi-supervised techniques, deep learning, text mining, social networks analytics, fraud analytics, and multiple modeling methodologies. His work has been published in well-known international journals, he has edited three special issues in business analytics in reputed scientific journals, and he regularly teaches courses in credit risk and analytics at all levels. He also blogs in Spanish at his website, www.sehablanalytics.com, and can be reached by Twitter at @CrBravoR.

Index

A

A/B testing, 169–170
Accuracy ratio (AR), 199
  AUC, linear relation, 67
  calculation, 66f
  defining, 66–67
Acquisition marketing campaign, 155
Active churn, 118–119
AdaBoost Variants, 250, 253
Adaptive Boosting (Adaboost)
    procedure, implementation, 57–58
Age split, entropy calculation, 48f
Agglomerative clustering, 74–75
Agglomerative hierarchical
    clustering, divisive hierarchical
    clustering (contrast), 74f
Algorithms, differences, 46
Always a share approach,
    assumption, 124
Always a share model, 128
Always a share perspective, 123–124
AMC. *See* Average misprediction
    cost and Average
    misclassification cost
Analysis, data denormalization, 29–30
Analysis of variance (ANOVA),
    usage, 51
Analytical approaches, 14
  insight, 1–2
Analytical-based fraud detection
    approaches, 136
Analytical churn prediction, 118
Analytical exercise, 144–145

Analytical model
    development/implementation,
    challenges, 17
  evaluation, 17–19
  validation/approval, 16
Analytical projects, ROI (jeopardy), 361–362
Analytical techniques, 28
Analytics
  application, 8
  capabilities, footprint access, 362
  categories, task-oriented
    perspective, 5t
  economic value, 355–359
  organizational facilitation, 2
  predictive analytics, 37–56
  ROI, 358f
    improvement, 364–372
  statistical approach, example, 11–12
  term, usage, 4–5
  types, 37
Analytics process model, 14–17
  preprocessing/post-processing, 15f
Analytics team, 19–23
  data scientists, 20–23
  profiles, 19–20
Area under the receiver operating
    characteristic curve
    (AUROC/AUC), 310
Area under the ROC curve (AUC),
    64, 67, 93, 199, 256, 297
  AUCIV, 337
  characteristic, 311
Area under the uplift curve (AUUC), 191
ARIMA, 39
Assignment decision, 46

Association rules, 69–72, 281
  economic impact, 72
Asymmetric AdaBoost, 250
Asymmetric loss, 261
At risk, meaning, 85
Attrition (defection, churn),
  118
AUC. *See* Area under the ROC
  curve
Average misclassification cost
  (AMC), 298–303
  approach, extension, 303
  calculation, 300–301
  case study, 304–309
  decrease, 306
  expected average misclassification
  cost, 301
Average misprediction cost (AMC)
  evaluation metric, 261–262
  minimization, 266–267

B

Back propagation learning, 54
Backward regression, usage, 44
Bad split/good split, 184
Bad targets, 179
Bagging. *See* Bootstrapping
  aggregating
Bart rate, 133
Basel Accord, 363
Basel guidelines, 140
Baseline hazard,
  specification/function, 91
Baseline model, cumulative
  incremental gains charts/Qini
  curves, 206f
Bayesian methods, 55
Bayesian networks, 134
Benchmarking studies, 59
Best matching unit (BMU), 78–79
Beta distribution, 329
Beta-geometric/negative binomial
  distribution
  (Beta-geometric/NBD)
  submodel, 126
Betweenness, 144
Bias, testing/controlling, 163–164

Big data
  determination, difficulty, 357
  economic value, 355–359
  leverage, 114
  management support, 369–370
  organizational aspects, 370–371
  ROI, 358f
  improvement, 364–372
  usage, 141, 145–146
Binary classification problem
  confusion matrix, 323t
  cost matrix, examples, 224t, 299t
Binary classification setting,
  challenges, 17, 19
Binary response target (modeling),
  linear regression (usage), 39
Binary target variable, likelihood cost
  function, 54
Biomedical clinical trial analysis, 157
Black-box models, 59
BMU. *See* Best matching unit
Boosting, 57–58, 199, 241
Bootstrapping aggregating (bagging),
  57, 199, 241
  uplift bagging, 195–196
Bootstrapping, usage, 62f
Bounding function, 40
  example, 40f
Box plots, 32
Breiman, Leo, 195
BSZ performance-tuning algorithm,
  263
Bucket testing, 169–170
Business
  applications, 114
  classification models, 254
  decision matching analytics,
  examples, 10t–11t
  models, development, 357
  problem, definition, 14–15
  rules, usage, 135
Business analytics, 3–9
  models, characteristics, 18t–19t
  profit-driven business analytics,
  9–14
Business intelligence (BI), 3–4
  formal definition, 4

C

C4.5 (algorithm), 46, 247
  implementation, 185
Campaign effectiveness, 202
  measurement, 168
Campaign effect measurement
  example, 166t
  overview, 164t
Campaign operation, fixed
    administrative cost,
    326–327
Candidate models
  accuracy/AUC, 319t, 320t
  H-measure, 321t
CAP. *See* Cumulative accuracy profile
CART (algorithm), 46, 47, 183, 247
  implementation, 185
Cascade correlation, 55
Causal conditional inference forest
    (CCIF), 196–198
  algorithm, 197
Causal conditional inference tree
    (CCIT), 196–198
  algorithm, 197
CDUT uplift decision tree, 213
Censoring
  occurrence, 82–84, 86
  presence, 89
Centrality measures, 96–97, 97t
Centroid method, 75
CHAID (algorithm), 46, 47, 183
Chaos, 46
Characteristics, dependencies
    (detection), 12
Chief analytics officer (CAO),
    impact, 369–370
Chief data officer (CDO), impact,
    369–370
Chief information officer (CIO),
    impact, 369–370
Child nodes
  balance, 185–186
  difference, 184f
    minimization, 184
  membership, 199
Chi-squared analysis, 47
Chi-squared divergence, 190

Churn
  action, 82
  customer churn
    (attrition/defection), 118
  indicator, 69
  rate, 126
  types, 118–119
Churner, 221
  node, 99
  prediction, 327
Churn prediction, 118–120
  data usage, 119
  KM analysis, 86
  right censoring, example, 82f
Class-dependent cost-sensitive (CCS)
    learning technique, 232–233
Class distribution, imbalance,
    256–258
Classification
  accuracy/error, 63–64
  algorithms, 257
  cutoff, 323–324
  dataset, example, 40t
  measures, 64
  problem, 5
  technique, tuning, 236
  trees, 58–59
Classification models
  building, cost-sensitive learning
    (usage), 226
  development, 116
  performance measures, 63–67
  predictions (average
    misclassification cost),
    299–300
  profit-driven evaluation, 298–337
Class imbalance problem, 257
Class labels, derivation, 304
Class probability estimates, 304
Closed-form formula, 38
Closeness, 144
Cloud-based solutions, 362
Cluster
  boundaries, 275
  centroids, 77
  distance, calculation, 75, 76f
  profiling, histograms (usage), 122f

Clustering, 74–81
  agglomerative clustering, 74–75
  countries, SOM (usage), 80f
  data, usage, 121
  divisive clustering, 74–75
  example, 76f
  hierarchical clustering, 74–76
  interpretation, decision trees
    (usage), 123f
  K-means clustering, 77–78
  limits, superimposition, 280f
  optimum, 77f
  scree plot, 77f
CLV. *See* Customer lifetime value
Codebook vector graph, 276f
  clustering limits, superimposition,
    280f
Coefficients, signs, 45
Collaborative filtering, 133
Collective inferencing, 102
  procedure, 98
Collinearity, reduction, 42
Commercial software
  disadvantage, 364
  open-source software, contrast,
    362–364
Company-wide data culture,
  370–371
Competing risks, 92
Component plane, 79, 80f, 81f
Conditional probability estimates,
  228–229
Confidence (measure), 70–72
Confusion matrix, 322–323
  examples, 63t, 222t, 323t
Conjugate gradient algorithm, 54
Content filtering, recommendations,
  134
Continuous outcomes, 198–199
Continuous uplift models,
  evaluation, 199
Control group, 162, 183, 187, 201f
  ranking, 203f
Control nonresponder (CN), 178
Control responder (CR), 178
Control response model (M_C), 172
Correlation plots, 199

Corruption perception index
  (CPI), 79
Cost-benefit matrix, 335
Cost-benefit ratio, 324
Cost distribution, 317
Cost-insensitive classification
  models, usage, 228–231
Cost-insensitive classifier, 231
Cost-insensitive evaluation
  measures, adoption, 256
Cost-insensitive objective function,
  optimization, 262
Cost matrix, 220–227, 228t
  continuous/smooth version, 345
  example, 225t
  misclassification costs, 225
  observation-dependent cost
    matrix, 303
  sensitivity analysis, 227
  simplification, 230t
  time-dependent cost matrix, 303
  values, calculation, 225
Cost measure, 247
Cost of Service (CoS), 272, 272t
  frequency, relationship, 277
  values, 273
Cost reduction criterion, case study,
  249–250
Cost-sensitive AdaBoost, 250
Cost-sensitive boosting-based
  approaches, 251t–253t
Cost-sensitive class distribution, 237
Cost-sensitive classification, 234–259
  approaches
    evaluation, 255–256
    structured overview, 234t
  class distribution, imbalance,
    256–258
  cutoff, 220–221, 307
  during-training methods,
    247–253
  evaluation, 255–256
  framework, 231–234
  implementations, 259
  post-training methods, 253–255
  pre-training methods, 235–246
  techniques, 222

Cost-sensitive cutoff, 230, 231
Cost-sensitive decision making,
  228–231
Cost-sensitive decision tree (CSDT),
  233, 247
  approaches, 248t
Cost-sensitive distribution, 240
Cost-sensitive learning
  post-training methods, 261–267
  sampling-based ensemble
    approaches, 242t
  training methods, 260–261
  usage, 260–267
  weighting approaches,
    243t–245t
Cost-sensitive regression, 259
  application, case study, 263–266
Cost-sensitive voting system, 247
Cost-sensitive weight update
  functions, 250
Credit defaults, reduction, 357
Credit rating model, building, 227
Credit risk
  analytics, 139–141
  management, 157
  modeling, 223
  models, ROC curves, 319f
  multilevel credit risk model
    architecture, 140f
Credit scoring
  context, baseline model, 336
  EMP, usage, 329–331
    case study, 332–334
  observation-dependent cost
    matrix, 334t
Cross-fertilization, 371–372
Cross-selling, 120
Cross-validation, 60
  usage, 62f
Cultural mismatch, 360–361
Cumulative accuracy profile (CAP),
  66, 66f
Cumulative distribution, 84f
Cumulative hazard function, 89
Cumulative incremental gains, 205
  charts, 206f
Cumulative uplift, 204–206

Customer
  activities, event log, 130t
  analytics settings, 45
  categorization, 178f
  creditworthiness, 372
  journey, 129–131, 130f
    analysis, 131
  leakage, 129
  lifetime, exponential distribution,
    126
  needs/opportunities, identification,
    357
  population, understanding, 121
  relationships, management, 141
  return, fraction, 4
  segmentation, 121, 123, 269
    three-group customer
      segmentation, 270f
  selection, 168–169
  survival probability, 124
  types, 159f
Customer churn, See *Churn*
  attrition/defection, 118
  management process, 326–327,
    326f
  prediction, MP/EMP (usage),
    325–329
Customer equity (CE), obtaining,
  128
Customer lifetime value (CLV),
  123–129, 220
  classification, three-cut strategy,
    268f
  context, 38
  contributions, 358
  dataset
    K-means clustering,
      components, 271f–272f
    variables, heatmaps, 278f
  dataset SOM
    codebook vector graph, 276f
    distance map, 276f
  definition, 267
  density maps, 275f
  distribution, 268f
  increase, 188
  modeling, 127

Customer lifetime value (*Continued*)
  prediction, 37
  scatter plot, 67f
  variable, 269–270
Cutoff points, 204
  accuracies/costs, 305t
  knowledge, absence, 209
  tuning, 303–304
  two-cutoff-point strategy, 308
Cutoff score, 210
Cutoff value, 344

D
Data
  clustering, 121
  collection, 161
    experimental design, 162f
  data-driven services, development,
    357
  data-pooling firms, impact, 365
  denormalization, 29–30
  information, difference, 3
  location-visitation data, 365
  management, footprint
    access, 362
  matrix, eigenvectors/
    eigenvalues, 33
  poolers, 139–140
  preprocessing, 29–37, 161
    activities, 368–369
  quality, 367–369
    dimensions, 368t
  RFID data, 366–367
  sampling, 235
  simulated data, PCA, 36f
  sources, 364–367
  stewards, 369
  textual data, 366
Database errors, 82–83
Database technology, adoption
  (acceleration), 2
  conversion, 3
Data scientists, 20–23
  communication/visualization
    skills, 22
  creativity, 22–23
  profile, 23f

  programming skills, 21–22
  quantitative skills, 21
Datasets
  CLV distribution, 268f
  distribution, 274
  examples, 6t, 7t, 63t
  K-means clustering, components,
    271f–272f
  missing values, 32t
  PCA calculation, 35
  relabeled dataset, 180t
  schemes, adoption, 60
  SOMs
    CLV, density maps, 275f
    distance map, 276f
  splitting, 59–63
  transaction dataset, example, 70t
  2D visualization, 273
  variables, 277
  visualization, PCA (usage), 36
DBUT. *See* Divergence-based uplift
  tree
Decay parameter, 344
Decision making
  improvement, 9
  toolkit, betweenness/closeness
    elements, 144
Decisions, conversion, 3
Decision trees, 28, 45–51
  algorithms, 247
  concepts, 45–46
  construction algorithm, efficiency
    (increase), 48
  decision boundary, 50f
  example, 46f
  forest, creation, 58
  growth (cessation), validation set
    (usage), 49f
  instability, 189
  modification, 247–248
  properties, 49–50
  splitting decision, 46–48
  stopping decision, 48–49
  tree-based approaches, 188–189
  usage, 123f
Default risk, 139
Defection (attrition), 118

Demographic variables, 117
Dendrogram, 75–76
  example, 77f
  plot, single linkage (usage), 279f
Density maps, 275f
Dependencies, detection/relation
    establishment, 12
Descriptive analytical models,
    examples, 7t
Descriptive analytics, 69–81, 138
Descriptive statistics, 31
Development base, 162
Development marketing campaign,
    155
Difference score method, 172–173
Dimensionality reduction, 35–36
Direct cost-sensitive decision
    making, 253–254
Direct methods, meta-learning
    methods (contrast), 233–234
Direct profit-driven segmentation,
    267–269
Discrete event time distribution,
    example, 84f
Disruptive technology, 144–145
Divergence-based uplift tree (DBUT),
    189–192
  robustness, 191
Divergence gain, 190
Divisive clustering, 74–75
Divisive hierarchical clustering,
    agglomerative hierarchical
    clustering (contrast), 74f
Do-Not-Disturbs (customer type),
    159–161, 178
  application dependence, 204
  identification, 170
  rank, 203
Double classifier approach,
    172–173
Downlift, 202
Down-selling, 120
Downside mean absolute deviation
    (DMAD), 261
Dummy variable, 174t
During-training methods, 247–253
Dynamic pricing, 157

E
EAD. *See* Exposure at default
E-AMC. *See* Expected average
    misclassification cost
Economic considerations, 359–364
Eigenvectors/eigenvalues, 33
Ellipse rotation, dataset usage
    (example), 34f
Ellipsoid, appearance, 33
Employee network
  defining, 143–144
  example, 143f
End user, utility/value, 3
Ensemble methods, 56–59
  evaluation, 59
  sampling-based ensemble
    approaches, 242t
Ensembles, 171, 193–198
Entities, grouping, 5–6
Entropy, 47
  calculation, 48f
  Gini, contrast, 47f
  nodes, 48
Epsilon-insensitive loss function, 261
Error amplitude, 345
Error-based evaluation measures,
    339–341
Error estimates, 62
Error minimization, weight
    minimization (contrast), 56
Estimation process, 226
Euclidean distance
  Manhattan distance, contrast, 75f
  metric, 78
Event log, example, 130t
Events, groups (finding), 5–6
Event time distribution
  cumulative distribution/survival
    function, usage, 84f
  exponential event time
    distribution, 87f
Expected average misclassification
    cost (E-AMC), 301
Expected churn, 118–119
Expected loss (EL), 139
  class prediction, association,
    228–229

Expected maximum profit (EMP)
  benefits/costs/profits, 333t
  fraction per model, 333t
  measures, 297, 298, 312, 325
    alternative, 324
  usage, 325–331
Expected number of days absent
    (EDA), determination, 142
Experimental design, 161–164
  example, 162f
  extension, 168–169
Expert-based approach, 135
Explaining, predicting (difference),
    12
Explicit networks, distillation, 364
Exploratory analysis, 31
Exponential distribution, 89, 126
  memoryless property, 87
Exponential event time distribution,
    87f
Exponential gamma, contrast, 90
Exponential model, 90, 91
Exposure at default (EAD),
    139, 321
  risk measurements, 140
Exposure risk, 139

F
False negative (FN), 223, 224
False positive (FP), 223
Featurization, 101
  examples, 101f
Filled nodes, correspondence,
    137–138
F-measure, 63
Fodina, 129
Forced churn, 118–119
Forecasting, 125
  impact, 5
Forward regression set-up, 45
FPCI. *See* Fundamental problem of
    causal inference
FPIC, impact, 209
Fraction per model, 333t
Fraud
  analytics, 134–138
  characteristics, 135

indicator, 69
  losses, reduction, 357
Fraud detection, 223
  analytical techniques, usage, 136
  applications, 256
  call detail record dataset, example,
    137t
  social network, example, 138f
  system, development, 138
Fraud percentage (FP), 50
  prediction, regression tree
    (example), 51f
Fraudsters, oversampling, 238f
Frequency variable, 235, 242
F-statistic, calculation, 51
Fundamental problem of causal
    inference (FPCI), 200

G
Gain, measurements, 48
Gain$_U$
  calculation, 186f
  size, 185
Gamma average values, 331
Gamma distribution, 88, 90
Gamma/Gamma submodel, usage,
    126
Gamma value, 328
Garbage in, garbage out (GIGO)
    principle, 29, 367
GARCH, 39
Generalized gamma, contrast, 90
Generalized Lai method, 177–183,
    211
  relabeled dataset, 180t
Genetic algorithms, 55
German Credit Data, 225
  cost matrix
    case study, 301–302
    example, 225t
  cost-sensitive class distribution,
    case study, 237–238, 245–246
Gibbs sampling, 102
Gini, 47, 247
  coefficient, 67
  entropy, contrast, 47f
Girvan-Newman algorithm, 97

Global minima, local minima
  (contrast), 55f
Good targets, 179
Gross response, estimation, 156
Guilt by association, 98

H
Hazard function, 83–84
  cumulative hazard function, 89
Hazard rate, 87, 88
Hazard shapes, 84–85, 85f
Heatmaps
  example, 278f
  usage, 277
Heuristic search procedures, 44
HeuristicsMiner, 129
Hexagonal SOM grid, rectangular
  SOM grid (contrast), 78f
Hidden layer, non-linear
  transformation function, 53
Hidden neurons, requirement, 55
Hierarchical clustering, 74–76, 78
  advantage, 76
  algorithm, application,
    277–278
  nonhierarchical clustering,
    contrast, 74f
  procedure (dendrogram plot),
    single linkage (usage), 279f
Histograms, 32
  usage, 122f
H-measure, 312–317
  impact, 321
Hmeasure R package, 331–332
Human decision making,
  automation/enhancement,
  357
Human resources (HR) analytics,
  141–146, 256
  application, 142, 145
Hyperbolic tangent, 53
Hypothesis testing, 86

I
ICET decision trees, 233
ICT services, 360
Identity theft, 136

Impurity, 46
  calculation, datasets (example), 47f
  measure, decision tree algorithm
    usage, 247
Independent and identically
  distributed (IID), 97–98
Independent variables, dependencies
  (detection), 12
Information
  adoption, acceleration, 2
  conversion, 3
  data, difference, 3
  retrieval, 36–37
Input selection, 36
In-sourcing, outsourcing (contrast),
  355, 356, 359–361
Interaction variables, advancement,
  175
Internet infrastructure providers,
  relationship mapping, 94
Internet services, growth/success, 2
Interpretability, 171
Inter-product dependencies, 129
Inter-purchase times, variation, 125
Inter-transaction patterns, 72
Interval censoring, 82–83
Intra-transaction patterns, 72
Item-item collaborative filtering,
  133–134
Iterative classification, 102

J
Jacard index, 133

K
Kane's variation, 181
Kaplan Meier (KM) analysis, 85–87
Kaplan Meier (KM) estimator,
  85–86
Kaplan Meier (KM) example, 86f
Kernel PCA, 37
K folds, 60
Kite network, 96–97, 96f
  centrality measures, 97t
K-means
  clusters, 272t
  usage, 269–273

K-means clustering, 77–78, 81, 121
  results, 270
  sample output, 123t
k-nearest neighbor approach, 133
KS-distance, 256
Kullback-Leibler divergence (KL), 190
  divergence-based splitting criterion, 193

L

Lai's method, 174, 177–183, 211
  relabeled dataset, 180t
Landing page, 131
Lasso regression, 39
Latent Dirichlet allocation, 134
Latent semantic models, 134
Leaf node, 46
  purity, 189
Left child node, observations, 186
Levenberg-Marquardt algorithm, 54
LGD. *See* Loss given default
Life value, 72
Lift (measure), 70–72, 71t
  prediction, 176–177
  score, 181–182
Lift curve, 65, 65f, 199
  noncumulative expression, 66
Likelihood cost function, optimization, 54
Likelihood function, 89
Likelihood-ratio statistic, 86
Likelihood ratio test, 89–90
Linear decision boundary, 42f
Linear regression, 28, 32
  dataset, 38t
  usage, 38–39
  variable selection, 42–45
Linear regression model, 187
  application, 188
  defining, 38
  estimation, 188
Linlin cost function (C_{linlin}), usage, 264f
Literacy, component plane, 80f
Loan obligation, default risk, 139

Local minima, global minima (contrast), 55f
Local model, 98
Local node behavior, description, 101f
Location-visitation data, 365
Logistic regression, 28, 32, 39–45, 99, 179
  bounding function, example, 40f
  concepts, 39–41
  linear decision boundary, 42f
  neural network representation, 52f
  properties, 41–42
  relational logistic regression, 100–102
  variable selection, 42–45
Logistic regression model
  formulation, 40
  interpretation, 41–42
  parameters, 41
Log-logistic distribution, 88
Log-normal distribution, 88
Log-normal gamma, contrast, 90
Log-normal model, 90
Log-rank test, 86
Loopy belief propagation, 102
Lo's method/approach, 174–177, 199, 211
  disadvantages, 177
  tree-based version, 186
Loss functions, 339–341
Loss functions, usage, 57–58
Loss given default (LGD), 321
  calculation, 330
  prediction, 37
  risk measurements, 140
  usage, 139
Loss risk, 139
Lost Causes (customer type), 159, 178, 204
  inclusion, 182
  rank, 203
Lost for good
  approach, 128
  model, 128
  perspective, 123–124

M

Machine failure prediction, 256
Macroeconomic data, 365–366
Manhattan distance, Euclidean
distance (contrast), 75f
Mantel-Haenzel test, 86
Map density, 274
Marginal class membership
probability, computation,
97–98
Marketing analytics, 114–134
Marketing campaign, running
(payoff), 210
Markov chain
analysis, 128
example, 127f
models, usage, 127
Markov decision processes, 134
Markov property, usage, 98
Matlab, 362
Matrix
binary classification problem, cost
matrix, 224t
confusion matrix, 63t, 222t
cost-benefit matrix, 335
data matrix,
eigenvectors/eigenvalues, 33
orthogonal basis, 33
singular value, 34
term-document matrix, SVD
transform (estimation),
36–37
unitary matrices, 34
user-item matrix, example, 132t
Maximal impurity, occurrence, 46
Maximum likelihood procedures,
usage, 89
Maximum profit (MP)
framework, 323–324
measures, 297, 322–334
basis, 329
usage, 298, 325–329
Mean absolute deviation
(MAD), 68, 261
calculations, 345
performance measures,
339, 340t

Mean squared error (MSE), 59,
68, 199
calculation, 50–51, 345
performance measures, 339, 340f
Memoryless property, 87
Merger, usage (decision), 75
MetaCost, 254–255
approach, example, 255t
Meta-learning methods, direct
methods (contrast), 233–234
Metrics, usage, 207
MicroCredit dataset
case study, 318–321
observations, example, 305
Misprediction cost, 265f
Minimal impurity
occurrence, 46
Misclassification costs, 320–321
average, 298–303
calculation, 300–301
expected average
misclassification cost
(E-AMC), 301
dependence, 224
estimation, 226
imbalance, 257
Misclassification, impact, 224
Missing values, 31–32
Model base, 163
size, decisions, 167
Model-based collaborative filtering,
analytical techniques
(usage), 134
Model-building process, 173
Model effectiveness, 202
campaign measurement, 164–170
issues, 166–168
Model effect measurement
example, 166t
overview, 164t
Model estimation, 180
aggregation, 181
Modeling
paradigm, shift, 166
techniques, 296
Mortgage sales process, customer
journey, 130f

Mouse movements, 132
Multiclass model, development, 181
Multidimensional analysis, OLAP
    facilities usage, 15–16
Multilayer perceptron (MLP) neural
    network, 52–53, 53f
Multilevel credit risk model
    architecture, 140f
Multipartite networks,
    137–138
Multivariate adaptive regression
    splines (MARS), 39
Multivariate testing, 169

N
Naïve approach, 172–173
Negative class observation,
    322–323
Neighbors
    local node behavior, features, 101f
    target behavior, features, 101f
Net response, 156
Networks
    centrality measures, 96t
    characteristics, 101
    model, 98
    neural networks, 28
    technology, adoption
        (acceleration), 2
Neural networks, 28, 52–56
    approximators, 53
    concepts, 52–53
    overfitting, prevention, 56
    patterns/decision boundaries,
        complexity, 55
    training (stopping), validation set
        (usage), 56f
    weight learning, 54–56
Neurons
    hidden neurons, requirement, 55
    operations, 52
    output neurons, usage, 54–55
Nonchurner, 221
    node, 99
    prediction, 327
Nondefaulter, classification, 332
Nonfraudsters, undersampling, 239f

Nonhierarchical clustering,
    hierarchical clustering
    (contrast), 74f
Non-linear transformation function,
    53
Non-normalized data table,
    normalized data table
    aggregation, 30f
Nonresponders, responders
    (contrast), 158
Normalized data tables, aggregation,
    30f

O
Observation-dependent costs
    matrix, 334t
    usage, 334–337
Observation-dependent
    cost-sensitive (OCS) learning
    technique, 232–233
Observations
    analysis, 5–6
    distance, respect, 33
    observation-dependent cost
        matrix, 303
    observation-dependent
        misclassification costs, 306
    observations per score group,
        LGD histogram/percentage,
        332f
    observations per segment,
        CLV/fraction, 268f
    term, usage, 8
Odds ratio,
    calculation/representation,
    41–42
Off-balance-sheet exposures,
    estimations, 139
OLAP facilities, 72
    usage, 15–16
One-*versus*-All coding, 299
One-*versus*-One coding, 299
Online social network sites, usage,
    93–94
Online transaction processing
    (OLTP), transactional data
    extraction, 4

On-premise analytics, advantage, 361–362
Open-source software, commercial software (contrast), 362–364
Operational efficiency, 171
Opportunity cost, 223
Optimization
  facilitation, analytics (usage), 9, 11
  procedure, byproduct, 43
  simplification, 41
Ordered outcomes, 198–199
Ordinal classification problem, cost matrix, 228t
Ordinary least squares (OLS)
  non-OLS models, negative values, 68
  regression, 39, 39f
  usage, problems, 39
Outlier detection/handling, 32
Output neurons, usage, 54–55
Outsourcing, 145
  analytics, benefits, 360
  in-sourcing, contrast, 355, 356, 359–361
Overfitting, 48–49
  prevention, 56
Oversampling, 238–239, 238f
  alternative, 237
  combination, 241
  synthetic minority oversampling technique (SMOTE), 239–246

P
Parametric survival analysis, 87–90
Pareto/dependent approach, 126
Pareto/negative binomial distribution (Pareto/NBD) model, 126–127
Partial spending behavior, 198
Passive churn, 118–119
PCA. See Principal component analysis
PD. See Probability of default
Pearson correlation, 133
  coefficient, 67

Performance
  calculation, dataset (example), 63t
  estimation, training/test set split-up, 61f
  evaluation, lift curve (usage), 65
  figure-of-merit, 64
  measure, cross-validation (usage), 62f
  metrics, 207–210
Persuadables (customer type), 159–161, 165–167, 178, 202
  identification, 170
  rank, 203
  uplift score, 208
PLV. See Prospect lifetime value
Poisson process, 126
Political campaigning, 157
Political rights, component plane (usage), 81f
Population distribution, 121
Post-processing approaches, 233
Post-training methods, 253–255
Power, 171
Predicted class labels, 300–301
Predicting, explaining (difference), 12
Prediction error, 260f
  linlin cost function, usage, 264f
Predictive analytical models
  examples, 6t
  performance measures, 68–69
Predictive analytics, 37–56, 138
  application, 136–137
  profit-driven predictive analytics, 221–234
  usage, 156
Predictive models, evaluation, 59–69
Predictor variable, 174t
Principal component analysis (PCA), 33–37, 366
  algorithm, 35
  calculation, results, 35
  Kernel PCA, 37
  usage, 270
  usefulness, 34–35

Probabilistic relational neighbor
   classifier, 99–100
 social network, example, 100f
Probability estimates,
   calibration, 258
Probability of default (PD),
   139–140
 risk measurements, 140
Probability scores, 181
Processing element, operations, 52
Profit-driven analytical techniques,
   220
Profit-driven analytics, 11
 ROC-based measures, 297
Profit-driven approaches, 13
 example, 11–12
Profit-driven association rules,
   280–283
Profit-driven business analytics,
   9–14, 359
Profit-driven descriptive analytics,
   267–283
Profit-driven evaluation, 338–346
 observation-dependent costs,
   usage, 334–337
Profit-driven model
   evaluation/implementation,
   296
Profit-driven predictive analytics,
   221–234
Profit-driven regression, 259
Profit-driven segmentation,
   267–280
 direct profit-driven segmentation,
   267–269
 K-means, usage, 269–273
 self-organizing maps, 273–280
Profit-oriented visualization,
   279–280
PROFSET model, 283
Proportional hazards, 91
 model, 91f
 regression, 90–92
Prospect lifetime value (PLV), 124
 values, 128–129
Purchasing behavior function, 159f
Purchasing rate, 126

p-value
 basis, 44
 calculation, 43
   Student's t-distribution, usage,
   43f
 representation, 43

Q
Qini curves, cumulative incremental
   gains charts, 206f
Qini measures, 208–210
Qini uplift, 204–206
Quadratic cost, 260f
Quantile uplift measures, 207–208
Quantile uplift ratio measures, 208
Quantitative association rules,
   282–283
Quantitative modeling, 145

R
Random base, 163
Random forests, 28, 58–59, 241
 uplift random forest, 193–195
Random model, power curve,
   66–67
Rebalancing ensemble methods, 235,
   241
Rebalancing methods, 235–241
REC. See Regression error
   characteristic
Receiver operating characteristic
   (ROC)
 analysis, 64–65, 64t
 curve-based measures, 310–334
 ROC-based measures, 297
 ROCIV measure, 297, 334
Receiver operating characteristic
   (ROC) curve, 64, 65t,
   199–200, 310
 construction, 336–337
 examples, 310f, 319f
 values, 140
Recency Frequency Monetary
   (RFM), 283
 analysis, 115–116
 framework, 143
 score, construction, 115f

values, 273
variables, 117, 121, 127, 272t
Recipient, utility/value, 3
Recommendations, types, 132
Recommender systems, 131–134
Rectangular SOM grid, hexagonal
    SOM grid (contrast), 78f
Recursive partitioning algorithms
    (RPAs), 45
Regression
    coefficients, signs (verification), 69
    cost-sensitive learning, 260–267
    evaluation measures, 340t
    regression-based approaches, 171,
        174–183
Regression error characteristic (REC)
    curves, 341–346
    data, 341t
    example, 342f
Regression error characteristic (REC)
    surfaces, 341–346
    data, 343f
    example, 343f
Regression models
    adoption, 340
    estimation, 12–13
    generalization performance,
        evaluation, 339
    performance measures, 67–68
    profit-driven evaluation, 338–346
Regression trees, 50–51, 59,
    198–199
    example, 51f
Relabeled dataset, 180t
Relational logistic regression,
    100–102, 100f
Relational neighbor classifier, 98–99
    probabilistic relational neighbor
        classifier, 99–100
    social network, example, 99f
Relationship variables, 117
Relaxation labeling, 102
Responders, nonresponders
    (contrast), 158
Response
    data, 162–163
    indicator, 69

modeling, 116–118, 121,
    155–158, 256
probability, increase, 170–171
rates
    decile graph, usage, 201f
    difference, 165
    target, 117
Results, business expert
    interpretation/evaluation, 16
Retention, 125
    marketing campaign, 155
Return on investment (ROI), 332,
    355, 357–359
    determination, difficulty, 357
    improvement, 364–372
    jeopardy, 361–362
    management support, 369–370
    organizational aspects, 370–371
Revenues, generation, 4
RFID data, 366–367
Ridge regression, 39
ROC. See Receiver operating
    characteristic
Root mean squared error
    (RMSE), 68
Root node, 45–46

S
Sales, increase, 357
Sampling, 30–31
    aim, 257
    application, 258
Sampling-based ensemble
    approaches, 242t
SAS, 362
SBUT. See Significance-based uplift
    tree
Scatter plots, 32, 67f
Scree plot, 77f
Self-organizing map (SOM), 78–81,
    273–280
    dataset distribution, 274
    interpretation, 277
    power, 279–280
    rectangular SOM grid, hexagonal
        SOM grid (contrast), 78f
    usage, 80f

Senior-level executives,
    cross-industry survey, 371
Sensitivity analysis, performing,
    72, 227
Sequence rules, 28, 72–73
    mining, transaction
        dataset/sequential dataset
        (examples), 73t
Sequential dataset, example, 73t
Significance-based splitting criterion,
    186–187
Significance-based uplift tree
    (SBUT), 183–189,
    199, 213
Simulated data, PCA, 36f
Single linkage, usage, 279f
Singular value, 34
Singular value decomposition (SVD),
    34, 134, 366
    transform, estimation, 36–37
Small-to-medium-sized enterprise
    (SME), 361–362
Social network
    analysis, 137
    analytics, 93–102, 138
    definitions, 94–95
    examples, 99f, 100f, 138f
    information, 117
    learner, components, 98
    learning, 97–98
    matrix representation, 95t
    metrics, 95–97
    sociogram representation, 95f
    variable, 127
Sociodemographic variable, 127
Sociograms, usage, 95
SOM. See Self-organizing map
Source data
    tables, merger, 29–30
Source data, identification, 15
Specificity, 63
Splits, 51
Splitting decision, 46–47, 75
SPSS, 362
Squared Euclidean
    distance, 190
Standard gamma model, 90

Statistical analysis, usage, 83
Stock prices
    prediction, 37
    variation, 344
Stopping decision, 46, 48–49
Stress-testing, 141
Structured analytics, application, 9
Structured data, analytics
    (application), 8
Structured dataset, 8t
Student's t-distribution, $n-2$ degrees
    of freedom, 43
Sum of squared errors (SSE), 188
Support (measure), 70–72
Support vector regression (SVR),
    260–261
Sure-Things (customer type), 159,
    178, 204
    identification, 170
    inclusion, 182
    rank, 203
Survival analysis, 5, 81–93, 120
    interpretability, 93
    measurements, 83–85
    models
        estimation, maximum likelihood
            procedures (usage), 89
        evaluation, 93
        extensions, 92
        usage, examples, 82
Survival function, 87
Survival probability, 124
Synthetic minority oversampling
    technique (SMOTE),
    239–246, 240f
    extension, development,
        240–241

T
Target variable, 174t, 299
    cost-sensitive estimate, 266
    unobserved/future value,
        estimation/prediction, 12
Task completion, technical
    perspective, 8
TCO. See Total cost of ownership
t-distribution, 187–188

Term-document matrix, SVD transform (estimation), 36–37
Text documents, analysis, 36–37
Text mining, 36–37
Textual data, 366
Three-cut strategy, 268f
Three-group customer segmentation, 270f
Time-dependent cost matrix, 303
Time horizon, selection, 124–125
Time series models, 39
Time-varying covariates, 83
Top node, 45–46
Torgo, Luís, 342
Total cost of ownership (TCO), 355–356
  calculation, example costs, 356t
  goal, 356
  reduction, 359
Total spending behavior, 198
Training set, error (decrease), 49
Transactional database, 94
Transactional data, extraction, 4
Transaction dataset, example, 70t, 73t
Transactions database, example, 282
Treatment, 155–156
  effects, 158–161
  group, 162, 183
  net effect, estimation, 154
  response model (M_T), 172
  variables, 174t
Treatment nonresponder (TN), 179
Treatment responder (TR), 179
Tree-based approaches, 171, 183–199, 211
Tree-like diagram, 75–76
Trees, optimization, 194
True lift, 165
True negative (TN), 223, 224
True positive (TP), 223, 224
t-statistic, 187–188
Two-cutoff-point strategy, 308
  example, 309f
Two-model approaches, 171, 172–174

U
Undersampling, 238–239, 239f
  combination, 241
Unexpected loss (UL), 139
Unified distance matrix (U matrix), 79
Unipartite networks, 137–138
Unitary matrices, 34
Unobserved/future value (estimation/prediction), 12
Uplift bagging, 195–196
  algorithm, 195
Uplift (plotting), decile graph (usage), 200–204
Uplift differences, maximization, 183
Uplift gain, 185
Uplift modeling, 13, 167
  approaches, 171
  case, 155–158
  data requirement, experimental design, 162f
  guidelines, 210–213
  implementations/software, 212–213
  methods, 170–199
  requirement, 158
Uplift models (M_U), 172
  comparison, 209
  cumulative incremental gains charts/Qini curves, 206f
  development, 155, 161
    two-step approach, 210–212
  evaluation, 199–210
  response rate curve, 203f
  uplift, decile curve, 205f
Uplift random forest, 193–195
  algorithm, 194
Uplift tree split, reevaluation (case study), 191–192
Up-selling, 120
Upside mean absolute deviation (UMAD), 261
U.S. Equal Credit Opportunities Act, 141
User interest
  measurement, 132
  representation, 132

User-item matrix, 134
  example, 132t
User-user collaborative filtering,
  133–134
Utility-based evaluation framework,
  343–344
Utility function, 344

V
Validation set, usage, 49f, 56f
VAR, 39
Variable
  external collection, 45
  selection procedure, application,
    176
  subsets, 44f
  term, usage, 8
Visual evaluation approaches,
  200–206
Visualization, 36, 360
  facilities, 72
Voting procedure, usage, 60

W
WARM. *See* Weighted Association
  Rule Mining
Wearout, 116
Web analytics setting, 72
Weibull distribution, 88, 88f

Weibull gamma, contrast, 90
Weibull model, 90
Weighted aggregate
  divergence, 190
Weighted Association Rule Mining
  (WARM), 283
Weighted average cost of capital
  (WACC), calculation, 125
Weighting methods, 235, 242,
  245–246
  application, 258
  overview, 243t–245t
Weight minimization, error
  minimization (contrast), 56
Weight parameter vector,
  closed-form formula, 38
Weight vector, 78–79
Wilcoxon test, 86
Within-network classification, goal,
  97–98
Workforce
  behavior, 145–146
  network, 144
World Wide Web, growth/success, 2
Wrapper approaches, 233–234

X
X-selling, 120
  campaigns, 125